The Invention of Illusions

The Invention of Illusions:
International Perspectives on Paul Auster

Edited by

Stefania Ciocia and Jesús A. González

**CAMBRIDGE
SCHOLARS**

P U B L I S H I N G

The Invention of Illusions:
International Perspectives on Paul Auster,
Edited by Stefania Ciocia and Jesús A. González

This book first published 2011

Cambridge Scholars Publishing

12 Back Chapman Street, Newcastle upon Tyne, NE6 2XX, UK

British Library Cataloguing in Publication Data
A catalogue record for this book is available from the British Library

ISBN (10): 1-4438-2580-8, ISBN (13): 978-1-4438-2580-1

TABLE OF CONTENTS

INTRODUCTION

STEFANIA CIOCIA
AND JESÚS ÁNGEL GONZÁLEZ

At the time of writing, it has been fifteen years since the publication of *Beyond the Red Notebook: Essays on Paul Auster* (1995), the seminal collection of essays edited by Dennis Barone which marked the beginning of sustained academic critical attention on the New York author. Barone begins his introduction by drawing attention to the remarkable speed of Auster's ascent in popularity—a sudden reversal of fortune that is part of the writer's own self-mythology—particularly on the score of the success of *The New York Trilogy* (1987), the trio of interconnected metaphysical detective novels which still remains his most widely read (and studied) work. In explaining the rationale for his collection, Barone hypothesises that the rapidity of Auster's rise to fame might have been the reason for the lack of scholarship on his work, and concludes his introductory essay with the prescient wish that his volume would promote the development of further criticism on Auster—a desire reiterated by Patricia Merivale who, in her appraisal of the state of Auster scholarship in a piece written for *Contemporary Literature* in 1997, could not help but remark, with undisguised puzzlement, that Auster critics had lagged behind those of other prestigious authors coming to prominence in the Eighties, such as J.M. Coetzee, William Gibson or even Don DeLillo.

Merivale's call for a more extensive academic response to the work of "an author with so impassioned a following in both North America and Europe" (Merivale 1997, 186) has not gone unheeded. In fact, as Barone had predicted, Auster scholarship witnessed "an exponential growth in the late 1990s" (Barone 1995, 1) and continues to thrive, not least because the twenty-first century has so far proven to be a very prolific time for this distinctive writer.

Since 1995, Auster has published seven novels (with another one, *Sunset Park*, scheduled for publication in November 2010) and a couple of biographical pieces; he has directed—or otherwise collaborated in the making of—four films, and has edited books as different as a collection of non-fictional pieces by National Public Radio's listeners (*True Tales of American Life*, [2001]) and Samuel Beckett's complete works (2006). He has retained—and indeed positively fostered with his many auto-intertextual connections—his staunch following, and has strengthened his popularity particularly in Europe, where he seems to have more devotees than at home—as shown by the several prizes he has received, such as the Spanish Prince of Asturias Award in 2006 or the French grade of Commander of the *Ordre des Arts et des Lettres* in 2007.

The fact that Auster acquired instant cult status by managing to strike a difficult balance between a strong intellectual appeal and mainstream success may perhaps be the true mark of his postmodernity, a label that he himself dislikes.[1] But now that the general theoretical debate has shifted from a definition and a critique of postmodernism to a reflection on whether or how we can claim to have entered a post-postmodern phase, Auster continues to make waves on the literary scene, garnering "the best reviews and the worst reviews of any writer I know"—as he said in an interview in *The Washington Post* (online edition)[2]—and attracting significant scholarly interest. Three of the contributors to this very collection have authored monographs on him: Aliki Varvogli has published *The World that is the Book. Paul Auster's Fiction* in 2001 with Liverpool University Press; Mark Brown's *Paul Auster*, written for the 'Contemporary American and Canadian Novelists' series for Manchester University Press, has come out in 2007, while James Peacock's *Understanding Paul Auster*, out in 2009 with the University of South Carolina Press, is the latest book-length study of this author to date.

Before them, critics in continental Europe had been faster to react to Auster's early success: Marc Chénetier had published *Paul Auster as the Wizard of Odds* (Paris: Didier, 1996), dealing exclusively with *Moon Palace* (1989), while Anne M. Holzapfel had focused her analysis on Auster's earliest fictional work in *The New York Trilogy: Whodunit? Tracking the Structure of Paul Auster's Anti-Detective Novels* (Frankfurt am Main: Peter Lang, 1996) and Bernd Herzogenrath had published *An Art of Desire. Reading Paul Auster* (Amsterdam: Rodopi, 1999), offering a Lacanian perspective on the writer's output. Two further thematic studies of Auster came out with Peter Lang in 2001 and 2002 respectively: Carsten Springer's *Crises: The Work of Paul Auster* and Ilana Shiloh's *Paul Auster and the Postmodern Quest*. They have recently been followed by Brendan Martin's *Paul Auster's Postmodernity* (London: Routledge, 2008), another monograph concerned with tracing the extent of the author's affinities with this cultural category.

This cursory account of the volumes devoted exclusively to Auster—an account that becomes much longer when works written in languages other than English are considered[3]—would not be complete without the mention of the collection of essays published in *Bloom's Modern Critical Views* series for Chelsea House in 2004; with this compilation of previously published scholarly pieces, Harold Bloom sanctions Auster's canonicity, somewhat reluctantly perhaps, but without a shadow of a doubt: in fact, in his concise introductory editorial comments, having voiced his reservations about Auster's greatness vis-à-vis those "elliptical literary artists" (Beckett, Kafka, Hamsun, Celan, etc.) who have inspired him, Bloom makes a generous and gracious admission: "If Auster evades me, I ... blame myself" (2).

Where does the present collection fit in, then, within the context of such a remarkable proliferation of critical activity around Paul Auster? In planning and putting together this book, our intention has been to follow the example of *Beyond the Red Notebook*, and of course supplement the recent monographs, with another polyphonic volume of original essays on those Austerian texts and themes in need of (re)assessment, either in the form of an updated summative reading which could draw connections between the author's early and later production, or of a fresh and thought-provoking alternative to previous analyses, or even—in the case of very recent work—of initial scholarly responses.

In order to do this—and in keeping with Paul Auster's transatlantic appeal and engagement with various media—we have deliberately sought collaborations from as international and eclectic an academic context as it has been possible: our contributors, both for their background and institutional affiliation, represent a number of different countries, cultural traditions and (inter)disciplinary approaches. We have also been especially keen to focus on Auster's twenty-first-century output, given how—in the wake of 9/11—questions about the importance and the power of narrative acts, the relationship between the personal and the public, the interplay between fiction and history, and the relevance of storytelling to the processing of traumatic or otherwise epochal events have now become more pressing than ever.

In the light of these topical concerns, more often than not and regardless of their individual starting point or specific object of analysis, the contributors to this volume have been naturally drawn to muse about Auster's position in the American canon and on the global literary scene, as well as to reflect on the trajectory of his oeuvre and his development as a consummate practitioner and theorist of the art of storytelling across different genres and media.

Unsurprisingly perhaps, one of the most recurrent issues to have cropped up in response to our call for papers, and to have then been reflected in the final selection of essays, has been the need to go beyond a reading of Auster as the endlessly self-referential postmodern writer, with a tried and tested repertoire of signature themes and narrative ploys, addressed at a captive audience of adepts. Admittedly, this is a cliché that Auster himself seems to have courted with some of his projects, most notably with the relatively recent *Travels in the Scriptorium* (2006), a short novel whose interpretation is substantially dependent on the readers' knowledge of Auster's previous work. And yet, as a number of chapters of this book make clear, this text has a depth of meaning unacknowledged by its early reviewers, who had generally decried it as a sign of Auster's terminally narcissistic involution, or an exasperation of the pared-down intellectualism that, two decades before, had made the fortune of *The New York Trilogy*.

Against this interpretative trend, several of our contributors have been eager to highlight the political drive of Auster's most recent production, particularly in those texts where collective concerns of historical magnitude appear to be dismissed in the same breath in which they are articulated. Consider, for example, the case of *The Brooklyn Follies* (2005): at a first glance, it has often been seen at best as a jolly, naïve celebration of the communal spirit fostered by New York's most populous borough, even in (or especially in) the wake of 9/11, for a brief mention of the terrorist attacks brings the novel to a close and thus frames, retrospectively, the entire narration. Incidentally, the text's focus on the various—however improbable and haphazard—local support networks sprouting in Brooklyn has probably exacerbated the disappointed response at the ostensibly inward-looking, more-rarefied-than-ever scope of *Travels in the Scriptorium*, perceived by some as an about-turn from a writer who had finally started talking about "real" people.

The easiness with which both *The Brooklyn Follies* and *Travels in the Scriptorium* have lent themselves to simplistic, dismissive readings might account for the fact that they are the most represented works in this collection, together with *The Book of Illusions* (2002), whose own popularity amongst our contributors is explained by its obvious status as a fruitful entry point into the discussion of Auster's interest in film. Besides, while they are possibly the two novels in Auster's corpus most in need of critical redress, both *The Brooklyn Follies* and *Travels in the Scriptorium* are in many ways, and for different reasons, very typical of the author's production. *The Brooklyn Follies* provides a remarkable example of Auster's storytelling at its most expansive and sentimental; at the opposite end of the narrative spectrum, *Travels in the Scriptorium* takes us back to the author's metaphysical roots, while being—at times quite literally—a compendium of his work.

In view of how representative they are of these two complementary drives in Auster's writing, it is no wonder that *The Brooklyn Follies* and *Travels in the Scriptorium* should have sparked such a flurry of exegetical activity in the present volume. Together with *Man in the Dark* (2008), these two very different narratives can be said to form a(n admittedly rather unlikely) second trilogy,[4] as argued by the two contributors who open our collection by configuring the three works as Auster's response not so much to 9/11, but to the ensuing "war on terror" and George W. Bush's foreign policy.

PAOLO SIMONETTI finds a further context for his analysis of the second trilogy in the debate about the state of realism after postmodernism. He argues that in his revisitation of genres such as the realist novel, the metafictional novel and the counterfactual history, Auster inscribes himself within the American, Hawthornian tradition of the Romancer, with its investment in the power of storytelling through the creation of fictions imbued with a deep historical and mythical consciousness. In her discussion of the same texts, ALIKI VARVOGLI also engages with Auster's commitment to fiction-writing, not as a way of affecting the world directly, but as a creative *process*—an ongoing, exploratory, dynamic activity—that helps us become aware of and test the boundaries between the real and the (im)possible. In particular, her reading of the three novels focuses on their relationship with the idea of America as utopia and dystopia.

ANITA DURKIN instead conducts her political reading of *The Brooklyn Follies* by pairing it to the earlier *Timbuktu* (1999) in an analysis of how configurations of place in the two novels are often tied in with the American history and practice of racial oppression. She also goes decidedly against the grain of common (mis)interpretations of Auster's unbounded faith in fabulation, when she argues that both texts under scrutiny present the dark side of storytelling in highlighting how books and writing itself have partaken and can still partake of oppressive politics. JAMES PEACOCK continues the examination of *The Brooklyn Follies* by performing an extended analysis of its complex engagement with the interconnected notions of originality, forgery and authenticity. Having suggested that this text might well be regarded as Auster's first post-postmodern novel, Peacock reads it as a celebration and perhaps even an enactment of the paradoxical notion of the "true fake", a catalyst for reconciliations of opposites when performance and imitation give way to the establishment and/or the discovery of deep, essential resemblances and sympathetic connections. In doing so, Peacock's piece foregrounds a theme that informs several other analyses in this collection: the relationship between creative ventures and the opening up of an ethical sphere.

The following chapter leads us into relatively uncharted territory in Auster's scholarship, as STEFANIA CIOCIA focuses on *Oracle Night* (2004) and sets out to query the author's gender politics with her focus on the role of women in his novels. In particular, Ciocia analyses the hidden implications of Auster's long-lasting affair with the trope of the *donna angelicata*, the beatific woman whose sudden appearance on the scene is often configured as a miraculous act of sense-making and provider of narrative closure, those least postmodern of portents which otherwise elude most Austerian characters.

GINEVRA GERACI's reading of *Travels in the Scriptorium* takes us back to the analysis of ethical questions, especially in relation to the authorial role, and the author's responsibility towards fictional creations and readers alike. Drawing on Ricoeur's hermeneutics for her theoretical background, Geraci complements her discussion of the Beckettian traces in *Travels* with an investigation of the Pirandellian legacies in Auster's adoption of an ironical stance and in the metatheatrical conventions discernible in that text. MICHELLE BANKS, instead, looks at a different manifestation of Auster's metafictional drive: his often much maligned auto-intertextuality, typically dismissed by negative critics of his work as postmodern narcissism and gamesmanship. Banks chooses to focus primarily on recurring characters as the clearest markers of the stability (or otherwise) of the fictional world created by Auster's entire oeuvre, and inevitably ends up discussing *Travels* as a hub of such reappearances. While seemingly hinting at the consistency of Auster's fictional world, the *retour de personnages* in *Travels*, as in other Austerian texts, actually destabilizes it, for there are often small, but clearly visible discrepancies in the characters' reincarnations from one narrative to the next. This move, Banks argues, underscores the presence of necessity, choice and chance in these fictional connections and, by extension, in our approach to the world and to our individual and collective hermeneutical projects.

ULRICH MEURER shares Banks' wide textual scope, for he provides a topography of how Auster's works inhabit a liminal space, often crossing boundaries between different media and between the fictional and the factual. This chapter builds up to the mapping out of Auster's most daring hybrid enterprises, i.e. those actualizations, in the real world, of projects originally charted only in fiction-writing, such as, for example, Auster's collaboration with the conceptualist artist Sophie Calle or the making of *The Inner Life of Martin Frost* (a film directed by Auster and based on a fictional film described in *The Book of Illusions*).

Auster's interest in cinema, and in its interplay with writing, is the subject of the next three pieces in the collection. The first is JESÚS ÁNGEL GONZÁLEZ's comparative analysis of Auster's "films about words" and novels about films. Having initially posited the movement from narrative fiction to film as a continuation of Auster's "opening of the fist" from poetry to narrative fiction, González argues that Auster's engagement with the cinematic medium is marked by the need to overcome the two-dimensionality of this artistic form. Auster finds this third dimension in his (both real and written) films by demanding the reader/viewer's moral and epistemological involvement in the creative and hermeneutical acts, through multiple viewings, through the identification of intertextual and metafictional connections or even, more generally, through an active subscription to the idea that we find meaning in our individual lives when we relate them to other people's stories.

Following this overview of Auster's fascination with cinema, and awareness of its limitation, is MARK BROWN's reading of *The Book of Illusions* and of the correlation between place and identity in this, as indeed in other, Austerian novels. Like González, Brown points out how Auster ultimately privileges the narrative form in spite of his interest in the cinematic medium—part of whose charm comes precisely from its insubstantiality and its dream-like quality. This lack of physicality also seems to run counter to Auster's investment in the importance of place in our self-perception and continuing development. In *The Book of Illusions* the word turns out to be more enduring than the image, and storytelling becomes a more powerful act than a physical journey of (self-)exploration involving either the discovery or the escape from one's past. It is in the stories woven by the various characters for themselves and for other people that we can trace the least evanescent of processes of identity formation.

ALAN BILTON also looks at *The Book of Illusions*, as an obvious starting point for his investigation of Auster's interest in the phantasmal nature of silent film. Having identified Raymond Griffith—a spectral figure in his own right since almost none of his films have survived—as the real-life source of inspiration for the novel's protagonist Hector Mann, Bilton proceeds to outline Auster's continuous thematization of the fragile balance and the paradoxical interplay between presence and absence both in life and art. Incidentally, this is a recurrent obsession in Auster's work; indeed, it can be said to underpin the original Austerian self-myth, the presence/absence of an "invisible" father figure, as well as the writer's ongoing preoccupation with posthumous, phantasmal narratives or the contrast between his (American?) fabulatory penchant and his (European?) Beckettian search for a naked form of language.

Finally, FRANÇOIS HUGONNIER focuses on that crucial dichotomy that runs through Auster's entire artistic career: the one between language and silence, the speakable and the unspeakable, and the writer's ensuing quest to find ways of articulating what cannot be said. Hugonnier recapitulates the recurrent concern with the limits of language in a discussion which, starting from Auster's beginnings as a critic and a poet, goes on to cover his development as a fiction writer up to as late a novel as *Invisible* (2009).

In the already mentioned 1997 review of Auster's early reception, Patricia Merivale asked when the critical dust would settle and allow for an equanimous assessment of the writer's production, lamenting a general inability on the part of the scholars to trace a sense of trajectory in his entire output, then dominated, even more than it is now, by the (academic and non-academic) readers' privileging of *The New York Trilogy* over his other works. With her call for a more comprehensive and balanced perspective on the place of the *Trilogy* in the Austerian canon, Merivale also put forth the idea that Auster at one point seemed to have changed direction, from the minimalist, intellectual postmodern writer of his narrative beginnings to a more "humanist" storyteller; a painter on a wider canvas with larger and more concrete ethical and social concerns, the explorer of the big American themes, say, of *Moon Palace* (1989), an early novel which alone can be said to have sparked as much critical activity as Auster's first foray into fiction.

More than a decade on, we can safely say that Auster has continued to cultivate this oscillation between, on the one hand, the philosophical musings on the fragility of the human predicament and the linguistic medium and, on the other, the extroverted celebrations of our imaginative, emotional and communicative resources; between a sort of asceticism in his choice of themes and language and an exploration of the accidental or necessary interconnections that make up the rich texture of our experience of the world, of one another and of ourselves. In fact, in later texts, such as *The Book of Illusions* or the second trilogy, Auster positively demands that we acknowledge the complementary nature of the two drives that underpin his writing: the productive tension between inside and outside, the locked room and the wide world, Self and Other, imagination and reality, presence and absence, linguistic abstractions and ethical actions. If anything can be surmised from the contributions of the different scholars taking part in *The Invention of Illusions* is that this constant dialectical

tension is still at the heart of Auster's work, and now matters more than ever.

As already mentioned, in composing this volume, our intention has been to write a *Beyond the Red Notebook* for the twenty-first century: if Barone's collection had set a benchmark and prompted a boom in Auster scholarship, *The Invention of Illusions* wants to reinvigorate that critical tradition which, in recent years—particularly at the level of book reviews—has occasionally been a little hasty and superficial, and therefore also ungenerous. It is perhaps now time to debunk, once and for all, the self-perpetuating myth of Paul Auster, Brooklynite bard of "Gothic good looks" (Akbar 2009) and easy charm, endlessly capitalizing on a few skilful narrative tricks, executed with the grace and levity of the seasoned magician, whose dazzling illusions ultimately leave no real mark on the audience. While, to phrase it in Merivale's terms, the critical dust won't settle until Auster puts away his trusted Olympia typewriter, this collection invites us to take another look at Auster as an inventor of illusions in the most positive sense of this word: not as short-lived, deceitful gimmickry, but rather as an imaginative testing of possibilities, a wilful establishment of real bonds between people, even if these bonds are rooted in the illusive—and elusive—world of storytelling.

The best example of this sort of connections is provided by Auster himself when Tom tells Nathan the anecdote of Kafka and the lost doll, such a powerful story that all the commentators in this volume who have dealt with *The Brooklyn Follies* have chosen to dwell on it. In telling us this least Kafkaesque of tales—the story of how the great writer spent three weeks composing letters from a missing doll, in order to cure its young owner from the sadness caused by her loss—Paul Auster reiterates once more his belief in the power of fiction to help us make sense, relate and somehow come to terms with the world inside and outside us. They might not be all-powerful remedies, but good stories, be they lived, acted out, told, read, seen, dreamt, imagined or experienced in any other possible way, perform an essential function in our collective and individual existence, as Auster himself declared when he received the Prince of Asturias award in 2006:

> From the moment we learn to talk, we begin to develop a hunger for stories ... human beings need stories. They need them almost as desperately as they need food, and however the stories might be presented ... it would be impossible to imagine life without them. That explains the particular power of the novel, and why in my opinion, it will never die as a form. Every novel is an equal collaboration between the writer and the reader, and it is the only place in the world where two strangers can meet

on terms of absolute intimacy. I have spent my life in conversations with people I have never seen, with people I will never know, and I hope to continue until the day I stop breathing. It's the only job I've ever wanted. (Auster 2006b)

References

Akbar, Arifa. 2009. Innocence of youth: How Paul Auster excavated his own past for his latest novel. *The Independent. Books.* October 30 2009. http://www.independent.co.uk/arts-entertainment/books/features/ innocence-of-youth-how-paul-auster-excavated-his-own-past-for-his-latest-novel-1811322.html (July 3 2010).

Auster, Paul. 1987. *The New York trilogy*. London: Faber and Faber.

—. 1989. *Moon palace*. London: Faber and Faber.

—. 1998. *Hand to mouth*. London: Faber and Faber.

—. 1999. *Timbuktu*. London: Faber and Faber.

—. ed. 2001. *True tales of American life*. London: Faber and Faber.

—. 2002. *The book of illusions*. London: Faber and Faber.

—. 2002. *The story of my typewriter*. New York: Distributed Art Publishers.

—. 2003. *3 Films: Smoke, Blue in the face, Lulu on the bridge (screenplays)*. New York: Picador.

—. 2004. *Oracle night*. London: Faber and Faber.

—. 2005. *The Brooklyn follies*. London: Faber and Faber.

—. ed. 2006a. *Samuel Beckett. The centenary editions*. New York: Grove/Atlantic.

—. 2006b. Speech of acceptance of the Prince of Asturias Award, Letters, 2006. http://www.fpa.es/en/awards/2006/paul-auster-1/speech/. (July 3 2010).

—. 2006c. *Travels in the scriptorium*. London: Faber and Faber.

—. 2007. *The inner life of Martin Frost (screenplay)*. New York: Henry Holt.

—. 2008. *Man in the dark*. London: Faber and Faber.

—. 2009. *Invisible*. London: Faber and Faber.

Barone, Dennis, ed. 1995. *Beyond the red notebook: Essays on Paul Auster*. Philadelphia: University of Pennsylvania Press.

Martin, Clancy. 2009. Love Crimes. The New York Times, November 15 2009. http://www.nytimes.com/2009/11/15/books/review/Martin-t.htm l?_r=1& pagewanted=print. (July 3 2010).

Merivale, Patricia. 1997. The Austerized version. *Contemporary Literature* 38 (1): 185-197.

Teodoro, José. 2009. Parallel worlds (unabridged): in the scriptorium with Paul Auster, March 23. http://stopsmilingonline.com/story_detail.php ?id=1216 &page=1 (30 May 2010).

The Washington Post. 2003. Off the Page: Paul Auster, December 16, 2003. http://www.washingtonpost.com/wp-dyn/articles/A60646-2003 Dec12.html (July 2 2010).

Wood, James. 2009. Shallow graves: The novels of Paul Auster. *The New Yorker*, November 30 2009. http://www.newyorker.com/arts/critics/ books/2009/11/30/091130crbo_books_wood?currentPage=all. (July 3 2010).

Notes

[1] Joint Q & A session with Pedro Almodóvar in Gijón, Spain, prior to the reception of the Prince of Asturias award, October 19, 2006.

[2] As an example, James Wood wrote in his review of *Invisible* for *The New Yorker* that Auster "does nothing with cliché except use it" and he gets "the worst of both worlds: fake realism and shallow skepticism". In contrast, Clancy Martin in *The New York Times* called the book "American writing at its best".

[3] In France, Annick Duperray had edited *L'œuvre de Paul Auster* in 1995 (Paris: Actes Sud, 1995), while 1996 saw an impressive three books published on *Moon Palace*: Catherine Pesso-Miquel's *Toiles roués et déserts lunaires dans* Moon Palace *de Paul Auster* (Paris: Presses de la Sorbonne, 1996), François Gallix's edition of *Lectures d'une oeuvre:* Moon Palace (Paris: Éditions du Temps, 1996) and Yves-Charles Grandjeat's edition of the collection *Moon Palace: Paul Auster* (Paris : Ellipses, 1996). Later on, François Gavillon wrote *Paul Auster: Gravité et légèreté de l'écriture* (Rennes: Presses Universitaires de Rennes, 2000), and Gérard de Cortanze published *La solitude du labyrinthe* (Paris: Actes Sud, 1997). More recently, Catherine Quarré Roger has published *Paul Auster: L'enchanteur désenchanté* (Paris: Publibook, 2006). Critics in languages other than English have also paid more attention to Auster's involvement with cinema, as can be seen in Beate Hötger's *Identität im filmischen Werk von Paul Auster* (Frankfurt: Peter Lang, 2002), Andreas Lienkamp, Wolfgang Merth and Christian Berkemeier's edition of *"As strange as the world": Annäherungen an das Werk des Erzählers und Filmemachers Paul Auster* (Münster: LIT, 2002) or Celestino Deleyto's *Smoke* (Barcelona: Paidós, 2000). Eduardo Urbina has collected his excellent articles on the relationship between Auster and Cervantes in *La ficción que no cesa: Paul Auster y Cervantes* (Vigo: Academia del Hispanismo, 2007).

[4] While *The Brooklyn Follies* is the odd-one-out in this trio, *Travels in the Scriptorium* and *Man in the Dark* are much more discernible as part of a "diptych", as Auster readily admits (Teodoro 2009).

CHAPTER ONE

LOSS, RUINS, WAR:
PAUL AUSTER'S RESPONSE TO 9/11
AND THE "WAR ON TERROR"

PAOLO SIMONETTI

> I cannot deny that September 11, 2001, creates
> and requires a kind of silence. We desperately
> want to "explain" what happened. Explanation
> domesticates terror, making it part of "our"
> world. I believe attempts to explain must be
> resisted.
>
> —Stanley Hauerwas

Up to the present day, Paul Auster has never described the 9/11 attacks in any of his novels (except for a brief prolepsis in *The Brooklyn Follies*, to be mentioned later), though, of course, as an American and a New Yorker, he has been strongly affected by the event, both personally and professionally.[1] In a NPR interview held on September 8, 2002, he stated that, from his point of view as a storyteller, the most interesting response to 9/11 was people's need to cope with their own traumatic experiences by telling stories about the event (NPR 2002). It is safe to assume that he himself did share the same need.

Despite Auster's opinion that it might take a long time for the terrorist attacks to find an appropriate literary dimension ("Fiction is slow", he reminded the NPR interviewer, "fiction doesn't happen the next week"), in the immediate aftermath of 9/11 a number of renowned writers of different ages and backgrounds—such as Jonathan Safran Foer, Jay McInerney, Don DeLillo, and Ken Kalfus, to name but a few—have explicitly dealt with the attacks in their works. Nonetheless, apart from some notable exceptions,[2] even the most interesting of so called "9/11 novels" share an understated, quite submissive tone.[3] Perhaps Theodor Adorno's famous (and often misunderstood) contention that "writing poetry after Auschwitz is barbaric" (Adorno 1955, 31) applies to this more recent historical event as well. More likely, the reason behind such reserve lies in the fact that, as Auster acutely observed in the same interview, "some of the greatest art about a particular time is told obliquely" (NPR 2002).

Auster has indeed preferred to deal with the theme in oblique ways, adopting narrative techniques and intertextual strategies which made the attacks and their aftermath some of the text's main preoccupations without depicting them in a traditional way. Since 2001, Auster has published six novels and a screenplay: many contain (explicit or implicit) references to 9/11, and an attentive reader can easily understand how this event and its social and political reverberations play a crucial role in the plot and the structure of at least three of the novels: *The Brooklyn Follies* (2005), *Travels in the Scriptorium* (2006), and *Man in the Dark* (2008).

The aim of this chapter is to investigate Auster's response to 9/11 and the subsequent "war on terror" as exemplified in these novels, which constitute a sort of trilogy about contemporary America. More generally, an analysis of Auster's most recent works would underscore the shift from a postmodernist sensibility to a new historical consciousness. According to Hayden White, the atrocities of Nazism and the concentration camps required just the high modernist style to be figured out in literature (White 1992). In a similar way, postmodernist fiction, characterized by self-reflexive inclinations from the Sixties to the Eighties, denied the consolation of good form and offered the fragmented plots and the schizophrenic language of a post-traumatic consciousness (Elias 2001). Now, in order to keep up with the media-saturated contemporary world, it seems that fiction has veered toward a new kind of realism, what James Wood contemptuously called "hysterical realism". Complaining that in recent "big, ambitious novels" such as Don DeLillo's *Underworld* (1997), Thomas Pynchon's *Mason & Dixon* (1997), or Salman Rushdie's *The Ground Beneath Her Feet* (1999), "the conventions of realism are not being abolished but, on the contrary, exhausted, overworked", Wood declared that this mode of narration "seems to be almost incompatible with tragedy or anguish". Somehow missing the point, Wood faults this writing style because "it seems evasive of reality while borrowing from realism itself" (Wood 2004, 179-80), failing to recognize the originality of a realism that, to quote Lance Olsen, "has moved through the blast furnace of postmodernity and come out on the other side, never able to be quite the same again" (Olsen 1990, 122).

Mimicking the language of television and media outlets, as well as the clusters of information endlessly connected in the World Wide Web, the most interesting among present-day novels do not define historical representation by accuracy of depiction; on the contrary, the contemporary is caught up with past times through the use of anachronistic allusions and self-conscious malapropisms, intentional slips and absurd exaggerations, so that the traditional strategies of "mimesis" are strongly challenged. From this point of view, an analysis of Auster's works since 2005 is indicative of a paradigm shift, and sheds new light on this author's complex and original liaison with history.

Loss—Auster's goodbye to postmodernist fiction: *The Brooklyn Follies*

As some critics have remarked, Auster's complex relationship with postmodernist literature mainly focuses on a problematic equilibrium between metafiction and the narrative strategies traditionally associated with realism (Barone 1995, Weisenburger 1995, Herzogenrath 1999). It is particularly difficult to place Auster's earlier novels in a specific trend, because they belong to different genres, ranging from memoir (*The Invention of Solitude*, 1982) to metafiction (*The New York Trilogy*, 1987), from post-apocalyptic (*In the Country of Last Things*, 1987) through picaresque (*Moon Palace*, 1989), to magic realism (*Mr. Vertigo*, 1994). It seems that Auster's fiction—not to speak of his poetry—inhabits a Hawthornean "neutral territory", a purely subjective (quite autobiographical) dimension always conscious of the difficult negotiation with a historical reality that, though progressively bracketed by metafictional strategies, violently reclaims its actuality through recent traumatic events.

Unlike Thomas Pynchon and Don DeLillo, "the mythic cousins of American postmodernism" (Cowart 2002, 7) to whom he is sometimes related, Auster considers himself a "realist" writer, and his works of fiction often include autobiographical elements and personal recollections. These are, nonetheless, as Dennis Barone writes, "kernels of reality buried in a text that everywhere seeks an effect of unreality", and their use becomes a parody "not of realism, but of irrealism" (Barone 1995, 6). "Realism" in Auster's works includes such irrational elements as chance, absurd coincidences, bizarre connections, secret relationships, "mirrors, twins, innumerable fathers and sons, reflections, ghosts, and eponyms" (Chénetier 1995, 38), and all other unlikely aspects of everyday life so dear to postmodernist writers, without nevertheless making Auster one of them. However, he cannot be easily related to the new generation of "post-postmodernism", as David Foster Wallace famously called "a certain subgenre of pop-conscious postmodern fiction, written mostly by young

Americans"—like Dave Eggers, Jonathan Safran Foer, Jonathan Lethem or Wallace himself—who attempt to "transfigure a world of and for appearance, mass appeal, and television", using "the transient received myths of popular culture as a *world* in which to imagine fictions about 'real,' albeit pop-mediated, characters" (Wallace 1997, 50). Surely there is continuity from Pynchon's analysis of history and its textual (paranoid) emplotment, through DeLillo's critique of the language of media and information dimming contemporary communications, to Auster's challenge to language *tout-court* as a means of interpretation and representation of experience. Yet the relation is not simply a derivative one.

The metafictional dimension of his works does not imply that Auster is not interested in history, and that his novels lack historical grounding; on the contrary, though in a 1996 interview he admitted that "historiography is a very murky subject", he confessed to be "a great reader of history", and that, especially during the writing of *Moon Palace*, he felt "compelled, again and again, to read and read and read and read more and more books about history" (Chénetier 1996, 29). He made clear that his interest in American past and present history dates back to the beginning of his career, and that *Moon Palace* is not his only "historical" novel:

> *City of Glass* is also about America. And certainly *Leviathan* and *Mr. Vertigo* are also about America. *The Music of Chance* may be less so on the surface, but that story, too, could only happen in America. (Chénetier 1996, 16)

Yet history in Auster's early novels is often "stylised", as Aliki Varvogli noted, "always subordinate to the artistic, aesthetic concerns of his texts" (Varvogli 2001, 117), a cardboard background behind the characters' actions and feelings rather than a character itself.

On a first reading, *The Brooklyn Follies* seems to conform to this trend, with its insistence on chance, coincidence, and human idiosyncrasy against the familiar background of Brooklyn. However, Auster specified in an interview that "the book had a very slow evolution" and that, though it was conceived before 9/11, it was written in its shadow, because the book "changed its shape as [he] wrote it and as the historical context changed" (ABC Radio National 2008). Through the novel's elaborate and complex plot, Auster managed to show how the promises and the good intentions glimpsed at the beginning of the new millennium "have been drowned in a whirlpool of suspicion and division" after the "collective amnesia" (Hellman 2006) derived from the dubious result of the 2000 elections, and then definitively annihilated by the New York attacks. Published after Bush's re-election in 2004 but set in the period of the contested elections that first brought Bush to the White House following the fiasco of the Florida ballot, the novel deals with 9/11 in an oblique way, as a collective experience of imminent disaster unconsciously shared by the main characters as well as by the whole New York population. For this reason, according to David Hellman, it is "probably the first authentic attempt to deal with the post-Sept. 11 world", though the story ends just some minutes before the first plane hits the World Trade Center, and the attacks are mentioned only in the last lines, when the narrator states:

> It was eight o'clock when I stepped out onto the street, eight o'clock on the morning of September 11, 2001—just forty-six minutes before the first plane crashed into the North Tower of the World Trade Center. Just two hours after that, the smoke of three thousand incinerated bodies would drift over toward Brooklyn and come pouring down on us in a white cloud of ashes and death. (Auster 2005, 303-04)

The 9/11 attacks literally close the novel, as well as, in Auster's own words, "a certain moment in our history" (La Clé des Langues 2009). Such an ending shapes the entire book as a sort of elegy of pre-9/11 America, the story of America's loss of innocence and the end of the nation's myth of invulnerability. Even the novel's first line, with the narrator just arrived in Brooklyn declaring to be "looking for some quiet place to die" (Auster 2005, 1), acquires a different significance, if one considers how 9/11's *memento mori* ominously looms just outside the narrative.

Significantly enough, Auster declared that only when he "found" the character of Nathan Glass—the first-person narrator of the story—he was able to "reconstruct the book", and began to conceive the novel as "a picture of life before 9/11", a "hymn to ordinary life" and to "all those little aches and pains of being alive" (La Clé des Langues 2009). When confronted with his duty as a writer in the face of a tragedy, Auster took upon himself "the onerous task of delivering up a literary balm to a wounded nation" (Hellman 2006) through the character of fifty-nine-year-old Nathan, who, at the beginning of the novel, convalescent from lung cancer, moves to Brooklyn in order to live the rest of his life in solitude and seclusion.

Though a retired insurance salesman, in the course of the novel Nathan reminds us of an old reclusive postmodernist writer—"You're a writer, Nathan", his nephew Tom tells him, "You're becoming a real writer" (Auster 2005, 147)—more similar to Thomas Pynchon or John Barth than to his own author, as a matter of fact. His acquaintances are on the same wavelength: his nephew Tom Glass is a failed-academic-turned-taxi-driver, convinced that his job gives him "a unique entry point into the chaotic substructures of the universe" (Auster 2005, 29), while Tom's new employer, the book dealer Harry Brightman, is a belated Borges, whose dream as a child was "to publish an encyclopedia in which all the information was false. Wrong dates for every historical events, wrong locations for every river, biographies of people who never existed" (Auster 2005, 125). In order to occupy his time, Nathan himself begins to write down "in the simplest, clearest language possible an account of every blunder, every pratfall, every embarrassment, every idiocy, every foible, and every inane act" (Auster 2005, 5) ever committed by himself or other people. The process of research and annotation for his "Book of Human Folly" threatens to expand in a rhizomatic way—"I abandoned my one-box system", Nathan desperately declares, "in favor of a multi-box arrangement that allowed me to preserve my finished works in a more coherent fashion", (Auster 2005, 7)—and resembles the umpteenth postmodern pastiche:

> I called the project a book, but in fact it wasn't a book at all. Working with yellow legal pads, loose sheets of paper, the backs of envelopes and junk-mail form letters for credit cards and home-improvement loans, I was compiling what amounted to a collection of random jottings, a hodgepodge of unrelated anecdotes that I would throw into a cardboard box each time another story was finished. There was little method to my madness. Some of the pieces came to no more than a few lines, and a number of them, in particular the spoonerisms and malapropisms I was so fond of, were just a single phrase. (Auster 2005, 6)

Nevertheless, to write such a book is no longer possible, as Nathan understands when he admits: "Even though I did my best to keep the tone frivolous and light, I discovered that it wasn't always possible" (Auster 2005, 8). In a similar way, Auster could not write the comedy he had in mind when he first conceived *The Brooklyn Follies*.[4] The jokes and circumvolutions of chance—"Call them parallels, call them coincidences" —are considered by Tom mere "external facts", and so "less important than the inner truth of each man's life" (Auster 2005, 15-16). It is difficult (and politically incorrect) to find bizarre links or make witty jokes in the face of events as tragic as the New York attacks, and even postmodernist writers feel less and less compelled to humour or clever linguistic plays while addressing recent history.

In 1990 Lance Olsen had already observed how "postmodernism has turned its sense of joking against itself and against its readers—the final centers of authority in this century", until "as we move into the last decade of our century, both postmodernism and the comic vision have once again been marginalized by our neoconservative culture" (Olsen 1990, 35). In the empty space left by the destruction of the towers, even postmodernist writers discovered themselves as realist writers[5] and felt the moral imperative of producing counternarratives to face the terroristic discourse of violence and fear (as devised by terrorists and politicians alike). In this regard Tom, while playing with the meaning of their surnames, ironically reminds his uncle that "we've entered a new era, Nathan. The post-family, post-student, post-past age of Glass and Wood. ... The *now*. And also the *later*. But no more dwelling on the *then*" (Auster 2005, 22). Auster makes thus clear that the new millennium requires an original approach to history and temporality, different from the witty linguistic plays of postmodernism, and in his most recent novels he tries to negotiate a new relationship between history and fiction.

At the end of *The Brooklyn Follies*, after having experienced the ups and downs of everyday life and having relinquished his initial solipsism, Nathan's literary project utterly changes when a sudden thought hits him: "Most lives vanish. A person dies, and little by little all traces of that life disappear", leaving only "a few objects, a few documents, and a smattering of impressions made on other people" (Auster 2005, 301). When Nathan is unexpectedly hospitalized for an alleged heart attack, forced to face the mourning of loss and the ineluctable actuality of death, he turns toward other people, their feelings suddenly more important than any bizarre encyclopedia he may long to write:

> My idea was this: to form a company that would publish books about the forgotten ones, to rescue the stories and facts and documents before they disappeared—and shape them into a contiguous narrative, the narrative of a life. (Auster 2005, 301)

As a bitter irony, this new project—which Nathan foolishly reputes "the single most important idea [he] had ever had" (Auster 2005, 300)—is probably doomed to failure as well, because, forty-six minutes after he leaves the hospital "feverishly planning the structure of [his] new company", the sky, until then "the bluest of pure deep blue" (Auster 2005, 303), would be full of the smoke coming from the crashed planes and the flaming towers. Yet, Nathan's project was apparently fulfilled, in the real world, by *The New York Times*. In the aftermath of 9/11, the newspaper published as a daily feature the so-called "Portraits of Grief": brief biographies of the victims that in few lines and sensationalistic titles related some generic facts of their lives. Auster himself confessed in an interview his interest in these profiles:

One felt, looking at those pages every day, that real lives were jumping out at you. We weren't mourning an anonymous mass of people, we were mourning thousands of individuals. And the more we knew about them, the more we could wrestle with our own grief. (Scott 2001)

However, as the author showed in his novel, a return to an ingenuous old-style realism is not a valid alternative to the metafictional exaggerations of postmodernist literature, neither is it an effective way to cope with trauma.

What chances remain, then, for literature to endure after 9/11 (and after postmodernism as well)? A partial answer may be found in an anecdote Tom recounts to Nathan during a car trip, regarding one of the precursors of postmodernist fiction, Franz Kafka. In order to comfort a little girl who had lost her doll, Kafka wrote her a number of letters pretending they were from the doll, informing the girl of its life far from home, and ultimately bidding her goodbye. It is important that Kafka writes the letters with "the same seriousness and tension he displays when composing his own work":

He isn't about to cheat the little girl. This is a real literary labor, and he's determined to get it right. If he can come up with a beautiful and persuasive lie, it will supplant the girl's loss with a different reality—a false one, maybe, but something true and believable according to the laws of fiction. (Auster 2005, 154)

Of course, literature may have a therapeutic function, as testified by Auster's novel and all 9/11 fiction (not to mention the recent studies of "Medical Humanities" and narrative medicine in particular), but it has to be taken seriously; "when a person is lucky enough to live inside a story, to live inside an imaginary world", says Tom, "the pains of this world disappear" (Auster 2005, 155). Reductionist as this view of literature may seem, "there's a message in it for us", as Tom reflects, "some kind of warning about how we're supposed to act" (Auster 2005, 153).

Ruins—Writing "Ground Zero": *Travels in the Scriptorium*

Critics have largely dismissed *Travels in the Scriptorium* as a belated (and largely failed) metafictional puzzle "swallowing its own tail until there is nothing left" (Zipp 2007), "self-regarding almost to the point of narcissism" (Royle 2006), and on the whole representing "a backward step from Auster's last novel" (Hickling 2006). Yet, Auster considers this work as constituting a "diptych" (Teodoro 2009) with his following novel, *Man in the Dark*, in which the American contemporary political situation is explicitly criticized, and this makes it worthy of a closer scrutiny. In depicting an amnesiac old man trapped in a room, spied on by hidden cameras and microphones, ridden by guilt and unsure about what he has forced his "operatives" to do, the novel reflects the paranoid mood and the confused feelings of American people towards the government's responsibilities for the 9/11 attacks and the "war on terror". Mr. Blank, the rather mysterious main character, "has no idea that a camera is planted in the ceiling directly above him" (Auster 2006, 1), neither is he aware of his whereabouts. "What he knows", says the narrator, "is that his heart is filled with an implacable sense of guilt. At the same time, he can't escape the feeling that he is the victim of a terrible injustice" (Auster 2006, 2-3), just like the average American citizen after 9/11.

In a way, the novel begins where *The Brooklyn Follies* ended, with an old man recovering from some disease, oppressed by old age as well as by a number of questions. The hospitalized Nathan had felt a very similar sense of oppression toward the end of the previous book:

> [L]ying in that boxed-in enclosure with the beeping machines and the wires clamped to my skin was the closest I have come to being nowhere, to being inside myself and outside myself at the same time. ... To be diminished in such a way is to lose all right to privacy. (Auster 2005, 297)

At the beginning of *Travels in the Scriptorium* Mr. Blank is sitting on a bed, "palms spread out on his knees, head down, staring at the floor", while "[h]is mind is elsewhere, stranded among the figments in his head as he searches for an answer to the question that haunts him" (Auster 2006, 1). He has at his disposal only a series of pictures, though the narrator distrusts what Mr. Blank sees, observing that "[t]he pictures do not lie, but neither do they tell the whole story" (Auster 2006, 3). Auster himself has always been suspicious of the "truth" of history and its representations, as he reflected in an interview:

> Most of our contemporary history comes out of newspapers, people recording what happens; and they *always* get it wrong. It happens so consistently, that you learn that everything you read in the newspaper is wrong—even though the journalist is trying his best, is not purposely distorting the facts. (Chénetier 1996, 29)

Right after that, he quoted the most (mis)represented event in American history, the Kennedy assassination, and refuted the widespread myth of a nation suddenly "stunned", where "everybody was grieving and there wasn't a dry eye in the nation". The record of his travel to Washington to attend the funerals is particularly revealing:

> A large number of the people there were only interested in getting good photographs. There were people climbing up into trees and yelling at each other about how to get the right angle. There was no sadness or bereavement that I could see. Just people out there in a kind of carnival atmosphere. (Chénetier 1996, 30)

Auster's anecdote exposes the origins of present-day obsession for media reproduction that obliterates any historical event in the precise moment when it happens. The Kennedy assassination represented "the shock of a communicational explosion", as Fredric Jameson described it, "a unique collective (and media, communicational) experience, which trained people to read such events in a new way" (Jameson 1991, 306, 355), and which, "by accidentally drawing attention to the lack of coherence and coordination in the plot of history" (Knight 2000, 114), inaugurated the new paradigm of paranoia in American fiction (Knight 2000, Simonetti 2009). From then on, every historical occurrence is already filtered, prefabricated, edited and ready for the market the very moment it happens, while at the same time it remains inevitably opaque and inaccessible to the public.

9/11 is one of such occurrences: quite everything we know about it comes from newspapers, reportages and interviews, though millions of people experienced it personally or in front of a TV set, listened to "true" reports from witnesses and survivors and read "true" relations from governmental authorities and experts. Yet many people still contend that all we know about it might be a lie, or, worse, a kind of governmental propaganda, as Auster himself has recently declared:

> Under the new Bush administration, one truly feels that the media is functioning as a kind of propaganda machine for the government. ... [O]ther organs of the media are just blatantly pandering to the public, giving them what they think the public wants, entertaining war coverage on cable TV. It's become impossible for me to look at that stuff anymore—it seems so tainted and biased and twisted. (Reed 2003)

In this regard, Auster's insistence on feigning absolute objectivity while relating the facts happening in the novel (which is presented as an objective report based on data gathered with highly reliable instruments) acquires different, ominous meanings:

It should be noted that in addition to the camera a microphone is embedded
in one of the walls, and every sound Mr. Blank makes is being reproduced
and preserved by a highly sensitive digital tape recorder. ...

It should be noted that a second camera and a second tape recorder have
been planted in the bathroom ceiling, making it possible for all activities in
that space to be recorded as well, and because the word all is an absolute
term, the transcription of the dialogue between Anna and Mr. Blank can be
verified in every one of its details. (Auster 2006, 8, 26)

Of course, nobody can verify such details in a work of fiction, and
Auster's irony is stressed by the fact that some of the characters refer to
obviously fictitious novels (some of them written by Auster himself) as
"reports", recalling in some way the infamous *9/11 Commission Report*
and the language used by the Bush government to legitimize military
operations. As Martin Butler and Jens Martin Gurr argued, the novel
"critically engages with a particular genre which, especially in a US
context, has been controversially debated in recent years", and in reading
Travels in the Scriptorium "one may only think of the reports allegedly
proving the existence of weapons of mass destructions in Iraq and thus
legitimizing the replacement of Saddam Hussein's dictatorship" (Butler
and Gurr 2008, 199).

The story gets complicated when the secluded Mr. Blank begins to
read a story set in an alternate world by one Trause (anagram of the author
and protagonist of another Auster's novel, *Oracle Night*) about one
Sigmund Graf, who, while prisoner in a cell with "the desert begin[ning]
just outside [the] window" (Auster 2006, 10) and subject to numerous
beatings by "the Colonel", writes a report of his (obviously failed)
mission; as a loyal operative for the mighty "Confederation", he has been
sent in "the Alien Territories" in order to investigate the suspicious
activity of an alleged traitor, notably called "Land", accused of stirring
unrest among the natives. The history of the troubled Territories,
originally inhabited by "the Primitives", traces that of the American
conquest:

Everything used to be theirs. Then the ships arrived, bringing settlers from
Iberia and Gaul, from Albion, Germania, and the Tartar kingdoms, and
little by little the Primitives were pushed off their lands. We slaughtered
them and enslaved them and then we herded them together in the parched
and barren territories beyond the western provinces. (Auster 2006, 75-76)

While reading the book, Mr. Blank, so far "reasonably certain that the
present moment can be situated sometime in the early twenty-first century

and that he lives in a country called the United States of America" (Auster 2006, 12), begins to doubt whether he is still there, while on the contrary the reader gradually understands that Auster is actually commenting on "contemporary America, the 'war on terror,' and prison camps in Guantanamo, Afghanistan, Iraq and elsewhere" (Butler and Gurr 2008, 198). Yet, as soon as Mr. Blank becomes acquainted with the story he is reading and considers it true, because "it sounds more like a report, something that really happened", he is contradicted again by another character, who tells him that "it's make-believe, ... [a] work of fiction" (Auster 2006, 78).

This is the very reason why Auster structures his novel as a mock-postmodernist romp, willingly exaggerating its metafictional dimension; by stripping language to the bone while reflecting on contemporary issues, Auster makes clear that the recent national events and the political responses to them have brought not only America, but also narrative itself to a sort of "Ground Zero". The story about the Confederation is, by Auster's words, "a weird political parable" (Owens, 2007); Mr. Blank, like his author, does not accept the situation it represents, and eventually he has the opportunity to change it. When the manuscript he is reading abruptly interrupts, he feels angry and frustrated:

> Mr. Blank tosses the typescript onto the desk, snorting with dissatisfaction and contempt, furious that he has been compelled to read a story that has no ending, an unfinished work that has barely even begun, a mere bloody fragment. What garbage, he says out loud ... regretting having wasted so much time on that misbegotten excuse of a story. (Auster 2006, 84)

Not a lover of postmodernist literature, definitely. "[W]here I come from", he adds, "stories are supposed to have a beginning, a middle, and an end", suggesting that the "bastard" author "should be taken outside and shot" (Auster 2006, 88). In *The Brooklyn Follies*, Nathan realized that in the face of tragedy he could no longer write his witty "Book of Human Follies", or any naïve biography of dead people. The (postmodernist) writer (as well as any reader trained on postmodernist assumptions) is trapped in his self-constructed works of fantasy and is violently forced by events to negotiate a new relationship between words and objects, facts and fiction, subjectivity and history.

Mr. Blank goes one step further. When he is asked to continue the story he is reading, "as an exercise in imaginative reasoning" (Auster 2006, 89), he finally utters what the reader at this point has already understood:

The Confederation... The Con-fed-e-ra-tion... It's all very simple, isn't it? Just another name for America. Not the United States as we know it, but a country that has evolved in another way, that has another history. (Auster 2006, 91)

Before he can "verbally write" the story, however, he needs to piece together language anew, since it is all in ruin and has reverted to a zero degree. The labels that at the beginning of the novel neatly designated the objects in the room are all scattered and confused, and the words no longer correspond to the things:

After a thorough investigation, he is horrified to discover that not a single label occupies its former spot. The wall now reads CHAIR. The lamp now reads BATHROOM. The chair now reads DESK. ...

It will not do, then, to call a chair a desk or a desk a lamp. To indulge in such infantile whimsy is to throw the world into chaos, to make life intolerable for all but the mad. (Auster 2006, 115-16)

After having performed the exhausting "symbolic undertaking to restore harmony to a broken universe" (Auster 2006, 118), Mr. Blank is finally able to imagine an appropriate ending for the story. Significantly enough, the plot he puts together deals with a phony war staged to unite a divided nation, and with the merciless mass extermination of troops and entire populations for the sole purpose of ensuring national security: "[W]hat better way to unite the people", twenty-first century American Mr. Blank reflects, "than to invent a common enemy and start a war?" (Auster 2006, 92). Besides, "[t]hese are treacherous times" (Auster 2006, 49), as anyone living after 9/11 knows all too well.

Yet, despite the fact that this alternate America has no black slaves and "more ethnic variety than here for that moment in history" (Auster 2006, 121), the dreadful picture does not change. The writer's attempt to create a counternarrative, a creative, heterogeneous language opposed to the one-way rhetoric of the terrorists and the one-way rhetoric of the government is doomed to failure. In Mr. Blank's sketch Land must die, "lying on his back with a bullet hole in his forehead and a swarm of flies and maggots crawling over his half-eaten face" (Auster 2006, 125), his regiment massacred by another Confederation army; and Graf himself, drawn into a "sinister scheme" in order to "unleash the war the government so desperately wants" (Auster 2006, 126), after having written his reputedly true "Firsthand Report" and understood his role as a patsy, "picks up a loaded revolver and fires a bullet through his skull" (Auster 2006, 128). As the narrator states at the end, "even if Mr. Blank is happy to have reshaped

the story according to his own design, he knows that it is a gruesome story
for all that, and a part of him recoils in terror from what he has yet to tell"
(Auster 2006, 125). Of course, "if you want to tell a good story, you can't
show any pity" (Auster 2006, 123), as Auster would prove in his following
novel.

War—A History of the Present:
Man in the Dark

Man in the Dark is perhaps Auster's most evidently political novel
(along with *Leviathan*), a book, as the author himself reckoned, full of
grief and rage for the dangerous direction America has taken during the
Bush presidency. Published on the eve of the 2008 presidential election
that would eventually salute Barack Obama as the US 44th president, it
begins where *Travels in the Scriptorium* ended, somewhat closing the
trilogy with another fictitious account of America's present history. As the
action of the previous novel takes place in one day, *Man in the Dark*
recounts the night which the insomniac retired literary critic August Brill
spends telling himself the story of Owen Brick, a magician inexplicably
catapulted in a parallel course of history. In Brick's world America is at
war not with terrorists but with itself, because, after the contested 2000
elections, a civil war has broken out, and several states have seceded from
the U.S.A in protest. Brick's experience is the literalization of a metaphor
lived by all Americans on September 11, 2001: "One minute you're living
your life, and the next minute you're in the war" (Auster 2008, 9).

Nonetheless Auster declared in an interview that the first source of
inspiration for his civil-war story was not 9/11 but the 2000 elections,
which stroke him as an outrage:

> I felt so frustrated, and disgusted, and angry, and depressed about what
> happened, because Al Gore won the election, he was voted president of the
> United States; and through political and legal manoeuvrings the
> Republicans stole it from him. I've had this eerie sense in the last eight
> years that we're out of the tracks of reality, we've been living in a parallel
> world. The world we asked for is one in which Al Gore is now finishing
> his second term, the US never invaded Iraq, and possibly 9/11 never
> happened either. And so I think this sense of living in a real/unreal world
> inspired me to make this story and tell it through Brill. (Miller 2008)

This is an uncharacteristically strong declaration for an author like Auster,
who in his long career has rarely written explicitly political works, nor has
been too interested in taking sides. It seems that, as critic James Bone

hinted, after 9/11 Auster has undergone "a new incarnation: intellectual 'engagé'" (Bone 2004). Every time he was interviewed on 9/11 and the "war on terror", Auster used to show his interviewers the framed cover of a poetry magazine hanging on his wall, headlined "U.S.A. out of NYC"; he made clear several times that he "would love to see New York break away from the United States and become an independent city-state", because New Yorkers "represent something more than just America" (Reed 2003). We can probably consider declarations such as these as the spontaneous outpouring of an outraged artist in the face of a national tragedy. Auster himself mitigated his position in the same interview, shifting the issue to the dimension of language:

> In a sense, this is of course an exaggeration, I'm not predicting a real civil war in the United States, but I do think we are in a civil war of a kind, not with bombs or bullets, but with words and ideas, and the country is very divided; and the two halves are unable to speak to each other anymore: there's no common language, there's no discourse available anymore. (Miller 2008)

Nonetheless, much of this rage filters through *Man in the Dark*, turning the book into a harsh commentary on present-day America.

If Auster is at times surprisingly well-disposed toward secession, he entrusts his doubts to his characters:

> Well, for your information, Mr. Stupid, Molly says, we're in a war, and New York started it.
> Oh?
> Yes, *oh*. Secession. Maybe you've heard of it. When a state declares independence from the rest of the country. There are sixteen of us now, and God knows when it will end. I'm not saying it's a bad thing, but enough is enough. It wears you out, and pretty soon you're just sick of the whole business. (Auster 2008, 29)

Brick's and Auster's mixed attitudes towards secession parallel the reflections of Nathaniel Hawthorne, who, during his last years, had to cope with civil war too, and it is significant that the father of American literature is a constant presence in this novel as well as in all of Auster's works. The author has often remarked that the nineteenth-century writer is one of his great favorites, to the extent that he has become "almost an obsession" (Owens 2007). Moreover, Auster is not only fond of Hawthorne the writer, but also an admirer of Hawthorne the man and the father, as he wrote in the introduction to *Twenty Days with Julian & Little Bunny by Papa*, a reprint of a tender and funny extract from Hawthorne's *American*

Notebooks where the famous writer recounts the three weeks he spent at home with his five-year-old son Julian. Indeed, Auster's fiction has inherited many of the themes explored by Hawthorne in his writing—the seclusion of the artist, the relationship between history and romance, the dark side of the human mind; in *Man in the Dark*, Brill's daughter Katya is writing a biography of Hawthorne's daughter Rose, and at one point the old critic inevitably reflects on the writer's attitude towards war, mixing past and present, facts and fictions in his mind:

> Hawthorne didn't care. If the South wanted to secede from the country, he said, let them go and good riddance. The weird world, the battered world, the weird world rolling on as wars flame all around us: the chopped-off arms in Africa, the chopped-off heads in Iraq, and in my own head this other war, an imaginary war on home ground, America cracking apart, the noble experiment finally dead. (Auster 2008, 49)

This is a very simplistic view of Hawthorne's complex stance on American politics; notably, the old writer was outraged by the outbreak of the civil war, and dealt with the topic in a witty and complex essay, significantly entitled "Chiefly About War Matters. By a Peaceable Man", aware that "[t]here is no remoteness of life and thought, no hermetically sealed seclusion, except, possibly, that of the grave, into which the disturbing influences of this war do not penetrate" (Hawthorne 1862, 43). Nonetheless, he never mentioned the civil war in a work of fiction, and was finally unable to find an appropriate language to transfigure it, if not through his essay and in some sketchy notes on his journal. By mentioning Hawthorne and evoking his doubts about war, Auster clearly suggests that Brill and his imagined story (as well as Auster's novel itself) are after the same task: to find an appropriate "literary" way to cope with war and death.

Like the aging Hawthorne absorbed in "the contemplation of certain fantasies" (Hawthorne 1862, 43) in the relative insulation of The Wayside in Concord, Brill, in his house in Vermont, tries not to think about war. The stories he invents during his sleepless nights serve to prevent him "from thinking about the things [he] would prefer to forget", such as the brutal death in Iraq of his granddaughter's boyfriend Titus, pushing it "as far away from [him] as possible" (Auster 2008, 2). Yet the "laws of fiction" invoked by Tom in *The Brooklyn Follies* do not allow any beautiful, tranquilizing lie, because it would not be persuasive. The bitter irony is that though in Brick's alternate world 9/11 never happened, the situation is far worse than any foreseeable outcome, with bombed-out cities and a second civil war ravaging the country. The unbelieving Brick asks a waitress: "[I]f I said the words *September eleventh* to you, would they have any special meaning?", and when the annoyed girl denies that they would, he becomes aware that inevitably "[o]ne nightmare replaces another" (Auster 2008, 31). It is not by erasing the event nor by pretending it never happened that one can successfully cope with trauma.

In a similar way, the frantic search for "responsibilities" that has been going on in public discourses since 9/11—and that resulted in a number of conspiracy theories about what actually provoked the collapse of the towers or who was really responsible for the plane crashes—is exposed by Auster's novel as senseless and futile: the only way Brick has to end the war is to kill the one person responsible for its outbreak, the one who "owns the war, [who] invented it" (Auster 2008, 10), that is, his own author, Brill. And this is clearly impossible. The point is that, as a sergeant says to an astonished Brick, "[i]t's not *who* so much as *what* … . We're not even sure of his name. It could be Blake. It could be Black. It could be Block" (Auster 2008, 9). It could be Bush, or Bin Laden, as well, but the result would be the same; it is impossible to trace the actual culprits when names and roles, rights and wrongs get so easily confused: "Is it North against South again?", a disoriented Brick asks himself, "East against West? Red against Blue? White against Black?", concluding that "[w]hatever caused the war … and whatever issues or ideas happen to be at stake, none of it makes any sense" (Auster 2008, 23).

It is similarly useless to think of a utopian country after a hypothetical secession; in Brick's world the seceding states promote an idyllic program that would never become real:

> Foreign policy: no meddling anywhere … . Domestic policy: universal health insurance, no more oil, no more cars or plans, a fourfold increase in teachers' salaries (to attract the brightest students to the profession), strict gun control, free education and job training for the poor … all in the realm of fantasy for the moment, a dream of the future, since the war drags on, and the state of emergency is still in force. (Auster 2008, 63)

Brill himself is well aware of the impossibility of the task, and his story is neither convincing nor feasible. Quite in the middle of the book he reveals that "the Brill character wasn't in my original plan":

> The mind that created the war was going to belong to someone else, another invented character, as unreal as … all the rest, but the longer I went on, the more I understood how badly I was fooling myself. (Auster 2008, 102)

At first, when he ponders on what direction the story should take, he is still undecided: "Hope or no hope? Both options are available, and yet neither one is fully satisfying" (Auster 2008, 88). Finally he becomes aware that only one ending is suitable, and comes to the same conclusion Mr. Blank arrived at in *Travels in the Scriptorium*: Brick must die, violently and abruptly, with a bullet in the leg and another "straight through his right eye and out the back of his head. And that is the end of Owen Brick, who leaves the world in silence, with no chance to say a last word or think a last thought" (Auster 2008, 118).

Brill knows all too well that a happy ending is not available:

> Does it have to end that way? Yes, probably yes, although it wouldn't be difficult to think of a less brutal outcome. But what would be the point? My subject tonight is war, and now that war has entered this house, I feel I would be insulting Titus and Katya if I softened the blow. (Auster 2008, 118)

If Brick's America is ravaged by a civil war, Brill's is haunted by the ghosts of actual wars, not only in Iraq and Afghanistan. It is worth remembering that, as Auster specified, the idea for *Man in the Dark* was also inspired by the killing in Lebanon of Uri Grossman, the twenty-year-old son of Israeli writer David Grossman, to whose memory the novel is dedicated. The event is mirrored in the novel by the final narration of the brutal killing in Iraq of Titus, a death as meaningless as that of Brick. Once again, Auster seems to share DeLillo's idea that the writer is no longer able to counteract the discourse of terrorism, to change the course of the present through art (*Mao II*, 1991); every narration inevitably breaks off, every plot leads only to death (*Libra*, 1988).[6]

In Auster's novel, all characters are in some way artists: the fictitious Brick is a magician; Brill is a retired literary critic who invents stories during the night, his daughter Miriam is a biographer, and his granddaughter Katya has frequented a film school in New York and now spends her days watching movies and analyzing them with her grandfather. At the end of the novel, the reader is told that Titus too, a former student at Columbia, has decided to go off to work in Iraq as a contractor because, as he says, "[e]very word I've written so far is crap" (Auster 2008, 173):

> I spend my days sitting in an office, answering the phone for a literary agent. What kind of life is that? It's so fucking safe, so fucking dreary, I can't stand it anymore. I don't *know* anything, August. I haven't *done* anything. That's why I'm going away. To experience something that isn't about me. To be out in the big rotten world and discover what it feels like to be part of history. (Auster 2008, 173)

Paradoxically, the words used by Titus to justify his decision recall those pronounced by another Auster character, Benjamin Sachs, the writer turned terrorist in *Leviathan*, who at one point in his literary career arrived at a very similar conclusion:

> I don't want to spend the rest of my life rolling pieces of blank paper into a typewriter. I want to stand up from my desk and do something. The days of being a shadow are over. I've got to step into the real world now and do something. (Auster 2004 [1992], 122)

Unlike Titus, who goes to Iraq in order to transport supplies, Sachs becomes a terrorist and begins to bomb replicas of the Statue of Liberty throughout America. No matter that he is careful not to hurt people; the writer senses "a sort of cosmic attraction" toward the terrorist, because "both knew that fundamental changes were needed", but the terrorist "was brave enough to put his ideas to the test" (Auster 2004 [1992], 224-25).[7] Both Titus and Sachs represent Auster's opinion about the futility of such an active but inconsiderate commitment, and both will eventually die without having accomplished their idealistic dreams. The solution, Auster implies, lies elsewhere.

How can the novelist, then, give sense, prominence, and a proper structure to the historical facts and to the present traumas that the language of media (not to speak of the fanatical blabbers of terrorists) inevitably flatten in the idle chatters of talk shows, in the jargon of newspaper "reports", or in the worn-out stereotypes of historical "realist" narratives? According to many commentators, after 9/11 we have definitely entered the "age of nonfiction";[8] all through his second "trilogy" Auster has tried to give back to literature its relevance and to find a way out of the impasse. He has deconstructed and mixed three different literary genres—the realist novel, the metafictional novel, and the counterfactual history (or allohistory)—in order to renegotiate a historical temporality that would reject the simplistic vision of a "boundless present" without repudiating the complexities of historicization across time (past, future or alternative) and space (real or imagined). From the overabundant and frivolous prose of *The Brooklyn Follies*, through the stripped-out, essential language of *Travels in the Scriptorium*, he has arrived at the mixed structure of *Man in the Dark*, merging first- and third-person narration, facts and fiction, the "real" world and an imagined (yet plausible) one, subjective and national traumas, complex, human characters and flat figures conscious of their own fictionality, while managing at the same time to restore a creative heterogeneity without sacrificing historical or emotional depth. In the end, we can conclude that Auster's realism relies

upon metafiction to represent reality, and what Stephen J. Burn wrote
about Richard Powers' *The Gold Bug Variations* (1991) may fit Auster's
most recent novels as well:

> By basing the novel upon a relatively traditional foundation, and then
> relying upon the codes of realism until the final pages, Powers [as well as
> Auster] attempts a synthesis of two apparently opposed modes of rendering
> the world. The realist dimension to his novels elicits the traditional effects
> of fiction—understanding, empathy with another's perspective—while the
> metafictional element draws the reader's attention outside the book, to
> recognize the way her own life story is constructed. (Burn 2001, 229-30)

In his post-9/11 novels Auster has tried, like Powers, to "reconcile
postmodernism and realism and escape the narcissistic inward spiral of
self-referring fiction", in order to cope with the traumatic events of recent
American history, and to reconfigure that "neutral territory" dividing the
narrator from the "Romancer", the space of biography from the territory
of fiction-writing.

In his attempt to reconstruct a "history of the present", Auster started,
of course, from his personal experience: all his three protagonists are
aging and disenchanted (writers), forced to cope with their own life and
feelings as well as with the national political situation; all face disease,
loss, and mourning, and all are in some way affected by war. Yet they
represent an evolution from Auster's early novels, whose characters were
mostly solitary and introverted, lonely outcasts such as Quinn (*City of
Glass*), or stubborn intellectuals like Fogg (*Moon Palace*). His most recent
novels testify to a renewed sense of community and to a continuous search
for sympathetic relations with people, probably also as a consequence of
trauma. From initial negative or dramatic situations, all characters find
later more and more comfort in the warmth of family, cherishing human
touch and compassionate feelings: Nathan comes out of his initial
solipsism and suicidal tendencies after having met his nephew and a
number of people who befriend him; Mr. Blank finds comfort in Anna's
tender and reciprocal love; and while the doubly fictitious Brick dies "in
silence" in the dark, Brill awakes in the morning after his painful wake
(the wake of postmodernism?), ready to face another day; his relationship
with his daughter and granddaughter sounds as the strongest note that
closes the novel.

References

ABC Radio National. 2008. The Book Show. Paul Auster and the writer's mind. 9 April 2008. http://www.abc.net.au/rn/bookshow/stories/2008/2211787.htm. (16 April 2010).

Adorno, Theodor. 1955. *Prismen*. Frankfurt: Suhrkamp.

Auster, Paul. 2002. Random notes-September 11, 2001, 4:00 p.m.; underground. In *110 stories: New York writes after September 11*, ed. Ulrich Baer. New York and London: New York University Press. 26-27.

—. 2004 [1992]. *Leviathan*. London: Faber and Faber.

—. 2005. *The Brooklyn follies*. London: Faber and Faber.

—. 2006. *Travels in the scriptorium*. New York: Henry Holt.

—. 2008. *Man in the dark*. New York: Henry Holt.

Baer, Ulrich. Ed. 2002. *110 stories. New York writes after September 11*. New York and London: New York University Press.

Barone, Dennis. 1995. Introduction: Paul Auster and the postmodern American novel. In *Beyond the red notebook. Essays on Paul Auster*, ed. Dennis Barone. Philadelphia: University of Pennsylvania Press. 1-26.

Bone, James. 2004. Dem old Bush blues. Times Online. 17 April 2004. http://entertainment.timesonline.co.uk/tol/arts_and_entertainment/article825554.ece?token=null&offset=0&page=1. (16 April 2010).

Burn, Stephen J. 2008. The end of postmodernism. American fiction at the millennium. In *American fiction of the 1990s. Reflections of history and culture*, ed. Jay Prosser. London and New York: Routledge. 220-34.

Butler, Martin and Jens Martin Gurr. 2008. The poetics and politics of metafiction: reading Paul Auster's *Travels in the scriptorium*. *English Studies* 89 (2): 195-209.

Chénetier, Marc. 1995. Paul Auster's pseudonymous world. In *Beyond the red notebook. Essays on Paul Auster*, ed. Dennis Barone. Philadelphia: University of Pennsylvania Press. 34-43.

—. 1996. Around *Moon Palace*. A conversation with Paul Auster. *Sources. Revue d'Etudes Anglophones* 1: 5-35.

Cowart, David. 2002. *Don DeLillo. The physics of language*. Athens and London: The University of Georgia Press.

DeLillo, Don. 1989 [1988]. *Libra*. London: Penguin.

—. 1992 [1991]. *Mao II*. London: Vintage.

—. 2007. *Falling Man*. New York: Scribner.

Donadio, Rachel. 2004. Oh, Sam Tanenhaus: new cerebral boss takes
    Book Review. *The New York Observer*, March 21.
    http://www.observer.com/node/48967. (16 April 2010).
Elias, Amy J. 2001. *Sublime desire. History and post-1960s fiction.*
    Baltimore and London: The Johns Hopkins University Press.
Geismar, Haidy. 2005. Building sites of memory: the *Ground Zero Sonic
    Memorial Sound Walk. Fabrication* 15 (2): 1-14. http://espace.library.
    uq.edu.au/eserv/UQ:135725/n15_2_002_Geismar.pdf. (16 April 2010).
Gorman, Michael. 2006. Introductory remark at the American Library
    Association 2006 Annual Conference, June 25. http://mg.csufresno
    .edu/papers/ forum_2/captioned_text.pdf. (16 April 2010).
Hauerwas, Stanley. 2003. September 11, 2001. A pacifist response. In
    Dissent from the homeland. Essays after September 11, ed. Stanley
    Hauerwas and Frank Lentricchia, 181-93. Durham and London: Duke
    University Press.
Hawthorne, Nathaniel. 1862. Chiefly about war matters. By a peaceable
    man. *Atlantic Monthly* 10 (57): 43-61.
Hellman, David. 2006. A twist of fate. *San Francisco Chronicle*, January 1.
    http://articles.sfgate.com/2006-01-01/books/17276806_1_nathan-glass-
    paul-auster-brooklyn-follies. (16 April 2010).
Herzogenrath, Bernd. 1999. *An art of desire. Reading Paul Auster.*
    Amsterdam, Atlanta: Rodopi.
Hickling, Alfred. 2006. Where's the exit?. *The Guardian*, October 14.
    http://www.guardian.co.uk/books/2006/oct/14/fiction.paulauster. (16
    April 2010).
Houen, Alex. 2004. Novel spaces and taking place(s) in the wake of
    September 11. *Studies in the Novel* 36 (3): 419-37.
Jameson, Fredric. 1991. *Postmodernism, or the cultural logic of late
    capitalism.* Durham: Duke University Press.
Knight, Peter. 2000. *Conspiracy culture: American paranoia from
    Kennedy to the X-Files.* New York: Routledge.
La Clé des Langues. 2009. The "Mechanics of reality": Paul Auster speaks
    about his works and inspiration. *The Brooklyn follies* and 9/11. 13
    January 2009. http://cle.ens-lsh.fr/39808285/0/fiche___pagelibre/. (16
    April 2010).
Miller, George. 2008. Faber & Faber. Paul Auster on *Man in the dark.*
    http://www.faber.co.uk/site-media/audio-snippets/auster_interview.
    mp3 (16 April 2010).
NPR National Public Radio. 2002. All things considered. Authors Auster,
    Rushdie reflect on September 11. 8 September 2002. http://www.npr.
    org/templates/story/story.php?storyId=1149638. (16 April 2010).

Olsen, Lance. 1990. *Circus of the mind in motion. Postmodernism and the comic vision*. Detroit: Wayne State University Press.

Owens, Jill. 2007. Powell's Books. Author interviews. The book of Paul Auster. http://www.powells.com/interviews/auster.html. (16 April 2010).

Reed, John. 2003. Paul Auster. The Brooklyn rail. http://www.brooklyn rail.org/2003/08/books/paul-auster. (16 April 2010).

Royle, Nicholas. 2006. Being Paul Auster. A trip through the teeming brain of the author. *The Independent*, October, 30. http://www.independent.co.uk/artsentertainment/books/reviews/travels - in-the-scriptorium-by-paul-auster-422147.html. (16 April 2010).

Scott, Janny. 2001. Closing a scrapbook full of life and sorrow. *The New York Times*, December 31. http://www.nytimes.com/2001/12/31/nati onal/portraits/31PORT.html?pagewanted=1. (16 April 2010).

Simonetti, Paolo. 2009. *Paranoia blues. Trame del postmodern americano*. Roma: Aracne.

Teodoro, José. 2009. Parallel worlds (unabridged): in the scriptorium with Paul Auster, March 23. http://www.stopsmilingonline.com/story_detail .php?id=1216. (30 May 2010).

Varvogli, Aliki. 2001. *The world that is the book. Paul Auster's fiction*. Liverpool: Liverpool University Press.

Wallace, David Foster. 1997. E Unibus Pluram. Television and U.S. Fiction. In *A supposedly fun thing I'll never do again*. London: Abacus. 21-82.

Weisenburger, Steven. 1995. Inside *Moon Palace*. In *Beyond the red notebook. Essays on Paul Auster*, ed. Dennis Barone. Philadelphia: University of Pennsylvania Press. 129-142.

White, Hayden. 1992. Historical emplotment and the problem of truth. In *Probing the limits of representation: nazism and the "final solution"*, ed. Saul Friedlander. Cambridge: Harvard University Press. 37-53.

Wood, James. 2004. Hysterical realism. In *The irresponsible self. On laughter and the novel*. New York: Picador. 178-194.

Zipp, Yvonne. 2007. The perplexing tale of Mr. Blank. *The Christian Science Monitor*, February 13. http://www.csmonitor.com/2007/ 0213/p16s01-bogn.html. (16 April 2010).

Notes

[1] In the days following 9/11 Auster published his personal recollection of the event in a short article entitled "Random Notes—September 11, 2001, 4:00 PM; Underground". On September 8, 2002, he participated in the National Public Radio program "All Things Considered," commenting—in an interview with Salman Rushdie—on the sociopolitical and psychological effects of the attacks. More recently, he took part as narrator in an audio guide project called *The Ground Zero Sonic Memorial Walk*, and he also helped the editors choose a selection of sounds and narratives from over 1,000 contributions sent by witnesses (Geismar 2005, 3).

[2] One of these exceptions is represented by Thomas Pynchon's *Against the Day* (2006), which, in going back to the violent struggles between anarchists and capitalists at the beginning of the twentieth century, provides, among many other things, Pynchon's bitter (yet lucid) considerations on post-9/11 America. Though its plot is not overly connected with 9/11, the novel represents one of the most original contribution to post-9/11 fiction published so far.

[3] In this regard, Ulrich Baer's anthology *110 Stories: New York Writers After September 11* is very significant. In his introduction, Baer suggests that there are three divergent ways in which novelists relate to the event; these three models are identified by Alex Houen as a "transformative realism" that "honours the 'shocking singularity' of the event while turning it into a story", a "seismographic registering of events, in which writing is *subject* to them as a form of unconscious, historical symptom", and "a departure from the real to the extent that it poses other possible worlds" (Houen 2004, 421). While Auster's mostly autobiographical article "Random Notes—September 11, 2001, 4:00 PM; Underground" belongs to the first two modes, his novels tend toward the third one, a "fictive world-making" that, in Houen's words, "is little in evidence throughout the volume, particularly in the novelists' responses".

[4] In this interview Auster declared his original plans for the story: "I don't know if any of you has read the little novel *Timbuktu*, but in my original plan the characters in that book, Willy and Mr. Bones, the homeless poet and the dog, were going to be characters in this story, which was going to be told in the third person, and I was going to begin with Willy and Mr. Bones going to Baltimore. I started right in there and I fell in love with these two characters". So he began to write another novel, "a little lyrical book, without much of a plot, just a little poem about these two beings". As a consequence, "by taking them out of the original structure for what became *The Brooklyn Follies*, everything fell to pieces. […] Everybody else was in the book: Harry, and Tom, and Honey, and Rory, and Lucy, but no Nathan. And it was only when I found Nathan that I could reconstruct the book and bring all these characters together again" (La Clé des Langues 2009).

[5] Many renowned writers have resorted to traditional strategies in tackling 9/11 and terrorism, like John Updike in *Terrorist* (2006), or Jay McInerney in *The Good Life* (2006), and even an experienced postmodernist writer like Don DeLillo has opted for an intimate though fragmented realistic style in *Falling Man* (2007).

[6] In his works, from *Players* (1977) to *Libra* (1988), from *Mao II* (1991) to his most recent *Falling Man* (2007), DeLillo has continually reshaped the character of the terrorist as an ambivalent trope of postmodernist discourse. His fictional terrorists stand out as "authors" of a plot in competition with the writer's own plot; this eventually entails the issue of whether and how literature can cope with events so devastating as to defy any representation.

[7] Very similarly, DeLillo, in *Mao II*, had created a link between the figure of the terrorist and that of the writer, the latter no longer capable "to alter the inner life of the culture" (DeLillo 1992, 41): "For some time now, I've had the feeling that novelists and terrorists are playing a zero-sum game. [...] What terrorists gain, novelists lose. The degree to which they influence mass consciousness is the extent of our decline as shapers of sensibility and thought" (DeLillo 1992, 156-57).

[8] *The New York Times Book Review* Senior Editor Sam Tanenhaus recently stated that "to some extent nonfiction has taken over some of the earlier attributes of the novel, which is story-telling" (Donadio 2004); quite similarly Michael Gorman, president of the American Library Association, at the opening of the 2006 annual conference referred to "the golden age of nonfiction we are currently enjoying" (Gorman 2006), quoting the large number of histories, biographies, and memoirs permanently on the bestsellers lists.

CHAPTER TWO

"THE WORST POSSIBILITIES
OF THE IMAGINATION ARE THE COUNTRY
YOU LIVE IN":
PAUL AUSTER IN THE TWENTY-FIRST
CENTURY

ALIKI VARVOGLI

As we approach the end of the first decade of the twenty-first century, it seems hard to avoid thinking of September 11, 2001 as the beginning of a new era. The repercussions of that day are still felt around the world and are far beyond the scope of this chapter, but it may not be too soon to suggest that 2001 will be used by future scholars as a convenient cut-off point in the study of American literature. This is not to say necessarily that 9/11 altered the course of American literary history, but rather to suggest that new factors began to shape the creation and reception of literary writing. The attacks created a powerful new thematology and new challenges for the writer of fiction who now had to "compete" with the power of the image and the immediacy of media reports. At the same time, readers and critics began to await the arrival of noted authors' 9/11 novels, hoping perhaps that fiction could shed a different light on events. Jonathan Safran Foer, John Updike and Jay McInerney obliged fairly quickly, and Don DeLillo followed soon after. However, alongside those novels that dealt directly with the attacks of September 11 and their aftermath, there were also all the other American novels published since 2001: seemingly unconcerned with the events, but bound to be contextualised in a post-9/11 climate. Some, such as Cormac McCarthy's *The Road* (2006), Philip Roth's *The Plot Against America* (2004) or Percival Everett's *Wounded* (2005), stood to benefit from such contextualisation, as long as they were not read as direct allegories of the events that haunted them. Others might have fared less well under this line of enquiry, unyielding if read as post 9/11 in any way other than the chronological one.

What are we then to make of Paul Auster's post-9/11 output? He has published an astonishing six novels since 2001, and even though they could be read as continuous with his body of work, the latter ones can also be seen to represent a new stage in his development as a writer. *The Book of Illusions* (2002) and *Oracle Night* (2004) contain many of Auster's earlier preoccupations: we have, among many familiar tropes, authorial doubles, a quest for an elusive creator, a mysterious notebook, literary allusions and self-reflexiveness, and little interest in the post-9/11 world in which they were published. *The Brooklyn Follies* (2005), *Travels in the Scriptorium* (2007) and *Man in the Dark* (2008), on the other hand, could well be thought of as a new departure, even though they too appear to share the author's earlier aesthetic and thematic concerns, and it is these three that I will be discussing. While the similarities between *Travels in the Scriptorium* and *Man in the Dark* are obvious, the connections with *The Brooklyn Follies* are not immediately apparent in the same way. I would argue that what unites the three books is that they are politicised to a degree not seen since 1992's *Leviathan*. In interviews in the past, Auster has said that he does not consider himself a political author, except in so far as every work of art represents a political act (Cortanze 1997, 98), but the two most recent books clearly show an angered engagement with the politics of George W. Bush and the war on terror. The political subtext of *The Brooklyn Follies* is perhaps a little harder to grasp. The novel is much closer to previous books in its preoccupation with nineteenth-century American literature, and questions about agency, contingency and free will, and as such it may appear to have rather more in common with the two books that preceded it than the two that followed it. In several ways, though, *The Brooklyn Follies* can be seen as a bridge connecting the earlier twenty-first-century novels with the later ones.

Paul Auster is often identified as a significant New York author, and one might have expected him to produce a more direct 9/11 novel. It is typical, though, of the writer once described as "the ghost at the banquet of contemporary American letters" (Birkerts 1992, 338) that he has chosen to approach the topic in a way that does not represent a clean break from his earlier aesthetic, philosophical and narrative choices. Auster once remarked that all his books are really the same book, "the story of my obsessions ... the saga of the things that haunt me" (Auster 1993, 285), and the three novels under discussion here help us to understand better than ever before how Auster's immediate historical context shapes these obsessions; the underlying concerns may remain unchanged throughout his oeuvre, but each new novel enables us to recontextualise those concerns. In the second half of the 2000s, Auster had become a vocal opponent of Bush and his policies. The man who was previously more interested in French poetry and questions of self in language was now giving interviews and speeches expressing his despair at the direction his country had taken. In *Leviathan*, when the author Benjamin Sachs felt angry at the political climate of the Reagan years, he decided to get out of his room and do something about it. He transformed himself into the elusive Phantom of Liberty and travelled the country blowing up replicas of the Statue of Liberty, and urging his fellow-Americans to wake up. Auster didn't quite take it this far, but he channelled his anger and disillusionment into a series of novels that imagine America as utopia and dystopia, though the two certainly do not correspond to pre- and post-9/11. As I shall be demonstrating, his concern is not so much with the attacks on US soil, but rather with what his country has done since. It isn't so much 9/11 that made him a more political writer and contributed to a change in his writing; it was rather Bush's war on terror that had that effect, and the distinction is a crucial one: where the 9/11 novel has to engage on some level with the US as the victim of outside forces, Auster's books cast the country as victim and aggressor, and as threatened from within.

The engagement with politics and world affairs may be new in Auster's writing, but the narrative strategies he has employed to explore these issues are themselves not new. Reviewing *The Brooklyn Follies* in *The Observer*, Toby Lichtig noted that "Auster's postmodern metaphysics are built around a host of ... recurrent themes ... and reading him can sometimes feel like moving through a checklist. In this sense, *The Brooklyn Follies* ticks all of the boxes" (Lichtig 2005). The same can be said of *Travels* and *Man in the Dark*, which also make use of familiar tropes; prominent among them are utopias and dystopias, the room, the manuscript, and the figure of the author (as character). The remainder of this paper will examine these tropes in the three novels in order to demonstrate that Auster's post-9/11 fiction can be read as both continuous with and divergent from his earlier writing. The old preoccupations are reframed and redeployed in a quest to explore the nature of reality, language and fiction, but also more specifically to explore America's fate since the "election" of George W. Bush in 2000.

Of the three novels under discussion here, *The Brooklyn Follies* is the one most grounded in the "real" world. Much of the action takes place in the streets, shops and cafes of Brooklyn and in rural Vermont, and there are references to the lived world of contemporary America. This is in contrast with both *Travels in the Scriptorium* and *Man in the Dark*, whose settings are largely imaginary landscapes of the mind and fictional ones of the textual page, the products of frail and insomniac authors and narrators. Yet of the three, *The Brooklyn Follies* is also the one that engages most extensively with the notion of utopia; not in the literal sense of "non-place" that we find in the other two books, but in the more traditional sense of an ideal place. Mark Brown observes that "Auster's fiction incorporates many unreal or unearthly places" (Brown 2007, 129), and goes on to note that Auster "has explored the fine line between utopias and dystopias in his work since ... *The New York Trilogy*" (Brown 2007, 129). Brown's study of Paul Auster's work was published in 2007, too late to include much discussion of *The Brooklyn Follies*, and before *Travels in the Scriptorium* and *Man in the Dark* were published. As such, it is useful in that it enables us to follow both the continuities and the changes in Auster's later writing. Brown discusses the two most prominent dystopian spaces in Auster's work: The City of the World model in *The Music of Chance*, and the country of last things in the novel of the same name. Although he acknowledges the political import of their frightening nature, he describes them primarily as places that "allow Auster to explore the extremes of human experience, and to show how ontological stability is constantly undermined by spatial instability" (Brown 2007, 130), rather than viewing them as spaces of political control and oppressive ideologies. At the other end of the scale, Brown identifies the "dreamlike states" achieved by Walt, Mr Bones, David Zimmer and Hector Mann in *Mr Vertigo*, *Timbuktu* and *The Book of Illusions* respectively as utopian places where "the individual is able to distort reality by wishing, dreaming and speaking of a better life" (Brown 2007, 154). Such a better life is also imagined in *The Brooklyn Follies*, but the Hotel Existence, the central utopian trope in this novel, is as notable for its differences as it is for its similarities with the earlier utopian spaces. References to imaginary places of retreat appear early on in the novel, when Tom explains to Nathan that his dissertation was about "Imaginary Edens", a study of "the inner refuge, a map of the place a man goes to when life in the real world is no longer possible" (Auster 2005, 15). The full significance of the notion of an "Imaginary Eden" does not become clear until the end of the narrative, because the mention of the 9/11 attacks on the penultimate page effectively asks the reader to re-contextualise and re-interpret the novel. In between the first mention of the inner refuge and the last chapter announcing 9/11, the idea of a utopian retreat is further explored in complex and occasionally conflicting ways, while its political overtones slip in and out of the book's discourse.

Tom's early discussion of his dissertation continues and amplifies two prominent features of Auster's writing: the author's retreat, and his fascination with nineteenth-century American literature. However, whereas in earlier novels the writer's retreat was imagined as a space where solitude could be overcome, and where the self could be temporarily reconstituted, as was the case with Quinn's confinement and his Emersonian writing at the end of *City of Glass*, or Nashe's philosophical musings in *The Music of Chance*, here the retreat is explicitly linked to socio-economic forces. Auster's earlier engagement with the American Renaissance was related to his desire to return to a more philosophical strand of American writing; as he said in an interview,

> [t]he novels of Melville and Hawthorne, the stories of Poe and the writings of Thoreau, for example, all of whom I'm passionately interested in,... had a metaphysical dimension, a philosophical dimension to them which I think has been forgotten and ignored. (Varvogli 2001, 4)

In *The Brooklyn Follies*, though, the retreats imagined by Poe and Thoreau are not mentioned for their philosophical implications, nor for their aesthetic potential: Tom considers these utopias "a sensible alternative" in a country that had "gone to hell" (Auster 2005, 16), and his views appear to echo those of his creator. Auster had not given any indication in his previous twenty-first-century novels that he thought his country was going to hell, but it is obvious that this time the discourse on America in the decades prior to the Civil War is to be understood as pertaining to the present. The author acknowledges as much; asked by *The Guardian* newspaper a few days before the 2008 presidential election to assess the cultural legacy of the Bush administration, he replied:

> These past eight years have been about the worst that I can imagine. For the first time as a writer I've addressed, here and there, the situation that we're living through. I'd never done that before and I guess because I've been so alarmed, so distraught, the pressure of this unhappiness has spilled over into my work at times. If McCain wins, I feel like going into a cellar for the next four years or going out in the streets every day and screaming. (*The Guardian* 2008)

It may be a little hard to imagine the author of *The Invention of Solitude* going out in the streets and screaming, but that is a measure of his despair. That he might have retreated into a cellar seems more in keeping with the idea explored in *The Brooklyn Follies* that the individual can dream of controlling his own fate by retreating into an imaginary space. The question still remains, though, whether this retreat into the Hotel Existence can be read as a turning away from the possibility of imaginative fiction that engages with contemporary politics. Harry Brightman describes the hotel as "a wild dream of removing ourselves from the cares and sorrows of this miserable world and creating a world of our own" (Auster 2005, 108), and this wild dream almost becomes a reality when Nathan and Tom come across, and attempt to purchase, the Chowder Inn in Vermont. Though the events of the plot prevent them from realising this dream, both Nathan and Tom meet with happy endings which offer ample compensation for the loss of their imaginary Eden. In other words, though they are denied the opportunity to retreat from "the sorrows of this miserable world", the world itself becomes less miserable for them. Followed to its conclusion, this reading of the novel would suggest that Auster engages in nostalgic revision of the pre-9/11 past, which would represent a major change in his outlook. This interpretation would imply that (at least before 9/11) a state of happiness was not only available, but indeed a preferable alternative to the retreat into an imaginary world; clearly a departure for a writer who has been preoccupied with the latter since he sent Daniel Quinn to live in a dustbin. Though it is tempting to assume that *The Brooklyn Follies* does indeed engage in this type of nostalgia, and does represent a change in Auster's oeuvre, a closer re-examination of the novel may uncover different meanings.

Many reviewers noted that the book we are reading is not dissimilar to the book within the book that Nathan is writing: a book of follies, a chronicle of mishaps and comic, lighthearted adventure. What is perhaps less obvious is the extent to which Auster has created distance between his authorial self and Nathan, the narrator of his novel. Because the narrative belongs to Nathan, who can be an endearing storyteller, it is as easy as it is tempting to ignore the gaps that allow that distance to be glimpsed. Early in the narrative, Nathan complains of his daughter that "it's a rare day when she speaks in anything but platitudes—all those exhausted phrases and hand-me-down ideas that cram the dump sites of contemporary wisdom" (Auster 2005, 2), but then proceeds to write in precisely the kind of language he has been mocking. In addition to being oblivious to his own shortcomings as an author, Nathan is also, unlike his creator, not given to "gloomy introspection", his only goal being "to keep [him]self entertained" (Auster 2005, 6). Such instances where the text allows us to see the difference between author and narrator occur mainly near the beginning of the book. Nathan soon takes over as the sole commanding force, and despite his limitations as a stylist, he has a complex and well-paced story to tell, making it harder for us to sustain the distinction between the story he is telling and the book we are reading. Occasionally, though, Nathan will make a pronouncement that jolts the reader out of their sense of security. After the main characters in his narrative have been happily paired up, Nathan observes that "With so many positive developments in the love department, the reader may be lulled into thinking that universal happiness reigned over our little patch of Brooklyn" (Auster 2005, 240), and by implication, the reader might be lulled into thinking that light-heartedness and happiness are the qualities that Auster associates with the pre-9/11 community in Brooklyn. This is clearly not the case: whereas Nathan delivers his warning only as a way of introducing the news that Nancy Mazzucchelli has broken up with her husband, Auster is hinting at the larger story that will shape the lives of his characters. Nathan records that Nancy's husband left on August 11, 2000, and it is here that a hint of the text's dramatic irony can be seen: the marriage breakup is supplanted by the good news that Nathan's lungs are clear, and his family and friends throw him a surprise sixtieth birthday party. But as happiness mounts, the presidential election also approaches, and of course the characters within the narrative are oblivious to its importance.

When the contested election takes place in November, Nathan almost brushes it aside, eager to get on with the family story he is now narrating, and unaware that his creator may be prioritising the election over the family drama. "The 2000 election disaster was just a few days down the road", he writes, "but ... even as these offenses were committed against the American people ..., I was preoccupied with only one thing: to hunt down Rory" (Auster 2005, 244). From this point onward, until the penultimate page, the story no longer concerns itself with political events, concentrating instead on the domestic and the familial, and the danger is to misread the novel as Nathan's story: a story of a family that went through hard times but ended up happy just before 9/11. This, however, is Auster's book as well as Nathan's, and their concerns do not always overlap. Nathan's story suggests that real life can be so felicitous as to overshadow the desire for utopia, while Auster's story acknowledges that Nathan's fictional real life is itself utopian. For instance, Nathan records a story told to him by Tom about Kafka's kindness to a little girl. Nathan concludes from that story that "when a person is lucky enough to live inside a story, to live inside an imaginary world, the pains of this world disappear. For as long as the story goes on, reality no longer exists" (Auster 2005, 155). Of course, what Nathan does not know is that he himself also lives inside a story, and his happiness will last until the end that story: even without 9/11, the end of the novel would have been the end of his luck. The book within the book allows Auster to evoke the utopian impulse only to shatter

it, not only in the obvious way by having the planes fly toward the World
Trade Center as the narrative draws to a close, but more subtly through the
covert reminders of Nathan's own status as a fictional narrating and
narrated self. As the Kakfa story reminds us, Auster has always been
interested in fictions as worlds that are complete in themselves, but the
real strength in his recent fiction lies in the way he has managed to sustain
that interest while engaging with the real world, whose problems he has
felt he can no longer ignore. *The Brooklyn Follies* was the first post-9/11
Auster novel to attempt this double engagement, but the project has
continued with the next two books, *Travels in the Scriptorium* and *Man in
the Dark*.

Whereas *The Brooklyn Follies* flirts with the possibility of a utopian
space, *Travels in the Scriptorium* and *Man in the Dark* owe more to the
dystopian vision first explored in *In the Country of Last Things*. Indeed,
these two books share with their predecessor a concern not only with
dystopia, but also with narrating and narrated selves, language and its
relation to reality, and a clear sense that the world they explore is
ultimately neither made up nor an exaggerated version of reality. Back in
1961, Philip Roth had noted in "Writing American Fiction" that the
American author was often tempted to retreat into "wholly imaginary
worlds" (Roth 2001 [1961], 172) in order to escape the intense
competition offered by real, every day American life. Paul Auster has
shown with these books that the retreat into imaginary worlds is an
effective way of addressing in fiction the "implausibilities" of reality
itself. As I have argued elsewhere (Varvogli 2008), the relevance of
Travels in the Scriptorium to a post-9/11 world is not immediate or
obvious. The narrative begins as a textual experimentation with point of
view as we are introduced to Mr Blank, who sits in a room being recorded
by a blinking camera fixed to the ceiling. This is an image that represents
not only the author's manipulation of his character, but also the reader's
role as voyeur and as reader of typographical marks on the page, suggested
by the camera's silent clicking every second. The narrative then continues
with an engagement with intertextuality; however, whereas in previous
novels the intertextual references opened up the work to more
interpretative possibilities, here the references are all to previous Auster
novels, suggesting that this is a book about his other books. In turn, the
book we are reading turns out to be the creation of another (fictional,
trans-textual) author, and the book ends in a *mise-en-abyme* that brings to
the fore the question of authorship and the layers of worlds within worlds
it contains. It would seem, then, that a novel of this kind, seemingly
interested in *textual* questions, has little to say about its creator's mounting

anger with the role of his country in world affairs, yet I would like to suggest that this is exactly what the novel is concerned with. Early reviews appeared to miss this point entirely, with Alfred Hickling, for example, representing many when he complained that "this existential parlour game" has been going on for too long, and that "the retreat to an unidentified room … feels like a backward step from Auster's last novel, *The Brooklyn Follies*, which signalled a welcome intent to get out more" (Hickling 2006). It was not until 2008 that Martin Butler and Jens Martin Gurr suggested a more sophisticated reading of the book, arguing that

> the self-referential mode of the novel highlights the poietic potential of literature as a "room of its own", as a site of both poetological reflection and ideological intervention in extratextual discourses. (Butler and Gurr 2008, 196)

and further suggesting that

> despite the initial impression of a hermetically sealed text depicting a world outside time and space, the novel frequently invites us to read it as an engagement with contemporary America, the "war on terror" and the over-ambitious project of maintaining Homeland Security. (Butler and Gurr 2008, 198)

As well as correcting the earlier misconceptions concerning the novel's perceived lack of engagement with the world, the article's emphasis on the war on terror and Homeland Security created a meaningful context for the book in which America was not the victim of terror, but the creator of plots and elaborate surveillance mechanisms. The theme of surveillance is best observed in the image of the room as prison, with the added twist that the reader is explicitly made complicit through the emphasis on the camera eye as the book's point of view.

The trope of the room has dominated Auster's work from the start. It has been a place of inner refuge and quiet contemplation, and a retreat from the physicality of life. Here, the trope is taken to extremes in order to suggest the risk of isolation and alienation from the world around the author. Mr Blank, the author character in the novel, knows he is in a room, but is unsure whether the room is in a house, a hospital or a prison (Auster 2006a, 2). He wonders if the room is locked, having not had the opportunity to investigate because "his mind is elsewhere, adrift in the past" (Auster 2006a, 2). With this image of the author adrift in the past and possibly locked away in a room, Auster is maintaining his old interest in authorial solitude while also contemplating the necessity of leaving the room in order to engage with the "real" life of a post-9/11 world. There are references to the fact that Mr Blank may be a willing participant in some kind of experiment, rather than a prisoner against his will, and here is where Auster takes the opportunity to question authorial roles: is the author "deliberately" isolated from the world around him? Are there forces he cannot comprehend fully that keep him from getting out of his room? Is the commitment to the literary and the imaginative a turning away from the "real", or can the two be reconciled somehow? To ask these questions in the aftermath of 9/11 is to examine the role of the American author, which Auster does in his usual oblique way.

Ostensibly, the novel is about an author locked away in a room, tormented by guilt over the fictional characters he has created and who are now plotting their revenge on him. During his confinement, he reads a manuscript that the careful reader will recognise as a story left undeveloped by John Trause in *Oracle Night*, and the whole narrative turns out to be written by another Auster character, Fanshawe. This is no textual or metafictional gaming, though. On the novel's first page, we meet the author as a frail old man who is "stranded among the figments in his head": an image that expresses the fear that the author is becoming irrelevant in the cultural climate created during Bush's "war on terror". When the narrator goes on to ask of Mr Blank "Who is he? What is he doing there?" (Auster 2006a, 1), we should suspect that the answer is to be found not in the novel's elaborate fictional layers, but in the wider debate about the role of fiction in the aftermath of 9/11. Indeed, it could be that novels such as this one that take the longer view and question the role of writing and fictional representation have more to tell us than the ones that opt for a direct treatment of America's new realities.

In its investigation of contemporary authorship, *Travels in the Scriptorium* combines the trope of the room with that of the manuscript. There are two manuscripts within the fictional world: the one that Mr Blank is reading, and the one that it turns out he is written into. While the latter serves to highlight issues of textual identity, the former is both an intertextual reference to another Auster novel and an engagement with authorship on a thematic level. As I have argued elsewhere (Varvogli 2008), the story within the story is not only a political fable, but also a kind of warning. The author of the "report" Mr Blank has been reading turns out to have been tricked by the system into producing a false account that can be used to justify war. As Butler and Gurr have shown, the very use of the word "report" for the embedded narrative draws attention to the instability and unreliability of documents used to justify George W. Bush's foreign policy (Butler and Gurr 2008, 198-99). In addition, the trick that has been played on the author raises questions of complicity and resistance: how far will the state go to silence the author, and how can the author avoid misappropriation or misrepresentation of his work? Auster is asking questions about the role and responsibility of the writer, and he is also contemplating the fate of the literary author in Bush's America. In a country ruled by a notoriously inarticulate but ideologically powerful president, the concept of discourse itself has undergone a crisis.

The theme of crisis and responsibility is taken up in one of the novel's main premises: Mr Blank's creations (who are characters from previous Auster novels) are referred to as his "charges" (Auster 2006a, 25), suggesting he is responsible for them, but they also become his "operatives", and he is tormented by guilt over the "missions" he has sent them on (Auster 2006a, 120). Now, the characters are coming back to call him into account, and several of them want revenge. What all of this suggests is that the book may be read not simply as an authorial stock-taking, but as a meditation on the responsibilities of the imaginative life, a theme also taken up in *Man in the Dark*. Near the end of the book, Daniel Quinn (from *City of Glass* and elsewhere) tells Mr Blank that one of his creations has proposed revenge in the form of torture: Mr Blank should be

> hanged and cut down alive, and his body shall be opened, his heart and bowels plucked out, and his privy members cut off and thrown into the fire before his eyes. Then his head shall be stricken off from his body, and his body shall be divided into four quarters, to be disposed of at our discretion. (Auster 2006a, 122)

The image of the author hanged, drawn and quartered can of course be read as a playful reference to "the death of the author", and it is continuous with previous similar references to authorship, such as the one in *City of Glass* where "Paul Auster" is deemed to have "behaved badly throughout" (Auster 1987, 132). However, this time the description is uncharacteristically dark and gruesome, although its significance only becomes apparent after one has read Auster's next novel, *Man in the Dark*.

Where *The Brooklyn Follies* opened with the narrator looking for a place to die and wanting to tell stories until his demise, and *Travels in the Scriptorium* opened with the image of a frail author in a prison-like room, *Man in the Dark* opens with an insomniac author/narrator who combines elements of the previous two. Like Nathan, he is drawn as a realistic character rather than as a textual function or an abstraction, but like Mr Blank he makes slightly mysterious references to his state of health: "I have been living in this house for more than a year now, ever since they released me from the hospital" (Auster 2008, 1), he informs us from the

start, giving an innocent explanation that also contains hints of something
sinister (who are "they"? why "the" hospital?). We learn that he suffers
from insomnia, and he spends his nights making up stories. What appears
as an innocent pursuit, though, also turns out to be much more disturbing:
the stories are meant to help him drown out memories of the horrific death
of his granddaughter's partner, Titus Small. In making up stories, he tries
to retreat to his own "Hotel Existence", as he explains:

> That's what I do when sleep refuses to come. I lie in bed and tell myself
> stories. They might not add up to much, but as long as I'm inside them,
> they prevent me from thinking about the things I would prefer to forget.
> (Auster 2008, 2)

His words here are clearly reminiscent of Nathan's conclusions regarding
the Kafka story, but in this much darker novel the consolations of form
and narrative are not seen to have the same power they had in *The
Brooklyn Follies*. In addition to telling himself stories, August Brill spends
a lot of time watching films with his granddaughter Katya, until he begins
to suspect that this amounts to "obsessive movie watching as a form of
self-medication, a homeopathic drug" (Auster 2008, 15). The reader can
relate this observation to the earlier point made about the escape into
storytelling, and assume that the two are watching movies as a way of
filling their heads with images in order to push out the mental pictures that
torment them. However, the full significance of the film-watching is
withheld until the end of the novel. Six pages before the end of the book,
Brill finally narrates the missing piece of his story, the one that has shaped
everything he has created, the one that has kept him awake and haunted his
narrative.

Before he arrives at that point in his narrative, though, he constructs an
elaborate tale of alternative history in which New York secedes from the
Union after the 2000 election. It is soon followed by other states on the
Eastern seaboard who create the Independent States of America, sparking
a civil war that tears the country apart. In this alternative America, a
character seeks to assassinate his creator (August Brill himself) in order to
put an end to this war. It is clear that this metafictional game, which shares
many features with *Travels in the Scriptorium*, continues and amplifies
Auster's reflections on the politics and morality of the imagination. Unlike
Travels in the Scriptorium, however, this time the author makes his point
in an explicit manner. Concluding the story of the night August Brill
witnessed the Newark riots in 1967, he writes:

> That was my war. Not a real war, perhaps, but once you witness violence
> on that scale, it isn't difficult to imagine something worse, and once your
> mind is capable of doing that, you understand that the worst possibilities of
> the imagination are the country you live in. (Auster 2008, 82)

Though perhaps Auster will never be an overtly political writer, this
passage must be the closest he has come to commenting on the state of his
country. That he has done so while extending his enquiries into the nature
of imaginative storytelling can help us to understand how his fiction of the
second half of the 2000s has been both continuous with and divergent
from his earlier writing.

Man in the Dark closes with a line from a poem by Rose Hawthorne:
"As the weird world rolls on" (Auster 2008, 180), but this is no literary
shrug meant to suggest helplessness or defeat. To get to the end, Brill first
has to tell the story of what happened to Titus Small. Small was abducted
in Iraq, where he was working for a private company, having accepted the
job despite his opposition to the war. When challenged by Brill, he
explained that "It's not a moral decision. It's about learning something ...
I have to change my life" (Auster 2008, 172-73). This information is
crucial: Auster does not make his victim a soldier fighting for his country,
and by avoiding any reference to patriotic sentiment he is better able to
highlight the blurred line between aggressor and victim. The story of what
happens to Titus Small does not serve to emphasise the brutality of the
Iraqis, but rather to show how a misguided young man failed to imagine
the horror he was going to participate in ("The more horrible, the better"
(Auster 2008, 173) he said before he took up the post). Auster contrasts
Small's failure of the imagination with a reality so brutal as to be almost
unimaginable, and yet real and documented on film. The video shows his
abductors beheading him and then stabbing his eyes out, the torture
described by Brill in gory detail. The reference is clearly to Daniel Pearl,
the journalist beheaded in Pakistan in 2002, and the question that Auster
appears to be asking is whether fiction, in literature or on film, can
alleviate the pain and help to explain the shock of such narrative images.
His later novels suggest that the role of the author is not to create
remedies, and that fiction does not aim to change the world. Writing in
The Observer in 2006, Auster asked:

> What purpose does art, in particular the art of fiction, serve in what we call
> the real world? None that I can think of—at least not in any practical sense.
> ... A book has never prevented a bomb falling on innocent civilians in the
> midst of war. (Auster 2006b, 23)

However, to acknowledge that literature does not change the "weird world" is not to accept that it is any less vital for that. Auster has been preoccupied with the meaning of authorship from the beginning of his literary career, and though this preoccupation is still prominent in his early twenty-first-century fiction, it has undergone many transformations. The earlier textual experimentations that gave rise to metaphysical and ontological questions about identity and the nature of the self have been transformed in the later novels into an interrogation of the place of literature itself in a rapidly changing world of globalised war and terror. The novels published between 2005-2008 show an increasing engagement with the world of American politics (which of course is also world politics), but the formal and aesthetic strategies that Auster has employed demonstrate an abiding commitment to the art of fiction. "Each world is the creation of a mind" (Auster 2008, 69) explains Lou Frisk to Brick Owen in the embedded narrative of *Man in the Dark*, and in this Borgesian formulation Auster offers a key to understanding his commitment to writing not as a means of directly representing the world, but as a creative process that seeks to abolish the boundaries between real and imagined, lived and constructed in language. Literature, for Auster, does not get written *while* "the weird world rolls on": it participates in that weird world and alters it just as it is itself altered by it.

References

Auster, Paul. 1987. *The New York trilogy*. London: Faber and Faber.
—. 1993. *The art of hunger: essays, prefaces, interviews*. New York: Penguin.
—. 2005. *The Brooklyn follies*. London: Faber and Faber.
—. 2006a. *Travels in the scriptorium*. London: Faber and Faber.
—. 2006b. I want to tell you a story. *The Observer*, November 5, Books section, 23.
—. 2008. *Man in the dark*. London: Faber and Faber.
Birkerts, Sven. 1992. *American energies: essays on fiction*. New York: William Morrow.
Brown, Mark. 2007. *Paul Auster*. Manchester and New York: Manchester University Press.
Butler, Martin and Jens Martin Gurr. 2008. The poetics and politics of metafiction: reading Paul Auster's *Travels in the scriptorium*. *English Studies* 89 (2): 195-209.
Cortanze, Gérard de. 1997. *La solitude du labyrinthe: essai et entretiens*. Paris: Actes Sud.

The Guardian. 2008. One book fair, hours of satire and the Dixie Chicks – Bush's cultural legacy. *The Guardian*, October 31, Comments and Features section, 6. Hickling, Alfred. 2006. Where's the exit? *The Guardian*, October 14, Books section, 17.

Lichtig, Toby. 2005. A city of dreamers. *The Observer*, November 20, Features section, 16.

Roth, Philip. 2001 [1961]. Writing American fiction. In *Reading myself and others*, 165-82. New York: Vintage.

Varvogli, Aliki. 2001. The world that is the book: Paul Auster's fiction. Liverpool: Liverpool University Press.

—. 2008. Ailing authors: Paul Auster's *Travels in the scriptorium* and Philip Roth's *Exit Ghost*. *Review of International American Studies* 3 (3) – 4 (1): 94-101.

CHAPTER THREE

WRITING IN THE MARGINS:
PLACE AND RACE IN *THE BROOKLYN FOLLIES*
AND *TIMBUKTU*

ANITA DURKIN

Since the beginning of Paul Auster's career as a prose writer, his fiction and nonfiction alike have gravitated toward questions concerning the status of the book, playing, in the process, with the boundary between art and life, between imagined and lived experience. While many critics examine such questions through postmodernist critiques of identity, relatively few examine how the concept of place contributes to such discussions.[1] Yet in *The Brooklyn Follies* (2006) and *Timbuktu* (1999), it is place in particular that probes the fluid divide between the book and the world, the space of the margins, and it is place, as a result, that likewise engages questions of political oppression, especially racially and ethnically motivated oppression. While *Timbuktu* probes specifically the confluence between perspectives on place and constructions of identity, *The Brooklyn Follies* examines the relationship between writing and the political world to which it addresses itself. Read in tandem, these two books, one written at the end of the twentieth century and the other written well into the twenty-first, ponder more directly than perhaps most other Auster works the precise relationship between reading, writing, and the political scenes that infuse both, suggesting, in the process, a necessary wariness of Auster's chosen medium. That is, *The Brooklyn Follies* and *Timbuktu* together indicate the potential complicity of books and writing with the oppressive politics of the American scene.

In *Playing in the Dark: Whiteness and the Literary Imagination*, Toni Morrison makes explicit the influence of race-based and ethnicity-based politics on the American literary tradition from which Auster emerges. Morrison defines "Africanism" in American literature as "the denotative and connotative blackness that African peoples have come to signify, as well as the entire range of views, assumptions, readings, and misreadings that accompany Eurocentric learning about these people" (Morrison 1992, 6-7). Together, these significations and their (mis)readings comprise the Africanist presence that is the subject of Morrison's analysis and the subject, as she finds, of many American literary texts. In fact, as Morrison explains, the Africanist presence helps to define the contours of the American canon, to shape and determine the concerns of its literature. She writes: "I want to suggest that these concerns—autonomy, authority, newness and difference, absolute power—not only become the major themes and presumptions of American literature, but that each one is made possible by, shaped by, activated by a complex awareness and employment of a constituted Africanism" (Morrison 1992, 44). Many of these concerns are also evident in Auster's oeuvre as a result of his self-conscious examinations of his own authorship, the definition of texts, and the fluid movement between narrative and life, the book and the world. As such, they signify both the innovative, theoretical aspects that distinguish Auster's works as contemporary, and the confluence between those works and the tradition of American writing that Morrison sees as steeped in the nation's experiences of race and ethnocentrism. In *The Brooklyn Follies* and *Timbuktu*, Auster similarly considers the intricate relations between American literature, oppressive politics, and those people who, as Morrison writes, "are by no means marginal or already completely known and knowable" (Morrison 1992, x-xi).

The distinction between the "book" and the "world" derives from Auster's first successful work of prose, his memoir, *The Invention of Solitude* (1982). Even in this very early work, meditations on place appear intimately tied to questions about the book, as is especially apparent in the memoir's latter portion, "The Book of Memory". Self-quarantined in a room at 6 Varick Street, Auster's narrator, A., ponders throughout "The Book of Memory" his impending authorship and the paternalistic overtones that color that position. Auster writes: "The outer world, the tangible world of materials and bodies, has come to seem no more than an emanation of his mind" (Auster 1982, 78). The uneasiness about the responsibilities of authorship that A. registers in *The Invention of Solitude* remains a prime concern in Auster's fictional follow-up to the (in many ways) seminal memoir, appearing to some degree in each of the three parts of *The New York Trilogy* (1987). As in "The Book of Memory", each of the three novellas that comprise *The New York Trilogy* examines the condition of authorship through the image of the room, the solitude of which encloses and in fact encases Auster's writer-protagonists, as many critics note. James Peacock writes of *The Book of Illusions*: "As with so many recurrent tropes in Auster's work, the room is ambiguous; it enables a productive solitude and silence, yet precludes the rich experience of life. It can be viewed as, in short, a deferral of life, a form of temporary death" (Peacock 2006, 60). Though writing of *The Book of Illusions* (2002), a much later novel, Peacock's assessment of the room finds confirmation in the various works of the *Trilogy*; in *Ghosts*, for example, Blue's unwavering commitment to investigate Black, commissioned by the mysterious White, leads to an existence lived almost exclusively within a room across from Black's, one filled by Blue's incessantly writing and analyzing the mundane activities of Black. John Zilcosky notes: "Blue reads what Black writes and also what Black reads (*Walden*), hoping in the manner of a 'classic' critic to 'solve' Black by going back to his literary sources" (Zilcosky 1998, 200). In *The Locked Room*, similarly, the narrator trails his childhood friend and accomplished author, Fanshawe, an excursion that ends, as the title suggests, with Fanshawe's self-exile in a locked room, the room in which he will die. Zilcosky summarizes the narrator's position: "The Narrator realizes that self-expression—storytelling—is difficult, if not impossible, in a world where subjective will is muddled in a pool of infinite possibilities. However, if every contingency, even death, is accepted as given, the story will begin to tell itself" (Zilcosky 1998, 203).

In *City of Glass*, the first installment of *The New York Trilogy*, Daniel Quinn accepts a commissioned investigation of Peter Stillman Sr. from his son, Peter Stillman Jr.. A writer of detective fiction rather than a career detective, Quinn nevertheless ardently searches for Stillman Sr., a man so certain of the possibility of finding a prelapsarian language that he imprisons his son in a locked room, isolated from all human contact, for much of his childhood. Not surprisingly, critics tend to read Stillman's mad and manic search for the perfect language as resonant with the archaic idea of the author-god, the writer incapable of and spurred by a semi-divine, innate talent to find and write the perfect words. Mark Ford, for example, writes: "Stillman's Utopian fantasies derive from his consuming desire ... that vision and expression be fused, even if the resultant work must remain either wholly private, or indistinguishable from life itself" (Ford 1999, 208). Despite a markedly different style and tone, *The Brooklyn Follies*, with its many comic elements, direct addresses, and jocose tone, resembles *City of Glass* in many ways, a fact suggested perhaps in the "subterranean link" between the title of the novella and the name of the novel's protagonist, Nathan Glass (Auster 2006, 246). Most important to the novel's presentation of place, *The Brooklyn Follies*, like *City of Glass*, picks up the idea of perfection and its possibly oppressive relationship to the act of writing. Stillman's quest for an edenic language is an extreme and obsessive form of the too great faith of Nathan and his nephew, Tom, in the "power" of books.

Nathan, the sixty-year-old divorced lung cancer survivor, makes clear from the beginning of his narration his love for books. He says: "Reading was my escape and my comfort, my consolation, my stimulant of choice: reading for the pure pleasure of it, for the beautiful stillness that surrounds you when you hear an author's words reverberating in your head" (Auster 2006, 13). One wonders if the "stillness" to which Nathan refers also suggests an implicit link between his seemingly harmless, almost guileless love of books and the "Stillman" of *City of Glass* who inflicts a terrible abuse upon his son in the search for the perfect authorial words that here bring Nathan such "comfort". In his own authorial ambitions, which comprise the text of the novel, Nathan is far less serious than Stillman, writing his memoir on "yellow legal pads, loose sheets of paper, the backs of envelopes and junk-mail form letters for credit cards and home-improvement loans" and titling it *The Book of Human Folly*, "a grandiose, somewhat pompous title—in order to delude myself into thinking that I was engaged in important work" (Auster 2005, 6, 5). Nonetheless, Nathan can easily conceive of an earlier incarnation of himself seeking to devote his life to the study of books, as he expected his nephew Tom, a one-time doctoral student, to do. Having encountered his nephew at Brightman's Attic, the used bookstore where Tom works and where Nathan stops periodically to browse, Nathan observes: "Back when I was his age, I had hoped to follow a path similar to the one my nephew had chosen. Like him, I had majored in English at college, with secret ambitions to go on studying literature, or perhaps take a stab at journalism" (Auster 2006, 13).

Faced, however, with a far less promising Tom than he remembers, wondering what has happened to the young man's projected path (graduate school, followed by an academic post), Nathan interprets Tom's "decline" in typical Austerian terms: "For Tom, everything hinged on having the guts to barrel himself back into the thick of the game. Otherwise, he would go on languishing in the darkness of his private, two-by-four hell, and as the years went by he would slowly turn bitter, slowly turn into someone he wasn't meant to be" (Auster 2006, 84). Imagining the inertia of Tom's ambitions in terms of a room, the "two-by-four hell", Nathan locates his troubled nephew at the complex site of writing that appears in so many of Auster's works, the site that is also the site of death, a necessary aspect of writing in Barthes' famous formulation. What is more, Nathan firmly links Tom's problems to a metaphor of place, and it is Tom's ideas about place that connect his story, *The Brooklyn Follies*, both with an abstract concept of the book and with a specific tradition of books, namely, American literature. In his introductory preamble to his reunion with Tom, Nathan introduces his nephew, in part, by way of Tom's senior thesis, "Imaginary Edens: The Life of the Mind in Pre-Civil War America" (Auster 2006, 14). As the young Tom explains to his uncle, "It's about non-existent worlds ... the inner refuge, a map of the place a man goes to when life in the real world is no longer possible" (Auster 2006, 15). The writing of Poe and Thoreau, "an unfortunate rhyme", Tom's capstone project for his undergraduate degree, provides a reading of these "imaginary Edens", an examination of ideal places (Auster 2006, 14).

Significantly, Tom connects the works of Poe and Thoreau through each author's reaction to the political climate of his time: he reads their work according to the attributes of the place, the country that surrounds them. As he tells Nathan, "[b]oth men believed in America, and both men believed that America had gone to hell, that it was being crushed to death by an ever-growing mountain of machines and money. How was a man to think in the midst of all that clamor?" (Auster 2006, 16). In Tom's reading, then, the ills of the world, the ills endemic to the place of these writers' residences, inspire their invention of new, imaginary places, free of such troubles, utopian retreats within the minds of Poe and Thoreau. Tom's reading, however, erroneously locates these imaginary Edens solely in the minds of these writers, for if that were the case, then Tom, living a century and a half later, could have no access to them. Rather, these imaginary Edens are not only thoughts; they are writings, available in the books put forth by Poe and Thoreau. If Tom can subsequently learn of these places, "map" them, as he puts it, then it follows that he must also be able to "see" them, and that these places, therefore, cannot be wholly imaginary, at least not in the sense of being limited to their creators' imaginations.

In fact, in many ways, what Tom desires in the midst of his depression is precisely to gain access to such imaginary Edens, to live in such places himself. That Tom finds an existence in an act of imagination particularly appealing is evident in the story he tells Nathan about Kafka and a little girl who has lost her doll. Meeting the girl in the park one day, Kafka listens to the girl's distress over the loss of her doll, and assures her that she will surely hear from the doll soon. Kafka then proceeds to write the girl letters in the guise of the doll, and Tom continues: "By that point, of course, the girl no longer misses the doll. Kafka has given her something else instead, and by the time those three weeks are up, the letters have cured her of her unhappiness" (Auster 2006, 156). Tom concludes: "She has the story, and when a person is lucky enough to live inside a story, to live inside an imaginary world, the pains of this world disappear. For as long as the story goes on, reality no longer exists" (Auster 2006, 156). In Tom's estimation, it is not only desirable to live in a story, but entirely possible, too, and what his anecdote about Kafka reveals is how invested he is in the notion that imaginary, idealized places are available, through books, for residence.

That Tom, several years after writing his senior thesis, still longs after the imaginary Edens on which he staked his undergraduate degree is evident throughout his dinner with Nathan and his boss, Harry Brightman. Throughout the evening, Tom expresses virulent disdain for the condition and "culture" of the United States, echoing the subjects of his thesis, Poe and Thoreau, in the process. Tom rants, in answer to the question of whether he is talking about politics:

> Among other things, yes. And economics. And greed. And the horrible place this country has turned into. The maniacs on the Christian Right. The twenty-year-old dot-com millionaires. The Golf Channel. The Fuck Channel. The Vomit Channel. Capitalism triumphant, with nothing to oppose it anymore. And all of us so smug, so pleased with ourselves, while half the world is starving to death and we don't lift a finger to help. I can't take it anymore, gentlemen. I want out. (Auster 2006, 101)

Tom's wanting "out" is Tom's desire for escape, not from a place so much as from his reading of that place, of its many failings. Moreover, Tom's catalogue of the grave and absurd issues that afflict his native country draws attention to the political subtext of *The Brooklyn Follies*. Tom and, to a lesser extent, Nathan each expressly criticize the political atmosphere in the United States at the end of the Clinton presidency and on the cusp of George W. Bush's election, and their comments throw into relief the temporal setting of the novel (mostly the summer of 2000, with a denouement that encompasses several months of 2001). In a sense, the follies that Nathan records in his memoir all take place on the brink of American disaster, both in terms of the 9/11 terrorist attacks themselves and in terms of the repressive foreign and domestic policies enacted in the attacks' wake. As such, Tom's rant against U.S. politics intertwines with a larger national narrative that implies Tom's correlative desire for an imaginary Eden as common in scope; his longing is likewise a longing potentially shared by many Americans discouraged by the aftermath of 9/11.

For sure, Tom's desire to escape the place that he inhabits in response to suffering and perversion within that place is hardly original. At the dinner table where Tom expresses his ideas about politics, Harry Brightman narrates his similar desire for an imaginary escape in the wake of World War II, a childhood fantasy called "the Hotel Existence" (Auster 2006, 103). In Harry's description, the Hotel Existence is the place to which he, as a ten-year-old boy, brings the children of Europe who have suffered extensively as a result of the war. Harry tells Tom and Nathan: "So I imagine this place called the Hotel Existence, and I immediately turn it into a refuge for lost children. I'm talking about European children, of course" (Auster 2006, 103). Interestingly, Harry's altruism appears, in his imagination, capable of transgressing the laws of space and time, a fact that, as an adult, he clearly recognizes. He says: "It didn't matter what country I was in. Belgium or France, Poland or Italy, Holland or Denmark—the hotel was never far away, and I always managed to get the kid there by nightfall" (Auster 2006, 104). Because it is somehow readily available, no matter where Harry imagines himself going to retrieve these lost children, the Hotel Existence, Harry's imaginary Eden, does not appear to be anywhere, for it is not bound to any single country, any single place. At the same time, being nowhere, the Hotel Existence is also simultaneously anywhere, and subsequently, everywhere: it is in France, it is in Belgium, it is in England, Italy, Spain, and any other place that Harry needs it to be. In traversing so fluidly national boundaries, the Hotel Existence suggests how ephemeral in fact such boundaries are, how possible to imagine their absence. In this sense, it is a confirmation of the bonds between Harry and the rescued children, bonds that exist regardless of their national origin, and gesture quietly toward the idea of common humanity.

The name that Harry assigns to his hotel also reinforces the idea of some kind of connection between human beings, one that disregards borders and, even more so, space and distance. As a young boy, Harry hears the word "existence" on the radio, and his conclusions about it are telling: "Existence was bigger than just life. It was everyone's life all together, and even if you lived in Buffalo, New York, and had never been more than ten miles from home, you were part of the puzzle, too. It didn't matter how small your life was. What happened to you was just as important as what happened to everyone else" (Auster 2006, 103). In his interpretation of the word "existence", Harry thus offers the possibility of a connection between peoples of far-flung and disparate places, a sense of "everyone's life all together". By naming his hotel after this (to the ten-year-old Harry) tantamount concept, he further implies that the heroics he imagines himself performing as benefit to the children of Europe are in turn related to this connection. To some degree, Harry's interpretation of "existence" appears as the inverse of Benedict Anderson's reading of nation-building: rather than inventing bonds between peoples based on geographical borders, Harry's Hotel Existence imagines a community based on the transcendence of geographical borders, even the utter neglect of them.[2]

Harry's description of the Hotel Existence, however, is clearly not as free of borders as Harry's reading of "existence" and the Hotel's propensity to be anywhere might indicate. After all, while various European countries may have been witness to the most fighting and thus the most destruction during World War II, fighting was also present in Africa and Asia, and surely, the destruction wrought upon Hiroshima and Nagasaki via the atomic bomb was comparable to the worst bombings inflicted upon Europe. Nevertheless, it is only to the devastated European nations that the ten-year-old Harry sends his imagined self. On the one hand, Harry's exclusion immediately undermines the apparent inclusion of his altruistic venture, the sense of borderless-ness that his Hotel Existence supports. On the other hand, Harry's exclusion of all but European children from his charitable rescue intimates the limits of dissolving borders, the fact that the postmodernist effort to weaken the boundaries between things—identities, ideas, places, and so on—does not eradicate the oppressive politics that such boundaries tend to support. Writing of *The New York Trilogy*, and most specifically, about *Ghosts*, Eric Berlatsky eloquently makes this point: "while postmodernism in general, and Auster in particular, work diligently to deconstruct self/other binaries in a theoretical sense, the material actuality of American racial history and its psychological after-effects prove more intractable to theoretical re-vision than it might initially appear" (Berlatsky 2008, 112). As Berlatsky argues, the history of American racism resonates throughout *The New York Trilogy*, despite Auster's deconstruction of color categories in *Ghosts*; some of this racism even translates into presentations of people of color as exotic and alien, especially in *The Locked Room* (Berlatsky 2008, 125). Nor is *The Brooklyn Follies* as a whole free of the racial/racist structures that Berlatsky finds in the *Trilogy*. Note, for example, the racism latent in Nathan's description of Harry's assistant, Rufus Sprague, a Jamaican immigrant and drag queen, as "exotic" and "alien", which echoes also Marco's sense of the exoticism of Kitty Wu's biography in *Moon Palace* (1989) and the stationary store owner of *Oracle Night* (Auster 2006, 221). Such characterizations (often perpetuated by the novels' protagonists) underscore the complexity of interracial and intercultural relations and indicate the often contradictory impulses—fear and curiosity, repulsion and attraction—that constitute racial encounters in much of American literature. In its exclusion of non-Europeans, Harry's Hotel Existence, despite the altruism of its conception, is also subtly racist and subsequently undermines the terms of its own being, the erasure of borders that it supports and yet resists.

Questions of the relationship between a fluid sense of place and political (especially racially, ethnically, or culturally motivated) oppression are evident throughout Auster's earlier novel, *Timbuktu*. Narrated from the perspective of Mr. Bones, the dog of a homeless and mentally ill writer named Willy G. Christmas, *Timbuktu* begins with Willy near death and chronicles throughout Mr. Bones' struggle to find his place in the world after his master's death. Again and again, Mr. Bones' saga picks up on themes of immigration and displacement, themes that, in twentieth-century American history, necessarily resonate with racial and ethnic stereotype and discrimination. The novel's sometimes explicit and sometimes implicit concern with immigration begins with Willy's parents, Jewish refugees from Poland. The narrator explains:

> Considering what the family had been through before it landed in America, it was probably a miracle that David Gurevitch and Ida Perlmutter managed to produce a son in the first place. Of the seven children born to Willy's grandparents in Warsaw and Lodz between 1910 and 1921, they were the only two to survive the war. They alone did not have numbers tattooed on their forearms, they alone were granted the luck to escape. (Auster 1999, 13)

Targeted as a result of their Jewish identity in Europe, evident in the reference to numbers tattooed on forearms, Willy's parents subsequently arrive in Brooklyn, where "it wasn't a new life they were starting so much as a posthumous life, an interval between two deaths" (Auster 1999, 14). If their lives as immigrants are posthumous, then it stands to reason that leaving the place of their birth, finding a new home, has been, for Willy's parents, a kind of death, one that foreshadows Mr. Bones' struggle to find a satisfactory place to live after Willy's demise. More importantly, it emphasizes again the relationship between place and political oppression: sentenced to death for being Jewish, Ida and David can only avoid their execution by leaving the place where the threat against them is being carried out; to leave a place is literally to save their lives. At the same time, if their escape from Poland leads to their posthumous existence in Brooklyn, then they have saved nothing; to leave a place is to die, even when emigration is meant to preserve one's life. In this regard, Willy's parents demonstrate simultaneously two seemingly conflicting attributes of place: that existence, one's being, is not dependent upon place (and therefore, escape is possible), and that existence is dependent upon place, that to leave is to die. These attributes of place frame the difficult journey upon which Mr. Bones embarks after Willy passes away.

Certainly, Willy's imminent death looms over the whole of *Timbuktu*, as does his vision of the afterlife, his own posthumous existence. Having exhausted himself in a trek to Baltimore, in hopes of passing along his manuscripts to his high school English teacher, Mrs. Swanson, Willy sits against the Poe house while Mr. Bones ponders the many words that Willy has spoken to him over the course of their time together, including an especially offensive warning against the victuals at Chinese restaurants. Willy tells Mr. Bones: "There's a Chinese restaurant on every block, and if you think mouths won't water when you come strolling by, then you don't know squat about Oriental cuisine. They prize the taste of dog, friend. The chefs round up strays and slaughter them in the alley right behind the kitchen" (Auster 1999, 5-6). Presumably, Willy, either not understanding or simply not appreciating an unfamiliar national cuisine, perpetuates the stereotype and urban legend of dog meat's prevalence in Chinese American restaurants. That he does so in spite of his parents' immigrant history is particularly ironic, although, as the narrator notes in reference to the Gurevitches, "[Willy] found them alien, wholly embarrassing creatures, a pair of sore thumbs with their Polish accents and stinted foreign ways, and without really having to think about it he understood that his only hope of survival lay in resisting them at every turn" (Auster 1999, 14). Indeed, in the prejudice of his warning to Mr. Bones, and in his impressions of his own parents, Willy rehashes on a microcosmic scale the long, sad history of immigrant discrimination within the United States, a history in which those already settled in the country warned the newcomers in a variety of ways: either don't be different or don't come. Willy's admonition to Mr. Bones thus echoes calls for immigrant assimilation, and posits a tenuous link between identity and place in its implicit injunction to act "American". Afraid of the unfamiliar, Willy adopts the very values that force his parents to lead posthumous lives after leaving Poland, values that subsequently ask Chinese immigrants to do the same.

Mr. Bones' acquiescing to take Henry Chow, a Chinese American boy, as his new master after Willy dies illuminates the consequences of Willy's ethnocentric stereotypes. Since Henry is not only Chinese American, but the son, also, of the owner of a Chinese restaurant, Mr. Bones "went against his master's teachings and wound up living by the gates of hell", for "Willy's prejudices had become his fears" (Auster 1999, 103, 104). Mr. Bones' sense of unease as Henry's charge derives in part from Willy's discrimination: as the narrator recounts, Mr. Bones feels a "pang of unknowing that pricked his soul whenever his tongue chanced upon an unidentifiable taste" among the restaurant's leftovers (Auster 1999, 104). He even concludes that "it was only by the skin of his teeth that he hadn't wound up as a bogus appetizer in a little white takeout box" (Auster 1999, 112). Beyond Willy's biases, Mr. Bones' restlessness during his sojourn with Henry stems from the fact that the boy's parents have forbidden their child to have a dog, thus forcing Henry to house Mr. Bones secretly in a box in the Chows' backyard. In combination, it is these two things that drive Mr. Bones from Henry after Mr. Chow's discovery of the dog's existence. As Mr. Bones reflects upon leaving, "what good was a home if you didn't feel safe in it, if you were treated as an outcast in the very spot that was supposed to be your refuge?" (Auster 1999, 112). The irony, of course, is that Mr. Bones' sentiment echoes the plight of immigrants to the United States, those who, like the Chows, like Willy's parents, were met with persistent prejudice and told, in any number of ways, that they were not welcome.

Much of Mr. Bones' experience throughout the novel allies him with the immigrant experience so central to his master's family, running parallel as it does to narratives of ethnic and racial oppression. Willy makes this fact explicit when he appears to Mr. Bones in a dream. Speaking of his mother, *Mom-san*, Willy tells his beloved and beleaguered pet: "Well, they tried to kill her, too. They hunted her down like a dog, and she had to run for her life. People get treated like dogs, too, my friend, and sometimes they have to sleep in barns and meadows because there's nowhere else for them to go" (Auster 1999, 120). In comparing the mistreatment of his dog to the mistreatment of his mother during the Holocaust, Willy implies two important things: first, that Mr. Bones' suffering is neither isolated nor anomalous, but is something shared by seemingly disparate beings, human and animal; and second, that the apparent differences between people and dogs are not so rigid as they may seem. Mr. Bones likewise emphasizes the latter point when he ponders the ramifications of humans gauging the intelligence of dogs:

> Dogs as smart as men? A blasphemous assertion. There'd be riots in the streets, they'd burn down the White House, mayhem would rule. In three months, dogs would be pressing for their independence. Delegations would convene, negotiations would begin, and in the end they'd settle the thing by giving up Nebraska, South Dakota, and half of Kansas. They'd kick out the human population and let the dogs move in, and from then on the country would be divided in two. (Auster 1999, 82-83)

Notably, Mr. Bones' projection of human reaction to the realization that dogs, because intelligent, are not so wholly different from people alludes to the prelude to the American Civil War, both in its suggestion that the country would have to split into two adjacent nations as a result of dogs' intellectual prowess and in its suggestion that people would sacrifice "Nebraska, South Dakota, and half of Kansas", all parts of the Missouri territory declared free by the notorious Missouri Compromise in exchange for the admission of a slaveholding Missouri as a state. Perhaps most importantly, Mr. Bones' vision of human reaction to canine cognitive ability gestures also toward the arguments of inhumanness made by southern slave owners as justification for slavery throughout its practice in the United States, and especially as the abolition movement progressed.[3] In comparing the mistreatment of dogs to the mistreatment of African Americans during slavery, Mr. Bones subsequently draws into relief the supposed "animalism" of non-whites used as an excuse for barbarous treatment by whites, a rhetoric of animalism that the Nazis likewise invoked in their attacks against Jews. Mr. Bones seems to at once reinforce those stereotypes via his comparison (suggesting that these oppressed peoples are like dogs) and to undermine them by highlighting the absurdity of human reaction to canine intelligence, a reaction founded on the erosion of seemingly rigid boundaries.

As arbitrary as such distinctions between human and dog and human and human may appear in Mr. Bones' narrative of canine independence, they nevertheless persist and incite, in the process, the abuse of Mr. Bones by humans, abuse that contributes to his downtrodden mood and results in his visitation from Willy. Mr. Bones, speaking in his dream, tells his master: "Just yesterday, I nearly got myself shot. I was taking a shortcut through a field somewhere, and a guy came after me in a red pickup truck. Laughing, too, I might add, and then he pulled out a rifle and fired" (Auster 1999, 118-119). Significantly, Mr. Bones further suggests that most people "wouldn't think twice about loading up their shotguns the moment a four-leg sets foot on their land" (Auster 1999, 119). In other words, according to Mr. Bones, humans attack him (with inordinate violence) when he inadvertently violates the boundaries of private property, when he wanders onto human land. In this regard, the connection between place and the mistreatment of others appears direct: violent behavior against Mr. Bones, a nonhuman, comes about as a result of his crossing boundaries of which he is unaware. Once again, the overlap between Mr. Bones' narrative and the narratives of immigrants and African Americans is evident; and his story, like the stories of similarly oppressed humans, emphasizes the relationship between a firm belief in the boundaries that separate one place from another and the unjust and frequently violent behavior that can accompany the enforcement of those boundaries.

The irony is that Mr. Bones' own sense of place is perfectly fluid, based not on arbitrary distinctions and imaginary lines, but on his experiences. Mr. Bones reflects that place is experiential, rather than physical, for

> he had only to hear the word *Denver* now for Wanda's laugh to start ringing in his ears again. That was *Denver* for him, just as *Chicago* was a bus splashing through a rain puddle on Michigan Avenue. Just as *Tampa* was a wall of light shimmering up from the asphalt one August afternoon. Just as *Tucson* was a hot wind blowing off the desert, bearing with it the scent of juniper leaves and sagebrush, the sudden, unearthly plenitude of the vacant air. (Auster 1999, 32)

Though he is aware of the names of the cities he has visited, Mr. Bones can only think of them in terms of what he has experienced during the course of his visits. As a result, the places appear less like bounded geographical entities and more like the sum of one's impressions about them, less like the usual information a city name might signify—size, population, topography, main attractions—and more like little more than a dog's or a person's memory. (In fact, Mr. Bones reinforces the idea of place as memory and memory as place when, after dreaming of Willy, he realizes "that memory was a place, a real place that one could visit", Auster 1999, 115). The fluidity of place conceived as memory rather than physical fact is evident also in the slip of place names into one another near the time of Willy's death. Within a short span of time, Baltimore becomes, as a result of where Willy chooses to rest after their long journey, Poe-land, which in turn becomes Poland, thereby allowing Willy to "get himself home again" (Auster 1999, 45). Despite his sense of place as fluid, as more an abstract entity than a concrete, undisputed presence, Mr. Bones is nonetheless subject to the oppression that arises from the firm belief in place as place, the belief in agreed upon boundaries and, therefore, their possible violation of them. As Berlatsky argues of *The New York Trilogy*, simply deconstructing boundaries—of color, in his reading, of place, in mine—does not render those boundaries subsequently powerless, does not make them appear, in practice, any less real.

Timbuktu's ongoing concern with the intertwining of questions of place with the political oppression of underprivileged groups is evident, too, in the book's title, though in a way that reaches well beyond the history of the United States. In the novel, Timbuktu, of course, is the afterlife to which Willy looks forward. The narrator posits: "by now there was no doubt in the dog's mind that the next world was a real place. It was called Timbuktu, and from everything Mr. Bones could gather, it was located in the middle of a desert somewhere" (Auster 1999, 48). Interestingly, Willy locates Timbuktu "in the middle of a desert", a description that links Willy's intended afterlife with the geographical Timbuktu located in contemporary Mali, a city that indeed lies well across the Sahara. In positing this connection, Willy also refers to the postcolonial history of Timbuktu. One of the last places on the African continent reached by Europeans, Timbuktu, until the middle of the nineteenth century, was little more to Europe than a set of myths, a series of stories passed on and on. Prior to its colonization, moreover, it was central to greater African trade, including the slave trade. Not long after the arrival of Europeans, the territory was, like so much of the continent, colonized, then declared independent as part of Mali. By conflating his afterlife with the geographical Timbuktu, Willy consequently references the city's pre-colonial implication in the practice of slavery and its postcolonial history. Willy's post-death destination is a site of individual and collective enslavement, connected with the enterprise that so thoroughly entwined a rigid sense of place (the boundaries of territories) with the often brutal oppression of people, imperialism. Willy's afterlife, as he describes it to Mr. Bones, is rife with these histories.

It is also rife with literary connotation, for Timbuktu, after all, is simultaneously the name of Willy's afterlife and the name of the book. As such, it refers to both at once, thus subtly equating the two. In this regard, the book, in a way, *is* a kind of afterlife, and it is the notion of the book as afterlife that so excites Nathan Glass near the end of *The Brooklyn Follies*. Hospitalized after what feels like a heart attack, Nathan converses with the various occupants of the nearest bed, who, each in turn, leave for another ward. As Nathan looks at their now empty place, he realizes that "the empty bed signified death, whether that death were real or imagined" (Auster 2006, 302). Sobered by this possibility, Nathan goes on to have "the single most important idea I had ever had, an idea big enough to keep me occupied every hour of every day for the rest of my life" (Auster 2006, 302). Struck by the absence of the men to whom he has spoken, Nathan ponders the fact that "[e]ventually, we would all die, and when our bodies were carried off and buried in the ground, only our friends and family would know we were gone. ... There wouldn't be any obituaries in *The New York Times*. No books would be written about us" (Auster 2006, 303). His solution, then, is "to form a company that would publish books about the forgotten ones, to rescue the stories and facts and documents before they disappeared—and shape them into a continuous narrative, the narrative of a life" (Auster 2006, 303). Excited, he observes that the families of the dead "would want to bring their loved one back to life, and I would do everything humanly possible to grant their wish. I would resurrect that person in words, and once the pages had been printed and the story had been bound between covers, they would have something to hold on to for the rest of their lives" (Auster 2006, 304). Insofar as he believes that the dead will therefore go on living in and through their commissioned biographies, Nathan suggests the possibility that books *are* a kind of afterlife. Like Willy's *Timbuktu*, an imagined place as well as a novel, Nathan's intended biographies intimate a posthumous existence, the continuation of a kind of life, even after death.

What is therefore evident in Nathan's exaltation of the power of books is his faith in them, a faith that Tom, with his imaginary Edens, undoubtedly shares. For, like Nathan, Tom effusively praises the book in a way that likens it to a quasi-religious entity, as is clear in his thesis title: by employing the term "Eden", the Old Testament garden into which God creates the first man and woman, Tom draws a latent connection between a biblical story of creation and the act of creation perpetrated by writers. As such, Tom's sense of writing seems bound up in a belief in spontaneous parthenogenesis and in works of literature as divine productions. This notion finds further confirmation in Tom's description of the works by Poe and Thoreau that he examines and dubs imaginary Edens in his thesis. As he tells Nathan: "What they give is a description of the ideal room, the ideal house, and the ideal landscape" (Auster 2006, 15). In locating their perfect places in a room, Poe and Thoreau, in Tom's reading, render the site of writing as an ideal space. While the idea of the room as a site of writing is well-established in Auster's oeuvre, Tom confirms his sense that Poe's and Thoreau's rooms are precisely this when he says that "[a]s long as a man had the courage to reject what society told him to do, he could live life on his own terms. To what end? To be free. But free to what end? To read books, to write books, to think" (Auster 2006, 16). As an imaginary Eden, Poe's and Thoreau's ideal room suggests literature as a doubly religious experience: not only is the act of authorial creation made godly creation via Tom's title; there is also a sense that Edens exist in books as sites of reading and writing simultaneously. In any instance, Tom's reading indicates the writer, the literary object, and the literary subject as enshrouded with a semblance of divinity, a sense of religiosity as somehow engaged with various aspects of the book. Tom's comparisons intimate, consequently, a subtle conflation of literature with religion, a positioning of the book as an entity worthy of worship.

The trouble with Tom's position is that, as Nathan notes, it keeps him from fulfilling his potential, traps him in his own scene of writing from which, working at Harry's and living alone, he seems unable to escape. The dystopian aspects of Tom's imaginary Eden (the perfect room) are evident in the abuse of his sister, Aurora, by her husband, David Minor. No doubt, David takes his religion very seriously. When Nathan first arrives in North Carolina, David greets him with the following assurance: "We're very open-minded in this neck of the woods. Even when others don't share our faith, we make every effort to treat them with dignity and respect" (Auster 2006, 251). Tellingly, David's church is the Temple of the Holy Word, an unaffiliated sect whose leader, Reverend Bob, preaches that "[i]f the Word is God, then the words of men mean nothing. They're no more significant than the grunts of animals or the cries of birds" (Auster 2006, 254). Minor explains: "To breathe God into us and absorb His Word, the reverend instructs us to refrain from indulging in the vanity of human speech" (Auster 2006, 254). What is especially interesting is that David's belief in some ways falls into line with postmodern theory, for human language, or "the words of men", as he misogynistically describes it, proves fallible and unreliable according to both the Reverend Bob's preaching and the practice of deconstruction. Nathan, too, inadvertently notes the tendency of language to obscure rather than illuminate meaning as a result of his interactions with Aurora's daughter, Lucy, who arrives at Tom's apartment wholly silent. Nathan says: "Round and round it went, the two of us traveling in circles, talking, talking, talking, but unable to answer a single question" (Auster 2006, 138-139). And, when Lucy begins to speak again, Nathan says: "I am expecting answers and revelations, the unwrapping of manifold mysteries, a great beam of light shining into the darkness. I should have known better than to count on language as a more efficient form of communication than nods and shakes of the head" (Auster 2006, 185).

At the same time, however, Nathan relies on words in his effort to understand Lucy's situation, as is clear in his and Tom's efforts to arrive at a plausible explanation for her arrival and her silence through talking. Likewise, David Minor, though opposed dogmatically to over-reliance on human language, nevertheless employs language as his primary source of power. As Aurora tells Nathan on their flight to Brooklyn: "He's not a violent person. His game is talk. Talk, talk, talk. And then more talk. He wears you down with his arguments" (Auster 2006, 263). In this regard, both Nathan and David recognize at once the futility of language and the power of language; the two ideas are not, for them, mutually exclusive. What is more, it is possible to read David's obsession with language as akin to Tom's and Nathan's fascination with literature, which is, in a very basic way, a fascination with language and its uses. The difference is that while David declares human language largely pointless and rejects, in the process, literature (as a result of one of the Reverend Bob's Sunday Edicts), Tom and Nathan regard language as it appears in literature quite important; in Tom's case, literature can even be an escape from political strife. At the same time, Auster's presentation of these apparently opposing viewpoints shows them as not terribly disparate, for, after all, the futility of human words coexists with the belief in the power of words, and the rejection of literature as a result of Minor's religious beliefs meets the religiosity of Tom's and Nathan's love of books.

Tellingly, these seemingly different interests—David's in his religion, Tom's in his books—appear to converge on a similarly oppressive point. Not long after Nathan remembers the substance of Tom's senior thesis, his argument that the perfect room, the scene of writing, is an imaginary Eden, David Minor locks Aurora into Lucy's vacant bedroom, where she remains for six months. Aurora relays to her uncle during their flight: "I was locked up in that room for six months, Uncle Nat. Locked up like an animal in my own house for half a year" (Auster 2006, 275). During that time, Aurora claims, "mostly what I did was think about how to kill myself" (Auster 2006, 275). Thus, the abstract death of the author becomes a literal death for Aurora, and her scene of writing, clearly, a scene of excessive abuse. Incredibly, David punishes Aurora's betrayal of his religion (via her claim that the Reverend Bob raped her) by confining her in what is actually one of the imaginary Edens that Tom identifies, an enclosed room. And certainly, locked in her daughter's room, Aurora is very much apart from other people, very much isolated from society. If being alone, being away from others in a stiflingly small space, is Tom's idea of the perfect escape from a troubling political landscape, then his idea of perfection, too, is bound up in the imprisonment of his sister by her husband. Consequently, the ideal place that, in Tom's reading, is both the space of the book and the space of the book's creation is also a place of terrible abuse. And insofar as David Minor represents the contingent of fanatically religious Americans, part of "the maniacs on the Christian Right" against which Tom pontificates, then Tom and all his literary ideals appear intertwined here with the very contingent of people from which he wishes to escape, his imaginary Eden complicit, even, in the abusive behavior from which it is to shelter him (Auster 2006, 101). Literature, postmodern or otherwise, appears to provide no escape, no release, and no relief from political oppression, as the American literary canon makes evident.

Tom's ideal place turns out to be, in the case of his sister, an instrument of abuse as well. The optimistic lenses with which Tom and Nathan view books—as objects of comfort, as objects of escape from difficult times—appear, then, as obscurant lenses that render them potentially blind to literature's sometimes complicity with acts of violence and abuse. And yet, when *The Brooklyn Follies* ends on September 11, 2001, Nathan ends his narrative with the stillness of the morning prior to the attack, subsequently limiting the narrative to perpetually twenty minutes before the first plane crashed into the World Trade Center. As Nathan concludes: "But for now it was still eight o'clock, and as I walked along the avenue under that brilliant blue sky, I was happy, my friends, as happy as any man who had ever lived" (Auster 2006, 306). By ending his narrative before the attack takes place and preserving, in the process, the novel's pre-9/11 temporal setting, Nathan ends *The Brooklyn Follies* on a supremely happy note and, by drawing attention to the fact that the story ends on September 11, seems to suggest that his narrative encompasses perhaps a happier, easier time. In this manner, *The Brooklyn Follies*, even with so much in it to suggest the limitations of books, becomes a kind of imaginary Eden in its own right, a literary escape for those Americans longing after a pre-terror existence.

Because it ends with one of the most important occurrences in recent American history, and is in some ways haunted by that history throughout, *The Brooklyn Follies* may seem a particularly American book from an atypically American author. Similarly, *Timbuktu*'s emphasis on narratives of immigration and narratives of race draws on two themes consistently identified as central to the history and culture of the United States. In combination with Auster's characteristically self-reflexive writing, a practice that derives more from continental traditions than the American canon, the American history in these novels shows the limitations of the book as well as the limitations of theory, and in a manner that negotiates Auster's own place and potential complicity in the American literary tradition. For despite deconstruction, oppressive identity politics remain; and despite a belief in books as sources of comfort and escape, books nevertheless at times contribute to violence and other forms of mistreatment. Indeed, as Morrison argues, the American literary canon is built upon the premise of political oppression; and as the field of postcolonial literary analysis also suggests, continental canons are likewise implicated in the imperial enterprise, a fact subtly communicated in *Timbuktu*. In this regard, these two novels in particular (and other Auster novels perhaps) attempt to mediate his relationship to tradition, to connect his innovative and postmodern style with the traditions from which it emerges without at the same time dismissing the oppressive politics latent in much literature. *The Brooklyn Follies* and *Timbuktu* by no means relegate such questions to the margins, but embed them in, make them necessary to, the texts themselves.

References

Anderson, Benedict. 1983. *Imagined communities: Reflections on the origins and spread of nationalism*. London: Verso.

Auster, Paul. 1982. *The invention of solitude*. New York: Penguin.

—. 1987. *The New York trilogy*. New York: Penguin.

—. 1999. *Timbuktu*. New York: Picador.

—. 2006. *The Brooklyn follies*. New York: Henry Holt.

Berlatsky, Eric. 2008. "Everything in the world has its own color": Detecting race and identity in Paul Auster's *Ghosts*. *Arizona Quarterly* 64 (3): 109-142.

Ford, Mark.1999. Inventions of solitude: Thoreau and Auster. *Journal of American Studies* 33 (2): 201-219.

Peacock, James. 2006. Carrying the burden of representation: Paul Auster's *The book of illusions*. *Journal of American Studies* 40 (1): 53-69.

Morrison, Toni. 1992. *Playing in the dark: Whiteness and the literary imagination*. New York: Vintage.

Zilcosky, John. 1998. The revenge of the author: Paul Auster's challenge to theory. *Critique* 39 (3): 195-206.

Notes

[1] Notable exceptions include work by Tim Woods, Steven Weisenberger, and, most recently, Mark Brown.

[2] In *Imagined Communities*, Benedict Anderson famously argues that nations are comprised of imagined communities, of people sharing a national identity shaped and solidified through the advent of printed media.

[3] American slave owners often invoked the seriously flawed judgment (one advanced as early as the eighteenth century by Thomas Jefferson in his *Notes on the State of Virginia*) that enslaved Africans were neither fully human nor capable of the intellectual reasoning supposedly inherent among the white majority, the same majority that ironically advanced such claims.

CHAPTER FOUR

FAKING IT OR MAKING IT?
FORGERY, REAL LIVES AND THE TRUE FAKE
IN *THE BROOKLYN FOLLIES*

JAMES PEACOCK

Born *Originals*, how comes it to pass that we die *Copies*?
—Edward Young

Edward Young's question, couched in a belief in the original, founders on biology. Heredity, or genetic transcription, seems to bear out Hillel Schwartz's view that "copying makes us what we are" (Schwartz 1997, 211) and reveals that in a profound sense we are never truly original. Whether one perceives the history of biological copying to be one of degeneration or regeneration depends on one's theological leanings. Evolution permits faith in progress; through a series of subtle adaptations, "copies" eventually come to supersede the "originals". Choosing to start with the Fall, on the other hand, occasions a narrative of degradation, of a spiritual template reduced to imperfect copies.

This degrading imitative process is allegorised by the Russian doll narrative structures familiar from Paul Auster novels such as *The Book of Illusions* (2002) and *Oracle Night* (2003). Even if one retains faith in the existence of an original real event, its recession and degradation in the continual re-telling of stories is inevitable and, paradoxically, suggests that a truly original story is one which is unblemished by virtue of being unspoken. In other words, it is *unknown* and, effectively, non-existent. Drawing on the work of Joseph Tabbi, one could argue that the original shares its elusiveness with the very cognitive processes by which reality might be recognised at all. Cognition "is always notoriously in the place where it's not", allowing one to perform everyday actions which would otherwise break down if the individual were to stop and reflect on them. Thus "reality is what one sees when one is not looking" (Tabbi 2003, 98).

Following this logic, even to make someone aware of real events by means of narration is to degrade those events, but the real paradox resides, as Auster knows well, in the fact that stories have to be told.

When storytelling is considered in these terms, the categories of "original" and "copy" collapse, and maintenance of the former category becomes simply a matter of confidence. What is under pressure is a belief in authenticity, always attended by the possibility that the narrative one encounters is not simply a tarnished reproduction, but a complete lie or forgery (which, as Michael Wreen points out, is not necessarily a copy of anything [Wreen 2002, 149], a point I return to later). Indeed, adherence to notions such as "authenticity", "authority" and "individuality" valorises the discourse of both the genuine and the spurious. Of course, returning to the genetic issues with which I began, everything and everybody might be a forgery, anyway. And where genetics or genesis fail to elucidate matters, law inevitably intervenes. "A forgery is still a making", states Ian Haywood, "its condemnation is a matter of interpretation and law" (Haywood 1987, 6).

The Brooklyn Follies (2005), a novel peculiarly concerned with originals and fakes, is as ramshackle and eccentric as its eponymous borough. Considerably less bleak than *The Book of Illusions*, less self-absorbed than *Oracle Night*, it imagines life inside narrative frames just like these novels, but this time the frames are connected by and within something more concrete: Brooklyn itself, a place where life is inevitably and at times joyously transfigured into performance in the eyes of one's neighbours. As its stories accumulate, one has to agree with the *Publishers Weekly* reviewer's observation that "the book's presiding spirit is Brooklyn's first bard, Walt Whitman, as Auster embraces the borough's multitudes—neighborhood characters, stunning drag queens, intellectuals manqué, greasy-spoon waitresses, urbane bourgeoisie". *Blue in the Face* (1995), which features "Brooklyn Residents" simultaneously being and *playing* themselves (Auster 2003, 174) is another key influence. Perhaps the most important intertextual reference, however, is Auster's editorial work on the National Story Project, which resulted in the short story collection *I Thought My Father Was God* (2001). With its unofficial epigraph—"We have never been perfect, but we are real" (xvi)—this collection epitomises the more sentimental, earnest pursuit and validation of "the real" evident in recent Auster work, particularly *The Brooklyn Follies* and *Man in the Dark* (2008). It is, nonetheless a "real" extraordinary enough to sound made up: "What interested me most, I said, were stories that defied our expectations about the world, anecdotes that revealed forces at work in our lives, in our family histories, in our minds and bodies, in our souls. In other words, true stories that sounded like fiction" (Auster 2001, xiv).

Within the bewildering sprawl of anecdotes and relationships (formally reminiscent once again of *Blue in the Face*), one theme serves as narrative adhesive, as well as a distillation of the author's concerns about authenticity, originality and reality, and that is the forgery. It is worth observing that copies and forgeries have long been recurring ideas in the literature of a "new" nation concerned with its own authenticity. In Herman Melville's most intriguing short story, Bartleby's polite refusal to check over his copies can be seen as a desire not to invest any personality in the text such that it is changed from a perfect copy to something resembling a forgery. And more recently William Gaddis' *The Recognitions* (1955) employs art forgery as a metaphor for postmodern pastiche and fakery in all its forms.

In *The Brooklyn Follies* the forgery, as well as supplying diegetic ingredients—Harry Brightman's shady past as a co-conspirator in the forgery of a deceased artist's "*next*" canvases (Auster 2005 45, original italics) and his latest scheme to forge a manuscript of *The Scarlet Letter* (127)—becomes the nexus for a number of questions implicitly posed by the novel. These questions, although related to aesthetic objects, are not merely aesthetic. Rather, they reconvene Auster's concerns with community and the social context of artistic production, concerns at the heart of the 1995 film *Smoke*, in such a way as to reinforce the intrinsically ethical character of the aesthetic. These concerns are reflected in the text's formal characteristics, primarily the episodic structure revealed in the idiosyncratic chapter titles: for example, "The Queen of Brooklyn" (80) and "Dream Days at the Hotel Existence" (166). Like the tales in Nathan Glass' *The Book of Human Folly*, which starts out as "a hodgepodge of unrelated anecdotes" (6), each chapter stands as an individual tale yet combines with others to participate in an aggregative vision, just as the individual must enter into social relations. To read *The Brooklyn Follies*, then, is to participate in the building of a community.

So some of the questions the novel poses, and this chapter sets out to answer, are: first, if one agrees with Charles Taylor that the contemporary notion of "authenticity" stems from an individual's untrammelled faith in "originality", that is, living one's life in a unique way (Taylor 1991, 29), can a life ever, as it were, be faked, even if like Harry Brightman one perpetually self-reinvents (Auster 2005, 32-33)? Clearly, the facets of Brightman's personality which earn him the affectionate epithet "rascal" from Nathan (52)—the changes of identity, the scams, the verbal gymnastics—make him a confidence man in the American mould, a successor to The Cosmopolitan, Yossarian and Dean Moriarty. Indeed, even his real name, "Dunkel", meaning "dark" in German or Yiddish, implies indecipherability and deception, as well as the potential for retreat into murky imaginative spaces, a point I return to presently. But if his conning accurately reflects a mercurial reality, can it be called fake? Secondly, if one attempts, like Nathan Glass in his *Book of Human Folly*, to redact the lives of individuals, does the act of representation render biography as forgery? And finally, if origin becomes ever more irretrievable and irrelevant, can intentional forgeries or simple cases of misattribution be just as valuable as originals by virtue of their aesthetic qualities, regardless of any ethical complications they may throw up? Is all art at heart forgery?

Our point of departure, as is so often the case in Auster's fiction, is etymological. *The Brooklyn Follies* is a text acutely aware of the double meaning of "to forge", just as *City of Glass* relishes the duplicity of "'cleave', which means both 'to join together' and 'to break apart'" (Auster 1987, 43). Meaning both "to create" and, in its now more familiar pejorative sense, "to create fraudulently", the duplicity of "to forge" prompts K. K. Ruthven to speculate:

> Instead of assuming a difference *between* 'literature' and 'literary forgery', therefore, we might consider each term as marking a difference *within* the category of the literary. (Ruthven 2001, 38)

Ruthven attributes literature's inherent fakery to a suspicion of rhetoric's persuasive power harking back to Plato (Ruthven 2001, 50). (As a brief digression, it is interesting to note Harry Brightman's playful suggestion that what we know as classical literature itself, "'Aeschylus, Homer, Sophocles, Plato, the whole lot of them ... was all a hoax'" dreamed up "'by some clever Italian poets during the Renaissance'" [Auster 2005, 125-26]).

Certainly, rhetoric and eloquence come in for criticism throughout *The Brooklyn Follies*. David Minor, Aurora's[1] domineering, evangelist husband (note how nomenclature puts him in his proper place), "expresses himself so well" (261) that he almost succeeds in robbing his wife of her autonomy altogether (259). He enacts, in effect, a form of linguistic colonisation. David is himself linguistically and ideologically colonised by the cult leader Reverend Bob, who represents for Minor the "'flesh-and-blood human father'" functioning as mouthpiece for divine instruction "'from the big boss himself'" (263). Auster's overt attacks on self-appointed authority figures in this novel are exemplified in his treatment of Minor, who, after the death of his father, stumbles from one surrogate father figure to another; from the marines, serving "Big Daddy America" in the Gulf War, to the consolations of "the biggest father of them all" (262). Aurora's mixed metaphors as she tells the story are indexical of the problem: authority is a fallacy when it is reduced to a series of rhetorical constructs or binary oppositions designed for control, not dialogue.

Explaining her subsequent relationship with Nancy Mazzucchelli to Uncle Nathan, Aurora distinguishes between eloquence and the genuine in the arena of truly dialogic love: "'The men I've been with, it was always about words. ... With us, I just have to look at her, and she's inside my skin'" (290). This is the "silence before the *Thou*—silence of *all* tongues" advocated by Martin Buber (2004 [1923], 37), a silence inevitable, because true love requires no expression, and necessary, because even to attempt to represent it in words would be to objectify it, to make it in Buber's terms an "It", and thus to destroy it. It is an underlying aspiration of Auster's work, though of course a deeply ironic one, seen in the symbolic "White Spaces" of his early poetry and in Benjamin Sachs' meditative silence after his fall in *Leviathan* (Auster 2001, 118). And as Nathan wryly observes, "not talking is about the hardest thing a person can do" (Auster 2005, 173).

Unfortunately, in taking Nathan into her confidence Aurora is trusting in someone whose disgust at linguistic unoriginality contributes to his own arrogant advocacy of authority and eloquence. Of his daughter Rachel he sneers:

> it's a rare day when she speaks in anything but platitudes—all those exhausted phrases and hand-me-down ideas that cram the dump sites of contemporary wisdom ... not once has she come up with an original remark. (2)

A cliché's egregiousness derives not from its "hand-me-down" nature (language is, after all, something one learns from others), but from its repetition without regard for shifting contexts. It is true that in becoming a semantic passepartout, a cliché loses significance, but *received* wisdom is not automatically to be mistrusted.

One notable aspect of Nathan's sentimental education—his transition from salesman of "life-insurance" (2) to writer and securer of "biography insurance" (301)—is the realisation that the kinds of everyday parapraxes which undermine individual linguistic authority and inspire *The Book of Human Folly* are not only folly, but apertures through which social interaction is enabled. For instance, when Nathan mistakenly asks for a "*cinnamon-reagan*" bagel and the man behind the counter instantly replies, "'we don't have any of those. How about a pumpernixon instead?'" (5), he experiences not only the betrayals into which language constantly tricks its users, but also a moment of human connection. The reader, in turn, gets a glimpse of the political subtext threading the novel; there *is* a kind of wisdom in associating Republican leaders with both consumption and cock-ups.

Although Auster would of course acknowledge that language forges meaning in both the positive and negative senses, the emphasis in *The Brooklyn Follies* is ultimately more ethical than linguistic, and casts light on another exhausted cliché, the American Dream. Just as *The Book of Human Folly*, "an account of every blunder, every pratfall, every embarrassment, every idiocy, every foible, and every inane act" (5) committed by Nathan, his friends and various historical figures, is antithetical to an ethos of self-fulfilment and success, so the greatest folly and the most egregious fakery is commitment to that individualist ethos without due consideration of one's constitutive social context. Like Charles Taylor, I hold that the affirmation of individual choice as an autotelic category, leading to what Taylor calls "soft relativism" (Taylor 1991, 18), becomes factitious without "horizons of significance" (Taylor 1991, 39), some more or less agreed context within which to articulate and measure choice. In *The Brooklyn Follies* these horizons are found neither in moral absolutes nor in the novel's key imaginative space—The Hotel Existence, "[t]he inner refuge ... a man goes to when life in the real world is no longer possible" (Auster 2005, 100)—but in lived social relations. A space like The Hotel Existence, as Auster texts from *The Invention of Solitude* (1982) have shown, only has validity in reference to the outside world; otherwise it becomes a myth of American pastoral, a retreat in a solipsistic or melancholic sense. After all, as Harry Brightman expresses it, existence must be "bigger than just life. It [is] everyone's life all together" (101). And existence happens in Brooklyn; Nathan arrives "looking for a quiet place to die" (1) but ends up learning how to live. Brooklyn exemplifies the oxymoron toward which the novel aspires: the *true fake* (not the empty postmodern ones encountered by Umberto Eco on his "Travels in Hyperreality" [1986, 8], those which attempt to improve on reality or make no attempt to engage with reality whatsoever). It is "New York and yet not New York" (48), a place genuinely itself yet able to contain otherness; a place of performance yet also of fundamental sympathies; a place where factual truths accede to ethical truths about the need to recognise our interconnectedness.

A significant aspect of the narrator's journey is his increasing appreciation of the true fake's worth. In the first part of the novel, before he has become fully immersed in Brooklyn life, Nathan Glass is an unreliable first-person narrator precisely because his claims to factual truthfulness and a desire for linguistic originality render much of his prose prolix. The reader knows from *City of Glass* that glass promises perspicacity while tricking the observer into self-reflection and misrecognition, so the fact that the narrator's surname is "Glass" should set alarm bells ringing. Not only does the name evoke Stephen Glass, the *New Republican* journalist who invented news stories for many years, but also another literary fabulist, Philip Roth's Nathan Zuckerman, the fictional writer who narrates novels such as *American Pastoral, The Human Stain* and *Exit Ghost*. Naturally, Glass pays lip service to candour: "Truth be told (how can I write this book if I don't tell the truth?), I put myself to sleep by masturbating" (66). Given its context, however, just after Nathan has referred to himself as "an aimless, disconnected lump of human flesh" (62), this utterance provides little assurance of a veracity with which one can actually engage. "Truth" here is onanistic and self-serving. Rather than revealing the interlocutory value of the book, its "character as *addressed*" and addressing (Taylor 1991, 35), the scene casts the reader as voyeur to a private act of physical and narrative self-gratification.

Nathan's assertions that he is representing the facts accurately remind the reader that "[c]laims of faithfulness in copying suggest ... the presence of the forger" (Grafton 1990, 8), especially when the prior reality being copied is, as is clear from previous readings of Auster's poetry and prose, always-already textualised. In other words, truth in writing is not synonymous with truth in the world, and mimesis therefore stands as the most disingenuous fakery. Nathan's masturbatory truth-telling is at best highly subjective, at worst a tacit admission of deception. Unlike Emerson's transparent eye-ball, this glass cannot see, or chooses not to see, everything: "So much for Glass's unerring eye" (Auster 2005, 91). As we shall see, it takes several tragic incidents, including a heart scare (295) to jolt Nathan from his solipsism.

Evidently, the Nathan Glass of the early chapters is a faker, partly because his pretence at faithful mimesis is a product of his solipsism and arrogance and partly because, as the criticisms of his daughter Rachel indicate, he is not prepared to accept that language is something one gets from others and therefore that nothing one says is irreducibly original. But while it is acceptable to employ the term *faker* in its colloquial sense to describe Nathan—as a poseur, a hypocrite—some more precise definitions are required before proceeding to an analysis of the two concrete examples of *forgery*, one pictorial, one literary, included in *The Brooklyn Follies*. So in the realms of culture and aesthetics exactly what is a forgery, and how does it differ ethically from a fake?[2] Bracketing off for the moment the treachery of the word *forgery* itself, already alluded to, Michael Wreen's succinct definition is a good place to start:

> A forgery has to be understood as a forged XY, and so the important thing is to define a forged XY. As I understand it, a forged XY isn't a genuine XY, but is represented as a genuine XY, and is so represented with the intention to deceive. (Wreen 2002, 152)

Whether or not as a child of postmodernism one maintains that *all* representation tends toward deceit, it is the intentionality specified in the final clause that distinguishes the forgery. "Y" stands for the artifact forged, which could as easily be a cheque or a letter of invitation as a Dutch masterwork. Wreen stipulates that the "Y" must be "an artifact-kind", meaning that it must possess "a source of issue", as opposed to natural objects such as plants or rocks which are "created out of pre-existing materials of some kind, as a result of the interplay of forces" (Wreen 2002, 153). Therefore, he argues, a natural object can never be forged, only faked (he offers the example of plastic fruit), unless, presumably, human manipulation renders it artifactual.

The status of "X" as the "source of issue" is somewhat more complex. Clearly, it could be the place holder for an individual artist or author, such as "Vermeer". However, attribution is not always to do with individuals or even specific groups:

> 'X' could range over anyone or thing—for example, any group, period, workshop, or company—that could be the creator, the originator, or, more generally, the issuer of something. Forged seventeenth-century Flemish paintings are possible, just as surely as forged Picasso paintings are. (2002, 153)

What is being referred to here, in citing "period" in particular, is *context*, and it is the implied distinction between the unique artist and the wider context which troubles, even if Wreen's expansion of the source of issue category tidily explains why a forgery need not be a copy of any pre-existing artifact. For while it is technically possible (and desirable in terms of exchange-value) to ascertain that a Van Meegeren is not a Vermeer, where does that leave us? Falsehood is, as Nicholas Barker reminds us, an entirely abstract concept (Barker 1990, 23), such that nothing material in the artifact itself makes deception tangible. Instead, we draw speculative inferences from phantasmal hints toward a false provenance. That is why Wreen can say quite accurately that "[n]othing about a painting per se makes it a forgery; only as a represented object, in a network of human intentional activity, can it be a forgery" (Wreen 2002, 161).

But human intention only complicates the issue further. Dominick LaCapra reminds us that one can only talk of authorial intention at all retroactively. What is more, any interpretation of authorial intention is based on "excessively narrow moral, legal, and scientific presuppositions" (LaCapra 1983, 37) and generated within a contested present which strives to explain a complex and equally contested past. In other words, a simple mapping of genuine or false authorship through documentary evidence is impossible, as is any appeal to a hypostasised "context" without awareness that no monolithic context ever really exists. In LaCapra's words: "For complex texts, one has a set of interacting contexts whose relations to one another are variable and problematic and whose relation to the text being investigated raises difficult issues in interpretation" (LaCapra 1983, 35). One's dialectical relationship with even the recent past makes the extraction of provenance and intention exceptionally difficult. Moreover, when confronted with "'creative forgeries' of things that have no 'original' but answer some abstract desire or value" (Barker 1990, 23), one has to accept that the aesthetic and social value of the forgery may eventually make provenance completely irrelevant. A supreme example of this would be James Macpherson's Ossian texts. While accepting that Macpherson's context will never be recovered without present inflection, it is nonetheless true that forged texts "cannot be dismissed as mere pale reflections of their originals. They are, at least, part, and not a negligible part, of the stemma of the text. They can also be deeply revealing witnesses of the 'sociology of the text', a mirror of the society which elicited the forgery" (Barker 1990, 27).

So if a work's source of issue transcends simple author attribution and is bound up in plural contexts which can never be fully accessed, is one to dismiss context and intentionality from the equation altogether? Absolutely not, if one augments Wreen's definition with this statement: forgery is deceit precisely when it seeks to *stand in for* context, thus seeking to deny the coalition of creative, social and cultural factors behind the original. Such forgery can be called "melancholic", in the specific sense of denying that which is past or lost. (Macpherson's fragments are not of this kind because of their use of authentic material, their actual connection with the Highland past.) David Lowenthal's claim that "[e]very relic displayed in a museum is a fake in that it has been wrenched out of its original context" (Lowenthal 1990, 17) is true in a rather pristine sense, but one needs to consider again intentionality. I would stress that the intention that really matters is the forger's intention to disavow a work's participation in the web of relationships which constitutes it (what Nelson Goodman dubs the "history of production" [Goodman 1976, 122]); to

deny its own position as a stemma of the so-called original and negate the
essentially dialogic relation of text and context. Forgery is paradoxical,
then: only by declaring itself as forgery, with its own context, history of
production, and connection to the original, does it achieve value. But in
declaring itself a forgery, it can no longer be called one.

My initial example from *The Brooklyn Follies*, Gordon Dryer's
forgeries of Alec Smith's paintings, demonstrates this paradox. It should
immediately be noted that the names in this novel are typically loaded, and
relate specifically to questions of authenticity. Alec *Smith*, the reclusive
genius whose intense, expressionistic canvases tremble "with an
incandescent roar of emotion" (Auster 2005, 40), is patently a maker, a
creator. Gordon *Dryer* embodies the aridity, lack of original productivity
and emotional detachment of one whose talents stretch only to usurpation.
(In passing, I suggest that Auster's work, at least as reflected in the critical
responses to it, sits somewhere between the "Romanticism, with its florid
gestures and pseudo-heroic impulses" of Smith's work and the
"abstractions" and "cold intellectualism" of Dryer's [43, 42, 43]).

When Smith dies by apparent suicide, Dryer suggests to his now lover
Brightman that they "continue to create Smith's work after the artist [is]
dead", to produce forgeries of the "final paintings and drawings of the
young master" (43). Dryer's efforts are astonishing:

> Dryer had reinvented himself as Smith's double, purging every shred of his
> own personality in order to slip into the mind and heart of a dead man. It
> was a remarkable turn of theater, a piece of psychological witchcraft that
> struck both terror and awe in poor Harry's brain. (44)

It might initially appear that in keeping Smith alive through his work,
whilst simultaneously reminding us of his death, Dryer is engaged in the
same process of prosopopeia as Auster himself in *The Invention of
Solitude*, allowing the departed to speak through the work in a "poetics of
absence" (Auster 1997, 114). Yet this superficial reading would ignore the
simple fact that none of Harry and Dryer's art world associates are
supposed to know that Smith is dead. Thus this forgery is a systematic
denial of loss which, unlike Auster's project, aims not to find an artistic
voice in a community of voices, but to steal a voice from its context.
Auster's poetics, though it requires these other voices, in no way aspires to
a complete purging of personality. Dryer's jettisoning of his own
individuality can be read as cynical incorporation of the required elements
of Smith's personality revealed through the work. There is nothing of
dialogue in this highly skilled forgery, nothing of the "guiding light of
sympathy" which enables *The Marble Faun*'s Hilda to produce her

exquisite copies of Renaissance paintings through "generous self-surrender" (Hawthorne 1961 [1860], 48, 51). Like Flower and Stone's wall in *The Music of Chance* (1990), which is nothing more than a decontextualization of an earlier structure—specifically, an Irish castle—Dryer's work is closer to Fredric Jameson's notion of "pastiche", cannibalised and depthless (Jameson 1991, 25). (This brief comparison indicates that such concerns are not only the province of Auster's recent fiction.)

For Auster, the encounter between the individual and the aesthetic object is, after Immanuel Kant and Martin Buber, similar to the meeting of human subjects in that it reveals a desire for the reality and the totality of the other. It is primarily affective and, as Kant describes in the *Critique of Judgement* (1978 [1790], 63-80), implies the suspension of a Cartesian cognate subject in order to disarm the calculating scientific faculties which reduce artistic beauty to sets of objective or ideational properties, "a sum of qualities" in Buber's terms (2004 [1923], 16). Dryer's forgery is entirely calculating: despite the obvious technical expertise, his success lies not in sympathy with the fullness of the work, but in dissecting its characteristics, "the harsh palette-knife strokes, the dense coloration, and the random, accidental drips" (Auster 2005, 44). This last element is the most telling: how can a deliberate reproduction hope to capture the spontaneity of the accidental? It is a dilemma, of course, repeatedly faced by Auster himself in attempting to represent the effects of chance, but the key point is that the accidental drips, irreproducible, provide the most powerful insight into the personal context of the work's creation. Though they tend to resist objectification or analysis, they are central to the affective power of the aesthetic encounter.

So Dryer and Harry's abandonment of the intricately interlinked personal and historical contexts which constitute the work, and the corruption of the aesthetic encounter, are bound up together. Any aesthetic differences between the original and the forgery are to be found not in the kind of detective-like, microscopic empiricism detailed by Nelson Goodman (Goodman 1976, 99-112) but in that unfathomable, ineffable moment of *being* with the work which is unrepresentable by the forgery. At stake, then, is not authorship as a substantive or hypostasised category. Neither is some kind of mystical, originary moment between artist and work, never to be repeated. Rather we are talking about an authorial subjectivity created by the work as the work is created, a reciprocal relationship impossible to reproduce through the forger's close and cynical observation but which nonetheless contributes to the viewer's affective experience.

What Auster attempts to show is how a truly dialogic aesthetics is historically contextualised, even if context is something which, as we have seen, cannot be fully captured positivistically. Moments of affective splendour such as Tina Hott's performance at Harry's graveside (Auster 2005, 222) achieve their power precisely by being placed against the backdrop of the "2000 election disaster" (244). When democracy fails, when political dialogue is so manifestly circumscribed, then the need to treasure these fleeting communal glimpses of beauty becomes even greater. To use Raymond Williams' famous term, it is as if true art (even art, like Tina Hott's, so obviously "fake" on the surface) sincerely embodies a "structure of feeling" (Williams 1977, 133-34) in a way a forgery makes no attempt to do.

When one considers Harry and Dryer's plan to forge the manuscript of *The Scarlet Letter*, some different issues arise. An apt place to start is Nelson Goodman's influential but much refuted thesis in *Languages of Art* (1976).[3] According to Goodman, an artwork can be called "autographic" "if the distinction between original and forgery of it is significant ... if even the most exact duplication of it does not thereby count as genuine" (Goodman 1976, 113). Painting is Goodman's primary example. Here, and Dryer's work confirms this, the forgery's aesthetic merits are irrelevant. "Allographic" arts are those such as music where any accurately rendered performance of a faithfully notated score, regardless of stylistic interpretation, counts as genuine. It is Goodman's faith in notation which undermines his thesis. Arguing that "[i]nitially, perhaps, all arts are autographic" and "an art seems to be allographic just insofar as it is amenable to notation", Goodman believes that the "transitory" nature of certain art forms, notably drama and music, requires notation "in order to transcend the limitations of time and the individual". This is why "in the case of literature, texts have even supplanted oral performances as the primary aesthetic objects" (Goodman 1976, 121).

Thus Goodman believes that *"sameness of spelling"* (original italics), employed here in the sense of "accuracy of transcription", is all that is required to render faithful a copy of a literary text or manuscript. Indeed, "nothing is more the original work than is such a correct copy" (Goodman 1976, 115, 116).[4] However, a unique manuscript is surely an example of the "autographic features" all "so-called allographic arts" possess (Margolis 1983, 170), which is precisely why it is a highly valued aesthetic object. Harry Brightman is very explicit about these features:

> It's not as if you just sit down with a printed version of *The Scarlet Letter* and copy it out by hand. You have to know every one of Hawthorne's private tics, the errors he made, his idiosyncratic use of hyphens, his

inability to spell certain words correctly. *Ceiling* was always *cieling*; *steadfast* was always *stedfast*; *subtle* was always *subtile*. Whenever Hawthorne wrote *Oh*, the typesetters would change it to *O*. (Auster 2005, 128)

Invoking the typesetters' activity reminds us that although to some extent authorship is being fetishised in the desire for the manuscript of the canonical text, the author is only one part of a complex historical, cultural and industrial network of creativity, exchange and indeed error. The vagaries of the printing industry help evoke Hawthorne's context and add to both the text's documentary interest and its aesthetic value. Thus Goodman's distinction between autographic (painting) and allographic (literature) falls down when one observes that autographic elements in both instances are themselves contextual, with a complex production history, and not simply productive of "patriarchal anxiety about legitimacy of descent". It is the production history, in fact, which overcomes "the limitations of time and the individual" (Ruthven 1991, 40).

In any case, Harry is "walking into a trap" (Auster 2005, 129). There is no Hawthorne forgery, only Dryer's plan to wreak revenge on Harry for implicating Dryer in the art forgeries years before (46). What has been perpetrated, then, is "an elaborate hoax within a hoax" (210). In terms of plot, Dryer's betrayal of Harry leads directly to Harry's death by, in all probability, a broken heart (208). Reflexively, if we agree with K. K. Ruthven that metafiction "revels in its own fictiveness" (Ruthven 2001, 51) and draws attention to its fakery (making it, in light of the paradox described earlier, something other than a forgery), the hoax-within-a-hoax playfully references the author's own fictive practices in earlier, heavily sedimented works such as *Oracle Night*. A nice joke, one might think, but the consequences are far-reaching and serious. The plot within a plot is literally deathly, so it could be that Auster is surreptitiously advocating a return to a more straightforward, broadly mimetic "realism", one which may in fact prove to be a greater imposture, in Baudrillard's terms a "counterfeit" mode of representation (Baudrillard 1983, 83). Is the reader also walking into a trap, then?

One response might be: only if one loses sight of how Auster's reality is textured. Auster considers himself a realist, and stresses that to reflect reality is to allow for the aleatorical and the fantastic (Auster 1997, 287). What is more, the very fabric of collective reality is narrative exchanges, so that an objective metanarrative is unavailable. The genuine therefore arises only through the sincerest possible attention to the interposed narratives of others and due respect for the potentially infinite overlapping contexts each individual brings. With their multiple narratives, the Chinese doll construction of *Oracle Night* and the more anecdotal form of *The Brooklyn Follies* might then be seen as two sides of the same coin, with one crucial difference. The former aspires to the lost hypotactic, miming the futile search for authority and pure reality through the regressive mining of layers. In contrast, the latter proceeds along the horizontal, the paratactic, on the assumption that an authoritative original is unavailable and new paradigms are required.

Nathan says "there is no escape from the wretchedness that stalks the earth" (Auster 2005, 189), but *The Brooklyn Follies* at least demonstrates that our primary coping strategy is the continuation of storytelling. The novel ends, significantly, on the morning of 11 September 2001, when "the smoke of three thousand incinerated bodies" drifts across Brooklyn (304) and human strength in adversity is under its greatest pressure. As Auster has suggested in an interview, a "family tragedy" of such magnitude cannot be conceived of at all without amassing stories:

> the accumulation of all those stories becomes, in some way, the reality of the experience for us, because it wasn't private, it was a communal event and we have to talk to each other and hear what each of us has gone through in order to get some sense of the totality of the experience. (*Fresh Air* 2004)

Although to use language in storytelling always risks misrepresentation, it also necessitates vehicularity, travelling between persons. So there is nothing of "postmodernist exhaustion" (Neagu 2002, 157) to Auster's writing in *The Brooklyn Follies*; rather it hankers after urgent participation in a shared sense of the experience of the material world as a composite reality. And whether or not his work is in "the realistic mode", one can site this novel within what Adriana Neagu dubs "the post-postmodern dominant ... the revigorating [sic] of humanist concerns through a re-evaluation of the ethics of writing and reading" (Neagu 2002, 150). What is at stake here is no less than the saving of a shared sense of reality fragmented by inconceivable violence.

The lesson Nathan Glass, Harry Brightman and Tom Wood all have to learn is that lives, like artworks, can be called fakes when they attempt to escape from reality into decontextualised imaginative realms constructed around a pre-eminent self. Like David Minor's religious fanaticism, Brightman's Hotel Existence is "built on a foundation of 'just talk' ... It's still just hot air and hopeless fantasy, an idea as fake as Harry's Hawthorne manuscript" (Auster 2005, 180-81). Similarly, the long, idyllic chapter called "Dream Days at the Hotel Existence" and set at the Chowder Inn in southern Vermont (166-200) is precisely that: Nathan's dream rendered in pseudo-poetic prose full of "cerulean dusks" and "languorous, rosy dawns" (166). Its present tense narration betrays the desire to retreat inward and arrest history, and it requires the sudden brutality of Harry's death to jolt Nathan and his companions back to reality (and Brooklyn). A similar effect is achieved by the sudden use of play script for the chapter in which the idea of the Hotel is first discussed (98-108). Formally and emotionally these scenes are as isolated as the Blithedale-like retreat Nathan and Tom briefly enjoy in Vermont. As a further example, Nancy Mazzucchelli, the object of Tom's ridiculous crush, is initially described by Nathan as "a sublime incarnation of the angelic and the beautiful" with "an unselfconscious abandon that allowed her to live fully in the moment, in an ever-present, ever-expanding now" (83). Clearly her present-ness is fetishised along with her beauty. This is before the men get to know her, at which point she ceases to be transcendent and becomes a socially and historically constituted being, complete with a past, as well as present marital difficulties (240).

To offset these examples of escapist fantasy, the novel offers three examples of true fakes rooted in sympathy and a sense of community. The first is described on the way to the Chowder Inn when Tom tells Nathan a story about Franz Kafka. In the final year of his life, resettled in Berlin, Kafka comes across a young girl during his afternoon stroll in the park. The young girl, "sobbing her heart out ... tells him that she's lost her doll" (153). Kafka immediately improvises a story about the doll: she has gone on a trip and has written him a letter to explain. Promising to bring it the following day, Kafka returns home and with "the same seriousness and tension he displays when composing his own work" (154) begins to compose the letter. Constructing an elaborate fairy story involving the doll's education and ending in her marriage, Kafka continues the letter-writing for three weeks until "the letters have cured [the little girl] of her unhappiness" (155). Tom's interpretation is revealing:

> "She has the story, and when a person is lucky enough to live inside a story, to live inside an imaginary world, the pains of this world disappear. For as long as the story goes on, reality no longer exists." (155)

Perhaps influenced too heavily by his undergraduate thesis on Poe and Thoreau, "Imaginary Edens: The Life of the Mind in Pre-Civil War America" (14), Tom fails to perceive that Kafka's story does not provide escape, another Hotel Existence, for the girl, but a means of continuing to live in the real world. Kafka's is a necessary fiction, or in Auster's words the deployment of a "lie in order to tell the truth" (Lewis 2005, 128). It is a fake which attains truth through its sympathetic understanding of the recipient's context and its efforts to relate.

Nathan arrives at acceptance of a similar truth as he lies in hospital following his heart scare. Whereas his previous job in life insurance reduced biography to detective work and financial recuperation (exemplified by his ironically named former colleague Henry Peoples, who demonstrates "all the warmth and personality of an extinguished lamppost" [Auster 2005, 246]), his latest project re-envisages biography as "a question of love" (302). We know from the first part of *The Invention of Solitude* that the project is empirically dubious, in that the belief in one's capacity "to rescue the stories and facts ... and shape them into a continuous narrative" implies a faith in objectivity masking an act of subjective representation (Auster 2005, 301). In fact, this is precisely what Nathan has done in this novel—taken the "random jottings" of his collection of follies (6) and produced a concatenated version. But there is little doubt that the ethical motivations behind the publication of "books about the forgotten ones" (301) are to be endorsed. In the desire to stick to the facts and "resurrect that person in words" (302), these biographies will prove to be only creative fakes. However, in realising that beauty, art and significance reside in "the ordinary, the unsung, the workaday" (300-301), Nathan's biographies participate in meaningful relations. They reconcile individuals to loss while retaining a sense of interconnecting contexts in "the smattering of impressions made on other people" (301) that they capture. Moreover, they are less a celebration of individual success or authenticity than a contribution to a sense of community and an attempt to capture a specific structure of feeling, post-9/11, in which attention to small, unique but connected individual lives increases in significance in the face of the grand narratives of religion and politics behind the terrorist act. So, to answer one of my earlier questions, not all art is at heart forgery or fake in the pejorative sense. Unlike Brightman and Dryer's forgeries, Nathan's biographies can be called true fakes because of the attempt they make to reflect their context and to contribute to community.

In terms of Auster's prose work, then, *The Brooklyn Follies* brings us full circle, back to the question of mourning central to *The Invention of Solitude*. If "The Book of Memory" counteracts, through its multitude of voices, the futility of private, biographical investigation in "Portrait of an Invisible Man", then Nathan's biographies offer something of a compromise: community biographies. Successful mourning is achieved not by striving for empirical facts, but by amassing stories about individuals such that an affective portrait is created. This is the approach of the novel itself, and it helps explain Auster's decision to finish with

9/11. Concluding with the catastrophe is not intended to undermine what
has gone before. Rather, *The Brooklyn Follies* serves as retroactive
preparation for that tragedy, as an act of mourning for real lives lost, and
as evidence that whatever horrors might be visited upon the citizens of
New York and the world, community and sympathy will endure,
overcoming hate and prejudice in the process.

If this sounds sentimental in both the philosophical and pejorative
senses, it reflects the tensions in Auster's approach. *The Brooklyn Follies*
might be considered Auster's first avowedly "post-postmodern" novel, in
that it largely eschews the introspective reflexivity of previous outings and
opts instead to paint on a broader canvas.[5] In setting the small lives of
individuals against the background of the 2000 election, it sits somewhere
between the "social novel" espoused by Jonathan Franzen (Franzen 1996,
37), descriptive of a particular culture at a particular moment in history,
and the affective novel which relates "how somebody felt about
something—indeed, how a lot of different people felt about a lot of
different things" (Wood 2001, 8). Its position is a somewhat uncomfortable
one, however. Brooklyn, as the supposed epitome of the lost ideal of *e
pluribus unum*,[6] may well be the most important horizon of significance
here and "community" the closest thing to a timeless, humanist value, but
the repeated, facile acts of self-reinvention that occur throughout the text
suggest an unflinching posthumanist emphasis on shifting identities. For
example, Aurora changes from pornographic actress to prim housewife
and Tom immediately accepts that "it was a different Aurora who sat in
front of him now" (Auster 2005, 74). Nathan insists that "[a]ll men contain
several men inside them, and most of us bounce from one self to another
without ever knowing who we are" (122-23). Such an idea is familiar from
previous Auster novels, notably *The Book of Illusions*, but is treated much
less dialectically here, to the extent that sudden self-transformation
becomes axiomatic and unproblematic in a way which seems to elevate
individual volition above the influence of community and history.
Although it does perhaps reinforce the point that the desire for authenticity
and the search for an original are futile impulses, its very facility begins to
feel like a confidence trick.

In one key scene, however, Auster successfully reconciles his humanist
and posthumanist tendencies and presents the most affecting of his true
fakes. When Rufus Sprague, aka Tina Hott, gives his lip-synching
performance at Harry Brightman's graveside, the literary mode is not
dissimilar to the "sentimental posthumanism" Paul Giles identifies in the
writing of David Foster Wallace (Giles 2007). Like the imaginary sweet
shop which supplies real sweets to the neighbourhood kids in *Blue in the*

Face (Auster 2003, 172), Rufus' performance as a transvestite "faux-singer", mouthing the words to Lena Horne's "Can't Help Lovin' Dat Man" (222), is not as Nathan says a "transcendent" moment in the sense of rising above reality (223), but a celebration of the fact that real lives can be fabulous. If one regards only the surface, it is the apotheosis of mimesis-as-fakery. "Decked out in full widow's regalia" (221), Rufus has paid as much attention to realistic detail as Gordon Dryer has to the characteristics of Smith's paintings. The wig is "like real hair", the breasts "like real breasts" and the legs too "long and lovely" to be a man's (222). Yet this is beyond mimesis: Rufus embodies "an idea of the feminine that surpass[es] anything that exist[s] in the realm of natural womanhood" and, in his "perfect representation of grieving widowhood", likewise proposes an *idea* of mourning (222). The excessive fakery of the performance is the point. It is an honest expression of Rufus' identity and permits the display of his private emotion by means of a role which is simultaneously an act of generosity to the assembled party. Though the performance is both "funny and heartbreaking" (222), it perfectly encapsulates the necessary embrace of otherness in the act of mourning, while defusing the anxiety which might ensue from the witnessing of private suffering made public. What is sovereign and enduring about human subjectivity, it seems to say, is precisely its performativity. And in contradiction to Nathan's belief that an individual bounces randomly between identities, Rufus demonstrates exquisite awareness of context, choosing an appropriate performance invested with the "inner light" of sympathy (222) to provide the others with a means of sharing grief. In the wisest utterance of his whole narration, Nathan sums up the ethical, affective qualities of this true fake: "It was everything it was and everything it wasn't" (222).

Such pathos is unusual in Auster's work. Although his fiction has always oscillated between introspective confinement (*Ghosts*, *Oracle Night*) and wider, more inclusive spaces (*Moon Palace*, *Mr Vertigo*), the publication of *The Brooklyn Follies* promised a shift toward optimism and a form of sentimental literary regionalism reminiscent of Betty Smith's *A Tree Grows in Brooklyn* (1943). So the arrival of *Travels in the Scriptorium* barely a year later was a surprise. After his most tender and magnanimous vision, Auster produced his most solipsistic novel to date. Gone was the interest in the small lives of the ordinary; *Travels* spoke much more of a celebrity writer's anxieties about public scrutiny and his possible legacy. Aliki Varvogli (2007) claims that "thinking small" is a common literary reaction to 9/11, a reluctance to tackle the large, historical or political issues and an emphasis instead on the local and the private. From this perspective, one might argue that *Follies* and its successor are different symptoms of the same problem. *The Brooklyn Follies*, however, does at least venture out of the locked room and into the streets to entertain the possibility of community. *Travels* symbolises a frustrating retreat into familiar puzzles, metafictional strategies and knowing fakery. *Man in the Dark* (2008) may represent a belated acknowledgement of these overtly postmodern strategies' limitations; recursive, uchronic narratives dominate the early chapters, but are ultimately abandoned in favour of "true" stories, touching domestic dramas and the all-too-real horrors of the Iraq War. If this signals a desire to reinvigorate the ethics of *The Brooklyn Follies*, then this is arguably a good thing. For all its failings in terms of prose style and occasional mawkishness, Auster would surely wish the novel to be remembered as "everything it was and everything it wasn't", his sincere attempt to create a true fake for the hard times.

References

Auster, Paul. 1987. *The New York trilogy*. London: Faber and Faber.
—. 1990. *The music of chance*. London: Faber and Faber.
—. 1992 [1982]. *The invention of solitude*. London: Faber and Faber.
—. 1997. *The art of hunger: essays, prefaces, interviews*. New York: Penguin.
—. 2001. *Leviathan*. London: Faber and Faber.
—. ed. 2001. *True tales of American life*. London: Faber and Faber.
—. 2003. *3 Films. Smoke, Blue in the face, Lulu on the bridge*. New York: Picador.
—. 2004. *Fresh air*. Sound recording. WHYY and NPR. New York, January 20.
—. 2005. *The Brooklyn follies*. London: Faber and Faber.
—. 2008. *Man in the dark*. London: Faber and Faber.
Barker, Nicholas. 1990. Textual Forgery. In *Fake? The art of deception*, ed. Mark Jones, 22-28. London: British Museum Publications Ltd.
Baudrillard, Jean. 1983. *Simulations*. Trans. Paul Foss, Paul Patton and Philip Beitchman. New York: Semiotext(e).
The Brooklyn Follies. 2005. *Publishers Weekly*. October 25. http://www. publishersweekly.com/article/CA6265342.html?pubdate=10%2F7%2F 2005& display=breaking. (17 March 2008).
Buber, Martin. 2004 [1923]. *I and thou*. Trans. Ronald Gregor Smith. London: Continuum.
Eco. Umberto. 1986. Travels in hyperreality. In *Faith in fakes: Essays*, trans. William Weaver, 1-58. London: Secker and Warburg.

Franzen, Jonathan. 1996. Perchance to dream: In an age of images, a reason to write novels. *Harper's Magazine* April: 35-54.

Gaddis, William. 2003. [1955] *The recognitions*. London: Atlantic Books.

Giles, Paul. 2007. Sentimental posthumanism: David Foster Wallace. *Twentieth-Century Literature* 53: 327-44.

Goodman, Nelson. 1976. *Languages of art: An approach to a theory of symbols*. Indianapolis: Hackett Publishing Company, Inc.

Grafton, Anthony. 1990. *Forgers and critics: Creativity and duplicity in western scholarship*. London: Collins and Brown.

Hawthorne, Nathaniel. 1961. [1860] *The marble faun*. New York: Signet.

Haywood, Ian. 1987. *Faking it: Art and the politics of forgery*. Brighton: Harvester.

Hoberek, Andrew. 2007. Introduction: After postmodernism. *Twentieth-Century Literature* 53: 233-47.

Jameson, Fredric. 1991. *Postmodernism, or, the cultural logic of late capitalism*. Durham, NC: Duke University Press.

Kant, Immanuel. 1978. [1790] *The critique of judgement*. Trans. James Creed Meredith. Oxford: Clarendon Press.

LaCapra, Dominick. 1983. *Rethinking intellectual history*. Ithaca: Cornell University Press.

Lewis, Tim. 2005. An audience with Paul Auster. *Esquire,* December.

Lowenthal, David. 1990. Forging the past. In *Fake? The art of deception*, ed. Mark Jones, 16-22. London: British Museum Publications Ltd.

Macpherson, James. 1996. *The poems of Ossian*. Ed. Howard Gaskill. Edinburgh: Edinburgh University Press.

Margolis, Joseph. 1983. Art, forgery and authenticity. In *The forger's art: Forgery and the philosophy of art*, ed. Denis Dutton, 153-71. Berkeley: University of California Press.

Melville, Herman. 2002 [1853]. Bartleby, the scrivener. In *Melville's short novels*, ed. Dan McCall, 3-34. New York and London: W. W. Norton & Company.

Neagu, Adriana-Cecilia. 2002. *Sublimating the postmodern discourse: Toward a post-postmodern fiction in the writings of Paul Auster and Peter Ackroyd*. Sibiu: Editura Universității "Lucian Blaga" din Sibiu.

Pillow, Kirk. 2003. Did Goodman's distinction survive LeWitt? *Journal of Aesthetics and Art Criticism* 61: 365-80.

Ruthven, K. K. 2001. *Faking literature*. Cambridge: Cambridge University Literature.

Schwartz, Hillel. 1997. *The culture of the copy: Striking likenesses, unreasonable facsimiles*. New York: Zone Books.

Smith, Betty. 1943. *A tree grows in Brooklyn*. New York: Harper and Brothers.

Tabbi, Joseph. 2003. Matter into imagination: The cognitive realism of Gilbert Sorrentino's *Imaginary qualities of actual things*. *Review of Contemporary Fiction* 23: 90-127.

Taylor, Charles. 1991. *The ethics of authenticity*. Cambridge, MA: Harvard University Press.

Varvogli. Aliki. 2007. Thinking small across the Atlantic: Ian McEwan's *Saturday* and Jay McInerney's *The good life*. *Symbiosis* 11: 47-59.

Williams, Raymond. 1977. *Marxism and literature*. Oxford: Oxford University Press.

Wood, James. 2001. Tell me how does it feel? *Guardian*, October 6.

Wreen, Michael. 2002. Forgery. *Canadian Journal of Philosophy* 32: 143-66.

Young, Edward. 1966. [1759] *Conjectures on original composition* Leeds: Scolar Press Ltd.

Notes

[1] *Aurora* as a name reflects the absolute uniqueness of the dawn and yet also its status as something endlessly repeated, copied day after day.

[2] If I employ the term *forgery* instead of alternatives like *counterfeit*, *pseudoepigrapha* or *supercherie*, it is for the sake of clarity, whilst acknowledging that within the realm of deception denoted by these terms, there are subtle conceptual and contextual differences. *Hoax* stands as a superordinate term along the lines of "act of deception", and can thus include the others. *Fake* I employ more generally, following Michael Wreen, to mean something unreal or simulated but not necessarily criminal or immoral.

[3] For a recent critical engagement with Goodman, see Pillow (2003).

[4] Goodman's criterion cannot account for, to cite one example, Thomas Wentworth Higginson and Mabel Loomis Todd's editions of Emily Dickinson's poetry, with their notorious punctuation changes. They are not forgeries, though they are clearly not accurate transcriptions of the original. Perhaps they are just examples of editorial insensitivity, but even this description feels unsatisfactory.

[5] One of the justifications put forward for citing a post-postmodern dominant in literature, as Andrew Hoberek explains, is the fact that popular culture has fully imbibed the knowing, ironic, reflexive strategies of high postmodernism (Hoberek 2007, 233).

[6] This might be one reason why New York secedes from the union in *Man in the Dark*.

CHAPTER FIVE

A DOOMED ROMANCE?
THE *DONNA ANGELICATA*
IN PAUL AUSTER'S FICTION

STEFANIA CIOCIA

Academic discussion of Paul Auster's work has not typically focused on his representation of women; as Mark Brown mentions in a footnote (!) in his monographic study of Auster, "[g]ender does not figure significantly in [his] work as a theme" (Brown 2007, 159, footnote 6). Indeed, a number of more pressing interests and recurrent topics come to mind when thinking of the Austerian oeuvre, whose most persistent concern can perhaps be summed up in the exploration of how the individual's relationship with language and with storytelling affects his (or, much less frequently, her) sense of self and of their place in the world. Besides, were we to abandon the metafictional and metalinguistic strand of Auster's work in order to look at his take on more material issues, such as, for example, fundamental human relationships, we would have to concede that the bond between father and son—an exclusively male connection—takes precedence over any other kind of interpersonal liaison, particularly in his early writing, as testified by the extensive, autobiographical meditation on fatherhood that is *The Invention of Solitude* (1982) or by the plot of *Moon Palace* (1989), whose main character's quest for identity unfolds as the (unwitting) discovery of his lost paternal lineage. Amidst these lost sons and their real or putative fathers, or—another frequent pairing—male authorial figures and their doubles, women very rarely occupy the central position in Auster's novels: only in *In the Country of Last Things* (1987) do we find a female protagonist and narrator in Anna Blume, who also plays a substantial role in the highly intra-intertextual *Travels in the Scriptorium* (2006). For all that her position is decidedly prominent in *Travels*, especially if compared to the cameos and walk-in parts of some of her fellow Austerian creations engaged in the mass *retour*

de personnages staged in this novel, the twenty-first-century Anna Blume
is no longer the undisputed heroine of the narrative: while her earlier
incarnation, set against a dispiriting post-apocalyptic scenario, had soldiered
on with the quest to find her missing brother, the new Anna seems to have
a diminutive mission instead, ostensibly acting as a carer—although
possibly also as a jailer—to Mr. Blank, the old and ailing male writer who
is at the heart of the story.[1]

Having said that, there *is* a particular kind of female figure—not quite
a heroine perhaps, but certainly instrumental to the development (or
otherwise) of the plot—who crops up repeatedly in Auster's novels, in the
guise of love interest of the male protagonist. Indeed, Auster has written
about the irresistible power of heterosexual romantic love—and therefore
about the relationship between men and women—just as often as he has
written about any other life-changing experience; what is more, in his
novels the characters who have lived through this rapturous event describe
it—briefly, for we are, by definition, in the realm of the ineffable—as a
miraculous and unexpected occurrence that has taken them by storm to
cast a flicker of signification on their existence. These protestations,
however typically succinct, are made with such earnestness and zeal,
particularly in their praise of the refining and beatific influence of the
loved woman, that readers would be hard-pressed not to make a
connection with aspects of the doctrine of courtly love even when the
allusion remains unspoken, as it normally does (with some notable
exceptions, as we will see later on). Codified at the court of Marie de
Troyes, daughter of Eleanor d'Aquitaine, by Andreas Capellanus's *De
Amore* (circa 1186-86), the theory of *fin amor* informed the poetry of the
troubadours in late twelfth-century Provence and its re-elaboration, a
generation or two later, at the hands of the Italian writers of the *dolce stil
novo*. This latter group of poets would endow the cult of the loved one
with distinctly religious undertones, creating the figure of the *donna
angelicata* (angel-like woman), most famously epitomized by Dante's
Beatrice.

In this chapter, I will look at Paul Auster's own love affair with the
trope of the *donna angelicata*, which he revisits, with subtle but significant
variations, throughout the course of his career. The roots of Auster's
fascination with the idea of the woman as a source of meaning and
inspiration to her man can be traced to his own personal experience, as can
be seen in the touching tributes to his second wife, Siri Hustvedt,
embedded in his fictional writing. Nowhere do we find a more explicit
tribute than in Auster's first novel, *City of Glass* (1985), where both the
author and Siri make a brief appearance, offering a glimpse of their marital

bliss; unsurprisingly, Auster has spoken of this entire text as "an homage to my wife. It's a fictitious subterranean autobiography, an attempt to imagine what my life would have been like if I hadn't met her" (Auster 1997, 278). This poignant, confessional statement remains securely outside the reach of the literary critic and is, all in all, perfectly sober and restrained. Not so, in Auster's novels, are the descriptions of the main characters' surrender to the power of romantic love, which are typically accompanied by knowing lapses into traditional amorous formulae, with all their metaphorical linguistic paraphernalia. Only this knowingness, to be found in the clear acknowledgment of the seemingly inevitable conventionality of certain expressions, injects a much needed postmodern corrective to what might otherwise sound like the wholehearted endorsement of chocolate-box feelings. After all, declarations of love in the time of postmodernism ought to flag up their citationality, as Umberto Eco reminds us in the 'Postscript' to *The Name of the Rose*:

> *I think of the postmodern attitude as that of a man who loves a very cultivated woman and knows he cannot say to her, 'I love you madly,' because he knows that she knows (and that she knows that he knows) that these words have already been written by Barbara Cartland. Still, there is a solution. He can say, 'As Barbara Cartland would put it, I love you madly.' At this point, having avoided false innocence, having said clearly that it is no longer possible to speak innocently, he will nevertheless have said what he wanted to say to the woman: that he loves her, but he loves her in an age of lost innocence.* (Eco 1984, 67)

Having said that, it is not always easy to tell when Auster speaks with his tongue firmly in his cheek, for he does seem to subscribe to the notion of the ineffability and the overwhelming charm of love, as testified by this gloss to his film *Lulu on the Bridge* (1998):

> Love is magic, after all, isn't it? No one understands what it is, no one can explain it. Pixie dust is as good an explanation as any other, it seems to me. ... In the end, metaphor might be the best way of getting at the truth. (Auster 1998, 146)

Still, whether Auster is being ironic here or not matters little, since, arguably, most contemporary readers would take these professions of faith in the power of love with a pinch of salt, *à la* Eco.

Postmodern self-awareness notwithstanding, the recuperation of the trope of the *donna angelicata*—however diluted, and divested of orthodox religious connotations, of course—is still likely to strike readers as potentially problematic, for it runs the risk of typecasting women into mono-dimensional roles: harbingers of private revelations and purveyors of secular salvation, these figures often have a short shelf-life, being marginalized—if not excised altogether—from the narrative, once they have fulfilled their inspirational mission. Auster's recurrent characterization of women as *donne angelicate*, or even as more active guides and muses, is without a doubt liable to being reductive. On the other hand, though, one might argue that—particularly in later novels such as *The Book of Illusions* (2002) and *Oracle Night* (2004)—the idealization of female characters is so blatantly a male construction that it cannot be read as anything other than Auster's exposure of men's tendency to project their fantasies and desires onto their female companions; indeed, Auster's own choice of incredibly loaded names—Alma (the Spanish word for *soul*) and Grace—for the main female characters in the two above-mentioned novels is so transparent that it must be duplicating willingly this dynamic at the authorial level: it is as if Auster-the-author were inviting us to read these characters as signs, i.e. as projections and embodiments of his intention (assuming, for a moment, that it were possible for the contemporary reader to fall prey to this intentional fallacy), rather than as realistic descriptions of real human beings.

On first glance then, Auster's representation of women seems to be bound—or even compromised—by the aesthetic as well as the ideological limitations of the vision of the female character as a portent and a mediator of signification, or at best as prompt and ancillary to the progress of the male quest for meaning. It is perhaps hard to dispel the legitimate reservations about the opportunity to revive this female stereotype which, in spite of being ostensibly flattering, tends to freeze women into crystallized figures. Yet, even so, I would argue that the fraught gender politics behind the male protagonists'—and indeed Auster's own—investment in the figure of the redeeming and inspirational female muse can also be seen as the inescapable consequence of the necessary strictures on plot development that are part and parcel of love narratives. In other words, ultimately it is because of his (tongue-in-cheek?) subscription to the imperious power of love that Auster seems to write himself into a corner every time he pens a beatific woman. In the following pages, I will articulate this thesis, tracing the development of Auster's fictional treatment of female characters; I will focus especially on his earliest, and most earnest, sketches of the figure of the woman-saviour in *The Locked Room* (1986) and in *Leviathan* (1992), two novels the similarities of whose set-up help highlight small but crucial variations in Auster's initial subscription to the notion of the redeeming power of love. Interspersed with passing references to other Austerian narratives, the second section of this piece will deal primarily with *Oracle Night*, where the male protagonist's investment in the idea of the *donna angelicata* is declared more explicitly than in any other text, even if—or perhaps as a consequence of the fact that—the main female character pointedly refuses to acquiesce to this role and, disturbingly, appears to be punished by the narrative for this all-too-human transgression.

* * *

The Locked Room, the third part of *The New York Trilogy*, first published as one volume in 1987, follows the rarefied, and highly intertextual and narcissistic model of its two predecessors, in the best tradition of metaphysical detective fiction. However, in spite of its having been described, when it was still its author's most recent fictional production, as "Auster's most realistic novel" (Salzman 1995, 162), *Leviathan* can be said to represent an equally apt companion piece to the last issue of the *Trilogy*, for the two narratives share a basic similarity in their plot development: in both cases the narrator of the story—a professional writer, in the guise of an anonymous character and the suggestively named Peter Aaron[2]—takes upon himself the task of researching and piecing together the life of a missing friend—Fanshawe (after the Hawthornian character) and Benjamin Sachs, both also fellow men of letters. Disappointed with the fundamental inadequacy of language as an epistemological tool, and with the remit of their literary calling, Fanshawe and Sachs choose to leave their old life behind in pursuit of a more radical quest for signification. Interestingly, not only are the two narrators then compelled to reconstruct the two anti-heroes' stories, but they find themselves filling in their friends' absence, to the point of replacing them in the marital bed and, in what turns out to be a pivotal moment in their own existence, falling in love with the other man's wife. As anticipated, the variations in the four characters' respective obsession with the limitations of language, their entanglement in each other's life and, last but not least, their experience of love throw light on Auster's early treatment of the encounter with the salvific woman.

Peter Aaron is the easiest character to discuss in this respect, because his story is merely ancillary to the telling of Sachs's tale, while his own personal trajectory remains relatively straightforward. Even if burdened with the task of reconstructing his best friend's terrible, self-imposed metamorphosis from successful writer to America's conscience as the anarchic, terrorist figure of the Phantom of Liberty, Peter Aaron writes his account of Sachs's tragic parable from a position of security. Unlike his (significantly anonymous) counterpart in *The Locked Room* who, as we will see, for a time is in serious danger of losing himself in his pursuit of Fanshawe, Aaron never really runs the risk of following in Sachs's ultimately self-destructive mission because he has already met his "happy ending" (Auster 1993, 103) in his second wife, Iris. Clearly, this female character, an English graduate student at Columbia University, is an anagrammatic homage to Siri Hustvedt, with whom she also shares her academic record. Besides, rather aptly for a wondrous and redemptive figure, Iris's name alludes to the ancient Greek goddess of the rainbow, the mediator between the gods and mankind. Aaron's romance with Iris is a textbook case of love at first sight, starting from the rapturous, impulsive first kiss, described as "one of the most impetuous things I have ever done, a moment of insane, unbridled passion" (Auster 1993, 103) to end with the inevitable, swift denouement of the amorous sub-plot:

> It was as though we were the first people who had ever kissed, as though we invented the art of kissing together that night. By the next morning, Iris had become my happy ending, the miracle that had fallen down on me when I was least expecting it. We took each other by storm, and nothing has ever been the same for me since. (Auster 1993, 103)

This is a real turning point in Aaron's life, for it secures his safe withdrawal from Sachs's direct sphere of influence—although, paradoxically, this miraculous encounter is made possible by Aaron's brief liaison with Fanny, Sachs's wife. Fanny's relationship with Aaron effectively prevents him from going back to Delia, his own estranged first wife, or to seek solace in the arms of his former lover, Maria Turner:

> There's no question that Fanny was directly responsible for this change of heart [i.e. Aaron's decision not to go back to Delia]. If not for her, I would never have been in a position to meet Iris, and from then on my life would have developed in an altogether different way. (Auster 1993, 88)

In what Aaron tellingly chooses to read—another instance of self-absorption in an Austerian male character?—as a "pure and luminous gesture of self-sacrifice" (Auster 1993, 89), Fanny acts as a first, minor, salvific creature. To paraphrase the relevant passage, she throws herself at Aaron to save him from himself, and then refuses to give in to his protestations of love and turn their affair into a long-lasting relationship. In this way, she sets Aaron free to fall in love with his rightful rescuer, the woman who will give meaning and wholeness to his life.

Before moving on to compare this blissful state of affairs with the plight of the anonymous narrator of *The Locked Room*, it is worth pausing to comment briefly on a different inspiring female figure in *Leviathan*, for it is with her guidance that the anti-hero Benjamin Sachs, unlike his earlier counterpart Fanshawe, does seem to find a sense of purpose in his otherwise desperate existence. The woman in question is Maria Turner, a photographer—and, yes, in the endless doublings and multiple entanglements charted in this novel, Aaron's erstwhile lover. Her projects are clearly reminiscent of those of real-life conceptual artist Sophie Calle, with their penchant for working with random constraints, pursuing arbitrary connections and exploring the power of coincidence (all themes explored by Auster himself). Taking the lead from Maria, "the reigning spirit of chance, the goddess of the unpredictable" (Auster 1993, 102), Sachs learns to appreciate the beauty and the intrinsically ethical nature of the gratuitous act, of the relinquishment of one's self in the immediate response to what life throws in our way. Under Maria's guidance, Sachs embraces the outside world as governed by Ananke, i.e. by the aleatory force representing the inherent necessity of things as they are; thus, in a way, Sachs's attitude can be viewed as a fatalistic version of the cognate Puritan idea of Manifest Destiny, which also makes no room for absolute arbitrariness or casual coincidence: if there is no real chance, then we must believe in the necessity of contingency and vice versa. If we do so, there follows that the whole world becomes a script to be scrutinized with paranoid eyes until the hidden meaning behind every occurrence is unveiled.

In a rocambolesque series of twists in the plot, too long to be summarised in detail in this chapter, Sachs's intellectual and physical engagement with Maria causes a fundamental shift in his view of the world: mystifying occurrences are made intelligible by a newly idiosyncratic hermeneutical thrust, unconnected events are all embedded in a cohesive plot by Sachs's defiance of the meaninglessness of coincidence in teasing out the necessity of contingency, and responding to it in tune. This is what triggers Sachs's abandonment of his old life, and of his writing, in order to author—or rather to give himself up to—a radically different narrative. Sachs's new text is woven directly into the fabric of life through the performance of gratuitous acts in the praxis and the mythology of the Phantom of Liberty. (Sachs's victimless bombings of the replicas of the Statue of Liberty scattered throughout the U.S. constitute a deliberately anonymous and unexplained wake-up call to his fellow country-people about the state of American democracy.)

While we are on the subject, it ought to be pointed out how Sachs's subscription to the necessity of contingency is not unlike the logic (or lack thereof) that romantic love is predicated upon: amorous language is full of metaphors suggesting the irresistibility of the passion that sweeps the lovers away, or takes them by storm, with the implication that the power of individual volition is reduced to nothing in these instances; there is a sense of inevitability and gratuitousness embedded in these ideas of self-abandonment. Of course, in the mission of the Phantom of Liberty, Sachs gives himself up to the spirit of the necessity of the contingent on a grand scale, in the social and political sphere, rather than in the private context of his personal, emotional life (although, as we have seen, these two dimensions are interconnected for Sachs, first through Maria Turner, and then through Lillian Stern, the last woman he gets entangled with and, more importantly, the person who—through her own association with a radical political activist in the making—sets Sachs on the final leg of his journey for signification).[3] A concluding remark remains to be made about the plot development in *Leviathan*: Sachs's is a story that, like many others in the Austerian canon, including the narrator's in *The Locked Room*, begins with a failure of marital faith, tied in to the lure of sexual transgression, and a subsequent fall—this time a spectacularly literal one, as Sachs plunges into the void from the fourth-floor of a building after a ruse to get Maria to embrace him. The whole story is thus set in motion by an attempted act of seduction, with lust—and not love—being the prime mover in the beginning of Sachs's plot. By contrast, its denouement comes about as a result of a course of action inspired by and inducing a blissful sense of plenitude comparable to the one typically experienced when finding love, as Sachs's description of his epiphany makes clear. We will get back to the significance of this narrative choice later on in this chapter.

The Locked Room also provides a brief, but eloquent, outline of the earth-shattering and sense-making power of love, with the meeting between the narrator and Sophie[4] (the young wife Fanshawe has walked out on) being described as a quasi-mystical epiphany and a life-changing experience, in accordance to the best conventions of romantic literature:

> I am tempted to use the traditional language of love. I want to talk in metaphors of heat, of burning, of barriers melting down in the face of irresistible passions. I am aware how overblown these terms might sound, but in the end I believe they are accurate. Everything had changed for me, and words that I had never understood before suddenly began to make sense. This came as a revelation ... . By belonging to Sophie, I began to feel as though I belonged to everyone else as well. My true place in the world, it turned out, was somewhere beyond myself, and if that place was

inside me, it was also unlocatable. This was the tiny hole between self and not-self, and for the first time in my life I saw this nowhere as the exact centre of the world. (Auster 1988, 232)

The problem for the narrator is that his love for Sophie, compelling and fulfilling as it clearly promises to be, comes laden with Fanshawe's dangerous legacy. It is, indeed, part of Fanshawe's carefully scripted plan, for, in the event of his disappearance, the writer had instructed Sophie to get in touch with the narrator (a one-time uncannily close childhood friend) and entrust him with his literary output. Fanshawe is acting here— deludedly, as it unsurprisingly turns out, in true postmodern fashion—as a megalomaniac, god-like, authorial figure, for the narrator's nomination as his literary executor is meant to be just a ploy to orchestrate the meeting between this old friend (and ideal replacement) and Sophie, and thus secure the blossoming of their romance. What Fanshawe has not reckoned with, blinded perhaps by the intensity of his quest for a prelapsarian language (a divine or Adamic idiom made of perfect correspondences and yielding utmost clarity, therefore very likely to promote the illusion that such flawless, tidy connections might be replicated in tying up the loose ends left by his disappearance), is that his plot still pertains to the imperfect, unpredictable world of human affairs and, even worse, that it requires the involvement of a character with whom he shares a deep, *prelinguistic* bond—a bond, that is, too deep to be erased. The anonymous narrator is thus a prime candidate not only to locate but, as Anne Holzapfel has convincingly argued, to *become* "the tiny hole between self and not-self" because of, and indeed through, his close connection with Fanshawe (Holzapfel 1996, 95 and ff.).

The narrator's predicament as the almost imperceptible space between presence and absence, identity and representation follows on as a natural consequence of his relationship with Fanshawe: he is his double, but also his biographer; his replacement, but also the investigator of his suspicious disappearance. He is Fanshawe's self (his alter ego), but also his not-self (his nemesis): enraged with his erstwhile friend, at one point the narrator describes himself as Fanshawe's appointed "executioner" (Auster 1988, 269), i.e. the man entrusted to carry out Fanshawe's will, being the sole judge of his literary inheritance, but also the man who puts Fanshawe to death, supplanting him in his own family and later refusing to disclose the fact that his friend is still alive. This is why reading and trying to understand Fanshawe's red notebook—the man's parting gift to the narrator in the way of explanation for his own linguistic quest, in the imminence of his suicide—would be a dangerous enterprise, as it carries the possibility for the narrator to comprehend Fanshawe completely, and thus put an end to the gap between the two characters. This merging of identity and full understanding, in its turn, would be a condemnation to take over Fanshawe's doomed, solipsistic search. The narrator escapes this fate when he chooses to tear the notebook apart and, presumably, head back home: the destruction of the written record of his double's enterprise constitutes the narrator's rejection of Fanshawe's quest and the quest for Fanshawe, which had initially tantalized him and dragged him into a spiral of dissipation, vindictiveness and self-hatred. While critics like Holzapfel have already dwelt extensively on the relationship between the two main characters in *The Locked Room*, their interpretations have perhaps tended to overlook the importance of the amorous plot in the economy of the story, for I would argue that it provides the ultimate reason why the narrator is in a position to turn his back on Fanshawe.

As we have seen, the text makes it very clear that the narrator can locate and reach the "tiny hole between self and not-self" in ways other than his identification with Fanshawe, i.e. in his love for Sophie, which is configured as an alternative route in the (endless) progress towards the erasure of difference. This is further demonstrated by the following account of the experience of falling in love as a "falling into each other", an event aptly described through a positive lapse into metaphoric language, which itself signals a linguistic subscription to the law of similarity (another instance of the privileging of sympathetic connections over an emphasis on alterity[5]):

> After that [the couple's first kiss], it is difficult for me to speak of what happened. Such things have little to do with words, so little, in fact, that it seems almost pointless to try to express them. If anything, I would say that *we were falling into each other*, that we were falling so fast and so far that nothing could catch us. Again, I *lapse into metaphor*. But this is probably beside the point. For whether or not I can talk about it does not change the truth of what happened. (Auster 1988, 233, my italics)

The revelatory, salvific potential of the amorous encounter is also implicitly reiterated in the narrator's realization that his inability to trust in Sophie, thinking that she might run back to Fanshawe if she discovered that he was still alive, had been his "greatest failure of all" and the reason for the degradation experienced during his pursuit of his missing friend: "If I had believed enough in Sophie's love for me, I would have been willing to risk everything" (Auster 1988, 239).

Earlier on in the story, the narrator had added a telling gloss to the account of his whirlwind romance with Sophie and their easy settling into the routine of family life:

> In some sense, this is where the story should end. The young genius
> [Fanshawe] is dead ... . His childhood friend has rescued the beautiful
> young widow, and the two of them will live happily ever after. That would
> seem to wrap it up, with nothing left but a final curtain call. *But it turns out*
> *that this is only the beginning. What I have written so far is no more than a*
> *prelude, a quick synopsis of everything that comes before the story I have*
> *to tell.* If there were no more to it than this, there would be nothing at all—
> for nothing would have compelled me to begin. (Auster 1988, 235, my
> italics)

While the narrator's metafictional remark explains that love is the prelude
to the story in *The Locked Room*, by the end of the novel it is clear that
love is also the condition for the telling of this tale, for without it, the
narrator would have completely lost himself in his pursuit of Fanshawe.
Paradoxically, however, the main plot is set in motion by the narrator's
lack of faith in the possibility of a happy ending, i.e. in the power of love
to provide security, meaning and, therefore, closure. In other words, love
sets the scene for the development of the main plot, while remaining at its
margins, and ultimately provides the condition for its telling; and yet,
without the narrator's *lack* of confidence in his wife's love for him there
simply would not have been any story to tell. Again, we will discuss the
full implications of this paradox in the final part of this chapter.

* * *

In *Oracle Night* lack of faith in love, and in the possibility for the happily
ever after that traditionally comes with it, becomes more radical, and it is
certainly the reason, rather than the condition, for the telling of the story.
At the very beginning of the novel, Sidney Orr—a promising writer in his
mid-thirties, who is still recovering from an unspecified, life-threatening,
debilitating illness—launches into a sustained account of his first
encounter with his future wife, Grace. Developed in a footnote, the
passage unfolds for five pages (thus becoming one of the longest,
paratextual narrations in the entire novel) and is mired in an obvious
contradiction, given how, for all his protestations that his love for Grace is
an ineffable epiphany, Sid insists in the attempt to articulate the
experience. In doing so, he provides an uncharacteristically detailed (for
Auster's standards) description of the beatific woman—"She was five feet
eight inches tall and weighed a hundred and twenty-five pounds. Slender
neck, long arms, and long fingers, pale skin, and short dirty-blond hair"
(Auster 2005, 16)—accompanied by the most overt reference to Beatrice,
and the tradition of courtly love, in Auster's work:[6]

I felt as if I had been thrust back into the world of the troubadours, reliving
some passage from the opening chapter of *La Vita Nova* (*...when first the
glorious lady of my thoughts was made manifest to my eyes*), inhabiting the
stale tropes of a thousand forgotten love sonnets. *I burned. I longed. I
pined. I was rendered mute.* ... There is no accounting for such an event, no
objective reason to explain why we fall for one person and not another.
(Auster 2005, 15, footnote 3)

Sid's description involves a series of intertextual references; significantly,
even the already-quoted mention of Grace's choppy hair is glossed with a
comparison to the curly mane in the drawings of Saint-Exupéry's creation
in *The Little Prince*. After a precise account of Grace's attire, and of the
exposure of "those long, smooth, infinitely feminine arms of hers" once
she removes her jacket, oblivious to the effect that this gesture has on her
ever more enraptured observer, Sid proclaims his desire to "go deeper than
Grace's body, deeper than the incidental facts of her physical self" (Auster
2005, 17, footnote 3) in what must surely strike the reader as an insatiable
urge to capture the woman's essence. Sid's dogged insistence in his
narrative enterprise is emphasised by his awareness of the futility of the
attempt; articulated through an extended discussion of the insufficiency of
language and a further reference to the conventional tropes of courtly
poetry, Sid's passionately argued belief in the ineffability of love casts the
entire footnote, retrospectively, as a form of apophasis, i.e. the invocation
of a subject through denial (in this case, the proclamation of the
impossibility that this subject should be even liable to verbalization).[7]
What is more, the proliferation of signs triggered by Sid's descriptive
endeavour, with its rich literary allusiveness, ultimately works only as a
marker of "his remoteness from Grace, his fundamental failure to
understand" (Peacock 2006, 67).

This is not so surprising when we think that *Oracle Night* is the only
Austerian novel to date whose central mystery—and therefore whose
narrative engine, so to speak—revolves around the story of the loved
woman rather than of the male lover, the narrator/protagonist who, in this
case, *presumes* to be able and to be entitled to tell the tale (thus prising
open the woman's secrets), even as he has otherwise acknowledged that
this gesture would be a breach of faith: "That was the power of Grace's
silence. If you meant to love her the way she demanded to be loved, then
you had to accept the line she'd drawn between herself and words" (Auster
2005, 50, footnote 6). While the early description of Grace is liable to a
more generous reading than the one that I have just articulated, for it
ultimately celebrates the unspeakable, enchanting power that Grace
commands over her husband, it becomes much harder to deny that Sid

crosses the line when he turns his writing to the composition of his (very plausible) speculations about Grace's past. These focus primarily on a supposed, troubled affair that Grace is imagined to have had before her marriage to Sid, and to have resumed during his near-fatal illness, with John Trause, the famous author (an anagram of Auster) and old friend of her parents, therefore a constant presence in her life.

Towards the conclusion of the novel, Sid puts down on paper his suspicions that Grace's wavering in the initial stages of her relationship with him might have been due to her reluctance to break it off with Trause who, on his part, once ousted in Grace's romantic affections, is only too happy—according to Sid's hypothetical reconstruction of the events—to befriend his younger rival and even mentor him as a fellow writer. The plausibility of this theory appears to be borne out by a spiteful remark uttered by Jacob, Trause's wastrel son, who nurtures a vicious, long-standing animosity towards Grace; just before the savage, physical attack which causes Grace to miscarry and virtually brings the narrative to a close, Jacob, who has barged in on the Orrs in a desperate search for money, reminds her sarcastically: "'After all, you're sort of my unofficial stepmom, aren't you? At least you used to be. Doesn't that count for something?" (Auster 2005, 200).

Incidentally, there is another, more convoluted explanation for Sid's paranoia: it is to be found in the power of the blue notebook, and therefore of writing at large, in *Oracle Night*. The blue notebook—possessed with magic properties, much like the blue stone in *Lulu on the Bridge*—can be regarded as the oracle in the novel, given how it predicts the future, and casts a spell both on who writes in it and who is written about in it. Whenever he writes in it, Sid becomes enraptured, and loses himself in its pages. Besides, whatever gets written in the blue notebook either is true or becomes true, literally or in indirect ways: as we will see in a moment, the Nick Bowen sub-plot prefigures Sid's disappearing acts, while Grace's miscarriage is foreshadowed by the story about the dead baby in the toilet. Even the intradiegetic narrative within the Nick Bowen sub-plot makes a similar point: in it, Nick Bowen reads a book by Silvia Maxwell called *Oracle Night*, whose protagonist, Lemuel Flagg, blinded while fighting in the Great War, recovers from his wounds to find out that he has acquired the gift of prophecy. On the eve of his wedding, Flagg foresees that his wife will betray him and, unable to withstand this blow, he kills himself. As the novel points out, Flagg's tragedy is compounded by the fact that his future wife is still innocent of any betrayal at this point. Close to the end of the novel, Trause shares with Sid the story of a French writer whose narrative poem about the drowning of a young child was followed by the death of his (the French writer's) five-year-old daughter in the waters of the Channel.

By the time Trause comments that "maybe that's what writing is all about ... Not recording events from the past, but making things happen in the future" (Auster 2005, 189), Sid is in the perfect state of mind to be convinced of the truthfulness of this statement—a fact that explains (albeit with a rather twisted logic) Sid's paranoia about Grace: as far as he is concerned, there are more than enough signs of her infidelity, even if the signs are mostly of his own making.[8] Sid's paranoia thus appears not to be completely groundless, given that his insecurity had been inflamed by Grace's brief, maddening disappearance in the middle of the novel. Aware that she has "put [him] through hell" (Auster 2005, 151), Grace nonetheless explains away her gesture as a sudden necessity in the face of the momentous decision she has had to make about whether to keep her baby, as Sid wishes her to, or whether to have an abortion, as she inclines to do, in the light of her rational consideration of their finances and of Sid's precarious recovery.[9]

An episode like this, paired to Grace's fierce sense of privacy and to her wilful reluctance to provide an explanation for her sudden decisions on considerable matters (her own proposal of marriage to Sid, the choice to keep her baby), should contribute to the readers' progressive realization that Sid's introduction of Grace as a beatific woman is nothing but an illusion, the projection of his desires, perhaps. In reality, the *ironically* named Grace does not conform at all to the model of the beatific woman as the purveyor of visions and revelations. On the contrary, Grace would appear to stand for the opacity, not the transparency, of signs, as testified by her very critical response to Sid's passionate oration for the Blue Team, a kind of secret society, a "tight-knit association of tolerant and sympathetic individuals" (Auster 2005, 44) that he had been chosen to join, as a young boy, at summer camp. Perplexed by Sid's enthusiastic panegyric to the gathering of fellow decent, idealistic, mutually supportive, superior human beings in the Blue Team (whose very name implies a belief in loyalty and integrity), Grace proceeds to debunk this mythical construction with uncharacteristic vehemence, maintaining that "[g]ood people do bad things" (Auster 2005, 46). Grace's gesture of reconciliation shortly afterwards, while obviously calling on the romantic cliché of the impetuosity of physical intimacy, is significantly phrased in terms of *tearing* and *breaking* rather than the more customary, metaphorical notion of the lovers' melting and blending into each other: "'The second we walk through the door, tear off my clothes and make love to me. Break me in two, Sid'" (Auster 2005, 47).

While the plot develops, it becomes more and more apparent that in *Oracle Night* love is not the condition for the writing of the story, as it had been in *The Locked Room*. In the earlier text, as we have seen, without love the narrator would have presumably lost himself forever: he does indeed lose himself for a period of time because of his momentary lack of faith in Sophie, and in spite of her unreserved leap of faith in their relationship.[10] By contrast, the inability to love *unconditionally* is the reason for the writing in *Oracle Night*. Both Sid and Grace utter conditional statements, which can be easily read as a strained attempt to persuade oneself of an unconvincing platitude and as an example of mild emotional manipulation respectively: "As long as Grace wants me, the past is of no importance" (Auster 2005, 187), Sid tells himself; "As long as you are not disappointed in me I can live through anything" (Auster 2005, 66), Grace tells him. Short of affirming the strength and solidity of their love, these declarations seem to mark its boundaries and define its limitations. The list of conditional statements includes also a blatant fallacy, articulated by Grace's "As long as you're dreaming, there is a way out" (Auster 2005, 116). The truthfulness of this statement is contradicted by the impasse reached by Sid in the intradiegetic narrative about Nick Bowen, the fictional story that he has started to write as an endeavour to get back to work. The Nick Bowen sub-plot is a re-elaboration of the Flitcraft episode in *The Maltese Falcon* (1930), but—contrary to Hammett's original tale, with its neat resolution—it remains unfinished, as Sid finds himself unable to write his two lovers out of the nuclear shelter which they have inadvertently locked themselves in. As already hinted, the narrative dead-end in this intradiegetic story is reflected, at the level of the main plot, by Sid's own repeated 'disappearing acts'—his failure to hear the phone, or to be seen by his wife—while he is writing in his blue notebook in the privacy of his room.

As James Peacock has suggested in his compelling reading of the Puritan legacy in *Oracle Night*, a piece that anticipates several of the points that I have so far made in my interpretation of the same novel, Sid's "immersion in writing leads to disappearance, estrangement from others, and especially from Grace" (Peacock 2006, 72). This troubling state of affairs seems to be connected with the nature of Sid's investment in his writing: the act is entrusted with the daunting task of restoring Sid's sense of (his *masculine*) self, which is significantly tied in with his ability to provide, as a traditional husband, for Grace. Even more worryingly, however, writing is also associated in Sid's mind with the assumption of a god-like authority, with the possibility to exert a degree of control in his life—control which he has otherwise lost[11]—and with the ability to fend off the horror and chaos of history. Besides the hypothesis about Grace's affair with Trause and the Nick Bowen sub-plot, which also contains barely disguised autobiographical elements, the other story that Sid writes in his blue notebook is a "little harangue" he furiously jots down as a response to "a dispatch from the bowels of hell" (Auster 2005, 99, 98), a newspaper article about the death of a baby, born in a toilet, and soon after discarded by his drug-addict mother. Yet, while writing to dispel the insecurity about one's ability to write (and therefore also to provide for one's family, in Sid's case) or writing as a cathartic response to the horror of "*the worst story [he has] ever read*" (Auster 2005, 98) are understandable gestures, Sid's determination to write down Grace's hypothetical liaison with Trause—an action he performs *after* her return from her sudden, mysterious disappearance and *after* her announcement that she will keep the baby—smacks of the perverse, and reads like an all too zealous attempt to understand (hence to control) Grace.

It is true that, as the narrative unfolds, Grace seems to become more and more of a cipher, as Sid resignedly admits during the long night of her disappearance: "Grace had become a blank to me" (Auster 2005, 150). Yet it is also true that this very blankness is what had attracted Sid to his future wife in the first place: he clearly indicates at the beginning of the narrative that he fell in love with "the sense of calm that *enveloped* her, the *radiant silence* burning within" (Auster 2005, 18, footnote 3, my italics). Thus Sid can be said to be implicitly subscribing to the long, patriarchal tradition that sees the woman as a blank page to be written on by the pen-penis of the male author (Gubar 1981, 247). On its part, however, Grace's penchant for *intentional* silence—an act of defiance against the requirement for the woman to reveal herself, or to let herself be spoken for by a man—is reiterated by the anecdote about her favourite toy, a doll named Pearl, who could speak, but chose not to (Auster 2005, 50, footnote 6). Pearl, of course, recalls the ambivalent, irreducible signifier in *The Scarlet Letter* (1850), and is an allusion to the proliferation of signs around and about Grace who, at no point in the narrative, shows any inclination to conform to the passive models of the muse, or the blank page, or the beatific woman. As we have seen, she repeatedly refuses to relinquish control over her story, by guarding her secrets and her independence very carefully, even to the point of putting Sid through hell, before marital harmony can be restored.

For this very reason, and possibly—another related point—because it is the one text centred on the mystery of its female protagonist, *Oracle Night* can easily be viewed as the novel where for the first time Auster has thematized the power games involved even in the most loving (heterosexual) relationships, particularly when the relationship in question involves a female artist, a woman who is a creative figure in her own right (not merely for biological reasons) and not just related to the artistic world by association. The latter had indeed been the case both for Sophie in *The Locked Room*, who is a music teacher, and for Iris, the English graduate student at Columbia, in *Leviathan*.[12] Figures like these make ideal female rescuers and sources of inspiration, for their artistic sensitivity can be channelled towards supporting their husbands rather than finding autonomous expression, or even giving rise to productive partnerships such as the short-lived collaboration between Maria Turner and Benjamin Sachs (which in turn originates and gives way to Sachs's final, solo artistic performance).

Interestingly, the female artists who light a spark in their male counterparts typically work in the realm of the visual, rather than the literary.[13] This is certainly the case for the women in *Oracle Night*: Grace is an illustrator, and Rosa Leightman—Nick Bowen's love interest in the intradiegetic narrative, whom Sid deliberately models on his wife—is securely heading in the same direction. Sid explains: "My first impulse was to make [Rosa] a photographer, or perhaps an assistant film editor—work that was connected to images, not words, just as Grace's job was" (Auster 2005, 19). Trause's beloved second wife Tina appears to belong to this category of women too, for she is a dancer-choreographer. Tina is in the best position to be idealized by her (older) husband, having died of uterine cancer—needless to say, an exclusively female disease—before her thirty-seventh birthday. It is in the face of such narrative details that the gender politics of this text *demand* to be untangled, for with Trause, as—to a lesser extent—with Sid, the novel does seem to suggest that the perfect woman is a dead woman. Amongst previous creative-female-characters-as-muses, two figures spring readily to mind: besides the photographer and conceptual artist Maria Turner, the other beatific woman connected with the world of visual performance is Kitty Wu from *Moon Palace*.

Kitty Wu is the dancer who miraculously irrupts in the world of Marco Stanley Fogg, the novel's protagonist. As he recalls, in terms that by now should sound incredibly familiar:

> I had resigned myself to a certain kind of life, and then, for reasons that were totally obscure, this beautiful Chinese girl had dropped down in front of me, *descending like an angel from another world*. It would have been impossible not to fall in love with her, impossible not to be swept away by the simple fact that she was there. (Auster 1990, 94-5, my italics)

As it is to be expected, Kitty remains incomprehensible to Marco, and the same is true of the other female characters in this novel who are configured

> as the other who cannot be absorbed into the subject. Kitty, who majors in dance, appears as a woman beyond Marco's apprehension. Marco likes to watch her body as she dances on stage, but at the same time he realizes that Kitty's illuminated body cannot be described; he says, "I did not understand it. Dancing was utterly foreign to me, a thing that stood beyond the grasp of words, and I was left with no choice but to sit there in silence, abandoning myself to the spectacle of pure motion" (96). Kitty's body is visible in the luminosity but could never be diminished to a representation. (Uchiyama 2008, 123)

Having literally saved Marco's life, and spent the best part of the novel in "superhuman harmony" (Auster 1990, 278) with him, Kitty exits the scene in the penultimate chapter of the narrative, when she decides to abort their child. In tearing their relationship apart, this gesture puts Marco in a position to complete his journey of self-discovery by embarking on a westward road-trip during which the identity of his long-lost father is finally revealed.

This is a crucial distinction in what is one of the many parallels between *Moon Palace* and *Oracle Night*: Kitty's abortion—an act of self-affirmation on her part—propels Marco onto the last leg of the adventure that, in disclosing the mystery of his origins, effectively marks the real beginning of his life (Auster 1990, 306). Grace's miscarriage, instead, appears to be a narrative necessity for opposite reasons, for its negative closure eliminates the danger of an illegitimate lineage for Sid who, in his speculations on Grace, had hypothesized that she might have been unsure of whether her unborn child had been fathered by himself or by Trause.[14] As James Peacock has pointed out, Sid's reaction to the news of Grace's pregnancy is related, in the first instance, to his desire to assert the indissolubility of their bond: having a child together, he feels, will finally assuage his fear of losing his beautiful wife. The hold on Sid of this train of thoughts is so strong that it supersedes even his paranoid suspicion that the child might not be biologically his own; in fact, the very possibility that the child might be Trause's makes it so much more important, for Sid, that Grace should make her own "leap of pure faith" (Auster 2005, 186) and choose to "embrace the baby as unequivocally her husband's, not John's" (Peacock 2006, 74). Rather predictably,

> [i]n a novel which incessantly oscillates between the desperate, paranoid-megalomaniac compulsion to create and an atavistic desire to erase and return to the blank page, Grace has to become the female victim who is

> required to sacrifice her part in creation to free the male writer from
> uncertainty. To put it bluntly, she needs to be wiped clean. (Peacock 2006,
> 74)

It seems that in Sid, the author who literally disappears within his
locked room, Auster has combined—and exposed, even if perhaps a little
too implicitly—the failing and the hubris of the two protagonists of *The
Locked Room*, without any of their redeeming qualities. Sid shares with
Fanshawe a solipsistic and, at times, megalomaniac authorial stance and,
like the narrator in *The Locked Room*, he fails to trust his wife. Grace, on
her part, is a much more complex, and significantly more fleshed out,
character than Sophie, whose unconditional love she is incapable of
duplicating. Even so, Grace's resistance to the leap of faith should not be
read as the reason for her final undoing in the violent beating that causes
her miscarriage, for it is the economy of the narrative in *Oracle Night* that
requires Grace to be wiped clean, and not Sid, who, as we have seen,
ostensibly embraces the prospect of becoming a father. This consideration
poses a rather troubling question: why does then Auster choose—or feels
the need—to resort to "the cruellest of narrative devices" (Peacock 2006,
74), co-opting Jacob as an amateur hit-man and unleashing wanton
destruction upon Grace? In this most inconclusive of tales, how can we
possibly justify and respond to the mindless violence that is visited upon
the female protagonist?

While it is hard to believe that Auster might have failed to realize that
Sid's final happiness, if not completely predicated on Grace's suffering, is
at the very least voiced *in spite of* her suffering, "it is equally unsatisfactory
to regard *Oracle Night* as an indisputably damning indictment of
masculine paranoia and dangerous insecurity, given that the male
protagonists are thematically and punningly linked to Auster himself (Orr-
ster? Auster-Trause? Austere, as in puritanical?)" (Peacock 2006, 75). In
the end, Grace's demise seems too high a price to pay even if, like
Peacock, we are prepared to give Auster the benefit of the doubt and
entertain the idea that in this novel he might be exposing the threats
inherent in the masculine need for control. This masculine desire is
described in *Oracle Night* as being fuelled by a fundamental fear not to be
able to live up to and comprehend the loved woman, and is subsequently
channelled into the act of writing. However soothing, the act of writing is
ultimately revealed to be painfully inadequate to offer any permanent
comfort or real solution, for it cannot provide a way out of the locked
room walled in by masculine solipsism and paranoia. In truth, Grace's
demise is too heavy an act of narrative retribution, even if we were willing
to concede that she is partly responsible for Sid's lack of self-confidence;

in a sense, the two are caught up in a vicious circle: with his jealousy and
wavering romantic faith (not to mention his indiscretion with Martine), Sid
makes a poor adept to the cult of the *donna angelicata*, while Grace
repeatedly and deliberately refuses to be pinned down to that role.

It is in this latter respect that *Oracle Night* appears to be an eminently
healthy, if belated, revision of this daunting trope, which is perhaps better
left to the realm of Provencal love poetry and of the *dolce stil novo*. Their
long-standing rarefied idealization of women provides a model of femininity
that—quite apart from its association with undesirable qualities, such as a
penchant for passivity and self-denial—is prohibitively difficult to live up
to in real life.[15] If nothing else, with this attitude *Oracle Night* marks a
clear departure from Auster's preceding novel, *The Book of Illusions*,
where there is a veritable proliferation of women as male projections and
fantasies—most notably in the figure of the mysterious muse Claire
(another name associated with light and intelligibility), who is shown
metamorphosing, for her man's benefit, from an "impulsive tomboy" to "a
glamorous, sophisticated, movie-star temptress ... [She] wriggles into a
narrow black cocktail dress, slips her feet into a pair of three-inch heels,
and we scarcely recognize her anymore. She cuts a ravishing figure: self-
possessed, confident, the very picture of feminine power" (Auster 2002,
258-59).[16] Alma, on her part, is also patently a construction, and overtly
unreal at that, given that her task is to lead Zimmer to the Tierra del Sueño
(the *Land of Dreams*), where—her mission accomplished—her life comes
all too aptly to an end.

By the same token, *Oracle Night* also marks a departure from the film
that had preceded it, *Lulu on the Bridge*. This film is the work where
Auster explicitly sets out to expose male cultural constructions of
femininity, rewriting, in the process, misogynist myths about women, such
as Pandora or Eve, seen as the originators of evil. In Auster's own words,
Lulu on the Bridge is

> about how men invent women. It begins with the very first shot—when we
> see that wall of photographs of women's faces. All those movie stars! I'm
> intrigued by the fact that for most of this century images of beautiful
> women have been projected on screens and have fed the fantasies of men
> all over the world. (Auster 1998, 149)[17]

The representation of women in Auster's later production thus sees the
creation of his most overtly fictional female figures, in the guise of the
muses and rescuers in *Lulu on the Bridge*, *The Book of Illusions* and *The
Inner Life of Martin Frost* (both the written film inside the novel and the
actual film). On the other hand, starting perhaps with *Oracle Night*, it also

heralds the emergence of more realistic and troubled female characters, or at least the acknowledgment—more hidden between the lines in *Oracle Night* than in *Lulu on the Bridge*—of the part played by men in fashioning restrictive models of femininity.

If *Oracle Night* is something of a tentative turning point in Auster's representation of female characters, perhaps it is no coincidence that in his following book, *The Brooklyn Follies* (2005), relationships, and the women involved in them, are more real and down to earth than ever before. Brimming with her innate self-confidence and bonhomie (aided, one suspects, by the wisdom that comes with age), the mature Joyce laughs at the proposal of marriage of the narrator-protagonist Nathan (another older character) and insists that their committed relationship should remain un-formalized. Women from a younger generation too eschew traditional gender roles: Nancy and Rory, having left their abusive/unsupportive husbands, end up together for what the narrative deliberately refuses to define as either a temporary experiment or a more permanent set-up. Nathan, on his part, is so incensed with his first wife that he cannot even bear to mention her name, in what reads like an ironic quotation of the *senhal*, the convention in the poetry of the troubadours that demands that the loved woman ought not to be referred to by her real name. The only woman who can be said to rescue her husband is the anything-but-ethereal Honey, who turns Nathan's nephew Tom from an introspective loner into a loving, jovial and self-assured man; yet, even in this case, on closer look, Honey cannot claim all the credit for Tom's transformation, for the real impetus for change in his life comes as a result of the gratuitous action of his employer, Harry Brightman, who leaves him an extravagantly generous monetary legacy.

However, none of these observations about *Oracle Night*'s role in Auster's later oeuvre offer a convincing explanation of why Grace needs to be the sacrificial victim in this text. The novel's implicit distancing from the courtly love tradition should not inevitably require the punishment suffered by Grace. The reason for her necessary disgrace is then to be found elsewhere, in the unwritten rules that govern a good (love) plot and, more specifically, a good Austerian (love) plot; read against texts like *The Locked Room* and *Leviathan*, the development of *Oracle Night* seems predestined both for its inscription in the Austerian canon, and on general narrative grounds: to the extent that Auster's narrators embark on the telling of somebody else's story, that somebody else needs to be a fallen and/or a missing person, which means, tautologically perhaps, that even Grace's final "leap of pure faith" into her relationship with Sid must really turn out to be a fall into her fate, in the sense of *doom* or *misfortune*. Besides, to paraphrase what Barbara Johnson has famously said of the plot of *Billy Budd*, the story of a fall is always also a fall into a story (Johnson, 1979, 576). Without the character's fall, there would be no plot: if the narrator of *The Locked Room* had matched Sophie's unconditional, unmotivated trust, there would have been no novel, as he readily admits when he says, in reference to his settling down with his wife, that "...this is where the story should end" (Auster 1988, 235). If Maria had not caused Sachs's terrifying plunge into the void, the chain of events that ultimately results in the self-appointed mission of the Phantom of Liberty would not have been set in motion in *Leviathan*.

It goes without saying that these characters' falls are incompatible with the presence on the scene of the *donna angelicata*. As I have posited in my introduction, in Auster the figure of the beatific woman is as frequent as that of the absent father, but the two are radically different in their impact on plot development: while the latter typically prompts the protagonist's quest for his origins, the sudden and startling apparition of the former, by definition, provides deliverance and therefore narrative closure, i.e. the "happy ending" (Auster, 1993, 103) that Peter Aaron sees in Iris. The search for the father marks the beginning of a story, while the miraculous encounter with the woman is inevitably bound with the conclusion of a story, for it fundamentally delivers the ineffable epiphany or, more prosaically, the traditional "and they lived happily ever after" beyond which there is nothing more to tell.[18] It is for very similar reasons that the Austerian falls are typically related to sexual transgressions or, more generally, to acts of seduction: after all, there is a long-standing, universal connection between sexual promiscuity and linguistic arbitrariness (or, to put it more bluntly, between infidelity and tale-telling, in the form of lies)[19] or, if we look at the other side of the coin, between romantic courtship and storytelling. While initially prompted by a survival instinct, Scheherazade's storytelling in the *Arabian Nights* is the ultimate act of seduction, parallel to, but not matched by, the bearing of three children to King Shahriyar in the course of their fabulous one-thousand-and-one-night romance. It is indeed on the strength of the fascination of her tales that Scheherazade finally finds the courage to ask for her life to be spared, with the result that, having won the King over, the storytelling can stop. And, to mention another illustrious text to thematize the seductiveness (and, later on, the treachery) of words, we only have to listen to Othello's revelation of the secret of his courtship of Desdemona: "...She thanked me / And bade me, if I had a friend that loved her, / I should but teach him how to tell my story / And that would woo her. Upon this hint I spake ... This is the only witchcraft I have used" (Shakespeare, 1997 [circa 1603-04], I, iii,

164-67,170). Love, by contrast, seems to demand silence, as testified by the parable of Martin Frost and Claire, whose life can only be rescued by the destruction of the manuscript that she has inspired. Once more, in a subtle variation of the motif later explored in *Oracle Night*, in order for the loved woman to survive, the writing has to be erased.

Is Auster's recurrent engagement with this theme a warning against— or at least an implicit acknowledgement of—the dangers that lurk in the solitary and solipsistic act of (male?) artistic creation, particularly when this act of creation hides an attempt to control the loved woman, or leads the male protagonist to self-destructive pursuits and to distance himself from the responsibility towards the other that comes with commitment to love? I would argue that the ambiguity and lack of closure in Auster's narratives leave enough room for disparate interpretative manoeuvres. It is up to the individual reader to decide whether the gender politics in Auster's work are deliberately and overtly problematic in order to generate a strong response, and it is up to the individual reader then to decide whether this is indeed the best strategy to be thought-provoking—in other words, whether there is enough distancing, on Auster's part, from old-fashioned stereotypes, so as to make sure that we question them and revise them, instead of merely perpetuating them. On the other hand, even as I am asking these questions, I cannot help but feel that there is something sadly reductive in approaching a writer's work by adopting an outlook that runs the risk of getting too close for comfort to a narrow-mindedly politically-correct version of literary criticism. Maybe Auster's main focus is—and why shouldn't it be?—on the weaknesses of his male authorial creations, and the pain and heartache that their women go through—and that, admittedly, are left unexplored—are no more and no less than a realistic by-product of the characters and situations in these narrative scenarios.

On balance, as we have seen, Auster is certainly aware of the burden that he places on his women, and of the futility and the narcissism that often accompany the male quests. This gender dynamics is best summarized in the words of the protagonist of one of his most recent novels, the aptly titled *Man in the Dark* (2008). As he lies in bed, sleepless, one of the most vulnerable and elderly authorial figures in Auster's work, completely dependent on his daughter and grand-daughter, whose own great suffering he willingly acknowledges, fully aware of the pain that he has inflicted on them himself,[20] August Brill declares that "women are the ones who carry the world. They take care of the real business while their hapless men stumble around making a hash of things" (Auster 2008, 21). While it is quite safe to say that women would prefer their men not to be hapless, and to provide some help with the task of carrying the world, this admission is, perhaps, a small step in the right direction.

References

Auster, Paul. 1988 [1985]. *City of glass.* In *The New York trilogy.* London: Faber and Faber. 1-132.

—. 1988 [1986]. *The locked room.* In *The New York trilogy.* London: Faber and Faber. 197-314.

—. 1990 [1989]. *Moon palace.* London: Faber and Faber.

—. 1993 [1992]. *Leviathan.* London: Faber and Faber.

—. 1997. Interview with Joseph Mallia. *The art of hunger. Essays, prefaces, interviews & the red notebook.* London: Faber and Faber, 274-86.

—. 1998. *Lulu on the bridge: A film by Paul Auster.* New York: Henry Holt.

—. 2002. *The book of illusions.* London: Faber and Faber.

—. 2005 [2004]. *Oracle night.* London: Faber and Faber.

—. 2007 [2006]. *Travels in the scriptorium.* London: Faber and Faber.

—. 2008. *Man in the dark.* New York: Henry Holt.

—. 2010 [2009]. *Invisible.* London: Faber and Faber.

Brown, Mark. 2007. *Paul Auster.* Manchester and New York. Manchester University Press.

Eco, Umberto. 1984 [1983] *Reflections on The name of the rose.* trans. William Weaver. London: Martin Secker and Warburg.

Fetterley, Judith. 1978. *The resisting reader. A feminist approach to American fiction.* Bloomington: Indiana University Press.

Gubar, Susan. 1981. "The blank page" and the issues of female creativity. *Critical Inquiry.* 8 (2): 243-263.

Holzapfel, Anne M. 1996. *The New York trilogy. Whodunit? Tracking the structure of Paul Auster's anti-detective novels.* Frankfurt am Main: Peter Lang.

Johnson, Barbara. 1979. Melville's fist: the execution of *Billy Budd. Studies in Romanticism.* 18 (4): 567-99.

Peacock, James. 2006. Signs of Grace: Paul Auster's *Oracle Night. English.* 55 (211): 65-78.

Salzman, Arthur. 1995. *Leviathan*: Post hoc harmonies. In *Beyond the red notebook. Essays on Paul Auster.* Ed. Dennis Barone. Philadelphia: University of Pennsylvania Press. 162-70.

Shakespeare, William. 1997 [circa 1603-04]. *The tragedy of Othello, the Moor of Venice.* Ed. E.A.J. Honigmann, London: Methuen.

Uchiyama, Kanae. 2008. The death of the other. A Levinasian reading of Paul Auster's *Moon palace*. *Modern Fiction Studies*. 54 (1): 115-39.

Notes

[1] One would think that neither of these possible occupations would involve masturbating one's charge, and yet this is precisely what Anna does for Mr. Blank—not before having praised him for the "well-lubricated erection" (Auster 2007, 20) that he has developed while she has been giving him his daily sponge-bath. It is difficult to conceive of this scene as anything other than an old man's fantasy, particularly in view of the suitably vague relationship between Anna and Mr. Blank.

[2] Besides sharing his author's initials, Peter Aaron is named after the biblical character who acts as a spokesman for Moses, a reference to the Austerian narrator's task of providing us with the story of Benjamin Sachs (himself comparable to the Old Testament prophet because engaged in a mission with near-messianic undertones).

[3] Again, notice the tellingly religious undertones of Sachs's description of his final epiphany: "All of a sudden, my life seemed to make sense to me. Not just the past few months, but my whole life, all the way back to the beginning. It was a miraculous confluence, a startling conjunction of motives and ambitions. I had found the unifying principle, and this one idea would bring all the broken pieces of myself together. For the first time in my life, I would be whole. ... I felt inspired, invigorated, cleansed. Almost like a man who had found religion. Like a man who had heard the call. The unfinished business of my life suddenly ceased to matter. I was ready to march out into the wilderness and spread the word, ready to begin all over again" (Auster 1993, 228).

[4] This is another case of *nomen omen*, for *sophia* means *wisdom* in ancient Greek.

[5] While metonymical language is predicated on the law of contiguity, whereby the metonym is related to the concept or object it refers to by close association (the part for the whole, for example), metaphor works according to the law of similarity, which entails the flagging up of a hidden correspondence between two concepts or things that otherwise share no intimate connection (as in the reference, common in poems of the *dolce stil novo*, to the loved woman as the "stella diana", i.e. the "morning star", or "Lucifer", that is the planet Venus). In this sense, metaphor clearly dwells on and emphasises the common traits between the two terms—say, the woman's and the star's brightness—and obscures their much more obvious differences.

[6] *Invisible* (2009), Auster's most recent published novel to date, begins with a reference to Bertran de Born, one of the most celebrated twelfth-century troubadours, as well as one of the damned in Dante's *Inferno*, for "having counselled Prince Henry to rebel against his father, King Henry II" (Auster 2010, 3). Born is the namesake of the villain in this novel. In *Invisible* Auster breaks the ultimate taboo in love narratives by telling us the story of an incestuous relationship, a topic that is perhaps better left for closer analysis to another essay.

For the purposes of the present piece, though, suffice it to say that here too, as in other Austerian novels, the ideal woman seems to be a projection, almost a double of her male lover: who better to understand bereaved and traumatized Adam Walker than his sister Gwyn, the person who shares with him an early, painful loss, i.e. the death of their younger brother Andy? Significantly, the novel never really reveals whether the affair between Adam and Gwyn has actually ever happened, or whether it is the bizarre product of Adam's imagination.

[7] "We all know that [love goes deeper than physical attraction], but the minute we go beyond a catalogue of surface qualities and appearances, words begin to fail us, to crumble apart in mystical confusions and cloudy, insubstantial metaphors. Some call it *the flame of being*. Others call it *the internal spark* or *the inner light of selfhood*. Still others refer to it as *the fires of quiddity*. The terms always draw on images of heat and illumination, and that force, that essence of life we sometimes refer to as soul, is always communicated to another person through the eyes. Surely the poets were correct to insist on this point" (Auster 2005, 17, footnote 3). Notice Sid's fundamental scepticism in metaphorical language.

[8] With these various sub-plots, the novel perhaps also flags up the responsibility of authorship for, whenever we tell a story, we do create a world, even if it is only an imaginary one. Conversely, imagination is often at the root of our decision making, and of the course of action that we subsequently embark upon: an aspiring medical student will presumably have imagined what their life would be like as a doctor and, in order to prepare for an important meeting or conversation, we typically try to imagine what might be in store for us, and to script the development of the events. The ability or the failure to act—in response to other people's circumstances—is also often dictated by the capacity for or a failure of empathy, i.e., ultimately, a failure of imagination. Notice too how—on the score of Maxwell's fictitious text, in a sense—the various uncanny coincidences, or self-fulfilling prophecies, in Auster's *Oracle Night* highlight failures of nerves on the part of the male characters: Sid hides in the notebook and Flagg refuses to face his destiny. Grace's miscarriage is the only event outside the control of the person who experiences it.

[9] Besides this one, there are further references to the motif of the descent to hell in *Oracle Night*: Nick Bowen enters his own "sliver of hell" (Auster 2005, 61) when he goes in search of Ed Victory, the man who—he hopes—can help him get a job; Sid thinks he has "drag[ged]" his wife "through hell by getting sick" (Auster 2005, 66), thus putting the two of them in financial troubles; the story about the dead baby in the toilet is described as "a dispatch from the bowels of hell" (Auster 2005, 98). The recurrence of such a trope is rather telling in a story that involves an alleged beatific woman.

[10] See this telling exchange between the narrator and Sophie, before the possibility of a romantic relationship between them has even been raised: "...'In the end, I suppose it boils down to whether or not you can trust me.' 'I trust you,' she said. 'I haven't given you any reason to,' I said. 'Not yet, in any case.' 'I know that. But I trust you anyway.' 'Just like that?' 'Yes. Just like that.'" (Auster 1988, 225).

---

[11] As he explains in the opening page of his narrative, as a result of his illness Sid has lost full control over his body, and is only just self-sufficient. Of course, another instance of lack of self-control is when Sid succumbs to the seduction of the beautiful Martine, one of the girls in the sex club owned by the Chinese entrepreneur M.R. Chang.

[12] A similar argument can be developed about Alma, the main female character in *The Book of Illusions*: she is writing the biography of Hector Mann, the silent film actor and director whose work begins the healing process for David Zimmer, the bereaved narrator and protagonist of the story. And, of course, even without taking into account her professional (and personal) relationship with Mann, Alma's own connection with the more passive side of the creative process is signalled by obvious signs of her own textuality, such as the already-mentioned meaning of her name, which is suggestive of her status as a male projection, and even more crucially, the blemish on her face. The birthmark is an unmistakable allusion to the eponymous short-story written by Nathaniel Hawthorne, a parable on the disastrous consequences of the male desire to author women, and a "brilliant analysis of the sexual politics of idealization" (Fetterley 1978, 22-3).

[13] On several occasions in his monograph, Mark Brown notes the redemptive quality of the female characters in Auster's oeuvre. As a matter of fact, having pointed out, as already mentioned at the beginning of this chapter, that "[g]ender does not figure significantly in Auster's work as a theme", Brown goes on to explain that Auster does "seem to suggest that female characters, particularly when they are artists, are more able to consistently bring appropriate strategies to their urban lives, and it is often through these women that his male protagonists achieve some sort of equilibrium between their inner and outer terrains" (Brown 2007, 159, footnote 6).

[14] The dramatic difference between the two story-lines is in tune with the general outlook of the two novels, itself borne out by the overt intertextual references that link them. The "Moon Palace" that gives the title to the earlier novel is a Chinese restaurant which, like Kitty Wu, summons up an entire host of metaphorical associations with the hopefulness of the frontier narrative, and the potential embodied by the feminine lunar realm. *Oracle Night*, instead, figures an eerie "Paper Palace", a stationery store owned by M.R. Chang, the man who later leads Sid to commit his own very real sexual transgression. Instead of bringing comfort and light, the Paper Palace is a threatening place where one comes undone and, of course, the location where Sid acquires the fateful blue notebook.

[15] At the risk of being accused of cynicism, and for all the admiration that is undoubtedly owed to the poetry of courtly love for its patent artistic achievements, it would be hard to deny that the celebration of the woman in this cultural tradition is, in a sense, no more than a foil for the lover's self-congratulatory praise of his own sophisticated accomplishments.

[16] Claire makes her appearance in *The Inner Life of Martin Frost*, one of Hector Mann's films. Martin Frost is the male writer who falls in love with Claire and who is also responsible for her apparition given how, as it is clearly intimated by the film's title, the whole story might just be taking place in his mind. This sub-

plot in *The Book of Illusions* is revisited by Auster in his 2007 film *The Inner Life of Martin Frost*, which develops the story between the writer Martin Frost and not one, but two muses, one of whom is played by Sophie Auster, Paul's own daughter. Thus, the notion of the woman-as-muse seems to have come full circle in the Auster family, with Sophie taking on a similar role to what had been, in *City of Glass*, her mother's.

[17] For a more in-depth analysis of this aspect of *Lulu on the Bridge*, and of how the film ultimately propounds the redeeming power of unconditional love, see Jesús Ángel González's piece in this collection.

[18] The counter proof of the validity of this theory comes from the fact that the disappearance, or the death, of the loved woman is also one of the recurrent narrative engines in Auster's novels: see, besides the already-mentioned disintegration of the relationship between Marco and Kitty, the death of the wives (and children) of Quinn and David Zimmer as a prelude to the stories told in *City of Glass* and *The Book of Illusions* respectively.

[19] This connection is flagged up with particular clarity in *The Locked Room*: far from gaining access to a prelapsarian world, the narrator's investigation of Fanshawe initiates a hellish descent into a degraded mock-semiotic dimension. This downward journey involves the breach of the Oedipal taboo, with the seduction of Fanshawe's mother, and the loss of oneself to a life of sexual promiscuity and linguistic arbitrariness, when the narrator traces his friend's steps back to France.

[20] Brill is another repentant sexual transgressor: at forty, after eighteen years of marriage, he ran off with a woman of twenty-six. After the failure of his second marriage, Brill was given a second chance by his first wife, hence—possibly—the particular harshness of his take on the respective wisdom of men and women.

CHAPTER SIX

A WRITER IN RECOIL:
THE PLIGHT OF MANKIND AND THE DILEMMA
OF AUTHORSHIP IN PAUL AUSTER'S
TRAVELS IN THE SCRIPTORIUM

GINEVRA GERACI

Ever since *The New York Trilogy* (1987), Auster's work has been haunted by the image of a writer secluded in a room, "the modern self in recoil"—according to the title Ihab Hassan chooses for the first chapter in his *Radical Innocence* (Hassan 1961, 11)—who, consistently with its evolution into a postmodern figure, has not dismissed a certain penchant for stubborn solitude and inward speculation. Whether this is doomed to become the death of the author is still to be decided.

Travels in the Scriptorium (2006) is a poignant effort to enlighten issues related to authorship and agency through Mr. Blank's uncanny and truly absurdist predicament: an old writer who is nursed or perhaps held captive in a room with apparently no way to escape. Mr. Blank is a weak author who has no longer control on his own characters, and a weak subject with a reduced ability to understand his situation and take action. This circumstance can be assumed as a starting point to illuminate a different side of the story. Exactly because he is a weak author who is challenged by his own fictional creatures and an insecure old man who can hardly deal with reality, Mr. Blank can finally face his ethical obligations as a forger of other people's destinies. As a non-assertive subject he may finally open himself up to the Other.

Therefore, despite the discomforting context, it is possible to read *Travels in the Scriptorium* as a tentative statement of purpose. While Mr. Blank's self-awareness is a problematic issue and his status as an author has become uncertain, Auster explores the problem of identity and authorship from an ethical perspective: an author is to fulfil an obligation to his or her characters, and to the reader who intends to interpret his or her art. This ethical horizon will be situated through Ricoeur's discussion of the hermeneutics of the self and the relationship between the self and the Other, as well as between the writer and the Other, as presented in *Oneself as Another* (1990).

In *Travels* this relationship between the self and the Other clearly materializes as a relationship between a suffering writer and his fictional creatures. The ethical dimension emerges through three key steps, each of which questions the notion of a central, ordering subject while supporting an idea of openness and relatedness:

- the adoption of meta-theatrical conventions that effectively dramatize the deeply dialogical nature of the relationship between an author and his work and, more extensively, between the self and the Other;
- a meditation on language as an ambiguous yet necessary tool that implies acceptance of chaos and incoherence, a door opening onto otherness;
- the use of irony as a form of ethical cooperation.

More specifically, *Travels* quotes the metatheatrical experimentation of Luigi Pirandello's *Six Characters in Search of an Author,* originally published in 1921, which effectively provides the framework for Auster's assessment of the asperities of authorship. The meditation on language is triggered by the intertextual relationships Auster's text establishes with absurdist literature and Samuel Beckett's *Endgame* (1958), which focuses on the crisis of the central subject and on the subsequent collapse of the subject's referential language. This aspect will be considered in the context of Auster's fascination with issues related to prelapsarian language, as already emerged in *City of Glass* (1985). Finally, the discussion on the use of irony will lead the argument back to Pirandello and his essay *L'umorismo* (1908).

However, as regards the complex connectedness of author and characters as already portrayed in *Six Characters in Search of an Author*, a distinction needs to be made. While in Pirandello's play the mysterious author is absent, in Auster's novel the writer still has a role to play, despite his weakness and lack of grasp of reality. In fact, his presence is necessary to recover the ethical dimension that is assumed here as a crucial element in the novel.

In the investigation of this interpretative hypothesis a premise might be helpful: before delving into the ethical possibilities of the non-assertive subject and distressed writer, his foibles and limits ought to be fully looked at and revealed. Auster portrays Mr. Blank's situation in the terms effectively defined by Ihab Hassan not only in *Radical Innocence* but also in *The Literature of Silence* (1967), namely a literature characterized by heroes who are fragile individuals often suffering physically and morally too. In particular, physical weakness and illness are traits Mr. Blank shares with some of Beckett's characters: *Travels* evokes *Endgame* in light of the character's inability to leave a closed room inside which nothing really happens and outside which nothing seems to exist.

Auster makes Mr. Blank an emblem of the human condition in Beckettian terms, while problematizing the status of authorship in a metafictional framework. The two levels constantly intersect, thus providing a complex perspective on man's willingness and ability to create his own life and on the writer's ultimate control over his art since, by a curious reversal of fate, he ends up being guided, and even manipulated by his own creatures. It might be interesting to note that the dramatic confrontation between Mr. Blank and his characters inscribes *Travels in the Scriptorium* into a metatheatrical tradition, but Auster gives it a self-referential twist when he imagines the confrontation taking place between his own characters, whom he has created over twenty years of writing, and his enfeebled and pathetic alter-ego.

Mr. Blank's characters have different attitudes towards their creator; Anna nurses him and seems grateful to be "alive": "...the fact is, Mr. Blank, without you I wouldn't be anyone" (Auster 2007, 22). On the other hand, James P. Flood, brought to fictional life by Fanshawe, the anti-hero of *The Locked Room* (1986), threatens Mr. Blank: "you're cruel ... cruel and indifferent to the pain of others. You play with people's lives and take no responsibility for what you've done ... I blame you for what's happened to me. I most sincerely blame you and I despise you for it" (Auster 2007, 53). Samuel Farr urges him to remember and forget at the same time, and is the one character who spurs Mr. Blank to find an appropriate ending for Trause's manuscript. Other characters are only mentioned, such as Stillman, both Jr. and Sr., and David Zimmer, while Fanshawe is the author of *Travels in the Scriptorium*, as we discover at the end.

Actually, the list of returning spectres is not confined to fictional characters but also includes the manuscript John Trause offers as a gift to Sid in *Oracle Night*, a short story entitled "The Empire of Bones" (Auster 2004, 144) that Sid ends up losing in the subway. *Travels in the Scriptorium* is also the title of a book published by Martin Frost, the protagonist of one of the unseen films by Hector Mann in *The Book of Illusions* (Auster 2002, 252). Interestingly, the film in question, *The Inner Life of Martin Frost*, tackles the complex relationship between author and character, and the apparent irreconcilability of art and life. While creating his fictional characters, Martin slowly destroys Claire, the mysterious flesh and bone woman he is in love with.

In providing a portrait of the artist as an old man, *Travels in the Scriptorium* reveals some intriguing features since, while Mr. Blank's sense of self is challenged, his ability to acknowledge his characters' pain increases. As the writer's control on his characters begins to fail, they become something new, fictional beings whose life expands outside the boundaries originally set by their author.

Ethics, narrative, authorship

The development of the characters' fictional life beyond the author's initial intent can be analyzed in the context of the hermeneutics of the self and of the relationship between the author and his work, an interaction Ricoeur considers in Hegelian terms. It is an extraordinarily precarious relationship because when the work of art becomes something detached from its author, it derives its own significance from the Other. Therefore, the work of art lives exclusively through the Other's mediation (Ricoeur 1992 [1990], 156). Ricoeur explains that narrative practices rely on this kind of interaction and that they are in a mimetic relationship with action, which gives them a prenarrative quality:

> …this close connection with the narrative sphere is reinforced by the form of interaction proper to practices. It is to the latter that the narrative gives the polemical form of a competition between narrative programs. (Ricoeur 1992 [1990], 157)

Therefore each narrative representation endorses a certain attempt at sense-making. This interactive competition between narratives has a deeply ethical nature because the narrative act is the effort to organize separate facts and provide them with meaning, and it is evidently different for each individual (Ricoeur 1992 [1990], 158). In particular, in dealing with a life that does not belong to him or her, the subject generates ambiguity, yet such ambiguity should be preserved and not solved:

> By narrating a life of which I am not the author as to existence, I make myself its coauthor as to its meaning. Moreover, it is neither by chance nor by error that, in the opposite sense, so many Stoic philosophers interpreted life itself, life lived, as playing a role in a play we have not written and whose author, as a result, retreats outside of the role. These exchanges between the multiple sense of the term "author" and "authorship" contribute

to the wealth of meaning of the very notion of agency. (Ricoeur 1992 [1990], 162)

In *Six Characters in Search of an Author*, the Father argues in a similar manner that "every man acts the part assigned to him—by himself or others—in this life" (Pirandello 1998 [1921], 31); in *Travels*, Auster investigates this interpretation of one's life as a performance in a role cast by a distant author transforming the metaphor into the literality of the novel's plot. By focussing on the author and on his "liabilities", Auster creates a figure who is at the same time a character—in Auster's text—and a creator—although his creatures were actually born of Auster's imagination. Thus the interplay of the notions of authorship, agency and identity produces a complex reflection game that finally undermines the solidity of each, although it does not diminish their relevance.

The subject remains a focal point that cannot be dismissed; the non-subject that is so frequently at the blurred centre of post-modern fiction requires to be dealt with. Non-subjectivity has been explored in several manners, from Musil's *The Man without Qualities* (1930-1943)—which Ricoeur also mentions (Ricoeur 1992 [1990], 149)—to the stolid non-hero in Jerzy Kosinsky's *Being There* (1970). In *Bartleby* (1989), Deleuze mentions Musil's *The Man without Qualities* as the epitome of a man who has no peculiarities nor preferences, like Melville's character (Deleuze 2006 [1989], 18). Bartebly is a looming presence in Auster's work (Varvogli 2001, 59-60), a character who, due to his stubborn "I would prefer not to", belongs to the category of unsubstantial beings haunting twentieth-century literature. Deleuze associates such lack of qualities to Blanchot's interpretation of Musil's hero as lacking not just qualities but substance too (Deleuze 2006 [1989], 18). Mr. Blank is closely related to such an inconspicuous personality. Yet, his state of dazedness and confusion, his metaphorical blankness is less a void than an existential condition compelling him to interact with those manifestations of his identity that are his characters. In doing so, he dramatizes the deeply dialectical nature of his identity.

Ricoeur argues that the notion of identity is defined by the dialectic relationship between *ipseité*, selfhood, and *mêmeté*, sameness; similarly *ipseité* relies on the dialectical relationship between Oneself and the Other (Ricoeur 1992 [1990], 13). *Anti-romans* first and post-modern experimentalism later have originated a negative narrative identity that has seen the disintegration of the plot on the one hand and of the character on the other, so that "as the narrative approaches the point of annihilation of the character, the novel also loses its own properly narrative qualities"

(Ricoeur 1992 [1990], 149). However, while the narrative level of the *ipse* weakens due to this absence of qualities, its ethical level becomes assertive. Defining the self in the traditional terms set by the philosophy of the subject is no longer possible, yet the tension between possession and dispossession, self-affirmation and self-effacement is fruitful and is exactly what animates much of Auster's fiction. It is the space of existential crisis in which the subject renounces its own primacy in favour of the Other's: "The irruption of the other, breaking through the enclosure of the same, meets with the complicity of this movement of effacement by which the self makes itself available to others" (Ricoeur 1992 [1990], 168). Being open to others adds an ethical perspective to the author's position, and in this sense many of Auster's anti-heroes start writing as a reconstruction process of other people's lives, sometimes to assuage a sense of guilt, sometimes to fill in the blanks—literally—of their own lives, more often to fulfil an ethical obligation.

A good number of Auster's novels begin with the protagonist being a victim of tremendous human wreckage—like David Zimmer in *The Book of Illusions* (2002)—or losing their grip on reality—like Jim Nashe in *The Music of Chance* (1991)—or purely and simply "looking for a quiet place to die" (Auster 2005, 1)—like Nathan Glass in *The Brooklyn Follies*. And many of them end up writing logs, records, autobiographical accounts of themselves or biographies of obscure "others". In *Travels*, Auster once again focuses on the nature of that moral obligation. Having dismissed the primacy of his own self, the most important question for Mr. Blank is not "Who am I?" but, in Ricoeurian terms, "What is my moral obligation to you, to the other?" (Ricoeur 1992 [1990], 168). The only way for him to fulfil such duty is to acknowledge his fictional creations and, perhaps, finish the unfinished story in Trause's manuscript. After all, Auster's fascination with indeterminacy and shifting boundaries between fiction and reality has never meant passive acceptance of purposelessness and individualism: "While he does not refuse to forsake the premodern notion of the individual so that a vestige of renaissance humanism can remain, he does examine in all of his fiction the consequences of actions taken in one's self-fashioning" (Barone 1995, 5).

Pirandellian and Beckettian legacies: *Travels* as (meta)theatre

The crisis of the central subject and the individual's unsuppressed need to be acknowledged is also the focus in Pirandello's *Six Characters*, where the author literally vanishes and the characters, like Mr. Blank's creatures, take over in a desperate effort to have someone recognize the significance of their sufferings. The parallel with Pirandello's play is further encouraged by the theatrical nature of *Travels*' setting, which can be conceived of as a play in which Mr. Blank's room resembles a stage, and where unity of time—a day——and of place—the room—are carefully preserved. The interior is the only reality we perceive as spectators, while the external space is evoked by the characters' words. Mr. Blank, finally turned into a character himself, is suspended in unchanging time and space:

> It will never end. For Mr. Blank is one of us now, and struggle though he might to understand his predicament, he will always be lost ... Mr. Blank is old and enfeebled, but as long as he remains in the room with the shuttered windows and the locked door, he can never die, never disappear, never be anything but the words I am writing on this page. (Auster 2007, 129-130)

The final words of the text reinforce a theatrical interpretation:

> He will fall asleep, and when he wakes up in the morning, the treatment will begin again. But for now it is still the day it has always been since the first word of this report, and now is the moment when Anna kisses Mr. Blank on the cheek and tucks him in, and now is the moment when she stands up from the bed and begins walking toward the door. Sleep well, Mr. Blank. Lights out. (Auster 2007, 130)

These seem to be stage directions, especially the imperative "Lights out", and they share a narrative quality with the ones Pirandello uses in *Six Characters*. Like Pirandello's, Mr. Blank's characters demand attention and recognition but also claim a freedom to act and speak well beyond the author's original intentions, so that Mr. Blank is finally directed by his own creatures. In *Six Characters* the following exchange is pivotal:

> DIRECTOR [*suddenly struck by a new idea, he steps in front of the* FATHER]: I should like to know, however, when anyone ever saw a character get out of his part and set about expounding and explicating it, delivering lectures on it. Can you tell me? I have never seen anything like that.

> FATHER: You have never seen it, sir, because authors generally hide the travail of their creations. When characters are alive and turn up, living, before their author, all the author does is follow the words and gestures which they propose to him. He has to want them to be as they themselves

want to be. Woe betide him if he doesn't! When a character is born, he at
once acquires such an independence, even of his own author, that the
whole world can imagine him in innumerable situations other than those
the author thought to place him in. At times he acquires a meaning that the
author never dreamt of giving him. (Pirandello 1998 [1921], 61-62)

The Father's words resonate with a tradition that imagines the work
of art as independent from the author in the same terms established by
Ricoeur's discussion on Hegel. The work of art detaches itself from the
author and becomes a living thing, as the narrator of *Travels* explains:

Without him we are nothing, but the paradox is that we, the figments of
another mind, will outlive the mind that made us, for once we are thrown
into the world, we continue to exist forever and our stories go on being
told, even after we are dead.

Mr. Blank might have acted cruelly toward some of his charges over the
years, but not one of us thinks he hasn't done everything in his power to
serve us well. That is why I plan to keep him where he is ... In a short
while, a woman will enter the room and feed him his dinner. I haven't
decided who that woman will be, but if all goes well between now and
then, I will send in Anna. (Auster 2007, 129-130)

The shift from 'we' to 'I' on the last page is interesting. 'I' indicates
that the narrator is taking responsibility for his narrative act and for the
choices it implies. Reversing roles has become an intoxicating game and
now the narrator cannot resist the temptation of sounding like a
condescending demiurge shaping reality—although fictional—according
to his will. Moreover, this final 'I' closes the circle that had been opened
when the story had begun with the 'eye' of the camera clicking and
following Mr. Blank on page one.

Once the characters take over, what happens to the author? Mr.
Blank's mysterious detainment recalls a Kafkaesque world of unspecified
crimes and incomprehensible punishments, while it is not clear whether he
is really punished or simply cured. Furthermore, for one eager to find out
what his condition is, he appears to be terribly helpless when it comes to
important questions, so after anxiously wondering whether he is being
held prisoner or not, he cannot bring himself to settle the matter:

Someone, perhaps several someones, has or have locked Mr. Blank in this
room and is or are holding him prisoner against his will. At least that is
what he concludes from the evidence of the two nails hammered into the
window sash, but damning as that evidence might be, there is still the

question of the door ... If he were thinking clearly, his next step would be to walk or to wheel himself over to the door and investigate the matter at once. But Mr. Blank does not move from his spot by the window, for the simple reason that he is afraid, so afraid of what he might learn from the door that he cannot bring himself to risk a confrontation with the truth. (Auster 2007, 36-37)

In *Travels,* Auster does not merely erase the fictional author, nor does the hidden narrator simply want to annihilate him, but rather he wants to confront him with the responsibilities of authorship. The author is not dead but has certainly reached a stage of crisis, and this condition is indeed being staged within the meta-fictional framework of the story, which develops as a one-act narrative with Mr. Blank in the spotlight, being judged by his characters and under the inexorable gaze of both the narrator and the reader. This multiplies the force of the panoptic mechanism that is symbolized by the room where he is under close scrutiny, nursed or perhaps held captive.

Flood judges him guilty and Mr. Blank himself—"I feel so ashamed" (Auster 2007, 22)—accepts the responsibility for his actions and consequently for his characters' destinies. However, if Mr. Blank is to be held responsible for something, one first has to know who he is. As his name immediately suggests, the question of identity is far from being settled, yet, problematizing the concepts of identity, authorship and agency does not necessarily imply denying that an individual, an author and an agent are there, rather that such concepts need to be reformulated.

Deprived of his former freedom as a writer, Mr. Blank loses part of his ability to understand and classify, as well as his control on knowledge. The deconstructive effect of his "blankness" and the progressive fragmentation of the epistemological process are accentuated by the deliberate blurring of boundaries between fact and fiction and, in particular, by the author, narrator and characters blending into each other. This is a meta-narrative strategy Auster has already applied, as Clara Bartocci explains in discussing the disruptive method whereby he disintegrates logocentrism, realism and linearity in *The New York Trilogy* (Bartocci 2000, 371).[1]

The complex network of relationships linking agency, authorship, identity and ethics outlines a landscape Auster has repeatedly investigated in his novels, often through the prism of absurdist literature. In meeting Mr. Blank, the reader is immediately introduced to the "figments in his head" (Auster 2007, 1), namely those questions—"Who is he? What is he doing here? When did he arrive and how long will he remain?" (Auster 2007, 1)—generating the same anguish that resonates in Beckett's *Waiting for Godot*, especially in Lucky's tirade pivoting around a hopeless possible answer: "for reasons unknown" (Beckett 1956, 43-44).

Auster's revision of Beckett's work is taken for granted by Steven Connor (Connor 1996, 166), while Aliki Varvogli discusses in more detail the analogies between Auster's *New York Trilogy* and Beckett's *Trilogy*. She stresses that in both *City of Glass* and *Molloy* (1951)

> a quest for a person turns out to be a search for one's own identity; the theme of the double, present in both narratives, underscores the increasing uncertainty of the two detectives concerning their own sense of self, while the fact that they both write reports about their undertaking raises the more complex issue of the search for one's identity in writing. (Varvogli 2001, 80)

In more general terms, Tim Woods remarks that, in defining "the epistemological paradox in which a subject often finds itself" (Woods 1995, 158), Auster draws inspiration directly from Beckett and his commitment to an art that respects otherness, openly quoting him in a passage included in *The Art of Hunger*: "'What I am saying does not mean that there will henceforth be no form of art. It only means that there will be a new form, and that this form will be of such a type that it admits the chaos and does not try to say that chaos is really something else ... To find a form that accommodates the mess, that is the task of the artist now'" (Auster 1992, 19). This was such a powerful source for Auster that he admits: "the influence of Beckett was so strong that I couldn't see my way beyond it" (Auster 1992, 275).

Faced with a Beckettian epistemological paradox, Mr. Blank is an author who has to find a form to accommodate chaos, too. His memory may be severely damaged and his ability to read reality strongly impaired, yet Auster's clueless and fragile alter-ego is a potentially open subject, an enfeebled yet ethically oriented writer.

Further Beckettian legacies: *Travels* as meditation on language

Once the ideas of controlling agency and authorship are questioned, the notion of a perfectly mastered language is too. Mr. Blank's reduced ability to use language effectively, to link words and objects, also works as a metaphor for the author's incapacity to control and successfully contain reality within the safe boundaries of a univocal, reassuring and transparent language.

Moving from the Pirandellian uncertain domain of authorship to the problematic realm of identity/agency and finally to the meditation on the nature of language, Beckett becomes a presence that, once again, requires to be acknowledged. First of all, the plainness of Mr. Blank's surroundings recalls the minimalism of Beckettian scenery. Despite the obsessive focus on objects, the prosaic descriptions and observation of action, the novel's setting is violently anti-naturalistic, as if those things were displayed and discarded at the same time as not really important. The room is as disturbingly aseptic and neutral as Mr. Blank's clothes, completely white as those worn by Stillman Jr. in *City of Glass*. The absurdist atmosphere recalls the dismal room where Hamm and Nagg hopelessly nag at each other in *Endgame*. The desert is outside but the inside has been deserted by all sense of human purpose. In this sense, Beckett's *Endgame* can be regarded as a helpful background for *Travels*: despite the mobility evoked by its title, stasis is a central question in Auster's text. For Mr. Blank, too, this seems to be the end of a game.

Apart from the setting, the two texts have other elements in common, such as the sense of impaired vision. In fact, Hamm's eyes are becoming weaker ("It seems they've gone all white", Beckett 1958, 4) and Nagg stresses "Our sight has failed" (Beckett 1958, 15). The extreme stasis of the characters is reinforced by the obsessive refrain "Is it not time for my pain-killer?" and, interestingly enough, the need to tell a story.

The room is outside real time and space, a non-referential place like Mr. Blank's room. This is the end of Hamm's life, the end of the game and of any form of life as everything seems to have died out: "But what in God's name do you imagine? That the earth will awake in the spring? That there's manna in heaven still for imbeciles like you?" (Beckett 1958, 53). This lost place is a degraded version of the new world depicted in Shakespeare's *The Tempest*, with Clov a sort of Caliban cursing the language he has been taught: "I use the words you taught me. If they don't mean anything anymore, teach me others. Or let me be silent" (Beckett 1958, 44).

Like Mr. Blank, Hamm is a narrator in terrible need of an audience. He bribes Nagg into listening to him for the puny price of a biscuit: "I hope that day will come when you'll really need to have me listen to you, and need to hear my voice, any voice" (Beckett 1958, 56). Hamm is concerned that the story he is telling might finish soon, "unless I bring in other characters" (Beckett 1958, 54) and also compels Clov to take part in this absurd game.

Hamm is aware that his words are lost in the nothingness that surrounds him and his fellows. Like Auster's hero, he is old and feeble, his weakness prevents him from moving or looking out of the window and his narrative is in fact an aside: "I'm warming up for my last soliloquy" (Beckett 1958, 78). While Beckett denies any hope that the soliloquy might become a dialogue, a narrative open to interaction, Auster leaves the matter open to speculation. Nevertheless, in both authors the logocentric subjectivity is dead, either in the form of the Maker or of the Author. In any case, both Beckett and Auster frequently choose ailing heroes, as Ihab Hassan has pointed out in reference to Beckett: "metaphysical clowns and jongleurs of solipsism; but they are also morbid quietists, cripples, impotents. They suffer from radical acedia" (Hassan 1967, 130).

The essentiality of the physical objects surrounding Mr. Blank corresponds to the very basic quality of the language used in the text, which is purposely simple and at times simplistic, an economy of expressive means that merely records what is going on. The use of the present simple reinforces the sense of constraint. It perfectly gives the sense of Mr. Blank being closely watched. This is the language that becomes naturally associated with the mechanical, cold and sterile eye of the hidden camera. It is a terribly skeletal language, with Beckett behind it as the master of spare style, so straightforward that it becomes allusive (Hassan 1967, 177).[2]

In *Travels*, the language the narrator uses to define his patient/prisoner is not merely concise; it has become so elusive that it might recede out of Mr. Blank's reach. The figure of the author as someone able to articulate an imaginative language shifts back once again: not only is Mr. Blank at a loss as to his past and present, thus displaying a limited ability to read reality; he also risks losing his ability to speak intelligibly. In fact, he experiences a reversal of man's prelapsarian condition: while Adam names the animals in the Garden of Eden, Mr. Blank is surrounded by objects already bearing their names written in black letters on white tape, with an unknown saboteur probably playing tricks on him and switching the labels. Someone is challenging his ability to use language in a conventional way and is reversing the situation in which Adam has not just named things but disclosed their real essence:

> But Mr. Blank is a man of order, and he is offended by the childish mischief-making of his captors ... It will not do, then, to call a chair a desk or a desk a lamp. To indulge in such infantile whimsy is to throw the world into chaos, to make life intolerable for all but the mad. Mr. Blank has not reached the point where he cannot identify objects that do not have their names affixed to them, but there is no question that he is in decline, and he understands that a day might come, perhaps soon, perhaps even tomorrow, when his brains will erode further and it will become necessary for him to

have the name of the thing on the thing in order for him to recognize it.
(Auster 2007, 104)

In response to a similar need to freeze linguistic reality, in *Six Characters* the Director tells the Prompter to follow the scenes and "try to pin down the speeches" (Pirandello 1998, 35), thus converting the function of prompting into the mechanical one of stenography, merely registering the characters' words.

In discussing *City of Glass* and Stillman's inspired and at the same time mad theorization on language, Aliki Varvogli argues that Stillman's theory reflects Emerson's argument in *Nature* (1836). Since nature is a projection of the human mind, language proceeds directly from the core of things: in giving things their names Adam "had gone straight to the quick of the word" (Varvogli 2001, 33).

If man is the one who originally names things and therefore rules over them, the reversal in Mr. Blank's case could not be more tragic. Yet, it dramatizes the necessarily imperfect nature of human language after the Fall: "the paradisiac language of man must have been one of perfect knowledge; whereas later all knowledge is again infinitely differentiated in the multiplicity of language, was indeed forced to differentiate itself on a lower level as creation in name" (Benjamin 1986, 326-327).

The episode of the switched labels and Mr. Blank's consequent perplexity is an example of the detachment and adequate distrust one should maintain in the face of things: despite his vulnerability, he knows those words are not to be trusted and the reader-observer knows that this is also true of Mr. Blank's words. In fact, if someone can switch the label so easily, it also means that language itself can be an ephemeral experience, so that when it is used to provide rigid definition and classifications, it becomes suspect. In the immanence of crisis, linguistic reality appears displaced, deprived of any ambition to totality (Rella 2001, 193), which is precisely what allows a new perspective to open up, a perspective in which art interrogates and deciphers rather than announces (Rella 2001, 194).

It is however undeniable that Mr. Blank makes a desperate effort to limit the damages of such a shifting use of language. After all, he does put the labels back to their original places, which proves that he tries to maintain an order of significance, a pseudo-system of meaning. Even after the paradisiac language has become something infinitely less accurate and pure, it still remains the unavoidable means whereby the world becomes intelligible. Language is inescapable, and we only go through things by going through it, as Benjamin explains:

> The language of this lamp, for example, does not communicate the lamp (for the mental being of the lamp, insofar as it is *communicable*, is by no means, the lamp itself), but the language-lamp, the lamp in communication, the lamp in expression. For in language the situation is this: *the linguistic being of all things is their language.* (Benjamin 1986, 316)

The subject *tout court* cannot be denied, despite all its shortcomings and fallacies; the linguistic subject cannot be dismissed. Similarly, the author may have become an enfeebled and ailing individual, but his commitment to language and sense is an enduring quality:

> From long experience, he has come to appreciate the importance of precision and clarity in all things, and during the years when he was sending out his charges on their various missions around the world, he always took great pains to write up his reports on their activities in a language that would not betray the truth of what they saw and thought and felt at each step along the way... (Auster 2007, 104)

Metafiction continues to fascinate Auster, who has invented another writer sending characters on "dangerous missions" in *Man in the Dark* (2008), where another old man, another physically suffering author contrives fictional plots to keep his mind at peace and thus avoid going through another sleepless night thinking of painful things in his real life. Metafictional Owen Brick's mission is to find and kill a certain Mr. Blake, Black or Bloch who deserves to die because he is the one who has invented the Civil War that plagues these parallel-dimension United States: "...he owns the war. He invented it, and everything that happens or is about to happen is in his head. Eliminate that head, and the war stops. It's that simple" (Auster 2008, 10).

The names are also suggestive. The name chosen for the evil creator of the war might be Blake—not dramatically different from Blank—and if it were Black it would still recall Mr. Blank's name as its opposite colour. Blank is not white, true enough, but a white page and a blank page can be the same. And isn't Bloch an innuendo to a possible writer's block? Brick, as a name for the story-within-the-story hero, is no less evocative, suggesting firmness, a feet-on-the-ground quality that seems to connote the character as a solid counterpart of Mr. Blank's evanescent will and inclination to fall prey to "the figments in his head".

In the disquieting universe of *Travels*, Mr. Blank's status is lowered in comparison to his characters'; he becomes an author who has no more control over his own creatures and who, conversely, moves in the realm of the "ironic mode" in which the hero is "inferior in power or intelligence to ourselves, so that we have the sense of looking down on a scene of bondage, frustration, or absurdity" (Frye 1990, 34).

Further Pirandellian legacies: *Travels* and irony

Irony is a rhetorical device relying on the perception of contraries, which also characterizes Pirandello's theorization of his own art as humoristic. Humour is for him "the sentiment of the opposite", not the mere perception of the opposite that characterizes the comic and implies a sense of superiority in the observer (Pirandello 1992 [1908], 126, 139). This feeling of the opposite triggers reflection and participation, the observer's awareness of the discrepancy between the ideal and the real. We do not laugh at Mr. Blank's shortcomings, we identify with his quandary and feel that we, too, are being watched and held responsible for other people's lives, which makes the affinities between Pirandello's humour and Auster's irony evident.[3] In fact, Pirandello grapples with the same ghosts haunting the house of many postmodernists: the perception of contradictions in multi-faceted reality and the collapse of a central subjectivity ordering events and values.

The destiny of Pirandello's characters, eternally wandering in search of an author and eager to represent their unwritten script resembles Mr. Blank's: "For Mr. Blank is one of us now, and struggle though he might to understand his predicament, he will always be lost" (Auster 2007, 129). His life suspended in an eternal, unchanging present, Mr. Blank thus becomes one of his characters, immutable and living only through the words of the story he finds himself enmeshed in. Mr. Blank eventually assumes the key feature of a fictional character, immutability, which tallies with the Father's meaningful remark in *Six Characters*:

> the author who created us, made us live, did not wish, or simply and materially was not able, to place us in the world of art. And that was a real crime, sir, because whoever has the luck to be born a living character can also laugh at death. He will never die! (Pirandello 1998 [1921], 13)

And he further explains: "A character, sir, can always ask a man who he is. Because a character really has his own life, marked with his own characteristics, by virtue of which he is always someone. Whereas a man … *a man* can be no one" (Pirandello 1998 [1921], 60).

So the narrative mode of *Travels* fully qualifies Mr. Blank as an ironic hero according to Frye's formulation in terms of bondage, frustration and absurdity. He is in some kind of bondage, although an apparently soft one;

his efforts to place past and present events as well as to perform any physical act of some relevance are continually frustrated by his memory loss and lack of strength; finally, his situation is typical of absurdist writing, where the sense of purpose of human efforts clashes against an inexorable sense of nothingness.

Like Pirandello's absent author, in *Travels* the central subjectivity has abandoned the stage that is the world; the ironic approach to Mr. Blank as a subject with limited knowledge and strength enables the characters to take over. The Six Characters had a "father", but they have lost him, a circumstance often occurring in Auster's novels and they offer a text—still to be written—an existence, a life to the actors who finally have to acknowledge them, so their story can be represented on the stage. They are humorous, according to Pirandello's definition, because they act in the chasm opening between reality and appearance, thus highlighting the contradiction between the said and the unsaid, knowledge and ignorance. They are, according to the author's abstruse formulation, naked masks. As Nino Borsellino writes in his introduction to the Italian edition of *Six Characters*, "Naked mask" is an adynaton (Borsellino 2001, xxvi), a hyperbole in the form of a paradox that expresses an enigma, "a stringing together of impossibilities" (Lanham 1991, 3), namely the expression of the character's unsolved mysteries and conflicts.

A mask reveals more than supposed "reality", which in fact covers up real experience. The mask, namely Art, has more truth in it because it can unveil real experience, not reality, which remains a fuzzy and non-identified object, but the experience we have of it. Similarly, theatre-within-the-theatre aims to denounce illusion and deception; it denounces that a murder has been committed and, as it is clear from *Hamlet* on, that the king is in fact a usurper.

This ability to disclose by veiling also belongs to irony in the terms defined by Jankélévitch, who qualifies it as an effort to be misunderstood in order to convince the other of what is supposed to be the truth and writes about the invisible visibility, the opaque transparency of the ironic mask (Jankélévitch 1997, 70). Similarly, when Pirandello defines humour as the "sentiment of the opposite", he aims to suggest the hidden workings of human nature behind a mask that may be laughable at first, but reveals its own deep tragedy a moment later, a tool that also deconstructs the observer's identity (Pirandello 1992 [1908], 148). Jankélévitch also argues that irony entails cooperation between the ironist and the target of the ironic discourse: the ironist operates on the same level as his counterpart, the former offers a tribute to the latter's ability to understand (Jankélévitch 1997, 72-73).

While Mr. Blank is in a disadvantaged position when compared with his creatures—and after all he is only experiencing what the characters themselves have experienced on their "missions"—the implied reader will possibly share the same insecurity, thus confirming an idea of irony as ethical cooperation shedding light on contradictions. Auster's ironic characterization of Mr. Blank as a subject with limited knowledge and ability to interpret reality combines closeness and distance, participation and detachedness. As Pirandello's naked mask, through distance and detachedness on the part of a potential observer/reader, this form of irony illuminates the contradictions and inadequacies of a character. At the same time, by closeness and emotional participation on the part of the same observer/reader, irony acknowledges the stubborn humanity of a character who will try and try again—to understand, to complete an unfinished story—even though he is doomed to fail.

This form of irony that displays while covering up and perorates through distrust is a form of adynaton as Pirandello's naked mask is. They both offer a subtle critique of order, authority and agency in an ethical perspective; in fact, irony has a fundamental role in the process of our inward refinement, and above all in our relation with the world (Jankélévitch 1997, 163). Ricoeur's ethical perspective combines with Jankélévitch's serious laughter, Pirandello's feeling of incongruities and Auster's pathetic anti-hero.

As a form of cooperation between the self and the Other, irony is a further means through which Auster develops his discourse on the ethical dimension. By enforcing acceptance and identification rather than a sense of superiority or estrangement, irony illuminates the possibilities of shared humanity and the urgency of ethical responsibility towards the Other and is both a rhetorical process and an epistemological approach.

Unresolved ambiguities: the writer in recoil

Mr. Blank starts fulfilling his ethical obligation through the ordering force of narration, taking part in what Ricoeur, as already discussed, calls "competition of narrative programs" (Ricoeur 1992 [1990], 162). He finally participates in a complex interplay between the self and the Other, between a pre-existing narrative and his own version of it. By working on Trause's manuscript, he becomes the co-author of Trause's story and provides a further meaning for the hero's life. Yet, the nature of this obligation cannot, and should not, evade ambiguity and contradiction.

The first contradiction lies in the fact that completing the manuscript represents at the same time an act of creativity and Mr. Blank's acceptance of the therapy suggested by his doctor which can easily be read as a form of control. On the one hand, Mr. Blank is irresistibly intrigued by the manuscript and tries to dissolve his frustration at its incompleteness by a voluntary act. On the other, if the room is a cell and the institution a form of dominion, he voluntarily submits to his own imprisonment since working on the manuscript is part of the therapy the institution is administering.[4]

The ambiguity of Mr. Blank's imprisonment/hospitalization is indirectly suggested by a passage in the manuscript in which the hero is imprisoned and then encouraged to write a report "to defend himself in writing" (Auster 2007, 30). Auster doubles the figure of the detained writer and through the *mise-en-abyme* is able to comment obliquely on Mr. Blank's difficulty. In fact, the manuscript's narrator, who is held captive by Colonel De Vega, is suspicious of his enemy's reasons to allow him to write, and assumes this is a means to serve the colonel's, and the authorities', hidden aims: "By allowing me to put the story in writing, he is gathering evidence, irrefutable evidence that will justify any action he decides to take against me … . It could be that he has already written to them about me, in fact, and that I am holding this pen in my hand now because they instructed him to put it there" (Auster 2007, 32).

The old writer's first response to the manuscript is one of intense discontent; he is "furious that he has been compelled to read a story that has no ending, an unfinished work that has barely even begun, a mere bloody fragment" (Auster 2007, 75). Samuel Farr, the doctor, urges him to finish the story—"You have the beginning. Now I want you to give me the middle and the end" (Auster 2007, 80)—as an exercise of "imaginative reasoning", which is however threatened by the procession of "figment beings who marched through his head at earlier points in the narrative" (Auster 2007, 80). The narrator deliberately draws the reader's attention to Mr. Blank's status as a culpable character in this narrative: "The damned specters …They're back again … My victims. All the people I've made suffer over the years. They're coming after me to take their revenge" (Auster 2007, 81). Notwithstanding his record as someone who has inflicted suffering and loss on his creatures, Mr. Blank is encouraged by Samuel Farr to engage once again in the task of telling a story. But this attempt, however, is frustrated by the end of the consultation, which provokes Mr. Blank's irritation:

> But I haven't finished! the old man shouts. I haven't come to the end!
> I know, Farr replies, but we're working on a tight schedule around here, and it can't be helped. We'll go on with the story tomorrow.

> Tomorrow? Mr. Blank roars, both incredulous and confused. What are
> you talking about? Tomorrow I won't remember a word I said today. You
> know that. Even I know that, and I don't know a blasted thing. (Auster
> 2007, 89)

So Mr. Blank's effort to finish the story is negated; once again the author's intelligence and will prove unsuccessful.

There seems to be a further contradiction between the ethical interaction of the self and the Other suggested by Ricoeur and the dismal condition of the writer in confinement. The creative and at times conflictive opportunities offered by this perspective of crisis account for the apparent contrast between commitment and retirement, the ethics and responsibility on the one hand and the writer's confinement or self-seclusion on the other. But this is fortunately a season of conflict and tension, not of sterile pacification. Mr. Blank is definitely guilty of irresoluteness and his whole situation has been read as a terribly self-indulgent comment on the part of Auster on the difficulties of writing.[5] There is a certain amount of self-indulgence indeed, yet Auster is also performing a form of self-irony and, therefore, self-criticism. Pirandello himself, a very active spectator at the rehearsals of his plays,[6] cannot resist the temptation of a pleased and ironic autobiographical remark when he has the Director burst out: "Rehearsing with authors present has always been hell, in my experience" (Pirandello 1998 [1921], 52).

Auster is trying to fulfil his own obligation as an artist through the self-reflexive use of the literary word; self-referentiality is a tool to delve into the eternal riddles man has to tackle, a context in which the ethical perspective, the individual's responsibility to his fellow-beings is crucial (Bartocci 2000, 380). Mr. Blank is not brave enough to check whether the door is locked or not and thus is guilty of shrinking away from reality. This is a self-mocking representation of the writer in recoil who is exclusively concentrated on himself and his art. So the initial effort to instil ethics—namely the relationship with the Other—into the aesthetic sphere and the narrative praxis remains suspended. Opening the door would mean going into the world outside, but Mr. Blank, for the moment, prefers not to.

The secluded and enfeebled writer turns in on himself but this forced stasis provides him with the opportunity to analyze the nature of his task as an artist, to try to collect the fragments of his experience into new forms. A new subject comes to light in this suspended time: Mr. Blank emerges as a weaker author who has lost control over his art and who has consequently gained stronger awareness of the ephemeral nature of authorship. In fact, not only do the characters live beyond their creator's original intentions, but the writer finds himself in a character's shoes: thrown into an incomprehensible world by a hidden and inscrutable author.

However, this weakness does not imply absence; it only suggests a different relationship with what the subject finds outside itself, where the space of relatedness opens up. This is a problematic self that experiences indeterminacy and uncertainty as an opportunity for facing and acknowledging the Other, thus an effaced self paradoxically becomes a space for relatedness and dialogism. As Franco Rella explains, "il sapere delle caducità, il sapere della discontinuità storica è dunque il sapere della rivoluzione e della transizione verso altri ordini" ("the knowledge of impermanence, the knowledge of historical discontinuity is the knowledge of revolution, of transition into a different order of things") (Rella 2001, 177).

In the fractured, desultory narrative of post-modernity, Auster is interested in developing a new kind of ethics, relying on individual responsibility and mutual acknowledgement, which is all the more necessary considering the lack of a central subjectivity, a primary and stable source providing a law for lost and paranoid individuals. Mr. Blank is deprived of his former status as an author, his characters compel him to face his sense of guilt and take the same path already trodden by other typical Austerian heroes-writers who realize they are bound to interact with others and sometimes to carry others' burdens. The crisis of a subjectivity ruling in splendid isolation allows the transition to an ethical perspective where the self certainly becomes less definite but significantly more open to the Other.

In the context outlined through Ricoeur's meditation on narrative practices shaped by the dialogue occurring between the self and the Other, the notion of crisis defines a space where authorship blends aesthetic intention and ethical momentum since, as the author's force decreases in terms of controlling agency, his ability to accept the cooperative nature of authorship and the dialogical character of identity increases.

As a writing-controlling subject, Mr. Blank might find himself stalled; yet, despite all his shortcomings and failures, he is still aware of the power of words and cannot evade his commitment to language. As an old and decayed Adam he cannot stop naming things, even though an invisible enemy is mocking him by switching the labels in his room, thus endangering his already fragile mental sanity. Rella argues that, after the corruption of pure Edenic language, the only possibility to restore the primary pureness of word belongs to the poet:

Solo la parola poetica, la parola di chi sa seguire le tracce degli dei fuggiti fin dentro l'abisso del tempo della miseria, del tempo senza fondamenti, è in grado di alludere alla condizione paradisiaca in cui l'anima, muovendo dall'Uno, può trovare nella differenza che lo costituisce quiete e riposo. (Only the poetic word, the word of someone who can follow the tracks of the gods who have fled as far as the abyss of time of misery, of time with no foundations, is able to suggest the paradisiac condition in which the soul, originating from the One, can find its peace and rest in the difference that substantiates it.) (Rella 2001, 188-189)

Ascribing an old and suffering fiction writer's work to a widely interpreted poetic category is perhaps not too hazardous. This ability to unveil the essence of things is a privilege, and perhaps a burden, that fully reveals the relevance of Mr. Blank's decision to open the door and leave the room or, conversely, refuse the world completely. At the same time, since *Travels* is a post-modern, absurdist, meta-fictional meditation on the complexities of agency on the one hand and authorship on the other, it seems that the only consistent ending is exactly the one Auster chooses. Tomorrow Mr. Blank's day will presumably once again consist of a series of frustrated attempts: to open the door, to understand who he is and what he must do, perhaps to complete an unfinished story.

Camus chooses the myth of Sisyphus as the emblem of the absurd man who is doomed to eternally try and to unceasingly fail, and American contemporary absurdist fiction stems from the same parable of perennial frustration (Galloway 1966, 5-20). Thus Mr. Blank is the perfect embodiment of a fragile individual faced with guilt, incoherence, and conflicts, the quintessence of post-modern contradictoriness. And yet contradictions and conflicts are likely to generate possibilities, a promise of future—perhaps never-to-be-attained—fulfilment. Auster effectively condenses the ineluctability of this destiny in *The Art of Hunger*, when he quotes something Beckett wrote in the forties: "To be an artist is to fail, and no other dares fail…" (Auster 1992, 169).

References

Auster, Paul. 1992. *The art of hunger*, Los Angeles: Sun & Moon Press.
—. 2002. *The book of illusions.* London: Faber and Faber.
—. 2004. *Oracle night.* London: Faber and Faber.
—. 2005. *The Brooklyn follies.* London: Faber and Faber.
—. 2007 [2006]. *Travels in the scriptorium.* London: Faber and Faber.
—. 2008. *Man in the dark.* London: Faber and Faber.

Barone, Dennis. 1995. Introduction: Paul Auster and the postmodern American novel. In *Beyond the red book. Essays on Paul Auster*, ed. Dennis Barone, 1-26. Philadelphia: University of Pennsylvania.

Bartocci, Clara. 2000. Ironia come strategia narrativa in *The New York trilogy* di Paul Auster. In *La forma breve nella cultura del Novecento. Scritture ironiche*, ed. Monique Streiff Moratti, Renzo Pavese, and Olga Simcic. 365-386. Napoli: Edizioni Scientifiche Italiane.

Beckett, Samuel. 1958. *Endgame and An act without words*. New York: Grove Press.

—. 1965 [1956]. *Waiting for Godot*. London: Faber and Faber.

Benjamin, Walter. 1986 [1978]. *Reflections: Essays, aphorisms, autobiographical writings*. Ed. with an Introduction by Peter Demetz. New York: Schocken Books.

Borsellino, Nino. 2001 [1993]. Introduction to *Sei personaggi in cerca d'autore*, by Luigi Pirandello, vii-xxxiii. Milano: Garzanti.

Connor, Steven. 1996. *The English novel in history, 1950-1995*. London and New York: Routledge.

Deleuze, Gilles, and Giorgio Agamben. 2006. *Bartleby. La formula della creazione*. Trans. Stefano Verdicchio. Macerata: Quodlibet. Originally published as *Bartleby, ou la formule* (Paris: Flammarion, 1989).

Foucault, Michel. 1995. *Discipline and punish. The birth of the prison*. Trans. Alan Sheridan. New York: Vintage. Originally published as *Surveiller et punir. Naissance de la prison* (Paris: Editions Gallimard, 1975).

Friedell, Deborah. 2006. Mr. writer man. Review of *Travels in the scriptorium,* by Paul Auster. *The Times Literary Supplement* (October 13), http://entertainment.timesonline.co.uk/tol/arts_and_entertainment/the_tls/tls_selections/fiction/article2305821.ece (May 12, 2010).

Frye, Northrop. 1990 [1957]. *Anatomy of criticism*. London: Penguin.

Galloway, David. 1966. *The absurd hero in American fiction*. Austin and London: University of Texas Press.

Harrison, Sophie. 2007. The content of his characters. Review of *Travels in the scriptorium* by Paul Auster. *The New York Times* (February 18), http://www.nytimes.com/2007/02/18/books/review/Harrison-Sophie.html (May 10, 2010).

Hassan, Ihab. 1961. *Radical innocence. Studies in the contemporary novel*. Princeton: Princeton University Press.

—. 1967. *The literature of silence: Henry Miller and Samuel Beckett*. New York: Alfred A. Knopf.

Jankélévitch, Vladimir. 1997. *L'ironia*. Trans. Fernanda Canepa. Genova: Il Melangolo. Originally published as *L'ironie* (Paris: Flammarion, 1964).

Lanham, Richard A.. 1991. *A handlist of rhetorical terms*. Berkeley and Los Angeles, California: University of California Press.

Pirandello, Luigi. 1992 [1908]. *L'umorismo*. Milano: Mondadori.

—. 1998 [1921]. *Six characters in search of an author*. Trans. Eric Bentley. New York: Signet.

Rella, Franco. 2001 [1981]. *Il silenzio e le parole. Il pensiero nel tempo della crisi*. Milano: Feltrinelli.

Ricoeur, Paul. 1992. *Oneself as another*. Trans. Kathleen Blamey. The University of Chicago Press, Chicago. Originally published as *Soi-même comme un autre* (Editions du Seuil, 1990).

Romei, Giovanna. 2001 [1993]. Notes to *Sei personaggi in cerca d'autore*, by Luigi Pirandello. Milano: Garzanti.

Varvogli, Aliki. 2001. *The world that is the book. Paul Auster's fiction*. Liverpool: Liverpool University Press.

Woods, Tim. *The music of chance*: Aleatorical (dis)harmonies within "The city of the world". In *Beyond the red book. Essays on Paul Auster*, ed. Dennis Barone, 143-161. Philadelphia: University of Pennsylvania.

Notes

[1] Clara Bartocci interprets the kaleidoscopic fragmentation of the authorial figure less as a parody of realism than as a parody of deconstructionism (Bartocci 2000, 374-375).

[2] Varvogli identifies this issue as a feature of Kafka's writing, where "the clarity imparted by this simple narration underscores the strange and often terrifying nature of the events" (Varvogli 2001, 75).

[3] In *L'umorismo* (1908) Pirandello actually distinguishes between humorists and ironists, but relies on a rather narrow idea of irony as a mere verbal expression of contradiction (Pirandello 1992 [1908], 147).

[4] Mr. Blank is forced into a panoptic mechanism by means of the camera recording his every movement and word. The meta-theatrical metaphor itself is a manifestation of the Panopticon as it highlights the centrality of the other's gaze relentlessly following the hero. As Foucault explains, the panopticon imagined by Bentham is comprised of cells that are "like so many cages, so many small theatres, in which every actor is alone, perfectly individualized and constantly visible … The panoptic mechanism arranges spatial unities that make it possible to see constantly and to recognize immediately … Visibility is a trap" (Foucault 1995, 200). Yet there is a difference: in the system described by Foucault, the awareness of being watched induces the prisoner to interiorize the precepts of the

guardian-institution, while Mr. Blank does not know he is being observed, but this does not make any difference in the end: "He has no idea that a camera is planted in the ceiling directly above him … Even if he knew he was being watched, it wouldn't make any difference. His mind is elsewhere, stranded among the figments in his head…" (Auster 2007, 1). A controlling power establishes a firm hegemony on the writer who has lost his status as a subject and finally becomes the object of close scrutiny. The therapy Mr. Blank is submitted to resembles the English model of correction through isolation described in Foucault's *Discipline and Punish*: "isolation provides a 'terrible shock' which, while protecting the prisoner from bad influences, enables him to go into himself and rediscover in the depths of his conscience the voice of good; solitary work would then become not only apprenticeship, but also an exercise of spiritual conversion; it would rearrange not only the complex interests proper to homo œconomicus, but also the imperatives of the moral subject" (Foucault 1995, 122-123).

[5] See some caustic comments by reviewers such as Sophie Harrison, "The Content of his Characters", review of *Travels in the Scriptorium* by Paul Auster, *The New York Times* (February 18, 2007), http://www.nytimes.com/2007/02/18/books/review/Harrison-Sophie.html. See also Deborah Friedell, "Mr. Writer Man", review of *Travels in the Scriptorium* by Paul Auster, *The Times Literary Supplement* (October 11, 2006), http://tls.timesonline.co.uk/article/0,,25339-2399052,00.html.

[6] See Giovanna Romei's notes to the play, in particular note 23 in Luigi Pirandello, *Sei personaggi in cerca d'autore* (Milano: Garzanti, 2001), 88.

CHAPTER SEVEN

"THE CONNECTION EXISTS": HERMENEUTICS AND AUTHORITY IN PAUL AUSTER'S FICTIONAL WORLDS

MICHELLE BANKS

In his esoteric early memoir, *The Invention of Solitude*, Paul Auster addressed what was to become one of the enduring preoccupations of his literary career. After the sudden death of his father he was compelled to notice like never before the relationships between things, and to allow the idiosyncrasy, operation, and burden of that "between" to become an object of primal focus. "The world", he writes,

> is not just the sum of things that are in it. It is the infinitely complex method of connections among them. As in the meanings of words, things take on meaning only in relationship to each other…it is possible for events in one's life to rhyme as well…The rhyme they create when looked at together alters the reality of each. Just as two physical objects, when brought into proximity of each other, give off electromagnetic forces that not only effect [sic] the molecular structure of each but the space between them as well, altering, as it were, the very environment, so it is that two (or more) rhyming events set up a connection in the world, adding one more synapse to be routed through the vast plenum of experience. (Auster 1988b [1982], 161)

This understanding of the world does not only include a measure of connection; it is itself connection. The world is more than a sum, he says; the world's very meaning is located in the relationships, proximities, and correspondences among things, events, and persons. But what Auster also expresses in that same text is the contradictory idea that while connections may seem like seductively whispered personal messages, attributing significance beyond simple existence is to indulge in imagination:

Like everyone else, he craves a meaning. Like everyone else, his life is so
fragmented that each time he sees a connection between two fragments he
is tempted to look for a meaning in that connection. The connection exists.
But to give it a meaning, to look beyond the bare fact of its existence,
would be to build an imaginary world inside the real world, and he knows
it would not stand. (Auster 1988b, 147)

Auster's works have consistently pursued these very multiple dynamics
of connection. His experiments in fictional representation have established
an intensely rhyming imaginary world, yet he likewise hesitates to confirm
a secure standing for that world. His oeuvre may be encountered by the
careful reader as producing a kind of overarching "supertext", a parallel
world that fulfills the attraction of his first fictional protagonist, Quinn
("What interested him about the stories he wrote was not their relation to
the world, but their relation to other stories" (Auster 1990a [1985], 8)), but
that overarching supertext delivers interrelations of doubt and anxiety
rather than intelligible, traceable paths to certainty. While Auster's texts
present many intertextual references (mostly to nineteenth century American
and French literature), their most intense intertextual relationships (by
"intense" I mean enduring, concentrated, and also puzzling) are with other
texts published under his own name. Martin Kreiswirth calls such a lasting
dynamic "*auto-intertextuality*" (Kreiswirth 1996, 162).

Crucially, Auster's auto-intertextual production demonstrates a
mutuality of senses of "world" held by different schools of thought, most
prominently the Geneva school of literary theory, and modal logic. What
interests me most about the fictional worlds, or world, of Auster's novels
are the phenomenological and material issues inevitably brought about by
this particular type of multi-textual connectivity. How are we to make
sense of the worlds, or world, produced in and by Auster's texts, and what
is at stake in recognizing either ontological sameness or ontological
difference between, say, *The Locked Room* and *The Book of Illusions*? In
other words, is it accurate to speak of "world" in the singular or in the
plural when discussing Auster's fictional productions? These questions are
not successfully answered by simply cataloguing the author's auto-
intertextual references (a seemingly ongoing list includes *The New York
Trilogy*, *In the Country of Last Things*, *Moon Palace*, *Mr. Vertigo*, *The
Book of Illusions*, *Travels in the Scriptorium*, *The Red Notebook*, *The Art
of Hunger*, *Smoke*, and *The Inner Life of Martin Frost*); instead, this
discussion will register a primarily ontological focus to consider the
multiple impacts of the fluctuating status of the fictional world(s)
presented across a handful of Auster's novels.

Taken together, his fictions present a persistent foregrounding of the processes of interpretative authority, hermeneutic pressures toward meaning, and the practices and conventions of fiction itself. My suspicion is that each of these concerns is in fact worked out through the author's unique infrastructure of ontological connectivity. In the above passage from *The Invention of Solitude* we see that Auster produces an undecided (undecidable?) flux of connective signification. Events, he says, can be recognized to rhyme and such rhyming alters the events and alters the fields surrounding the events; yet, he points out, the process of establishing significance from whatever rhyme is generated is not so straightforward or so certain. What is at stake here, then, is the balance of hermeneutics in general—*existence* balanced against further *meaning*.

***

"To be existent without existing" is how Thomas Pavel describes the condition of the fictional world (Pavel 1986, 31). Modal realists such as Pavel, Ruth Ronen, and Lubomir Dolezel hold that fictionality can be explained in terms of, in Ronen's words, "a definite and universal logico-semantic model" (Ronen 1994, 86). A useful way to think about a world encountered in a work of fiction is via the notion of "possible worlds" in philosophy. Philosophers use concepts of possible worlds to describe the world as a complex modal structure, one consisting of several sub-systems of worlds, each of varying degrees of possibility or accessibility relative to the actual world. Literary theorists have adapted this concept to describe the status and structure of the imagined worlds of fiction. A work of fiction actualizes a world which is analogous with, derivative of, or contradictory to the world in which we live.

The logico-semantic model of the fictional world depends upon two broad-spectrum propositions. First, this model states that worlds in fiction are subject to global semantic constraints, that is, the same logical modality will govern all sentences that form the work. Second, the fictional world will be logically and ontologically parallel to the actual world.

To consider the first proposition—a coherent fictional world will be made through a consistent logical modality, one that governs all sentences in the work—we cannot underestimate the role played by characters, or fictional existents, in performing the work of semantic constraint. Dolezel's account of the logical status of characters according to the provisions of "possible worlds" modalities explains that the constituents of fictional worlds are granted a definite ontological status, the status of "nonactualized possibilities". For example, "while Hamlet is not a man to be found in the actual world, he is an individualized possible person inhabiting an alternative world, the fictional world of Shakespeare's play. The name 'Hamlet' is neither empty nor self-referential; it refers to an individual of a fictional world" (Dolezel 1998 [1997], 16). The character and the world are indelibly linked and each fosters the other's consistency and coherency. Hamlet's status is tied to his position within his domain: he is "of" his domain and his domain garners its own consistency from the coherent presence of characters.[1] Because the conventional understanding of the operation of, say, a sequel or the novels in a trilogy is that any subsequent productions will repeat and extend the representational field of the prior novel, we should assume that the same logical modality will govern the extended field projected in the subsequent novel and that this consistent modality will by a large measure be enacted through consistency of fictional existents. It would appear, then, that a large-scale fictional cosmos such as Auster's would be subject to the same logical modality governing all sentences in all works in which certain characters recur.

Paul Auster's use of characters, however, troubles the very grounding of such global semantic assurances. Even in his most contractually-secure connected construct, *The New York Trilogy*, the legitimacy of ontological reference is challenged. Just a few pages into the third volume, *The Locked Room*, we learn that apparently Quinn, the lost soul protagonist of the first volume, *City of Glass*, had been extra-diegetically hired by Sophie (Fanshawe's wife) to track down Fanshawe after his disappearance. This is disorienting information. We think to ourselves: *But Quinn wasn't a real detective; he just got a phone call meant for a detective agency, and on a self-destructive whim impersonated a detective. How could he have taken another case?* Also, near the end of *The Locked Room* the narrator is down and out in Paris. One night in a bar he sees a "tall, athletically built" man who is "obviously American", has "sandy hair and an open, somewhat boyish manner" (Auster 1990b [1985], 347). He decides this man is Fanshawe, his childhood best friend for whom he has been searching. Deciding this, the narrator experiences immeasurable happiness: "I exulted in the sheer falsity of my assertion", he says, "I was the sublime alchemist who could change the world at will. This man was Fanshawe because I said he was Fanshawe, and that was all there was to it" (Auster 1987c, 348). The narrator, aware that he is not in fact looking at his long-lost childhood friend and mythical twin, revels in the arbitrariness involved in assigning one man another man's name. This alone is enough to confuse ontological certainties within the fiction—the story's narrator enjoys "changing the world at will"—but then the world gets even more ambiguous when he addresses the sandy-haired man as "Fanshawe" and the stranger responds, "'My name isn't Fanshawe. It's Stillman. Peter Stillman'" (Auster 1987c, 349). *Wait a second*, we think, *he can't be "Peter Stillman" either.* Or more precisely, he can't be *either* of the Peter Stillmans. In the fictional world of *City of Glass*, Stillman Sr. is an old man whose demeanor could hardly be called "boyish" and he was reported to have committed suicide at the end of the first volume, and the last time we saw Stillman Jr. he was practically immobile, such was the strain of conscious effort necessary for him to speak and perform the most basic of movements, hardly "athletically built" or likely to patronize Parisian cafes. *This* Peter Stillman cannot be either of the Peter Stillmans from *City of Glass*. So who is he and does it matter?

One reason why his status matters is that these recurrences of "Peter Stillman" (and "Quinn") in *The Locked Room* throw ontology—the world of this novel, retrospectively the world of *City of Glass*, and whatever world we are prompted to imagine might include the projections of both novels—into semantic jeopardy. With the reappearance of "Quinn" in particular, readers want the worlds to make sense *together*. Conventionally, when information reflective of a previous volume, especially information relating directly to fictional existents, is disclosed in a subsequent volume, readers expect that subsequent information to be true to certain knowledge-contexts established in the earlier, primary works, in this case the first volume of *The New York Trilogy*. We assume, in short, that the same modality will govern sentences in a trilogy just as in the operation of a work limited to a single novel. This is part of the genre's implicit promise. This practice of semantic making-sense-together is tested the moment "Quinn" resurfaces but fails to assume the standing of the first "Quinn". Absolutely, the two Quinns may indicate *something* of referential sameness, but they do not and cannot belong to the same logical modality. However Auster has extended this representational field, he has not done so in order to secure a coherent, continuous, and certain fictional world.

Literature, of course, has long been understood to operate within an assembly of social and historical forces concerning the interaction of various voices, codes, discourses, and images, an assembly that has little to do with necessary coherency, continuity, or certainty. Intertextual theory reminds us that a text ought not to be regarded as a self-enclosed or self-sufficient system, something whose borders are absolute; rather, we understand a text to be an open caucus that both invites and is constitutionally incapable of resisting a certain traversal of reference and influence. The very notion of the intertextual relationship rests upon an active, although not necessarily deliberate, movement over unavoidable borders. But the second controlling convention of the logico-semantic model of world reconstruction is that "a fictional world is not a possible world *ramifying* from the actual state of affairs, but a world logically and ontologically *parallel* to the actual world" (Ronen 1994, 91-92). As a *parallel* world, the fictional world is governed by the notion of closedness; that is, we tend to attach to fictional worlds a sense of autonomy, a sense which is both intuitive and logical. Any fiction's logical inferences are derived from "a set of possible states of affairs", and as such are "confined by that set's boundaries" (Ronen 1994, 29). Ronen concludes that "despite being heavily anchored to 'world knowledge,' and regardless of the degree to which fiction relies on real entities, the time and space of fiction form a domain in an autonomous world" (Ronen 1994, 198). This means that bordering strategies ("a set of possible states of affairs") establish and monitor logical relevance, in other words, categories of inside and outside. Despite aspects of representation and reception which compel us to recognize a certain mutability of borders and limits—the passing of text into text and back again and so on—the notion of the fictional world is in part founded upon implicitly secure boundaries. Even if those boundaries only enact separation from the actual world, the fictional world's identity is necessarily wrapped up with models of closedness, parallel autonomy, and confinement.

Encountering a fictional world means learning and remembering scales of encompassment. A world, after all, implies a swirling, wide expanse of perception, environment, understanding, and history. That wide swirling expanse, though, has important detectable limits and certain things will remain logically absent. In a fictional world, *something* is being demarcated, separated off, called distinct. An *outside* is made as well as an *inside*.[2] If we take into account the ontological rigor endorsed by Ronen, a fictional world becomes something *known* for and by its borders. Connected fictions, however, should by all rights repeat and extend their representational fields, *their worlds*, regardless of whatever borders are conventionally enacted at the conclusion of any individual novel; connected fictions impel more *inside* and attempt to alter what had been, earlier, the fiction's tacit *outside*. The borders between novels in a connected construct are decidedly not neutral sites and the security of the fictional worlds projected within will be subjected to trials of authority simply by and through the action of their connection.

Such an explicit testing of fictional ontology continues for Auster beyond his early trilogy. The texts which make up *The New York Trilogy* were originally published in 1985 and 1986. Auster followed the trilogy with *In the Country of Last Things* in 1987. In this short, dystopic walk through the refuse and horrors of a nonrepresentational, temporally ambiguous twentieth-century city, protagonist Anna Blume is searching for her lost brother William, and while scavenging she finds a passport that once belonged to someone named Quinn. In *Moon Palace* (1989), the protagonist's best friend, David Zimmer, carries on a long-distance relationship with a woman named Anna Blume who, while travelling with her brother William in a foreign country, mysteriously drops out of contact with Zimmer. The novel's protagonist loses touch with Zimmer, but does mention running into him years later, having learned that Zimmer is married, has two children, and is a literature professor at a California university. The protagonist of Auster's 2002 novel, *The Book of Illusions*, is called David Zimmer too. This David Zimmer is a literature professor in Vermont and is recently widowed—his wife Helen and his two sons died in a plane crash. In Auster's 2006 novel, *Travels in the Scriptorium*, a character named Anna Blume claims to be the widow of David Zimmer, who, she says, died because of a bad heart. Half of these statements fit with earlier representations of characters named "Anna Blume" and "David Zimmer", and the other half contradict what we "know". Zimmer's bad heart, for example, fits with the conceit of *The Book of Illusions*. In the last pages of the novel we discover that David Zimmer left the text of the book in the hands of his lawyer, only to be published after his death. He was prompted to write the book after suffering two heart attacks. However, the Zimmer of *The Book of Illusions* was married to Helen, not Anna.

How might readers reconcile these overt yet dubious repetitions of characters? Or, more to the point, how do we understand the larger domain, the *world*, if the ontological status of its own "constituents", its own "fictional particulars" is thrown into question?[3]

Brian McHale asks this question of the general postmodern literary impulse. McHale approaches Italo Calvino's *Invisible Cities*, a single text that posits the contiguity of multiple incommensurate and somewhat mutually exclusive worlds, through the double lens of, first, Michel Foucault's definition of "heterotopia", and second, the works of novelists who have created other *heterotopian*-like spaces, or "zones", in order to consider what kind of space can afford such incommensurate accommodation. Thomas Pynchon's *Gravity's Rainbow*, for example, imagines a zone wherein metaphors are literal and the happenings of various media (movies, comics) are deemed historically real; such fragmentary possible worlds coexist, in Foucault's phrasing, "without law or geometry" (Brian McHale 1987, 45). McHale's concept of the postmodern "zone" is a tempting one to make sense of Auster's ontological disruptions, as its constitution seems to offer an analogue to such unruly (or unruled) representations of space and time as David Zimmer's inconsistent status, but there is, however, a substantial impediment to declaring the space of Auster's fictional cosmos a postmodern "zone". That is, as a *sum,* Auster's texts suggest disregard for consistent space and time, law and geometry, but for the most part each individual work taken alone does not. Looked at in isolation *The Book of Illusions* is no more heterotopic than *The Old Man and the Sea.* It is only when we attempt to reckon with the fictions together, when we assume and seek out connection among and between the individual novels that the question of the qualitative or quantitative distribution of fictional space even presents itself.

Characters, of course, *can* recur in different texts by the same author (Faulkner's Yoknapatawpha novels being the most pressing American example). This convention is known as *retour de personnages.* The tendency in the *retour de personnages* convention is for characters to be identical, or functionally identical, across texts.[4] This is not the case with at least some of Auster's *retours.* Quinn cannot be considered identical across *City of Glass* and *The Locked Room*, as his relationship to private detection in the first novel is one of impersonation rather than profession as it seems to be in the third.[5] We might consider Auster's repeated references to Anna Blume as instances of the *retour de personnages* convention, and assume that "Anna Blume" indicates the same Anna Blume in each of the novels in which this name appears, thereby securing a coherent and consistent larger fictional world. But the presence of "David Zimmer" complicates our attempt to establish Anna Blume as a marker of ontological uniformity. The life or death status of a fictional character in a largely mimetic fictional world—even one stretched over multiple texts—must follow a chronologic temporality. While Auster's fictions may destabilize ontological *certainty*, they are by genre closer to realism than to science fiction, horror, the fantastic, or any other genre in which a character may exhibit a rotating pulse rate. David Zimmer, then, cannot be a functionally identical character in *Moon Palace* and *The Book of Illusions* and *Travels in the Scriptorium* because he cannot live and die and live again with impunity. And it follows that if Anna Blume is linked so closely to him (by marriage, according to *Travels in the Scriptorium*), this association throws her possible coherent status into question, making neither figure entirely stable in all or in *any* of the worlds in which their names appear.

We may move toward a more straightforward answer to the problem of, for example, David Zimmer's marital status and university affiliation by reflecting upon the emphasis Auster himself typically puts upon the names of his fictional existents. Dolezel draws our attention not only to the relationship between a fictional existent and her domain, but also between her domain and her own name. "The thread that holds together all the embodiments of an individual in all possible worlds", Dolezel writes, is "the proper name as rigid designator" (Dolezel 1998 [1997], 18). Dolezel follows the model put forward by Saul Kripke in *Naming and Necessity*, namely, "let's call something a *rigid designator* if in any possible world it designates the same object" (Dolezel 1998 [1997], 18). Just as the fictional world is held together by threads of sameness (logical modality), the fictional existent is held together by sameness, in this case sameness of name. The semantic distinctiveness of the proper name has an original moment or "baptism" and then the name is reinforced ("passed from link to link") and its rigidity is confirmed. If we take *City of Glass*, for example, we can agree that Quinn is as much Quinn on page 100 as on page 1. Multiple connected texts carry the possibility, however, of confusing or disrupting this chain of rigidity. In the possible world of *City of Glass,* the name "Quinn" functions as a rigid designator, but we see a noticeable slackening of this former rigidity when "Quinn" is used to designate some other or different fictional constituent in the possible world of *The Locked Room* or *Mr. Vertigo* or *Travels in the Scriptorium.* Because the repetition of name invites the initial assumption of ontological contiguity, we have here at the very least a *de-rigidizing* of the authority of names, as something typically held together unravels even just slightly, but we cannot yet account for either the plurality or the singularity of logical modality.

Perhaps these departures from ontological stability are minimal after all.[6] In grappling with the conventional assumptions of fictional worlds, Pavel notes:

> Contradictory worlds are not so remote as one might expect. Not only is physics still divided between the theory of relativity and quantum mechanics, not only is light simultaneously made up of particles and waves, but our everyday world hosts such impossible entities as psyches, desires, dreams, and symbols. Consistent worlds originate in a strong idealization, and our commitment to coherence is less warranted than it appears. (Pavel 1986, 50)

In short, if the actual world as phenomenologically experienced and as empirically and scientifically known evidences such deep inconsistencies and indeterminacies, then the fictional world might just as well too. Maybe this is all just to say that Auster is accurate when he describes his fictions as realist, surprising many critics who emphasize the extent to which his fictional worlds are ruled by the representation of coincidence. With undertones of American capitalist ideology working through motors of chance (opportunity, luck), the presence of the unpredictable, and the random finality of death (or life), coincidence for Auster not only serves to advance the plot, but also to advance projects of existential and phenomenological questioning, and he defends this texture of his fictional worlds as a testament to his own real-world experiences. He explains in interviews that he feels morally obligated "to write about the world as I experience it", and as such, he says, "I consider myself a realist. Chance is part of reality" (Paul Auster 1997b, 290-91). We could consign these confluences of *character names*, then, to the realm of Austerian coincidence: they are repetition of surface name only, signifying the operation of chance. Auster might say, for example, that it is entirely possible that in any world (whether the fictional world of an individual novel or the actual world) there *could be* a licensed private detective in New York City named Quinn, or that "David Zimmer" isn't so unique a name as to guarantee that one such David Zimmer could not be married to an Anna within *one* fictional domain while another Zimmer in *another* domain (even one whose creation is attributed to the author-name "Paul Auster") be married to someone called Helen.

Clearly, an attempt to settle the logical modality among or between Auster's various fictions is a less than straightforward endeavor. Whether approached through the conventions of fictional practice (*retours de personnages*), the experimentation of postmodernism (heterotopic zones), or through an examination of names and naming (rigidity versus chance), the variable status of an Auster character reveals a far greater variability, that of the ongoing production of an expansive yet self-undermining fictional cosmos.

* * *

Auster's recent novel, *Travels in the Scriptorium*, raises the most radical ontological challenges of all his books. Like John Barth's *LETTERS*, it is a severe disquieting of whatever security is conventionally enacted by fictional boundaries. What this novel also does, however, is offer paradoxically implicit promises of stability, certainty, and even final authority.

In this short, abstract parable of authorship, Mr. Blank wakes up one day in a room with no memory, apparently facing a slew of criminal charges all resulting from his abuse of certain past Auster characters. He is visited by a revolving door of characters from Auster's canon; for the most part, they claim to be "operatives" sent on "missions" by Mr. Blank, and with the exception of Anna Blume who acts as a kind of nurse-maid, they seem to be attempting to settle some kind of score with the feeble, forgetful, imprisoned old man. Quinn, for example, is the last "operative" to visit Mr. Blank. He tells him: "You sent me on more missions than anyone else", and reminds Blank of certain connections, sometimes tenuous, between himself and Fanshawe, the Peter Stillmans, Anna Blume, and Molly Fitzsimmons, Quinn's aunt and the wife of Walt Rawley (*Mr. Vertigo* concludes with Walt Rawley completing his memoirs and announcing that he will send the manuscript to his wife's nephew, Daniel Quinn) (Auster 2006, 133-134).

Quinn tells Mr. Blank that Blank "retired" him in 1993 and that since then he has been travelling the world (Auster 2006, 134). Even if Mr. Blank is confused and uncertain as to Quinn's status, any reader of *City of Glass* (Auster's most read novel) immediately recognizes Quinn to be in fact a fictional existent belonging to a specific and previous fictional world. Having Quinn report that since his last appearance in one of Auster's fictions he has been travelling the world, Auster slyly insinuates that there exists a domain, a world, for Quinn to travel and that characters from his past novels *continue* in some kind of quasi space and time beyond the borders of the novels themselves. With the promise that Quinn is still out there, somewhere, travelling around, still claiming a kind of ontological status, Auster builds up his text-actual, parallel world and extends its field even beyond the novels' combined authority.

If Quinn's exchange with Mr. Blank helps to build up a larger, more expansive text-actual world, Blank's meeting with Flood threatens that world's coherence and stability. Whereas Quinn's visit is rather tranquil and comforting, Flood's exchange with Blank is aggressively intense. Two elements of this exchange are ontologically problematic. First, Flood introduces himself as a former inspector with Scotland Yard and questions Mr. Blank about a dream: "My dream, Mr. Blank. The one you mentioned in your report on Fanshawe" (Auster 2006, 56). After being prodded to remember, Blank finally concedes: "The dream never really happened. It's nothing but words on a page—pure invention. Forget about it, Mr. Flood. It's not important", to which Flood replies: "It's important to me, Mr. Blank. My whole life depends on it. Without that dream, I'm nothing, literally nothing" (Auster 2006, 59). While, like Quinn, Flood seems to have maintained a kind of existence in the years between *The Locked Room* and *Travels in the Scriptorium*, he appears to Mr. Blank in crisis over his limited being (he was never a main figure in any of the fictions; the only mention of Flood has been a single reference to a character in

Fanshawe's novel, *Neverland*, and so this one reference constitutes his entire—till now—being). Because Mr. Blank has apparently read Fanshawe's novel, Flood appeals to him for information:

> Unfortunately, except for concluding that certain events in the book were inspired by similar events in Fanshawe's own life, you say nothing about the subject, nothing about the plot, nothing about the book at all. Only one brief aside—written in parentheses, I might add—which reads as follows. I quote from memory: (*Montag's house in chapter seven; Flood's dream in chapter thirty*). (Auster 2006, 58)

What Flood is quoting from is in fact *The Locked Room*. The unnamed narrator of the final novel in *The New York Trilogy*, the same unnamed narrator who we retrospectively learn to have "authored" the trilogy's first two texts, states exactly these words on page 324 of *The Locked Room*. So, while Flood has not read the fictional novel, *Neverland*, he has apparently read the actual-world novel, *The Locked Room*. This indicates Mr. Blank to "be", then, the unnamed narrator of *The New York Trilogy*, and further implies that all novels ("reports") published under the name Paul Auster were in some sense written by this alternate persona who qualifies therein as the implied author of all of Auster's many fictions.[7] "Revealing" such an implied author in *Travels in the Scriptorium* allows Auster to enact extensive connectivity among his texts: all texts become linked through the figure of Mr. Blank. The ontologically problematic aspect of such a gesture, though, is that by making a fictional existent out of a theoretical construct and by placing him in a domain (albeit an absurdist domain) to be shared with other, past fictional existents, the larger text-actual world is made even less secure than it is by the somewhat simple inconsistencies of status (marriage, profession).

The second ontological problem issued during Mr. Blank's conversation with Flood involves more direct claims made in *The Locked Room*. Flood claims that Fanshawe used him as a character in *Neverland*, but Flood seems not to have read the book himself. He says to Mr. Blank: "you must have read *Neverland* yourself, and in that you're one of the only people in the world to have done so" (Auster 2006, 133). The narrator of *The Locked Room*, however, had previously (according to the temporality suggested in *Travels in the Scriptorium* and according to publication chronology, 1987 versus 2006) informed readers that "By now, everyone knows what Fanshawe's work is like. It has been read and discussed, there have been articles and studies" (Auster, 1997c, 267). Why, nineteen years later, are we presented with this inconsistency of world-modality? The narrator of *The Locked Room* reports that Fanshawe's novel was published to critical fanfare and that it has inspired numerous studies; clearly in the fictional world of *The Locked Room* lots and lots of people have read *Neverland*; the world in which we can safely say no one has read *Neverland* is the actual world. *Travels in the Scriptorium* seems to resolve some ontological issues of multi-textual connectivity and seems to offer at least some grounding of authority (the revelation of an implied author and the promise that Quinn's world continues to exist), but the novel refuses to settle firmly on those hinted-at groundings (Flood, never a real character in the past, has become a character whose knowledge seems to originate not in any past fictional world, but in a version of the actual world). Some repetitions build up, other break down.

In thinking about the generic and historical identity of the sequel in particular, Thomas Carmichael points out that with the emergence of popular mass narrative, repetition increasingly became tied up with various forms of authority, thereby entangling connection in cultural modernity's larger crisis of representation. The narrative logic implicit in repetition is inevitably bound in an exchange of representational authority, as any subsequently-related text's claim to authority "ironically rests upon its intertextual traces. Every image and figure in the sequel stands in differential relation to an earlier representation with which it is affiliated and from which its authority derives" (Carmichael 1998, 175). Semiotics, of course, tells us how highly unstable intertextual traces, or even auto-intertextual traces can be, so attempts to locate and identify any semblance of final authority, while a compelling and often compulsive endeavor, may not yield satisfying or entirely intelligible results. In *Travels in the Scriptorium*, for example, an ostensibly new character such as Mr. Blank seems to derive authority from within the confines of the new novel, while a character such as Quinn stands in far greater differential relation to at least one previous fictional construct. Quinn's presence (as well as those presences of other repeated figures) contaminates Blank's status, pulling him into an ironic exchange with multiple other novels and with those novels' own claims to referential authority; the repetition of past fictional existents effectively draws Mr. Blank and the fictional world he inhabits into an ironic exchange with the past, disrupting any new assurances of ontological uniformity or authority.

Martin Kreiswirth has identified such a distinctive fluidity of authority that is logically a product of the connected natures of fictions taken to be or presented as related via their world(s). He finds, for example, that Faulkner's Yoknapatawpha is "constituted not by authoritative and authenticating narrative statements from a single novel or story, but from a collection of such utterances drawn together by the reader from a number of texts" (Kreiswirth 2002, 111). Because Yoknapatawpha is repeated in multiple texts, it is constituted by multiple texts. Aspects of its constitution derive their authority from different and multiple utterances and any semblance of a total or final Yoknapatawpha will necessarily be drawn together and collected from the various source representations. Auster's fictional cosmos, of course, is not as insular, apparent, or even as stable-seeming as Faulkner's fictional county (it does not, for example, follow the rigid designation of place name), but his repeated engagements with the properties, features, borders, and various underpinnings of fictional worlds do compel a certain constitution by collection. In other words, just as Faulkner's world of Yoknapatawpha draws authority from narrative statements spread over multiple works, any attempt to identify a consistent cosmos accommodating David Zimmer, Fanshawe, Anna Blume, Mr. Flood, Walt the Wonder Boy, and so on, will require a connective strategy and will require, too, a collecting agent. Whether understood as the response of a really-real, historically situated individual or as a text's theoretically encoded or implied construct, it is clear that whatever ontological designation we assign individual existents produced in and by Auster's texts, the condition of their connection will locate a decisive dimension in the role or person of the reader. That is, connection only works if the reader *recognizes* connection. A reader of *Travels in the Scriptorium*, for example, is charged with negotiating a highly unstable field, and such hermeneutic negotiation takes its cue from recognition. But, importantly, *Travels in the Scriptorium* is in many ways a book for Auster's previous readers, and any reader who begins his or her Auster experience with *Travels* rather than with any one of its earlier-published auto-intertexts will simply not notice this highly charged field and will likely not, for example, question how David Zimmer can be married to Anna Blume.

This is what Michael Zeitlin calls "the imaginative flux of reading" and what Kreiswirth calls reading's "extra-textual 'wild card'" (Zeitlin 1998, 162; Kreiswirth 2002, 166). Wide-ranging ontologically suggestive projects like Auster's bring to the fore key questions of reception order and knowledge influence. What effects will such potentially (or inevitably) unpredictable ordering exert over the reader's understanding of the larger fictional world being projected? To borrow a question Kreiswirth asks of Faulkner's works: "How are we to concretize the fictional cosmos of Yoknapatawpha from these discursive instabilities?"[8] Whether arranged by choice or by chance, the production of the *world* will be affected. This underlines, then, the dynamics of both choice and chance at the heart of the world's very identity. The world is not a given. *Travels in the Scriptorium* comes into circulation with certain ready-significations depending upon readers' past knowledge of other Auster-authored works enacting immediate referential over-determination. Such *over-determination* without the stabilizing force of generic designation, however, produces much greater *indeterminacy*. We find in Auster's texts an insistence upon some kind of relationship, yet there is nothing to either standardize or guarantee connective authority (as opposed to, say the "contractual" relationships between the *Trilogy* texts issued under the name "trilogy"). *Travels in the Scriptorium*, far from resolving the unruliness of authority and memory, presents new challenges and indeterminacies to the ontological and receptive stabilities of the author's previous fictional worlds and suggests that "world" is a truly unstable concept.

***

If "world" is demonstrated to be an unstable concept, what consequences will there be for its ultimate production? At the end of *The Locked Room*, Fanshawe presents the narrator with a notebook that supposedly resolves the narrator's many questions. The contents of the notebook are not reproduced in the text and in fact immediately after reading the notebook, the narrator rips it up and throws it away. His most cogent statement on Fanshawe's notebook is this:

> If I say nothing about what I found there, it is because I understood very little. All the words were familiar to me, and yet they seemed to have been put together strangely, as though their final purpose was to cancel each other out. I can think of no other way to express it. Each sentence erased the sentence before it, each paragraph made the next paragraph impossible. It is odd, then, that the feeling that survives from this notebook is one of great lucidity. (Auster 1987c, 370)

Clearly this characterization of Fanshawe's writing is to apply equally and self-reflexively to Auster's own text, the whole of the trilogy, the three novels gathered and considered together. *The New York Trilogy*'s interdiscursive patterning likewise performs a surface self-cancellation; when added up or looked at together these fictional worlds flirt as much with retrospective impossibility as with the construction of a total structure (*Ghosts* can be read to "cancel out" *City of Glass*; *The Locked Room* makes *Ghosts* and *City of Glass* "impossible"). Robert Briggs has noticed this same overturning dynamic at play in the *numbering* of Auster's trilogy. Briggs argues that with the publication in 1993 of a text called *The Red Notebook* under the name Paul Auster, *The New York Trilogy*'s identity was irrevocably altered. After several playfully provocative calculations and additions of even more related texts, Briggs reaches the following calculation: "Trilogy = (3 as 1) +1 +1 +3 + 1 + 2 = 11 as 9" (Briggs 2003, 220). From the possibility of producing these numbers he surmises that "Auster's *The New York Trilogy* is a trilogy is a fiction" (Briggs 2003, 220). A "trilogy", after all, is called a trilogy in order to name a set of three, and according to the pattern of assemblages Briggs has tracked down the construct originally designated "*The New York Trilogy*" can no longer be securely considered a set of only three: because *The Red Notebook* advertizes itself (by its auto-intertextual title at least) as necessarily connected to the trilogy, for Briggs, this new text effectively cancels out the generic status of the trilogy.[9]

I don't mean to suggest that Auster's first fictions set out a script for his subsequent experiments with logical modality and ontological operations, but there does seem to be an analogous dynamic still at work in his engagements with connection and with connection's provocative disruptions of authority (*Travels in the Scriptorium* in some ways makes *The Book of Illusions* "impossible", and so on). Concretizing *together* the fictions of Paul Auster prompts a hermeneutic that seems to demand we regard the proposed world as either a lucid impossibility or as unqualified fiction, both of which indicate the greater proposition: world-as-illusion.

Eduardo Urbina has noted that through its evocation of *Don Quixote,* Auster's *The Book of Illusions* takes stock of our mutual desire to believe in impossible things—in illusions. Storytelling and writing, he says, provide certain "consolations" as these illusions "provide meaning, identity, and redemption" (Urbina 2006, 65). I further recommend we read this production of world-as-illusion to indicate equally a vision of the world as enduringly and intrinsically revolutionary. Considered together, Auster's texts produce a kind of ontological "literalization" of Bakhtinian dialogism.[10] The fictions, as well as the works of non or quasi-non fiction, produce a seemingly continuous exchange of characters, views, scenarios, all without apparent resolution (time will tell if *Travels in the Scriptorium* marks Auster's pseudo "burial" of these past characters). The development of the novel issued forth a renewal and an increased flexibility of language, and as Bakhtin puts it, the most important thing that the novel may be said to introduce to previous classical genres is "an indeterminacy, a certain semantic openendedness, a living contact with unfinished, still evolving contemporary reality (the openended present)" (Bakhtin 1981 [1975], 7). The pattern of multi-textual interdiscursivity in Auster's canon manifests exactly this indeterminacy and crucially this is in his texts a semantic and ontological openendedness.

Bakhtin finds that "no living word relates to its object in a *singular* way: between the word and its object, between the word and the speaking subject, there exists an elastic environment of other, alien words about the same object, the same theme" (Bakhtin 1981 [1975], 267). He refers here explicitly to the "word", but of course *dialogue* is not limited in his thought to verbal or linguistic expression, and I recommend we consider the conceptual focus behind dialogism rather than only the concerns of language; specifically, I want to see what may be gained by taking "word" to bear the equivalency of "fictional existent". In Auster's multi-textual universe, characters exist in "an elastic environment", an environment that sometimes creates conflictual semantic relationships between the projected worlds of the texts. And, as Bakhtin continues,

> any concrete discourse (utterance) finds the object at which it was directed already as it were overlain with qualification, open to dispute, charged with value, already enveloped in an obscuring mist—or, on the contrary, by the 'light' of alien words that have already been spoken about it. It is entangled, shot through with shared thoughts, points of view, alien value judgments and accents. The word, directed toward its object, enters a dialogically agitated and tension-filled environment of alien words, value judgments and accents, weaves in and out of complex interrelationships, merges with some, recoils from others. (Bakhtin 1981 [1975], 276)

Because Auster's is for the most part an *auto*-intertextual project, Auster himself is responsible for the extent to which referents—characters or character names—are "already" "overlain with qualification". Past qualifications of the name "Quinn" or the name "Anna Blume" are his own, but this as we have seen does not necessarily simplify matters. This author's undertaking of multi-textuality is by and large a process of taking advantage of the sign's standing as "open to dispute" and then extending that more general "obscuring mist" to envelop the greater world of his fiction. On one hand, Auster seems to take control of his own "dialogically agitated and tension-filled environment", while the other hand issues forth greater indeterminacy of receptive understanding. His characters, like words for Bakhtin, are constituted in part by their *ongoing* interrelationships; they are known in and through the complexity of their mutual existences, at times merging with previous versions of themselves, at other times recoiling from these past constitutions.

Citing the multiple discrepancies of base-level signification that can be tracked across the many texts set in Faulkner's fictional domain, Kreiswirth describes Yoknapatawphan textuality as "compulsively transgressive": "no sooner is one element, feature, or structure stabilized or repeated, than another is destabilized and deformed. Each text sets limits whose horizons are traversed and problematized by the addition of other texts" (Kreiswirth 1996, 166). He suggests we regard Faulkner's textual transgressions in lines along Michel Foucault's thinking on transgression, that is, as a mode of thinking unwilling to stabilize certain basic borders, distinctions, and limitations. "Transgression", Kreiswirth summarizes, "implies a writing that is perpetually testing the limits of its own regularity; not for the sake of either stability or instability, but for a positive 'contestation' of 'values' that 'carries them all to their limits'" (Kreiswirth 1996, 167). I can think of no better characterization of Auster's repeated references to his own past characters than as a testing of regularity, a testing of limits and borders. Much that is *regular, regulating,* and *regulatory* about fiction is subjected to trials of coherency and ontology in the course of the author's re-introductions of fictional beings. References to Anna Blume or Fanshawe or David Zimmer outside their original domains, inside a semantically new domain create static in terms of both textuality and ontology, testing recognized limits not just of fictional worlds but of fiction itself.

No fictional production under the name Paul Auster is safe from some kind of traversal and transgression by other Paul Auster texts. Such unsafe semblances of ontology testify to the unavoidably contested and disputed (in both Foucault's and Bakhtin's terms) nature of any "values" associated with any manifestations of *being*, be they fictional or actual. And so the discrepancies involving David Zimmer's marital status or the publication status of Fanshawe's novel remain ultimately unsettled and open to dispute, emphasizing the incompleteness of the present moment and the fragility of all existence within the unfinished (fictional) world.

Many of Auster's representational practices are thoroughly wrapped up with these operational dynamics of connection. The traditional boundaries and integrities of fictional ontology may be jeopardized by such textual attachments, or a fictional world may in fact be enhanced and enriched through this mode of representational expansion. Either way, by compulsively insinuating doubt into his own hermeneutic field, Auster asks us exactly what is at stake when we approach phenomenologies and ideologies of connection. His fictions challenge our underlying assumptions about "fitting" on multiple fronts—formal, phenomenological, ideological— and thus challenge coherent meaning itself. Paul Ricoeur's hermeneutical philosophy indicates what may be at stake in imagining fictional worlds. Ricoeur insists that what must be interpreted in a text "is a *proposed world* which I could inhabit and wherein I could project one of my ownmost possibilities" (Ricoeur 1991 [1986], 86). This is a space wherein readers may carry out individual projections of individual possible selves, simultaneously reminding them of the real, physical world and their places in it. The hermeneutical endeavor for Ricoeur, a perspective I find particularly appropriate when considering Auster's multi-textual fictions, is about creating possibilities.

The world is not a sum; the world is a "method of connections". And the method by which Auster brings together fictions and their worlds is a method that underlines both choice and chance, refusing to limit the action to one or the other. Connections attained through either/both motor(s) (chance *or* choice; choice *and* chance) add, as Auster writes in *The Invention of Solitude*, "one more synapse to be routed through the vast plenum of experience". The idiosyncratic natures of both such routes and experiences are suitably played out over multiple textual productions and depend dramatically upon reader recognition. Readers, just like the subject of Auster's memoir, crave meaning in any or all recognized connections and existential rhymes. Auster insists that the rhyme exists, "the connection exists", but cautions against attributing stable or authoritative meaning; he cautions against looking "beyond the bare fact of its existence". By signaling anxiety and indeterminacy of world-status, by blending worlds without harmonizing those worlds, Auster's connected fictions produce a hermeneutic enterprise that ultimately makes a case for the far-reaching significance of the simple existence of a dynamic like connection. The bare fact of existence may be as close as we can get to *meaning*, and this, as Auster's fictions indicate, is considerable in itself.

References

Auster, Paul. 1988a [1987]. *In the country of last things*. New York: Viking.

—. 1988b [1982]. *The invention of solitude*. New York: Penguin.

—. 1989. *Moon palace*. New York: Viking.

—. 1990a [1985]. City of glass. In *The New York trilogy*. 3-158. New York: Penguin.

—. 1990b [1986]. The locked room. In *The New York trilogy*. 235-371. New York: Penguin.

—. 1997a [1993]. The red notebook. In *The art of hunger: Essays, prefaces, interviews and "The red notebook"*. 341-380. New York: Penguin.

—. 1997b. Interview with Larry McCaffery and Sinda Gregory. In *The art of hunger: Essays, prefaces, interviews and "The red notebook"*. 287-326. New York: Penguin.

—. 2002. *The book of illusions*. New York: Henry Holt.

—. 2006. *Travels in the scriptorium*. New York: Henry Holt.

Bakhtin, M. M. 1981 [1975]. Discourse in the novel. In *The dialogic imagination: Four essays*. ed. Michael Holquist. trans. Caryl Emerson and Michael Holquist, 259-422. Austin: University of Texas Press.

—. 1981 [1975]. Epic and novel: Toward a methodology for the study of the novel. In *The dialogic imagination: Four essays*. ed. Michael Holquist. trans. Caryl Emerson and Michael Holquist, 3-40. Austin: University of Texas Press.

Booth, Wayne C. 1961. *The rhetoric of fiction*. Chicago: University of Chicago Press.

Briggs, Robert. 2003. Wrong numbers: The endless fiction of Auster and Deleuze and Guattari and... *Critique: Studies in Contemporary Fiction* 44 (2): 213-224.

Carmichael, Thomas. 1998. "After the fact": Marx, the sequel, postmodernism, and John Barth's *LETTERS*. In *Part two: Reflections on the sequel*. ed. Paul Budra and Betty A. Schellenberg, 174-188. Toronto: University of Toronto Press.

Cohn, Dorrit. 1999. *The distinction of fiction*. Baltimore: Johns Hopkins University Press.

Concise Oxford English dictionary. 1995. 9th , rev. ed. New York: Oxford University Press.

Dolezel, Lubomír. 1998 [1997]. *Heterocosmica: Fiction and possible worlds*. Baltimore: Johns Hopkins University Press.

Eco, Umberto. 1979. *The role of the reader: Explorations in the semiotics of texts*. Bloomington: Indiana University Press.

Harshaw, Benjamin (Hrushovski). 1984. Fictionality and fields of reference. *Poetics Today* 5 (2): 227-251.

Ingarden, Roman. 1973[1937]. *The cognition of the literary work of art*. Evanston, Ill.: Northwestern University Press.

Kreiswirth, Martin. 1996. "Paradoxical and outrageous discrepancy": Transgression, auto-intertextuality, and Faulkner's Yoknapatawpha. In *Faulkner and the Artist*. ed. Donald M. Kartiganer and Ann J. Abadie, 161-180. Jackson: University Press of Mississippi.

—. 2002. Intertextuality, transference, and postmodernism in *Absalom, Absalom!*: The production and reception of Faulkner's fictional world. In *Faulkner and postmodernism*. ed. John N. Duvall and Ann J. Abadie, 109-123. Jackson: University Press of Mississippi.

McHale, Brian. 1992. *Constructing postmodernism*. New York: Routledge.

—. 1987. *Postmodernist fiction*. New York: Methuen.

Pavel, Thomas G. 1986. *Fictional worlds*. Cambridge, Mass.: Harvard University Press.

Ricoeur, Paul. 1991 [1986]. *From text to action*. trans. Kathleen Blamey and John B. Thompson. vol. 2. Evanston, Ill.: Northwestern University Press.

Ronen, Ruth. 1994. *Possible worlds in literary theory*. New York: Cambridge University Press.

Ryan, Marie-Laure. 1991. *Possible worlds, artificial intelligence, and narrative theory*. Bloomington: Indiana University Press.

Urbina, Eduardo. 2006. Reading matters: Quixotic fiction and subversive discourse in Paul Auster's *The book of illusions*. In *Critical reflections: Essays on golden age Spanish literature*, ed. Barbara Simerka and Amy R. Williamsen, 57-66. Lewisburg: Bucknell University Press.

Zeitlen, Michael. 1998. Donald Barthelme and the postmodern sequel. In *Part two: Reflections on the sequel*, ed. Paul Vincent Budra and Betty A. Schellenberg, 160-173. Toronto: University of Toronto Press.

Notes

[1] Fiction theorist Dorrit Cohn agrees that it is the presence of characters which most identifies fiction as fiction. She writes that "it is by its unique potential for presenting characters that fiction most consistently and most radically severs its connections with the real world outside the text" (Cohn 1999, 16).

[2] Even the more general concept of *world* independent of its status in fictional texts suggests both an excess and a strategy of limitation. In addition to indicating the associative unadulterated excess—"the universe or all that exists; everything"—*The Concise Oxford English Dictionary* lists meanings which imply important principles of separation and distinction, for instance, "all people; the earth as known or in some particular respect" and "all that concerns or all who belong to a specified class, time, domain, or sphere of activity (*the medieval world*; *the world of sport*)". *World* indicates all known aspects of the earth, and at the same time indicates a particularity of knowingness. By way of the term *world*, we are dealing with as close to total encompassment as can reasonably be imagined or asserted, but it seems that even in notions regarding the world's totality there is an *of* indicated, an *of* which erects and enacts apparently inevitable borders and bordering tendencies.

[3] I have opted to focus on textual inter-connections made by and through recurring characters, or at least character names, as character-stability bears the greatest significance to the surrounding stability of the fictional world. There are, of course, many other intriguing connections among Auster's texts. *Oracle Night*, for example, presents an especially provocative connective opportunity. In this novel, a writer purchases a notebook whose blueness is as intensely determined as *The New York Trilogy*'s red notebooks. The detective novel Auster says he published at

the outset of his career under a pseudonym and which is collected in *Hand to Mouth*, is attributed to "Paul Benjamin" which is also the name of the main character in the film *Smoke* for which Auster wrote the screenplay, and in *Smoke*, Paul Benjamin tells the same story that Auster tells in *The Locked Room* (about Bakhtin smoking one of his manuscripts). The scenario of Auster's recent film, too, *The Inner Life of Martin Frost*, was originally described in *The Book of Illusions* as a film made by the imaginary silent film star Hector Mann. And certainly Auster is known for recurring motifs such as artist-characters, the Fall, Brooklyn settings, story-telling, and so on. Over time, such repetitions have produced expectations in Auster's readers, and readers now may approach a new Auster novel as a kind of ludic game of recognition.

[4] Yet another way we may attempt to stabilize the logical modality of these different ontological assumptions is via Umberto Eco's concept of "transworld identity" (Eco 1979, 229). Fictional entities *can* migrate between fictional worlds, and in the case of "transworld identity" even between worlds authored by different writers (an author can "borrow" a fictional entity from one fictional universe and transpose the character into his or her own fictional world). This is a concept whose operation is founded upon the governing of difference. There are acceptable levels of difference, and unacceptable levels of difference; Eco measures these in terms of "essential or accidental properties" (Eco 1979, 239). Accidental differences occurring between texts are admissible. If a fictional character's "essential properties", however, are different from one book to the next, this negates his or her possible "transworld identity" status. When "the very notion of self-identity" is challenged, such as in self-contradictory works of science fiction or the avant-garde, this will, in Eco's understanding, "*undermine* the world of our encyclopedia rather than build up another self-sustaining world" (Eco 1979, 234).

[5] Brian McHale asks how far postmodernist fiction can be "pushed" before it begins to destabilize rather than consolidate fictional ontology, and argues, for example, that John Barth's *LETTERS* "carries the *retour de personnages* too far" (McHale 1987, 58).

[6] Marie-Laure Ryan's "principle of minimal departure", establishes limits on the fictional world. The "principle of minimal departure" states that the world of fiction is by and large constructed by readers to bear the closest possible resemblance to the reality already occupied and known: "we reconstrue the central world of a textual universe in the same way we reconstrue the alternate possible worlds of nonfactual statements: as conforming as far as possible to our representation of AW [the actual world]" (51). For Ryan, this means that as readers we habitually and implicitly project everything we know about the actual world onto the text's fiction-making statements, and so onto the world they suggest. We "make only the adjustments dictated by the text" (51); in other words, when we can't avoid making adjustments (Ryan 1991, 51).

[7] See Wayne Booth's 1961 *The Rhetoric of Fiction*. Chicago: University of Chicago Press, 71.

[8] Kreiswirth uses "concretize" in keeping with Roman Ingarden's terminology (Kreiswith 1996, 166).

[9] Briggs concludes his discussion and calculations self-reflexively by reintroducing un-decidability into his own reading. He wonders if his final calculation is the result of having carefully followed, sorted, and traced Auster's overall project, or whether it is something he "made up on the spot" (Briggs 2003, 222).

[10] Auster told Sinda Gregory: "Of all the theories of the novel, Bakhtin's strikes me as the most brilliant, the one that comes closest to understanding the complexity and the magic of the form" (Auster 1997c, 304).

CHAPTER EIGHT

LIFE TRANSMISSION:
PAUL AUSTER'S MERGING WORLDS,
MEDIA AND AUTHORS

ULRICH MEURER

I. Merging worlds

In 1967, in the wake of a long lasting agony which at the latest had set in
with Russian formalism, the author was finally declared dead by Roland
Barthes. From now on, meaning was not the result of a writer's intention
or experience any longer. Instead, it would become a function of a given
text's structure, of its joints and gaps, which had to be detected by the
reader. This highly polemic and utopian postulate was particularly directed
against the tradition of the *explication du texte*, then widespread in French
literary studies and criticism. While formalism or, two decades before
Barthes, Wimsatt and Beardsley's attack against the *intentional fallacy* had
successfully contributed to marginalizing the naïve identification of a
text's meaning with the authorial biography, French universities still
taught methods to explain the one by means of the other.[1] Thus, although
somewhat belated, Barthes' strict separation of the two concepts and his
empowerment of the recipient mark a significant change in literary criticism.

However, this accomplishment of structuralism was once again called
into question by post-structuralism and its dissolution of every system's
and text's centre, external boundary and non-textual adjacencies.
Integrated into an endless process of universal signification, the text loses
its coherence, limits and status as different from "reality" or the author's
biography. Accordingly, trying to comprehend the structure of a work of
art can no longer come to a halt at its margins, as Roland Barthes had
demanded. The play of signifiers reaches out to a whole world of signs
which unquestionably also includes the (likewise sign-formulated) life of
its author. This "life", being diegesis all along, cannot be reduced to

physical data or actual experience, but is constituted by discursive strategies and fictional elements that shape and at the same time destabilize its contours. On the one hand, the perpetual deferral of the signified thus adds to the author's erasure, while, on the other, he literally comes back into play since his new "essence"—being constituted of "inessential" signs—aligns him with every other cultural artifact and especially with his text.

With postmodernism almost undauntedly instructing our understanding of the ever-tenuous and manifold relations between the "real" and the "imaginary", it is therefore no longer Roland Barthes' dated separation of *facta* and *ficta* or the cancellation of all biographical traces from the text's structure which promise a deeper insight into the nature of the literary. All the same, one can diagnose an increasing complexity in contemporary arts as well as in their academic analysis which, in turn, challenges post-structuralism and its hieratical abandonment of the real. For although postmodernism has not, and by definition cannot, come to its end,[2] the classical Derridean stance of a limitless process of signification now seems to be qualified by a return of the empirical author and also by a playfully ironic, but at the same time earnestly probing, influx of "reality" into his or her work. John Zilcosky states that, in American book-culture, the notion of the "author" as a single personality is probably more entrenched now than it was twenty-five years ago:

> Within a shrinking industry, publishers construct increasingly convincing and compelling personalities on book jackets, and present-day readers … ardently pursue their authors and popular book signings and readings. Moreover, a professional industry now flourishes around authors such as Barthes, Foucault, and Derrida. (Zilcosky 1998, 196)

Aside from such marketing strategies, the literary text itself newly allows reality to appear—albeit with reservations. Having lived through post-structuralism, literature is aware of the complicated inter-play of different ontological spheres; it therefore develops modes and constructs which still make a difference between fact and fiction without separating them. Instead of sealing off texts from their context or declaring every context a text, such constructs keep *investigating* the ontological status of "text" and "world". They positively flag up their blurred differences as well as interdependencies that now lend a certain concreteness to the fictitious and simultaneously enrich the authentic with the unassertive potentiality of fiction.

Given this oscillating absence/presence of demarcations, authors like Paul Auster install their writing in the spacious and undifferentiated zone opening up between fictionalized life and biographical fiction. In contrast, for example, to Robbe-Grillet or Raymond Federman, who infuse their oeuvre with an overall ontological "porosity", Auster does not refer to such a broad factual substructure:

> Technically speaking …, each time I use the first person I push myself far away and see myself from a certain distance. Like a patient in the operating theater. I use the biographical mode, taking myself as an example. (Auster quoted by Coppersmith 1998)

Thus, Auster's texts often aim at a comparatively dense and self-contained fictionality which even verges on the parabolic.[3] Nevertheless, his work is punctured by sudden irruptions of actuality, for instance when his first novel has one "Paul Auster", "a tall dark fellow in his mid-thirties, with rumpled clothes and a two-day beard, [holding] an uncapped fountain pen, still poised in a writing position", (Auster 1987, 92-93) along with his wife and son appear as the protagonist's dialogue partner. As Dennis Barone points out (citing William Lavender), "biographical projections" such as these follow and at the same time turn over the concept of a fluctuating region of signs: they "'are kernels of reality buried in a text that everywhere seeks an effect of unreality.' The result is a parody 'not of realism, but of irrealism. To the postmodern statement that fiction is not truth, it opposes a new paradox: fiction cannot lie'" (Barone 1995, 6). It thus seems quite factoidal to assert that in Auster's quest for identity all representation is under erasure, the stable difference between subject and referent being "always already" tentative and authorial identity being transformed into an inter-play of signifiers.[4] The obvious ambiguity of what is "true" and what is "imagined" life in Auster's work is more likely to show how experience and narration constitute the terminals of a creative area of tension in which an experimental reconstruction of the formerly deconstructed self can take place. In this respect, "Paul Auster" appearing in Paul Auster's texts does not put into practice the transformation of the referent into an illimitable representation; rather, "Auster quite literally rejects theory's imperative to die or disperse" (Zilcosky 1998, 197). He plays on the post-structuralist concepts by realizing the paradox of a *whole variety of equally personal and true compossible worlds.*

Certainly, such entrées of "Paul Auster" or diverse alter egos in Auster's novels only mark a special case of the author's overall strategy to incessantly blur the boundaries between "fact" and "fiction". In one way or another, almost every text implements various diegetic levels which thereupon merge and become permeable: characters from a hypodiegetic level may encounter their hyperdiegetic creators (Owen Brick who in *Man*

in the Dark receives the order to kill August Brill, the man who made up
Brick and the fictional civil war he has blundered into from yet another
reality). Authors may be confronted with their novels' characters (Mr.
Blank who in *Travels in the Scriptorium* is kept hostage by his, or Paul
Auster's own, fictional "charges"). Figures from an imaginary space may
enter the narrative's "reality" (the muse Claire who in *The Inner Life of
Martin Frost* visits her artistic protégé). Minor characters may reappear as
central figures in another diegesis (David Zimmer who in *Moon Palace* is
Marco Stanley Fogg's roommate and then becomes protagonist in *The
Book of Illusions*). In light of Auster's later work noticeably intensifying
such operations, this list could be continued almost *ad infinitum*.
Occasionally, this process even gives way to irritatingly complex layering-
structures when for example Paul Auster (2007, 46) uses Mr. Blank as his
"persona" and as a fictitious character interrogated by one James P. Flood;
Flood is a former inspector of Scotland Yard and character from yet
another (intradiegetic) novel titled *Neverland* (here James M. Barrie comes
to mind), which was written by a man called Fanshawe; Fanshawe is
obviously created by the author Blank, but at the same time is the
namesake of Nathaniel Hawthorne's homonymous first novel's
protagonist, and also a character from Auster's early novella *The Locked
Room*. Here, four or five ontological spheres intermingle with, and loop
back into, each other.

It is precisely this overflowing multiplicity and complexity of schemes
that eliminates the gaps between various diegetic levels "inside" the text
and also between "reality" and "literature", an excessive intra- and
intertextual cross-linking which develops such a strong gravitational force
that in the end even the author—or at least a processed version of him—
gets into the event horizon. What at first sight appears like the mere
coupling of related but non-identical literary phenomena, transgressing
diegetic levels on the one hand and closing the ontological breach between
author and text on the other, thus reveals itself to be perfectly
consubstantial, the "quality" of the crossed borders being the same in both
cases. While Barthes has rightly exiled the authorial subject from the text,
stating that "writing is that neutral, composite, oblique space, ... the
negative where all identity is lost" (Barthes 1977, 142), the text itself, by
mingling (its) ontological strata, invites the author back in.

II. Merging media

However, Paul Auster's novels and movies do not only cross borders by
transforming diegesis into a multi-layered narrative structure or by

applying various intertextual references which either allude to Auster's proper oeuvre or to his literary (and cinematographic) precursors. In addition to this admittedly long established procedure—which bloomed no later than with the *Siglo de Oro*[5]—Auster interlaces his texts with an incessant treatment of mainly visual media. His first published book, *The Invention of Solitude* (1982), introduces a trick photograph taken in Atlantic City during the 1940's which shows five views of Samuel, Auster's father, simultaneously sitting around a table in still and ghostly contemplation. And from then on, the author repeatedly deals with optical techniques of representation as thematic backdrop, metaphor or starting point for intermedial reflection. Most notably, the second chapter of *The Book of Illusions* sketches out meticulously a whole series of films that the novel's gray eminence Hector Mann has starred in during the 1920's. In fact, entire portions of the book revert to "writing movies" in order to communicate what the sensation of looking at a (fictional) film would be (González 2009, 21), as well as to film criticism, actors' biographies and cinema history; when the novel's main topics can be subsumed as the illusionary essence of being and a person's always endangered presence in his own life, nothing seems better suited to convey these topics than the equally shadowy and flickering nature of projected images on the screen.

The Brooklyn Follies also deals with cinema, albeit in a more restrained manner. Time and again the intimate conversation between the aging protagonist Nathan Glass and his companion Joyce refers to films as their common interest. Nathan makes fun of the actor James Whitmore's flat remarks about getting old while watching a 1950's Western called *The Outriders* (Auster 2005, 294); Joyce astonishes her partner "with her encyclopedic knowledge of old Hollywood films and her talent for identifying every minor and forgotten actor who flitted across the screen" (Auster 2005, 277). Then there is the Chowder Inn in southern Vermont, decorated with eight-by-ten black-and-white photographs of Hollywood comedy stars, one room being devoted to the Marx Brothers, another to Buster Keaton, a third to Laurel and Hardy. And, finally, it is a video of Charles Chaplin's 1936 classic *Modern Times* which Nathan hopes will tease the first verbal reaction out of his nine-year-old niece Lucy who refuses to speak (Auster 2005, 141). Especially this last paradigm of intermedia reference demonstrates how deliberately films are introduced in Auster's texts: in *Modern Times* the tramp talks for the first time, so that the end of cinema's silent era—intentionally protracted by Chaplin—coincides with the struggle for human communication examined in the novel. Thus, the cinematic image, the technical reproduction of sound, verbal expression and their representation through "mute" characters on the page are silhouetted against each other, producing a constellation of differences which implicitly provides insight into the medial possibilities of "showing" and "telling".

Subsequently, Paul Auster's *Man in the Dark* (2008) treats movies as a form of self-medication after experiencing traumatic events (the death of the central character's wife, his car accident, or the beheading of his granddaughter's boyfriend Titus Small by Iraqi terrorists, which is depicted in Auster's text as a video of poor quality on the internet). In order to cope with these events, August Brill and his granddaughter Katya spend days in front of the TV watching rented DVDs—Renoir, De Sica, Ray, Ozu—another opportunity for Auster to confront the written word with the movie and the streaming video image and their respective ability to display the imaginary and the unspeakable.

Finally, the novel *Travels in the Scriptorium* (2007) has the writer Mr. Blank captured on a series of time-lapse-photographs taken by his characters with an automatic camera, the shutter clicking silently "once every second, producing eighty-six thousand four hundred still photos with each revolution of the earth" (Auster 2007, 1). This peculiar allusion to both modern surveillance techniques and early Muybridge-like chronophotography—every motion of the author being closely watched and analyzed by his creation—is mirrored by the fact that Blank in his cell is furnished with a stack of three dozen black-and-white portraits showing the characters of his novels.

So far we have been dealing with what Irina Rajewsky calls *intermedia references* in a narrow sense, a text's mention of photography or film either as evocation of their representational techniques or as incorporation of a specific genre's or movie's plot elements. In contrast to *media transitions* (the process of transferring a "source-text" into a different medium, the way film adaptations of literature or novelizations do) and *media combinations* (the co-operation of at least two different media taking part in a single work's signification process but still being present in their respective materiality, as it is the case with operas or comic books), intermedia references can be defined by their limitation to only one medium which does not employ but merely *simulates* or *thematizes* another form of representation (Rajewsky 2004, 37f). Paul Auster's novels incorporate other media primarily as their topic; being "literature" and therefore bound to the written word, they cannot functionalize photography or film as material units. Moreover, with the exception of *The Book of Illusions*, the texts seldom try to reproduce elements of filmic narrative structures like zoom, montage, or cross-fading. This comparatively restricted variant of intermediality is also adopted in Auster's movies[6] which—even though they are often engaged with literary or "writerly" subject matters—invariably limit their representational practice to the "plain image" without for example embedding lettering or another analogue system of signification.[7] Nevertheless, mentioning non-textual media in a literary text has a twofold effect: on the one hand, as Rajewsky points out, such "explicit system references" are closely connected with metatextual and metafictional strategies. They reflect the construction, mediality and materiality of a given text, thereby foregrounding the medial condition of every possible perception of the real (Rajewsky 2004, 49). In this way, the "textuality" of the text becomes visible. On the other hand, the example of Mr. Blank's photographs in *Travels in the Scriptorium* demonstrates how the more recent instances of such rather "conservative" intermedia practices are often correlated with an ontological "border traffic" that merges the text's diegetic levels. A discussion of the medial nature of the written is thus short-circuited with an examination of the authorial and fictional.[8]

Yet, on closer inspection one comes across various instances in Auster's oeuvre which clearly go beyond the simple evocation of another medium. The preeminent paradigm for such a correlation of media that implements their difference also on a material level is of course Auster's feature film *The Inner Life of Martin Frost* which actualizes a fictitious movie from *The Book of Illusions*. Whereas the novel's central character David Zimmer gives us a scene-by-scene breakdown of this imaginary film made by Hector Mann in 1946 (described as the only part of the director's secret productions that Zimmer gets to see before the whole work of a lifetime is destroyed), five years later it is Paul Auster himself who authors "that same" film, transforming a novelistic movie into a real-life one.[9] With *The Inner Life of Martin Frost* one has thus switched over to Rajewsky's concept of *media transitions* characterized by the engagement and physical presence of two different media, even though Auster's movie—based on a "written film" and therefore being located in a strange interspace between filmic adaptation and "remake"—complicates the concept considerably.

At the same time this procedure is of course associated with a challenge of the factual/fictional; once more, the author and his invention become indistinguishable when both Hector Mann and Paul Auster father the same film which nevertheless can only be read in the first case but actually seen in the second. And, as was argued earlier, this crossing of an ontological gap does not necessarily imply or hint at reality's constructedness (for it seems to be authored or at least mediated like any other ontological level) or dissolve reality in a universe of signs. Instead, the passage from written to real-life movie contributes to its concreteness and endows the film with a hitherto unknown objectivity. Whether Paul Auster enters his own texts as a character or has a thirty-second appearance in the final scene of Haas's movie version of *The Music of Chance*, whether he brings an imagined work into being or animates other artists to do the same, Auster's work always makes an effort to counterbalance the "postmodern" loss of depth and distinctness with a manifest transfusion of world and self. "Instead of writing himself out of history in favor of either a 'series of specific and complex operations' (Foucault) or a virtuosic reader (Barthes), Auster experiments, in fictional practice, with the possibilities of life after authorial death" (Zilcosky 1998, 197).

III. Collaborations

Auster's apparent urge to interconnect word and world as well as his resulting awareness of the medial already leave their mark on the narratives' production process, as his well-known refusal to write on a computer indicates. Jotting down the initial ideas for a planned novel in a small notebook and then transcribing these handwritten notes on a manual 1960's Olympia typewriter is a method which highlights Auster's conscious handling of the material that "formulates" his work. Again the accented physicality of the pencil and typewriter-imprint which shuns the weightless, disembodied, and perpetual flux of the digital tends to solidify the sphere of signification. Just as in the prose of Auster's friend and fellow author Don DeLillo, the crafted symbol, the indention that a writing-tool leaves on the sheet of paper, the way a word looks on the page can not be understood as mere "traces" which in terms of Derrida point to an absent *signifié* (Meurer 2007, 217).[10] They are—or at least simulate— almost magical graphic elements endowed with the power to re-implant writing into the realm of the material. This heightened materiality of the written word is brought about by a most willful manipulation of media and opens out into an extensive artistic practice which confines itself neither to literature nor to Auster's proper body of work. The complex interrelation between the mingling levels of reality and the alteration of media affects a wide range of artworks (films, paintings, graphics, comic books, music, etc.) which are based on Auster's novels but need not necessarily be Auster's own work.

To begin with, a book like *The Story of my Typewriter* (2002) reflects that same ontological/medial concept. It combines an essay retracing Auster's professional affection for his typewriter and several "portraits" of this piece of hardware rendered in oil by Sam Messer. The text ponders *in extenso* on the reliability and sheer materiality of the heavy and slightly unhandy instrument: "[it] was comfortable to the touch, it worked smoothly, it was dependable" (Auster and Messer 2002, 15-16). Auster depicts it as an essentially "modern" tool almost in line with Van Gogh's *Peasant Shoes*[11] and stresses the historicity of the typewriter by describing its acquisition in 1974 or the difficulties to procure ink ribbons in a time when such machines are "the last surviving artifacts of twentieth-century *homo scriptorus*" (Auster and Messer 2002, 23) and threatened with extinction. Finally, he even transforms the typewriter into a sort of super-object by confronting its exceptional longevity with transient quotidian articles like pencils and pens, cars, refrigerators, shoes, sweaters and jackets, watches, alarm clocks and umbrellas. In turn, Messer's paintings adopt this object-related trait. The artist converts the represented writing tool into a bas-relief protruding from the two-dimensional surface of the canvas by applying thick lumps of paint directly from the tube or working at the rough layers with a palette knife. Moreover, the little bronze sculpture which Messer made of Auster's typewriter and which was given to all purchasers of a limited edition of the book marks yet another medial change and increase of material concreteness. Even the book itself, with its thick and glossy Japanese Matte paper, accentuates this overall "objectification". It is further supported by a detailed editor's note about the title pages being set by Auster's Olympia typewriter, about the text being composed in Bodoni (the first of the Modern type designs which express the beginning of the Industrial Revolution) and Berthold Bodoni Antiqua respectively, and about the book being printed and bound in China and manufactured by Asia Pacific Offset in a trade edition of 5000 copies (Auster and Messer 2002, 71).

Similar strategies of furnishing texts with a heightened substantiality are employed in many of Auster's "intermedial ventures" and collaborations—be it his preliminary work for at least two comic books (Karasik's and Mazzucchelli's *City of Glass* and the short episode *The Day I Disappeared* drawn by Jacques de Loustal[12]) or his literary/musical collaboration with the band One Ring Zero.[13] The transposition from word to image generally causes a representation to shift from the realm of abstract concepts to concrete visualization. In the case of *City of Glass*, a "surprisingly nonvisual work at its core, a complex web of words and abstract ideas" (Spiegelman 2005, i), the process becomes all the more crucial for the novel to acquire a referentiality that seemingly manages to escape the mere differential structures of the written. However, the particular design of the "graphic novel" *City of Glass* adds various medial levels to this process of solidification. Firstly, it adopts other forms and instances of artistic representation by incorporating graphics and painting: Albrecht Dürer's engraving of *Adam and Eve* (also known as *The Fall of Man*, 1504); the 1563 version of Pieter Brueghel the Elder's *Tower of Babel*; Picasso's ink drawing of Don Quixote, made in 1955 for an issue of the magazine *Les LETTRES françaises*; John Tenniel's Victorian illustrations for Carroll's *Through the Looking-Glass*; the famous "Well Scene" or "Shaft of the Dead", a Paleolithic cave painting from Lascaux. Secondly, the comic book makes use of several different styles. Time and again, the altogether cinematographic, strong and rich-in-contrast ink drawings are superseded by passages of fine pencil- or childlike crayon-images, by sequences of geometrically simplified icons, nervous expressionistic sketches, or technical cartographic reproductions. In this context it is conspicuous that the change in style is often motivated by a transition from the narrative's diegetic to another—hypodiegetic—level (Coughlan 2006, 838-839), thus interconnecting a "hierarchy of sketchiness" with a "hierarchy of presence" (Coughlan 2006, 843). Finally, the order of panels contributes to the book's overall exhibited mediality and materiality. Whereas at times the panels dissect the page into nine regular rectangles that put into practice Peter Stillman's machine-like and strangely self-distanced monologue,[14] at other times they grow to full-page images which decelerate the "reading" process. This draws attention to the altered conditions of reception and to the rhythm of viewing pictures, until in the end the panels begin to sway, drift apart and dissolve into a completely blackened page.

Even the musical adaptations of Auster's work—his lyrics set to music by the "Lit Rock" band One Ring Zero for their song "Natty Man Blues" and also several tracks on Sophie Auster's debut album—happen to show certain traces of such materiality. Here, the newly gained "thingness" or object-quality of the written word owes mainly to the compositional style and arrangements of One Ring Zero, known for their slightly clanking and handmade kermis-sound. Although not in the least disapproving of electric or electronic instruments, the band's music is characterized by the use of acoustic sounding bodies like an accordion, claviola (a sort of melodica designed by Ernst Zacharias in the 1960's), metallophone, cajón, toy piano and megamouth (a small plastic megaphone found at toy stores). All these instruments possess a peculiar and diminutive mechanical charm associated with a child's innocent world of objects. The seemingly "unprofessional" music's timbre is intensified by recordings of power drills, bread machines, kitty litter stroked with a scooper and a wide array of other everyday sounds looped and altered to create a specific acoustical texture. Even synthetic sounds or noises are produced with the help of

instruments that own a certain aura of vintage machinery—the jones-O-
phone, a heavy eight-stringed electric guitar, or the theremin, designed in
the 1920's by Russian scientist Leon Theremin, which emits sound when
the musician waves his hands across an electro-magnetic field.[15]

IV. Double Game

All the above-mentioned works of art have in common that they transcend
Paul Auster's oeuvre and extend themselves into actuality by colonizing
the space between Auster's texts and another artist's work. Once more,
this strategy expands the sphere in which fiction and fact mingle: when at
first the intercommunion of different diegetic levels inside a literary text
generates a space that soon also includes the author's extra-textual
biography and reality, now the field widens again to comprise the work of
another artist; and while at first any operation questioning the fixed
boundaries of fiction or the ontological status of the written is limited to
the literary, now the task of rendering the word tangible is transferred to
what Roman Jakobson calls "intersemiotic translation". Whether one
considers the amalgamation of ontological strata, the authorial presence in,
or the affiliation of further individuals to his work—in all three cases Paul
Auster tends to combine, or initiates the combination of, the merging and
expansion of worlds with a correlative merging of media. In this respect,
the dialogue between Auster's fifth novel *Leviathan* (1992) and a series of
artworks by the Parisian conceptualist Sophie Calle constitutes a seminal
moment. The resulting textual/visual construct incorporates factual
elements on the part of both Auster and Calle and it transforms the usual
linear adaptation process into a multiform constellation whose various
units determine and reflect each other.

Dealing with the precarious conversion of life into art on various
levels, *Leviathan* adopts Calle as matrix for one of its characters, Maria
Turner, "twenty-seven or twenty-eight at the time, a tall, self-possessed
young woman with closely cropped blonde hair and a bony, angular face"
(Auster 2001 [1992], 59). While Auster's description of Maria makes it
hard to suspect that she might be modeled on the long-haired, brunette and
rather soft-featured Sophie Calle, the artistic projects she plans and
executes unmistakably refer to her real-life archetype.[16] In fact, the novel's
list of Maria's ventures reads like an almost comprehensive professional
CV of Sophie Calle, borrowing no less than eight of her previous projects:
To Follow (*Paris Shadows*, 1978-1979), *The Striptease* (1979), *Suite
vénitienne* (1980), *The Detective* (*The Shadow*, 1981), *The Hotel* (1981),
The Address Book (1983), *The Birthday Ceremony* (1980-1993), and *The*

Wardrobe (1985-1992). Moreover, Paul Auster invents two additional projects, *The Chromatic Diet* and *Days Under the Sign of B, C & W*. These projects possess a certain likeness to the work of Calle by submitting the artist Maria "who lived her life according to an elaborate set of bizarre, private rituals" (Auster 2001 [1992], 60) to contingent behavior guidelines such as restricting her to food of a single color for any given day of the week. Intrigued by her fictionalization, Sophie Calle responds to Auster's schemes and draws on the novel's imaginary artistic patterns as sources for her own upcoming works. Aside from playfully "correcting" the novel's passages that deal with her biography and inserting the respective pages in the binding of her own book *Double Game*, she appropriates *Leviathan* by re-enacting the projects of her invented alter ego and turning them into genuine sets of photos as well as written documents (Calle 2007 [1999], 10-31).

So far, this unique dialogue seems to oscillate between two antipodal effects: on the one hand, the insertion of historical personages into the novel's plot indicates a certain gain of "reality" and seems to lift the text to a higher ontological level (even if—according to the rules of historiographic fiction—such characters are relegated to secondary roles).[17] On the other, Sophie Calle translates Auster's literary schemes into her own life "in order to bring Maria and me closer together" (Calle 2007 [1999], 10), a convergence that lends a touch of fictionality to her self and biographical work. At the same time, it is precisely the concreteness of Calle's (albeit camouflaged) presence in *Leviathan* which emphasizes the novel's purely textual constitution. And reciprocally, Calle's acting out Auster's schemes retroacts as strategy of actualization and solidification of the fictional. Thus, the double games take place in an ontological no-man's-land in which "fictionalization" and "factualization" inevitably bring forth (and *are*) their respective opposites.

The cooperation's third step expands this equivocal zone: when Sophie Calle commissions directives for a further project, Paul Auster provides her with his *Gotham Handbook—Personal Instructions for SC on How to Improve Life in New York City (Because she asked ...)*. The text assigns her with several tasks like smiling at, or talking with, strangers in the street, giving out food or cigarettes to homeless people, and cultivating a spot in the city. At first glance, this remittance work leaves the realm of the fictional altogether and transcends Auster's novelistic oeuvre. Instead of taking Calle as a subject, Auster becomes the author of her actions and thus engages directly in the real. Whereas the above-mentioned collaborations with painters, comic book artists or musicians enhance the materiality of imaginary narratives *ex post*, the *Gotham Handbook*—

although a written text—constitutes an instruction manual and therefore demands its physical implementation. Accordingly, when Calle invites Auster to do what he wants with her, for a period of up to a year at most, he objects that he does not want to take responsibility for what might happen when Sophie acts out the script he has created for her (Calle 2007 [1999], 234-5). He prefers to compile a comparatively short and cautious, if not anticlimactic list of duties,[18] obviously leaving Sophie Calle a little disappointed: "I wonder if Paul got his idea for these instructions ... by reading the twelve steps of an Alcoholics Anonymous program, or whether he based them on a community service order. Anyway, I have a duty to obey. That was the agreement" (Calle 2007 [1999], 246). She tries to follow meticulously the given instructions and even adds some constraints concerning the project's documentation as if to outweigh the *Handbook's* somewhat uninspired harmlessness: "Paul didn't ask me to count the smiles I give. Unquestionably an oversight. I add this item to the *Handbook*" (Calle 2007 [1999], 246). However, the manual's diffident flatness does certainly not result from a lack of imagination or audacity on the part of Paul Auster but marks the difference between the act of conceptualizing or expanding the boundaries of fiction and being exposed to the uninhibited forces of reality. While Sophie Calle states that she has "no other choice but to submit", in fact it is she who knowingly exposes Auster to the imperative of the real. Thus, the reluctance of his instructions to extend too far into the "world" has nothing to do with Auster cocooning in the safe domain of fiction. Instead, it tries to relocate the author and his text inside the artwork's demarcation lines, because only "in what Maurice Blanchot calls pure textuality can the bar dividing the signifier from the signified be obliterated" (Bronfen 2001, 297). In any case, this is the place which is also occupied by Calle herself when she finally turns her *Handbook*-based experience into a "documentation" consisting of graphically designed texts and several series of photographs.

Strangely, this latter repatriation of reality into the written word and image is seldom discussed by literary critics who refer to Calle's and Auster's liaison, the more striking as the book *Double Game* (in most instances the only material basis for exploring their collaboration) solely presents texts and pictures of Calle's "real" ventures.[19] It is not unmediated reality which provides the project's core but the process of re-mediation, making the artwork visible in the first place; outside the realm of signs the well-matched players Auster and Calle—both practicing a cheerful oscillation between fact and fiction (Bronfen 2001, 300)—have no common ground whatsoever. The comparatively simple act of "materializing" fictional entities may elevate their ontological value. But first and foremost it is the employment of de- as well as re-mediating operations, the double game of seesawing into and out of the real, which is apt to probe the *signifié*'s connection with any fictional entity or culturally produced *signifiant*. In this sense, *Double Game* deliberately exhibits its medial and material qualities just like the works of Sam Messer, Karasik & Mazzucchelli or One Ring Zero do. The preceding process of collecting data from physical reality is already shaped by the constant use of media— Sophie Calle documents her artistic undertakings through photographs, written notes and transcriptions from a voice-activated tape-recorder (Martin 2000). The finished book also presents itself as a hybrid object positioned between materiality and mediality. On the one hand, its tactile quality seems to be intentionally emphasized by the burgundy satin ribbon holding the cover closed or by the dark red linen of the jacket's spine and back embossed with silver letters. The impression of "thingness" is further heightened by the smaller pages of *Leviathan*'s Faber & Faber edition inserted in the binding, by the volume's sometimes colored paper and its unusual weight. On the other hand, the book's medial status becomes evident in the overall combination of text and image: several different font sizes and printing types, their changing colors as well as the alternation of continuous and footnote text constantly remind the recipient of his or her special apperception as a reader. At the same time, the pictures—"partially re-edited and reconfigured from earlier gallery and museum exhibitions to fit the pages of the book" (Martin 2000)—produce a perceptional shift. The sheer variety of images (from black-and-white to color photographs, from scrapbook facsimiles to city maps, from contact prints to copies of letters and newspapers, from film stills to handwritten notes) transforms the reader into a viewer. All these features of materiality, textuality, and iconicity clearly indicate a refeeding of the actual into a nevertheless mediated artifact which, thus, is poised on the threshold between fact and fiction, between autobiography and the invention of self.

V. Interferences

The constant introduction of factual material in both Paul Auster's and Sophie Calle's fictional/artistic works and their accentuated mediality bring into play a concept which in the end can be seen as the main point of convergence: the nexus of inter-ontology (merging worlds) and intermediality (merging media) is established by an instance of *disturbance* or *interference* which in equal parts characterizes the one and the other. Whereas the self-contained fictional text is said to transport its recipient to a world differing from his or her own, this illusionary cosmos is suddenly perforated by supposedly non-diegetic elements. These elements interfere with the formerly closed system and attract notice to the underlying "principle of difference" on which the possible worlds' structure depends. Likewise, a medium can be defined as the foundation of an artistic form which is brought to attention and gains visibility solely in moments of interference. When letters collide with images, when they become illegible, when a text imitates a movie, when the filmstrip is ruptured, when noise outweighs information—the elementary fact becomes apparent that every perception needs mediation and that no medium whatsoever functions without interference. It is this interference with the fictional status of narratives, the factual status of lives and the independently operating medium that produces apertures through which alternative ontological concepts and media can enter. In this respect, Auster and Calle's collaboration does not create distinguishable entities—a novel, a conceptualist artwork—facing and complementing each other, but generates a set of permeable membranes which cross the two respective works' interior structure and also the space between them. Just as Paul Auster's borrowings from reality interfere with, and penetrate through, the porous boundaries of the imaginary, just as Sophie Calle's borrowings from the imaginary infiltrate reality (only to be re-translated into medial representations), their interstice constitutes yet another zone of indetermination crossed by *ficta*, *facta*, and *media*.

The resulting routes of *inter-ontological*, *inter-medial*, and *inter-personal* "border traffic" circumscribe an ideal terrain for questioning the post-structuralist paradigms described at the outset. While for instance Paul de Man argues that the binary opposition between fact and fiction is no longer relevant and that in any differential system it is the assertion of the space *between* the entities that matters, the interspace evoked by de Man can exist, only inasmuch as a work of art "suggests the continuing relevance of such an opposition, even if it be a problematic one" (Hutcheon 1995, 80). Accordingly, Paul Auster and Sophie Calle erect unstable constructs which reflect, and interfere with, our shaken confidence in empiricist and positivist epistemologies,

> shaken, but perhaps not yet destroyed. And this is what accounts for the skepticism rather than any real denunciation; it also accounts for the defining paradoxes of postmodern discourses. I have been arguing that postmodernism is a contradictory cultural enterprise, one that is heavily implicated in that which it seeks to contest. It uses and abuses the very structures and values it takes to task. (Hutcheon 1995, 72)

Leviathan and *Double Game* may blend "true" (auto-)biographical and "imaginary" components, but they clearly insist on their conceptual autonomy. They may arrange for the confrontation of different representational techniques, but in doing so they constantly allude to the process of mediation. This strategy of avoiding reconciliation or dialectics and retaining the unresolved contradiction (Hutcheon 1995, 72-73) problematizes the possibility of simple factuality and pure narrative. On the other hand, neither the novel nor the artist's book goes to such lengths as to abolish them altogether. Instead, their coupling—perhaps the ignition point for Auster's own examination of the "essence" of reality via media—demonstrates how late postmodern art both suffers the loss of substantiality in the strata of its representations and at the same time appropriates elements of reality (biographic data, documentary material, contingent patterns of chance) in order to enrich texts as well as images with a similar share of objectivity. Like *Leviathan* and *Double Game*, Paul Auster's and Sophie Calle's preceding and subsequent works thus seem to have the same paradoxical effect of lending contours to fictitious artistic forms as well as to the real by interfering with their boundaries.

References

Auster, Paul. 1987. *The New York trilogy* (*City of glass*). London: Faber and Faber.

—. 2001 [1992]. *Leviathan*. London: Faber and Faber.

—. 2002. *The book of illusions*. New York: Henri Holt & Co.

—. 2005. *The Brooklyn follies*. London: Faber and Faber.

—. 2007. *Travels in the scriptorium*. New York: Picador.

—. 2008. *Man in the dark*. New York: Henri Holt & Co.

Auster, Paul, Paul Karasik, and David Mazzucchelli. 2005. *City of glass, the graphic novel*. London: Faber and Faber.

Auster, Paul, and Sam Messer. 2002. *The story of my typewriter*. New York: Distributed Art Publishers.

Barone, Dennis. 1995. Introduction: Paul Auster and the postmodern American novel. In *Beyond the red notebook: Essays on Paul Auster*, ed. Dennis Barone, 1-26. Philadelphia: University of Pennsylvania Press.

Barthes, Roland. 1977. The death of the author. In *Image—music—text*, 142-148. London: Fontana.

Bronfen, Elisabeth. 2001. Gendering curiosity. The double games of Siri Hustvedt, Paul Auster and Sophie Calle. In *Bi-Textualität*.

Inszenierungen des Paares, ed. Annegret Heitmann, Sigrid Nieberle, Barbara Schaff, and Sabine Schülting, 283-302. Berlin: Erich Schmidt.

Buchholz, Linda. 2005. Wahre Geschichten—die Doppelspiele von Sophie Calle und Paul Auster. *Literaturblatt*, no. 1 (January/February), http://www.literaturblatt.de/heftarchiv/wahre-geschichten-die-doppel spiele-von-sophie-calle-und-paul-auster.html (December 7, 2009).

Calle, Sophie. 2007 [1999]. *Double game*. London: Violette Ltd.

Coppersmith, Fred. 1998. Constructing the self in Paul Auster's Leviathan. http://www.unreality.net/writings/academic/Eng436-1.pdf (January 8, 2010).

Coughlan, David. 2006. Paul Auster's City of glass: The graphic novel. *Modern Fiction Studies* 53 (4): 832-965.

Fluck, Winfried. 1997. "Nach der Postmoderne": Erscheinungsformen des amerikanischen Gegenwartsromans. In *Projekte des Romans nach der Moderne*, ed. Ulrich Schulz-Buschhaus and Karlheinz Stierle, 39-63. Munich: Fink.

González, Jesús Ángel. 2009. Happy accidents: An interview with Paul Auster. *Film/Literature Quarterly* 37 (1): 18-27.

Hutcheon, Linda. 1995. Historiographic metafiction. In *Metafiction*, ed. Mark Currie, 71-91. New York: Longman.

Jameson, Fredric. 1984. Postmodernism, or the cultural logic of late capitalism. *New Left Review* 146: 53-92.

Jannidis, Fotis, Gerhard Lauer, Matias Martinez, and Simone Winko, eds. 2000. *Texte zur Theorie der Autorschaft*. Stuttgart: Reclam.

Khimasia, Anna. 2007. Authorial turns: Sophie Calle, Paul Auster and the quest for identity. *Image [&] Narrative* 19, http://www.image andnarrative.be/autofiction/khimasia.htm (December 7, 2009).

Martin, Julie. 2000. Maria, Myself and I. *New York Times Book Review* (July 9, 2000), http://www.nytimes.com/books/00/07/09/reviews /0007 09.09martint.html (December 7, 2009).

McHale, Brian. 1987. *Postmodernist Fiction*. London, New York: Methuen.

Meurer, Ulrich. 2007. *Topographien*. Munich: Fink.

Paech, Joachim. 2000. Artwork—text—medium: Steps en route to intermediality. Paper presented at the ESF conference "Changing media in changing Europe", May 26-28, in Paris, France. http://www.uni-konstanz.de/FuF/Philo/LitWiss/MedienWiss/Texte/ intern.html (December 23, 2009).

Peacock, Jim. 2006. Carrying the burden of representation: Paul Auster's "The book of illusions". *Journal of American Studies* 40 (1): 53-69.

Rajewsky, Irina O. 2004. Intermedialität 'light'? Intermediale Bezüge und die 'bloße Thematisierung' des Altermedialen. In *Intermedium*

Literatur. Beiträge zu einer Medientheorie der Literaturwissenschaft, ed. Roger Lüdeke and Erika Greber, 27-77. Göttingen: Wallstein.
Spiegelman, Art. 2005. Picturing a glassy-eyed private I. Introduction to *City of glass, the graphic novel*, by Paul Auster, Paul Karasik, and David Mazzucchelli, i-iii. London: Faber and Faber.
Zilcosky, John. 1998. The revenge of the author: Paul Auster's challenge to theory. *Critique* 39 (3): 195-206.

Notes

[1] See the introduction to Roland Barthes' "Death of the Author" in Jannidis, et al. 2000, 181.

[2] It is, indeed, hard to detect concrete evidence for a closure of postmodernism or defining characteristics of a possible post-postmodern era. While the end of postmodernism has been postulated no later than 1986 (see Wilhelm Schmid's article on the "Return of Reality" [*Tagesspiegel*, November 6, 1998]), one could well argue that its basic "ontological" dominant still persists. As opposed to modernism's "epistemological" stance which asks about the interpretation of the world and the position of the subject in it, postmodernism deals with the general status of being and the constitution of reality (McHale 1987, 10). Thus, although these fundamental questions might nowadays be answered in a different way than during the 1960's, and *deconstruction* seems to have been replaced by *reconstruction*, contemporary literature can be interpreted in terms of what Winfried Fluck has called "postmodern realism" (see Fluck 1997, 49 and ff.). For a more comprehensive discussion of a potential persistence of postmodernism, see Meurer 2007, 21-24.

[3] For a concise discussion of the literary (as well as religious) concept of the "parable" in Auster's novels, see Peacock 2006, 61 and ff.

[4] See for example Khimasia 2007.

[5] Thus, many of the *topoi*, motifs and characters in Paul Auster's fiction can be traced back to Miguel de Cervantes whose influence is broadly discussed in many of Eduardo Urbina's publications. See *La ficción que no cesa: Paul Auster y Cervantes*. Vigo: Editorial Academia del Hispanismo, 2007; Parodias cervantinas: el Quijote en tres novelas de Paul Auster (La ciudad de cristal, El palacio de la luna y El libro de las ilusiones). In *'Calamo currente': Homenaje a Juan Bautista de Avalle Arce*, edited by Miguel Zugasti. RILCE (Universidad de Navarra) 23, No. 1, 2007. 245-56; Reading Matters: Quixotic Fiction and Subversive Discourse in Paul Auster's The Book of Illusions. In *Critical Reflections: Essays on Golden Age Spanish Literature in Honor of James A. Parr*, edited by Barbara Simerka and Amy R. Williamsen. 57-66. Lewisburg, PA: Bucknell UP, 2006.

[6] Paul Auster has co-directed and written the script for Wayne Wang's *Smoke* and *Blue in the Face*, has directed two films (*Lulu on the Bridge* and *The Inner Life of Martin Frost*) and by some means or other has been involved in various projects

from short to feature film. For a more exhaustive discussion of Auster's film work see González 2009 and also Chapter 9 in the collection at hand.

[7] In this context, Auggie's photographic project in the film *Smoke* can be seen as yet another instance of *intermedia reference*: the introduction of photographs takes place on a strictly diegetic level, while the images—as paper prints—are materially absent in the film. Nevertheless, their narrative function as "nostalgic" markers of elapsing time is accompanied by their capacity to draw the viewer's attention to the medium: cinema's basic technical disposition is photographic as well.

[8] So far, this chapter's analysis of Paul Auster's intermedial strategies has been restricted to the realm of *symbolic* intermediality. Its "conservatism" derives from a specific limitation of medial inscriptions: they all function as a mere "subject or theme on the level of narration or depiction" and do scarcely reflect on, or expose, *material* intermediality, "where the representational layer itself ... reappears constitutively in a different medium" (Paech 2000).

[9] Another of Hector Mann's "lost" films is titled *Travels in the Scriptorium*—in a peculiar way *The Book of Illusions* seems to instruct and pre-form Auster's later works.

[10] DeLillo himself declares to feel a "pleasure in the construction of sentences and the juxtaposition of words—not just how they sound or what they mean, but even what they look like" (DeLillo quoted by Vince Passaro [*New York Times Book Review*, May 19, 1991]).

[11] See Jameson 1984: Jameson's essay compares Van Gogh's eminently "historical", "material" and "modern" painting (as it is analyzed in Heidegger's *Der Ursprung des Kunstwerkes*) with Warhol's "postmodern" *Diamond Dust Shoes* which, in contrast, deny all depth and materiality.

[12] The story appears in volume II ("Strange Stories for Strange Kids") of the *Little Lit* comic book series, edited by Art Spiegelman and Françoise Mouly and published in 2001.

[13] Auster and sixteen other writers provided the lyrics for the band's album *As Smart As We Are*, published in 2004.

[14] See Spiegelman 2005, iii: "When I got to the pages that captured Peter Stillman's memorable speech to Quinn, my jaw dropped. It was an uncanny visual equivalent to Auster's description of Stillman's voice and movements ... . By insisting on a strict, regular grid of panels, Karasik located the Ur-language of comics: the grid as window, as prison door, as city block, as tic-tac-toe board; the grid as a metronome giving measure to the narrative's shifts and fits".

[15] See http://www.oneringzero.dreamhosters.com, the bands official website that includes a catalogue of "unusual instruments" used by One Ring Zero.

[16] See also Buchholz 2005. However, the discrepancies in appearance between Maria and Sophie are so strongly marked and conspicuous that they deliberately seem to point at the masquerade staged by Auster.

[17] See for example Georg Lukács's *The Historical Novel* and Hutcheon 1995, 82.

[18] Julie Martin calls them "goody-goody acts worthy of the blond bimbo on the cover of [Calle's] book", in fact Sophie herself "in a long blond wig wearing a blue

camisole demurely sitting in bed with blue-and-white sheets covered with blue bees" (Martin 2000).

[19] Elke Buchholz's article considers the project completed with the two artists having dinner at the end of Calle's stay in New York City.

CHAPTER NINE

IN SEARCH OF A THIRD DIMENSION:
PAUL AUSTER'S FILMS FROM *SMOKE*
TO *THE BOOK OF ILLUSIONS*

JESÚS ÁNGEL GONZÁLEZ

While Paul Auster's literary work has frequently been the object of scholarly research, the same cannot be said of his work as a scriptwriter and director. And yet Auster's interest in film dates back to his student years in Columbia University, when he started writing reviews for films by Jean-Luc Godard or Milos Forman in *The Columbia Daily Spectator*. Later on, during his apprentice years in Paris, he toyed with the idea of joining the *Institute des Hautes Études Cinématographiques*.[1] In fact, for a time, he hesitated between pursuing a career as a writer or a film-maker, and apparently becoming a writer was a question of personality and chance rather than a matter of choice:

> First of all, I was extremely shy. And I simply didn't know how to go about it. It seemed a lot easier to write than to make films. All I needed was a pencil and a piece of paper, whereas film-making was something I had no access to. (González 2009, 19)

He also wrote scripts for silent films, one of which was a "long, exhaustingly complex screenplay for a silent film (part Buster Keaton, part philosophical tap dance)" (Auster 2003, 173), but they have unfortunately disappeared. He even had his first contact with the film industry in Paris, because he worked for an anonymous film producer ("a well-known film producer of the old style" who "had backed good films and bad films, big films and small films, art films and trash films", Auster 2003, 203, 206). His job was to summarize a script into "seven pages of frantic, nonstop action, a bloodbath wrought in pulsing, Technicolor prose" (Auster 2003, 206) and then translate it from French into English. He even received an offer for an acting role in one of the producer's movies, for which he would have needed to take fencing and riding lessons, but he refused.[2]

In the end Auster decided to follow his literary vocation, but after his success in fiction-writing, the film industry came to call on his door again, this time with offers for cinematic versions of his novels. Philip Haas adapted *The Music of Chance* in 1993 and there were different proposals for adaptations of "The Locked Room", "City of Glass" and *Mr. Vertigo* which finally did not come through. On Dec 25, 1990 Auster published "Auggie Wren's Christmas Story" in *The New York Times*, a very unconventional Christmas story which Wayne Wang offered to direct for the big screen. Auster ended up writing the script for *Smoke* (1995), which in turn led to his role as co-director for *Blue in the Face* (1995). However, Auster didn't seem to be thoroughly convinced of the potential of films. In the interview with Annette Insdorf published with the scripts of these two films, Auster mentions his doubts:

> I also have certain problems with them. Not just with this or that particular movie, but with the movies in general, the medium itself ... The two-dimensionality, first of all. People think of movies as "real", but they're not. They're flat pictures projected against a wall, a simulacrum of reality, not the real thing. And then there's the question of the images. We tend to watch them passively, and in the end they wash right through us. We're captivated and intrigued and delighted for two hours, and then we walk out of the theater and can barely remember what we've seen. Novels are totally different. To read a book, you have to be actively involved in what the words are saying. You have to work, you have to use your imagination. And once your imagination has been fully awakened, you enter into the world of the book as if it were your own life. You smell things, you touch things, you have complex thoughts and insights, you find yourself in a three-dimensional world. (Auster 1995, 6)

Auster sees traditional film as simulacra, in Baudrillard's sense of the word (incidentally, *Simulacra and Simulation* was published in English in 1994, one year before *Smoke*'s release date): the apparently seamless way in which they represent reality masks the lack of depth both of the process and of reality itself. In actual fact, the cinematic medium, as a simulacrum (i.e. a sign with no corresponding referent), conceals reality at the same time as it pretends to be showing it to the audience. Following this idea, this chapter analyzes Auster's films as an effort to add that third dimension that films seem to lack, a way to offer "the real thing" instead of the "simulacrum of reality" that most films provide instead.

In *Smoke*, Auster's approach to that search is to let the characters speak, to give them time to show their emotions, following the example of "realistic" film directors like Renoir, Ozu or Bresson, who "allow their characters to unfold before our eyes, to exist as full-fledged human beings" (Auster 1995, 6). The characters in *Smoke*, therefore, are given enough space and time to be understood by the audience: Paul is a writer who has lost his pregnant wife and suffers from writer's block; Rashid is a black young orphan who has come across some money stolen by two thieves (Robert Goodwin and the Creeper), and who takes refuge in Paul's house; Auggie, finally, is the owner of a tobacco shop and amateur photographer who tells Paul a "true" story about how he stole his camera from a blind woman's house after pretending to be her grandson. The film constantly addresses questions of moral responsibility. Should Rashid keep the stolen money? Should Auggie have kept the camera? Should he have lied to the blind woman? And these questions are tied to other more general ethical and epistemological issues: should Paul "steal" Auggie's story and present it as true in the newspaper? Should fiction be true to reality? Should one take people's images or stories for fictional purposes? What is the moral responsibility of the artist?[3]

The moral and epistemological purpose lying behind these questions is crucial not just in *Smoke*, but in Auster's other films as well. For Auster and Wang, in fact, ethics and aesthetics were connected from the very beginning: "[the approach in *Smoke*] was a moral decision as well as an aesthetic one ... we thought we had a mission to do something human" ("Commentary" in the DVD version of the film).[4] But in the end, all the answers to the moral questions are extremely paradoxical and unconventional: stealing becomes a way of giving, because Auggie's stolen camera serves an artistic (and, arguably, moral) purpose, and the stolen money helps Auggie's and Ruby's daughter; lies become truths, because Auggie's story becomes true for the listener, just as his lies had become true for Ethel, the blind woman; facts become fictions, because Auggie's story is based on a real robbery and on "real" characters like Robert Goodwin and the Creeper; and fictions become facts, because Paul (the character)'s story and Paul (Auster)'s story are both published in a newspaper ("the paper of record", as he said in that interview, Auster 1995, 3).

Whatever the ethical paradoxes, the moral and aesthetic decision to let the characters take their time and show their personality through dialogues is consistent with the ideology of the film: Auggie's view of life is opposed to the "rat-race", the fast rhythm of the capitalistic world outside: "you've had two heart-attacks, and I'm still waiting for my first" (Auster 1995, 34), Auggie tells Vinnie. The cigar store acts as a metaphor for Park Slope, the area of Brooklyn where different races can meet and lonely disoriented characters have the time to relate to one another and establish

family-like relationships.[5] The title of the film also acts as a reminder of
this ideology: smoking and letting people smoke is a sign of tolerance,
"undogmatic behavior", as Auster says (Auster 1995, 14), and smoke
seems to represent human relationships, friendship as something intangible
but present, constantly connecting and influencing the characters.

This ideology is reinforced by a classical visual approach, reminiscent
of the studio era, which gives priority to mise-en-scène and long takes
over editing. As a result, the film has only sixty-eight scenes, unlike
typical Hollywood films, which normally have over two hundred. The
slow tempo that this approach entails is also reproduced in Auggie's
"picture project", the series of photographs that Auggie has been taking
every day from the same corner, and which acts as *mise-en-abyme* for the
whole film. At first, Paul doesn't know how to respond to it, but Auggie
tells him: "You'll never get it if you don't slow down, my friend" (Auster
1995, 44). Paul starts taking his time and appreciating the changes, until
the images painfully bring back the past when he notices the picture of his
dead wife.

Frosh and Deleyto have used Roland Barthes' theory of photography to
explain Auggie's way of capturing reality: Auggie's project is an example
of *punctum*, the arrow or revelation that goes from the photography,
affects the viewer emotionally and reveals the true nature of reality, as
opposed to *studium*, the more conventional way of photographic
representation. Whereas *studium* is superficially realistic, *punctum* is not
just a copy, but the emanation of the real thing.[6] According to Paul Frosh,
Auggie's pictures are anything but artistic:

> One of the most troubling things about Auggie's albums in *Smoke* is that
> they represent an *oeuvre* based entirely on a mechanized and automatic
> process. This process is similar to the serial repetitiveness that one finds in
> industrial production ... the same results could be gained from a computer-
> operated camera. (Frosh 1998, 332-333)

The goal may not be artistic, but, for Frosh, it is certainly realistic: "reality
reproduces its own image through the neutral agency of a mechanical
device" (Frosh 1998, 332). Auggie's only explanation is a quotation from
Macbeth ("tomorrow and tomorrow time creeps on its petty pace"), which
in the story is interpreted by its narrator ("Auggie was photographing time,
I realized, both natural time and human time", Auster 1995, 152). In the
film, however, there is no explanation, just Paul's sad reaction when he
sees the picture of his dead wife. After all, photography is as elliptic as
poetry and the use of black and white pictures stylizes the project, pushing
it away from the simulacrum of superficial realism (*studium*) into reality

itself (*punctum*). As Auster himself had said several years before in *The Art of Hunger*: "poetry is like taking still photographs, whereas prose is like filming with a movie camera" (Auster 2003, 303).

This scene is one of the few instances where the film departs from the original short story. In the story, the pictures do not affect Paul emotionally but trigger off his imagination instead: "I could imagine stories for them", says Paul (Auster 1995, 152). Thus, Auggie's picture project has an apparently different function in the original story: instead of capturing reality, the pictures become a springboard for fiction. After all, the story is told from Paul's point of view, and he, a novelist, takes the side of fiction.[7] But Auggie's "picture project" cannot be properly understood without Auggie's story at the end of the film. When Paul tells him about his writer's block, Auggie offers to give him a "true" story that he makes up using elements of the previous events (the robbery scene, the newspaper headlines, Rashid's story and Paul's beating). Although Paul is deceived at the beginning, in the end he realizes that Auggie has invented the story and gives him credit for that: "Bullshit is a real talent ... To make up a good story a person has to know how to push all the right buttons" (Auster 1995, 149).

According to Deleyto, the film shows a contradiction between two theories of representation, incarnated by Auggie's project (realistic) and the final story (fictional): "Auggie presenta un cierto compromiso con la realidad, Paul con el arte" (Deleyto 2000, 112) [Auggie is showing his commitment to reality, whereas Paul shows his commitment to art]. However, both scenes seem to show different aspects of Auggie as a creator: Auggie the photographer and apparent fact-recorder is also, and fundamentally, Auggie the story-teller and fiction-maker.

Besides, the editing process intensifies the effect of the story on the audience. In the published script, Auggie's story is interrupted by fragments of the dramatized action, so that the reader can see both Auggie's face telling the story and the images of the story being told. The final result in the film is more interesting from a metafictional point of view: while Auggie tells the story, the film just shows the faces of the story-teller and the listener, with the camera very slowly getting closer and closer as the story proceeds until, in an extreme close-up, it shows just the mouth of the story-teller, underlining the fact that words and dialogues are the core of the film, and underscoring the words "better than any off-screen music could" (Alleva 1995, 19). Interestingly enough, the countershot of that close-up is not the listener's ears, but his eyes. After all, this is a film, and even though it is a film of words and dialogues, it still is a visual show. Consequently, the film ends with words turned into images, with Paul Benjamin's story for the newspaper dramatized in black-and-white images, a brilliant counterpoint to a "movie about words" (as Wayne Wang described it). The story is also enhanced by the musical soundtrack: a song by Tom Waits with suggestions of artistic moral responsibility and absence of guilt: "and it's memories that I'm stealing/But you're innocent when you dream".[8]

Thus, to the list of moral and epistemological paradoxes mentioned before (lies and truths, stealing and giving, facts and fiction) we have to add a metafictional paradox: images become words (because the pictures taken by Auggie create stories and emotions in Paul's mind and are then transformed into words) and words become images (because Paul Benjamin's story for the newspaper is shown in images). Interestingly, Paul Benjamin's "written" story is shown in black-and-white images, like (black) written words on (white) paper, and like the black and white photographs of Auggie's project. The final story is in fact an example of the power of fiction to offer a "truer" layer of reality: the viewer is attracted towards the story-teller as a character and towards the story itself as an artifice, a fact emphasized by its visual treatment and repetition, but this artistry does not necessarily make the story less "true". The use of black and white acts as a reminder of the connections and contrasts between both hypodiegetic stories and stylizes them, pulling them away from simulated reality and bringing them paradoxically closer to a deeper essence of the Real.[9]

Auster has described his move from poetry to prose as an "opening up" process that took him from very personal poems which were like "clenched fists" to a narrative which opens itself up and involves other characters and experiences. Mark Brown has related this process to Auster's shift from novels to films and, specifically, from *Smoke* to its companion film *Blue in the Face*. Film is a collective medium by its very nature, and this is particularly true of Auster's first experience as a director. *Blue in the Face* started out with the improvisations of the actors while shooting *Smoke*, which led to Auster writing some situations and scripted scenes. The producers decided to go ahead with the experiment and the whole process ended up with the writer turning director and many situations being created collectively.[10]

This experience of communal artistic production reproduces in fact the main theme of the film: the importance of communities and relationships versus individualism, cold capitalism and globalization.[11] As we have already mentioned, Brooklyn had been offered as a model against Manhattan in *Smoke*, as shown in the very first scene of a train crossing slowly to Brooklyn. In *Blue in the Face* this borough becomes more than just a setting to represent a model of urban life. As Deleyto points out, it becomes a synthesis of the best values traditionally associated with the city (place of knowledge and communication) and the country (peace and innocence). Mark Brown identifies *Smoke* and *Blue in the Face* as practical examples of Raymond Williams' model of urban life: "Auster presents a mode of urban living, not in the dystopian mold that we've become used to … but more in the way of affirmative and positive relationships of communal support through informal social groupings; that is, family and friends" (Brown 2003, 127).

In *Blue in the Face* real Brooklyn residents read statistics and give their opinions about the city, with one of the characters emphasizing the contrast between a dehumanized Manhattan and Brooklyn ("Look, this is Brooklyn, we don't go by numbers", Auster 1995, 232) and Lou Reed making the contrast between Brooklyn and the car-dominated suburbs ("Long Island … was terrible, absolutely terrible. I mean, at least in Brooklyn you could walk around", Auster 1995, 239).

As in *Smoke*, the cigar store acts as center and metaphor for the model of urban life represented by Brooklyn. When Vinnie receives an offer to sell the cigar store, Auggie makes its importance as a place of social cohesion very clear:

> Sure, it's a dinky little nothing neighborhood store. But everybody comes in here. I mean, not just the smokers. The kids come in, the school kids, for their candy … old Mrs. McKenna comes in for the soap opera magazines … Crazy Louie for his cough drops … Frank Diaz for his *El Diario* … fat Mrs. Chen for his crossword puzzles. I mean, the whole neighborhood comes in here. It's a hangout, and it helps to keep the neighborhood together. Go twenty blocks from here, twelve-year-old kids are shooting each other for their sneakers. I mean, you close this store, and it's one more nail in the coffin. You'll be helping to kill off this neighborhood. (Auster 1995, 257)

Besides, the attempted sale of the cigar store is equated with the sale of the Brooklyn baseball team (the Dodgers), when Jackie Robinson's ghost (as mentioned before) convinces Vinnie not to sell the store. The Dodgers sale in 1958 to Los Angeles deprived Brooklyn of one of its most important elements of cohesion. "It was like a family" says one of the Brooklyn residents, and singer Lou Reed reminds us of its importance: "the Dodgers leaving Brooklyn … is a reason why some of us are imbued with a cynicism that we never recovered from" (Auster 1995, 238). Baseball as a collective sport involving people's feelings and commitment to a place is another metaphor for the kind of urban model that Auster seems to be proposing. The fact that teams can be bought and sold without taking into account people's feelings or values like loyalty and commitment (to a team, to people, to ideas) is a powerful illustration of the capitalistic society criticized by the film, a global society where money comes first and feelings last. It is a money-centered view ("Dollars and Cents", as one of the characters says) versus a humanistic view of life, sport or art ("Dollars and Sense", as shown in one of the film's intertitles).

As we can see, then, *Blue in the Face* expands and comments on the issues in *Smoke* (almost like a musical epilogue) to the point that it even explains the meaning of its title. Bob, a photographer played by independent film director Jim Jarmusch, goes to smoke his last cigarette with Auggie, and they both relate smoking to friendship, sex, and even the contrast between life and death: "a reminder of your mortality ... it reminds you that to live is also to die" (Auster 1995, 260).

Blue in the Face does not just expand the issues from *Smoke*, it also corrects them to integrate groups and opinions that were excluded in the first film, specifically racial minorities and women. Although *Smoke* promotes racial integration, as shown in the relationship between Paul and Rashid, or Auggie and Ethel,[12] it is also true that all the non-white characters play a secondary role as spectators of the two white men who are the main center of attention. The same could be said about women: in *Smoke* they are secondary characters who only appear as fans (April), objects (erotic magazines read by Rashid) or dangers to the harmonious all-male situation (Ruby). This derogatory attitude is verbalized by Auggie in the script when, quoting Rudyard Kipling, he says that "a woman is just a woman, but a cigar is a smoke" (Auster 1995, 23).

Apparently Auster was aware of these exclusions, because *Blue in the Face* gives these groups a voice: a black character (played by Malik Yoba, the same actor who had played the villain in *Smoke*) accuses the men at the cigar store of lacking racial identity: "You all want to be white" (Auster 1995, 238); and a woman (Sue) accuses the all-male group of excluding women and treating them unfairly ("Is that what this is about? You guys sit around here and talk this trash all day?" Auster 1995, 218), before slapping one of the characters (and the male and white writer-director, presumably) in the face.

The solutions offered by the film are various. The racial confrontation takes the form of a musical contest, with a white character singing country music and the African American answering with a rap, before the crisis is saved by a Caribbean tune in Spanish which they all sing together and which reinforces the anti-capitalistic message: "A mí me llaman el negrito ... porque el trabajo para mí es enemigo". [They call me little black man

... because work is my enemy.] Similarly, the exclusion of women is corrected with the appearance of the characters played by Roseanne Barr and Mel Gorham. Roseanne carries her TV *persona* (the strong woman who created the expression "domestic goddess" for housewives) to play Dot, who complains to her husband Vinnie of her role as a housewife and of lack of communication in their relationship ("the problem is that you never, ever, listen", Auster 1995, 272). Mel Gorham plays Auggie's Puerto Rican girlfriend (Violet) and she also complains of Auggie's lack of commitment to their relationship. Both female characters fight back and manage to turn the tables on their men: Vinnie decides to go to Las Vegas with his wife and Auggie ends up marrying Violet and having a child in the final scenes of the film ("I was passing out cigars myself ... free of charge. It was a boy. We named him Jackie", *Blue in the Face*, not in the published script).

Auggie and Violet's interracial marriage is an example of the kind of integration and tolerance that *Blue in the Face* proposes. However, the film is not as naïve as all of this may sound: if *Smoke* is about dialogue, about stories, words and dialogue as a way of solving conflicts, *Blue in the Face* is about confrontation, shouting and singing: "I talk myself blue in the face, and still it don't do no good", says Violet (Auster 1995, 226) in the words which provide the film with a title, showing that words and dialogue do not necessarily solve conflicts. If *Smoke* is about lies and stories being told, *Blue in the Face* is about truths being shouted and sung. Or, as Auster says, "The characters are embattled, highly opinionated, relentless in their anger. And yet ... the film is genuinely amusing, and one walks away from it with a feeling of great warmth" (Auster 1995, 161).

Peter Brooker has written that "the utopian moments of joyful union work ... because they qualify and are in turn qualified by the tension demonstrated elsewhere" (Brooker 2000, 111), and Auster himself has called *Blue in the Face* a "situationist comedy" (González 2009, 22) relating it both to sit-coms and to the situationist artistic movement. It is both a musical comedy and a crazy dada-like experiment, while it is also an expansion and correction of some of the moral, racial and gender issues appearing in *Smoke*.

The interest in male perception of women continues in Auster's following film, *Lulu on the Bridge* (1998), an unusual combination of thriller, fantasy and love story which continues Auster's quest for the third dimension of film. Auster himself has written that "to a large degree, the film is about how men invent women" (Auster 1998, 149), because in the script he rewrites the myths of women as the creators of evil, from classical myths like Pandora and Eve to the modernist rewriting of Lulu, trying to present a view which is not gender-biased. As one of the characters says in the film, probably stating Auster's own intention, "Who decided that Pandora is a woman? Men. That's the trouble. It's a man's story. And men—excuse the expression—don't know shit" (Auster 1998, 74-75). Therefore, Celia (played by Mira Sorvino) is a new Pandora who opens all the boxes and is not afraid to pick up the mysterious blue stone found by Izzy (Harvey Keitel); and she is also a new Eve who offers the stone to Adam/Izzy ("Oh, come on. Don't be afraid. It's the best thing. It really is. It's like nothing else", Auster 1998, 40). However, her curiosity does not bring about evil and destruction but communication, love and renewal: "You feel more alive, don't you? Yes ... more connected ... to myself ... to everything that's not me ... to you" (Auster 1998, 41).[13]

Celia is also a new Lulu, because she is an aspiring actress who plays the Lulu part in a remake of G. W. Pabst's *Die Busche der Pandora* (1929), the silent film based on Frank Wedekind's plays. In the original cut, Auster included five scenes which showed the shooting of the film-inside-film, but those scenes (scenes 46, 53, 59, 60 and 61, and most of scene 48 in the script) were cut out in the version released in cinemas, although they have been included in the American DVD of the film released in 2006 as "Deleted Scenes".

Those deleted scenes seem to be crucial in order to understand Auster's myth-rewriting intentions. Auster says that he was attracted to the original Lulu story because "Lulu is a completely amoral, infantile creature, a person without compassion" (Auster 1998, 150), who brings about death to all her lovers. But he decides to write a new Lulu story, the story of a Lulu who cares, and he provides the film-inside-the-film scenes in contrast to the "good Lulu", the Celia character. Thus, scene 46, where Lulu has casual sex with a painter named Black, comes right after Celia and Izzy's genuinely sincere love story.[14] Later on, scene 48, where Lulu complains of Peter's manipulative intentions ("He turns me into a success, and then, the more I succeed, the farther he can push me away from him. It's his way of getting rid of me", Auster 1998, 84) is followed by the scenes where Izzy, who has also helped Celia become a star, gives proof of his love. Finally, scene 53, which shows Lulu accidentally killing her lover, is followed by the scenes of Celia killing herself rather than betraying Izzy.

Apart from these "intertextual" connections between the original Lulu story and the "new Lulu", the scenes have further "intratextual" meaning, to use Carl Springer's terms. That's to say, these scenes also show the audience the hidden aspects of Celia's personality in a way similar to the clips that Celia has shown to Izzy previously. On the surface, these clips are examples of Celia's work as an actress, but they also provide the audience with insights into her personality: she plays a victim, a clown, a nun and a prostitute, which are all more or less hidden aspects of her personality. Similarly, when Celia plays Lulu we are able to perceive the complexity of Celia's character in a subliminal manner: Celia is an extremely positive character (which makes love at first sight between Izzy and her believable), but Celia as Lulu is selfish, dangerous, in command, thus acquiring "a new dimension, that of her evil side" (Springer 2001, 200).

Of course, we cannot forget that, as we find out in the end, most of the film can be interpreted as a fantasy created by Izzy, who, in the gates of death, gets a chance to live a second life and redeem himself. Seen in that light, Celia as Lulu could also be understood as a projection of Izzy's psyche, a version of the old Izzy (colder, isolated) created by Izzy himself. Carl Springer has written that the film's theme is "[Izzy] Maurer's identity crisis and his attempt at identity formation" and that "the concept of the ideal identity formation for Maurer … lies in embracing both the good and bad sides of himself as they have been projected into Celia/Lulu" (Springer 2001, 202). However, according to Auster himself, the purpose of the dream is religious or moral rather than psychological, or redemption rather than identity formation: "When [Izzy] dies at the end, he's a different man than he was at the beginning. He's managed to redeem himself in that final shot" (Auster 1998, 145). Before his accident, Izzy was a "lone wolf" (as Kalina Ivanov, the costume designer, says, Auster 1998, 168), a character unable to communicate with the others, despite his musical talent,[15] but he gets a second chance. One of the means for Izzy's redemption is reevaluation and acceptance of his good and bad sides as can be seen in the scenes with Dr. Van Horn, "an interrogating angel … the figure standing between Izzy and the gates of death" (Auster 1998, 148). Accordingly, the Lulu scenes can also be understood as part of Izzy's reevaluation process, his admission of his previous sins and mistakes.[16]

The other way for Izzy to redeem himself is unconditional love. In the end, like Auster's previous films, the moral message of *Lulu on the Bridge* is that connections between people are the only way of redemption. Both the blue stone and the bridge of the title are, like smoke itself, metaphors for connections, friendship, love and understanding. As Auster said, talking about the blue stone, "Love is magic after all, isn't it? No one understands what it is, no one can explain it. Pixie dust is as good an explanation as any other … And so is the blue stone … In the end, metaphor might be the best way of getting at the truth" (Auster 1998, 145-146).

Critics have emphasized the differences between *Lulu on the Bridge* and the *Smoke/Blue in the Face* pair, but the "realistic" approach of the latter and the "fantastic" approach of the former might be different ways of searching for that third dimension or "getting at the truth", as Auster has explained: "the magic isn't just simply a dream. It's real, and it carries all the emotions of reality ... Just because a story is told 'realistically' doesn't make it more realistic. And just because a story is told fancifully doesn't make it far-fetched" (Auster 1998, 145-146). As we can see, Auster's films are all moral tales, stories of moral responsibility where the characters need to consider the ethical implications of their acts. Izzy is forced to evaluate his past and to accept his mistakes as part of his redemption process, just as Auggie redeems his theft by art (his picture project), Rashid uses the stolen money to pay for his mistakes, Cyrus redeems himself by work, or Paul learns to accept the others and therefore recovers from his loss.[17] And, as in *Smoke*, the moral messages are as paradoxical as the nature of film itself: stealing (in this case, the briefcase and the blue stone) becomes a way of giving and sharing love (through the blue stone); and saving others (when Izzy lies to Van Horn and denies knowing Celia) is the only way of saving oneself, as Auster himself has pointed out: "You find your essence in relation to others. That's the great paradox. You don't take hold of yourself until you're willing to give it away" (Auster 1998, 147).

Both Celia and Izzy stand a trial for their love. In Izzy's case, it is Van Horn's questioning, where he risks his life by refusing to give Celia's name. In Celia's case, the trial is Van Horn's interrogation again, but also the Lulu play, which offers her an amoral role model ("She doesn't care what people think of her. That's what gives her her power. She has no pretensions. She doesn't play by the same rules as everyone else", says Celia of Lulu, Auster 1998, 65), but she chooses not to follow it. Their love survives all the tests, and they both end up sacrificing their lives for each other's sake. Right after Celia jumps from the bridge, Izzy jumps from the window risking his life to save her.[18] We cannot forget that it is Izzy's unconscious which makes Celia sacrifice her life. Izzy's process of redemption is over, and when he is ready to die for her, she dies for him.

The moral purpose and the love of paradox are not the only common features of Auster's films; they also share a metafictional interest in film and images. In *Smoke*, the photograph of Paul's wife is like an arrow which goes directly to Paul and affects him emotionally, as we have seen. *Lulu*, in turn, starts with Izzy looking at the pictures of famous actresses, among them Vanessa Redgrave, who plays Catherine Moore, the film director in the film; Louise Brooks, who played Lulu in Pabst's film; and Mira Sorvino, Celia in the film/fantasy. The whole fantasy created by Izzy is then the result of looking at these images, just like the blue stone is created by the piece of plaster coming from the ceiling when he is shot. Auster has related this scene to the power of images, not just still images, as in the first film, but images in movement, movies:

> It begins with the very first shot—when we see that wall of photographs of women's faces. All those movie stars. I'm intrigued by the fact that for most of this century images of beautiful women have been projected on screens and have fed the fantasies of men all over the world. That's probably why movie stars were invented. To feed dreams. Izzy invents a new life for himself through the medium of a picture. There's Mira Sorvino's face on the wall—and the movie begins. In a way, it duplicates what we all experience when we watch movies. We walk into a dark place and leave the world behind. We enter the realm of make-believe. (Auster 1998, 149)

This interest in showing the way film works, or in dealing with theories of representation and reception applied to film, seems to have been a big concern of Auster's in *Lulu on the Bridge*. Auster said in an interview from 1989 that, when he started writing fiction, he intended to "open up the process, to expose the plumbing" of writing (McCaffery and Gregory 1992, 14), and probably all his fiction can be explained as an expansion of this original intention. The scenes from the Lulu film inside *Lulu on the Bridge* are Auster's best attempt to date at exposing the "plumbing of cinema", the implications and complications of film-making. They were all filmed with different degrees of "metafictional transparency", from scene 46 (where the spectators can see the entire set with all the technicians making the film)[19] to scenes 59, 60 and 61, where "*Catherine [the director], the crew and the equipment are not visible. We experience what happens as unmediated action*" (Auster 1998, 115). Scene 48 is a combination of both techniques, and scene 53 is shown from the director's point of view, with her own occasional reaction shots. "*The scene feels more like theater than film, and the artificiality of the environment is felt throughout*" (Auster 1998, 99). The effect of these different presentations is double: it underlines the technical complexity, the fact that film is a collective creation where many specialist workers are needed, but it also emphasizes the artificiality of the stories being told, calling the viewer's attention to the stories themselves (both the Lulu story and the Celia story) as aesthetic artifices.

Therefore, to the intertextual and intratextual functions of these scenes, mentioned before, we have to add a third, metafictional function. Auster has explained that he decided to eliminate these scenes because in the first screenings "people got confused, it just diluted the film, rather than make it more interesting" (González 2009, 23). But, without them, all these functions have been lost, "the cuts affect the logical structure of the whole film" (Springer 2001, 202), and the references to the myths and the Lulu film have all but disappeared. Auster has said that his mistake was writing and filming the scenes. However, from the analysis of the deleted scenes it appears that he may have made a mistake, not as a scriptwriter, but as the director who decided to deprive the film of the rich subtext that the Lulu story provides.[20]

The preoccupation with the images of women created by men which lies behind *Lulu on the Bridge* may have had something to do with Auster's involvement in his last project with Wayne Wang. One of the most conspicuous frames traditionally used by men to look at women is pornography, and Wang's *The Center of the World* (2000) is a nearly pornographic film about a woman who sells her body for a weekend to a rich young man. The film was shot in digital video with amateur actors ans its main theme is the relationship between sex, money, love and power. Auster and his wife, Siri Hustvedt, wrote a screenplay based on Wang's story, but they found the result so "morally repulsive" (González 2009, 23) that they decided to take their names off the film. It is impossible to know what Auster and Hustvedt's screenplay might have been like, but the fact that the club where the female protagonist works is called *Pandora's Box* is an obvious hint at *Lulu*. Auster's interest in pornography as a demeaning act can also be seen in *The Book of Illusions*, when Hector Mann acts in pornographic shows with a mask covering his face, so that "he could go on killing himself" (Auster 2002, 177).[21]

Maybe because of Auster's decision to "expose the plumbing" of writing, practically all his novels involve at least one writer or one artist and deal with the process of artistic creation as a major or minor theme. After his experience with films, Auster decided to include a film director and discuss the process of film-making. *The Book of Illusions* (2002) deals with the search for a missing silent film director, Hector Mann, and describes some of his films in full detail. The narrator of the novel is David Zimmer, who recovers from the tragedy of losing his wife and children by searching and researching the missing Mann films. This quest ends up becoming a search for Mann himself, in which he is helped by a mysterious woman named Alma. The description of Mann's "written films", as Hal Hartley, the American film-maker and Auster's friend, has called them, takes up almost one third of the book and pushes Auster's search for the third dimension of films one step ahead.

Mr. Nobody is Hector Mann's last silent film and on the surface appears to be a silent comedy about a man who drinks a potion and becomes invisible, but, as in Ralph Ellison's *Invisible Man*, invisibility becomes a metaphor and the film becomes a "film about the anguish of selfhood" (Auster 2002, 53), as interpreted by Zimmer.[22] Like another film described in the book, *The Prop Man*, it is also a parable of Hector Mann's problems with his producers, who were actually making it impossible for audiences to see his films and turning them, in effect, invisible.[23]

The Inner Life of Martin Frost is the only talking film described in detail in the book and is the story of a writer who, alone in an isolated house, is visited by Claire, another mysterious woman like Alma. He falls in love with her, but as the story he is writing progresses, she becomes weaker and weaker until she dies. This written film shares with Auster's previous film, *Lulu on the Bridge,* the dream-like quality:

> In spite of appearances, the setting of the film was not Tierra del Sueño or the grounds of the Blue Stone Ranch. It was the inside of a man's head— and the woman who had walked into that head was not a real woman. She was a spirit, a figure born of the man's imagination, an ephemeral being sent to become his muse. (Auster 2002, 243)

Lulu on the Bridge offered a series of obscure clues to intimate the fantastic nature of what was happening to Izzy. Some of the clues were visual, like the abstract nature of the "limbo scene", and others were verbal, like the song at the beginning ("Dreams can be reality") or some hints dropped in a few dialogues ("Are you a real person … or a spirit?", Auster 1998, 45). *The Inner Life of Martin Frost*, in turn, uses some suggestive images ("a pot of boiling water, a puff of cigarette smoke, a pair of white curtains fluttering in the embrasure of a half-open window. Steam, smoke and wind—a catalogue of formless, insubstantial things … the camera is telling us not to trust in the surfaces of things, to doubt the evidence of our own eyes", Auster 2002, 255), but it also offers some unmistakable quotations about the nature of perception from philosophers like Berkeley (*"the various sensations or ideas … cannot exist otherwise than in a mind perceiving them"*, Auster 2002, 250) and Kant (*"things which we see are not by themselves what we see"*, Auster 2002, 264).

The Inner Life of Martin Frost had started out as a project for a half-hour TV film for a German film producer. When Auster backed out of the project, he decided to use the script and turn it into one of the films directed by Hector Mann. As it appears in the book, this written film becomes much richer than in its previous isolated form, because it interacts with the main story of the novel and acts as *mise-en-abyme* of the diegetic story by means of a semantic network of analogies and contrasts. For example, Claire's death in the written film prefigures Alma's in the novel (just like *Mr. Nobody* prefigures Hector's disappearance in the main story); and if Martin Frost (whose name evokes cold) rescues Claire from the dead by burning his story, Frieda (cold again) buries Hector by burning his films in the novel, but she also kills Alma by burning Alma's own book.[24] But the films and the book have already rescued David ("In eight short days, she had brought me back from the dead", Auster 2002, 316) just like Claire had been saved by Martin and Izzy had been saved by Lulu.

Likewise, if Claire in the film is "a spirit", Alma's name (*soul* in Spanish) also suggests her spiritual, dream-like nature ("Alma had walked in and out of my life so quickly, I sometimes felt that I had only imagined her", Auster 2002, 315). As a matter of fact, all the clues about the nature of perception which suggest the unreal quality of the Martin Frost story may be applied to *The Book of Illusions*, explaining one possible meaning of its title. The entire Alma-David story, including their trip to Tierra del Sueño (Land of Dreams, another obvious hint), might have been an illusion, a fantasy created by David Zimmer himself. Consequently, David recovers part of the story with the help of a hypnotist and he admits he has "no proof, no evidence to support my case ... Who would have believed such a story if I had tried to tell it?" (Auster 2002, 316). Accordingly, the title of Zimmer's own book is *The Book of Illusions*.

Just as in *Lulu*, regardless of whether the story is real or not, the important thing is the effect of the hypodiegetic story on the characters: as we have already seen, they are all stories of rebirth and redemption and yet, paradoxically, rebirth in Auster's stories is intimately related to death (Peacock 2006, 56). When Hector comes back to life in *Mr. Nobody*, he doesn't recognize himself: "He is not looking at the old Hector. He is someone else now" (52); Izzy is saved, but he dies in the last scene of the film; Alma kills herself after having rescued David from the dead; and Claire is "horrified" after being rescued by Martin "What are we going to do? she says. Tell me, Martin, what on earth are we going to do?" (Auster 2002, 268). *The Book of Illusions* is, in fact, a book of life and death, because like Chateaubriand's *Memoirs from Beyond the Grave* (which Zimmer works on before finding Hector's films), it is both the fictional book published by a dead Zimmer "from beyond the grave" and the real book published by Auster.[25] If *The Book of Illusions* is David Zimmer's testament, *The Inner Life of Martin Frost* can also be understood as Hector

Mann's metaphoric testament: Hector decides to purge his guilt by making art which nobody will see. However, since he knows that the only way to redemption is love rather than art, in *The Inner Life of Martin Frost* he rewrites his own story and destroys art for love's sake. This is the moral lesson learned by David Zimmer, Hector Mann, Izzy Maurer or Paul in *Smoke* and one of the clues lying behind Auster's search for a third dimension: smoke-like connections, bridges between people are the only way of rebirth and redemption, even though death is always fatally waiting. This combination of humanism and nihilism is at the bottom of Paul Auster's films, and, in fact, of his entire oeuvre.[26]

These written films then have a thematic function, establishing relations of analogy, similarity and contrast between the diegetic story and the hypodiegetic ones. But these stories are obviously different from other stories-within-the-story that Auster is so fond of, because the medium described is different from the language used to narrate them, a very post-modern way to call the reader's attention towards the frames, the different languages in which the stories are told, as James Peacock has pointed out: "The very title boldly refers to itself as an aesthetic artifact. Uniquely, this book of illusions chooses to foreground a particular medium of representation and framing—cinema" (Peacock 2006, 54).

Auster had already encountered this problem of transposition between media in *Moon Palace*, where Blakelock's painting *Moonlight* is described in full detail in words and plays a fundamental role in the main character's transformation. In *The Book of Illusions*, this translation from film discourse to literary discourse becomes a *tour de force* for Auster, who tried to reproduce in words the effect of film images:[27]

> The camera holds on the door for a second or two, and then very slowly starts pushing in on the keyhole. It is a lovely shot, full of mystery and anticipation, and as the opening grows larger and larger, taking up more and more of the screen, we are able to look through into Hector's office. (Auster 2002, 42)

Auster does not just describe images, he also summarizes, describes and provides shot description using the specialized language of translation between film discourse and literary discourse: the language of scripts ("It is a jagged, efficiently orchestrated montage, combining close and medium shots in a succession of slightly off-kilter angles, varied tempos, and small visual surprises", Auster 2002, 245).

Robert Scholes defined the main difference between literary narration and cinematic narration as a contrast between visualization and conceptualization:

The reader's narrative process in dealing with printed fiction is mainly
oriented towards visualization. This is what the reader must supply for a
printed text. But in cinematic narrative the spectator must supply a more
categorical and abstract narrativity ... A well-made film requires
interpretation, while a well-made novel may only need understanding ...
[Film] must achieve some level of reflection, of conceptualization, in order
to reach its optimum condition as narrative. (Scholes 1982, 67, 72)

In order to be able to follow Auster's hybrid tales, the reader must then
go back from words to the "original" images in the process of
visualization, or image creation, that characterizes the reading of fiction.
However, we are dealing with "written films", so Auster also tries to
accomplish the conceptualization that is typical of "well-made" films by
providing the necessary interpretation of the images:

Before the body, there is the face, and before the face there is the thin
black line between Hector's nose and upper lip. A twitching filament of
anxieties, a metaphysical jump rope, a dancing thread of discombobulation,
the mustache is a seismograph of Hector's inner states, and not only does it
make you laugh, it tells you what Hector is thinking, actually allows you
into the machinery of his thoughts. (Auster 2002, 29)

He also provides the critical commentary and, very significantly, the
audience reaction: "We no longer know what to expect. The story has
shifted into another register, and one minute after laughing our heads off,
we find ourselves in the middle of a tense, melodramatic scene" (Auster
2002, 263). The combination of the description of images and sound and
the critical interpretation has, at its best, an intensely poetic effect:

The camera pans from a close-up of Martin's face to a wide shot of the
trees. The wind is blowing again, and as the leaves and branches tremble
under the assault, the sound amplifies into a pulsing, breathlike wave of
percussiveness, an airborne clamor of sighs. The shot lasts three or four
seconds longer than we think it will. (Auster 2002, 246)

Therefore, with the description of these films, Auster continues his
investigation into the differences and similarities between the visual and
literary languages which he had started in *Smoke*. Always fond of paradox,
now that he is writing a novel, Auster makes Martin the novelist burn his
story for love's sake, belittling literary language: "It's only words. Thirty-
seven pages—and nothing but words" (Auster 2002, 268); and he makes
David, the writer and film critic, praise the directness of visual language:

the mustache is the instrument of communication, and even though it speaks a language without words, its wriggles and flutters are as clear and comprehensible as a message tapped out in Morse code ... such is the code of images. The meanings are understood at a single glance. (Auster 2002, 29-30)

Just like the use of black-and-white stylized both Auggie's pictures and the final sequence in *Smoke,* pulling them away from superficial reality into a different, deeper kind of reality (*punctum* as opposed to *studium*, to continue with Barthes' terms), the absence of colour has a similar effect in *The Inner Life of Martin Frost:* "all those things had been real. Now, in the black-and-white images of Charlie Grund's camera, they had been turned into the elements of a fictional world. I was supposed to read them as shadows" (Auster 2002, 243). Silent films go a step further, because they "were like poems, like the rendering of dreams, like some intricate choreography of the spirit", due to the absence not just of color but also of words, which "relieved the images of the burden of representation" (Auster 2002, 15) and pushed the story definitely into a different world. A world that, paradoxically, is a truer rendition of reality than the "simulacrum of reality" that Auster thinks most Hollywood films are: "The paradox was that the closer the movies came to simulating reality, the worse they failed at representing the world—which is in us as much as it is around us" (Auster 2002, 14).[28]

With the description of these written films, then, it seems that Auster is providing the other side of the coin of the black-and-white sequence at the end of *Smoke.* If that film ended with words turned into silent black-and-white images (the novelist becoming film-maker), now Auster turns black-and-white images into words (the film-maker becoming novelist). Apparently, Auster has finally found a solution to the problem of the two-dimensionality of films that he complained about after *Smoke* and *Blue in the Face.* David Zimmer is talking about silent comedians, but his words can also be applied to Auster's own film work:

[they] had understood the language they were speaking ... ... we no longer had to pretend that we were looking at the real world. The flat screen was the world, and it existed in two dimensions. The third dimension was in our head. (Auster 2002, 15)

Whether writing scripts, directing films or writing about imaginary films, Auster has always tried to place that third dimension in the viewer's mind, trying to provide the necessary abstraction or conceptualization that characterizes the best films, according to Scholes. Whether his films are realistic or fantastic, in color or black-and-white, silent or with sound, comedies or tragedies, described with words or shown with images and sound, they always attempt to achieve the viewer's involvement by bringing up moral and epistemological issues and by providing the opportunity for second readings or viewings, metafictional reflections and frames, and a network of connections between different stories and characters. Thus, paradoxically, they may not simulate reality the way most Hollywood films do, but, like the *punctum* described by Barthes, they show a deeper layer of the Real: "the world—which is in us as much as it is around us".

References

Alleva, Richard. 1995. Reel people, real people. *Commonweal*, Sept 8.

Auster, Paul. 1995. *Smoke and Blue in the face: Two films by Paul Auster*. London: Faber and Faber.

—. 1998. *Lulu on the bridge: A film by Paul Auster*. New York: Henry Holt.

—. 2002. *The book of illusions*. London: Faber and Faber.

—. 2003. *Collected prose*. London: Faber and Faber.

—. 2006. *Travels in the scriptorium*. London: Faber and Faber.

Barthes, Roland. 1980. *Camera lucida*. London: Vintage.

Blue in the Face. 1995. Directed by Wayne Wang and Paul Auster. Miramax.

Baudrillard, Jean. 1994 [1981]. *Simulacra and simulation*. Michigan: Michigan University Press.

Brooker, Peter. 2000. The Brooklyn Cigar Co. as dialogic public sphere: Community and postmodernism in Paul Auster and Wayne Wang's *Smoke* and *Blue in the face*. In *Urban space and representation*, ed. Maria Balshaw and Liam Kennedy, 98-115. London: Pluto.

Brown, Mark. 2003. "We don't go by numbers": Brooklyn and baseball in the films of Paul Auster. In *The Brooklyn film: Essays in the history of filmmaking*, ed. John B. Manbeck and Robert Singer, 127-147. Jefferson, NC: McFarland.

Bruder, Schlafes. 2002. Assoziationen zu Text, Tod und (T)raum in Austers Moon Palace, Timbuktu und Lulu on the Bridge. In *"As strange as the world": Annäherungen an das Werk des Erzählers und Filmemachers Paul Auster,* ed. Andreas Lienkamp et al., 147-158. Münster: LIT Verlag.

Buñuel, Luis. 1984. *My last sigh*. New York: Vintage Books.

Deleyto, Celestino. 2000. *Smoke: Estudio crítico*. Barcelona: Paidós.

Frosh, Paul. 1998. Filling the sight by force: 'Smoke', photography and the rhetoric of immobilization. *Textual Practice* 12 (2): 323-340.

González, Jesús Ángel. 2006. The west in *Moon palace*. In *Exploring the American literary west: International perspectives*, ed. David Río *et al.* 291-302. Bilbao: Servicio Editorial de la Universidad del País Vasco.

—. 2009. Happy accidents: An interview with Paul Auster. *Literature/Film Quarterly* 37 (1): 18-27.

Hötger, Beate. 2002. *Identität im filmischen Werk von Paul Auster*. Frankfurt am Main: Peter Lang.

Irwin, Mark. 1994. Memory's escape: Inventing *The music of chance*—A conversation with Paul Auster. *Denver Quarterly* 28 (3): 111-122.

Lulu on the Bridge. 1998. Directed by Paul Auster. Miramax.

McCaffery, Larry, and Sinda Gregory. 1992. An interview with Paul Auster. *Contemporary Literature* 33 (1): 1-23.

Peacock, James. 2006. Carrying the burden of representation: Paul Auster's *The book of illusions*. *Journal of American Studies* 40 (1): 53-69.

Rimmon-Kenan, Shlomith. 1983. *Narrative fiction: Contemporary poetics*. London: Routledge.

Smoke. 1995. Directed by Wayne Wang. Script by Paul Auster. Miramax.

Scholes, Robert. 1982. *Semiotics and interpretation*. New Haven: Yale University Press.

Spiegelmann, Art, and Françoise Mouly, eds. 2001. *Little lit: Strange stories for strange kids*. New York: RAW Junior.

Springer, Carl. 2001. *Crises: The works of Paul Auster*. Frankfurt: Peter Lang.

The Center of the World. 2001. Directed by Wayne Wang. Screenplay by Ellen Benjamin Wong (pseudonym). Story by Wayne Wang & Miranda July and Paul Auster & Siri Hustvedt.

The Music of Chance. 1993. Directed by Philip Haas. Miramax.

Turner, Wilbert. 2003. Tony, Auggie, and the Mook: Race relations in cinematic Brooklyn. In *The Brooklyn film: Essays in the history of filmmaking*, ed. John B. Manbeck and Robert Singer, 71-81. Jefferson, NC: McFarland.

Williams, Raymond. 1973. *The Country and the City*. Oxford: Oxford University Press.

This chapter is based on a previous article printed in *Literature/Film Quarterly* Vol. 37:1 (2009) @ Salisbury University, Salisbury, MD.

Notes

[1] He actually got to the point of getting the application forms, but he did not finally apply. Wim Wenders, the German film-maker, was also living in Paris at the time and did try to join the IDHEC, but failed the entrance exam.

[2] Auster appeared as an actor in the adaptation of *The Music of Chance*. His role was extremely short, but he had to do about ten takes and then redo the dialogue in a studio over twenty times. After that, he has just lent his hands and his typewriter, which appear at the end of *Smoke*, typing the words "Auggie Wren's Christmas Story by Paul Benjamin".

[3] These last questions are particularly relevant in Auster's case, since most of his novels refer openly to other novels and stories, "stealing" characters, plot lines and ideas from them.

[4] This connection between ethics and aesthetics in film may remind us of a well-known statement in Bernardo Bertolucci's *Before the Revolution*: "Style is a moral fact … a 360-degree circular travelling shot [is] one of the most intensely moral … things in the history of cinema".

[5] Most of the characters (Paul, Rashid, Ruby, Ethel) have lost a relative and these emotional voids are represented visually in physical handicaps: Cyrus lacks an arm, Ruby lacks an eye, and Ethel her eyesight.

[6] Barthes's *punctum* and *studium* are similar to two of the successive phases of the image that Baudrillard proposes: "it is the reflection of a profound reality", and "it masks and denatures a profound reality" (Baudrillard 1994 [1981], 6).

[7] "Auggie Wren's Christmas Story" is much shorter than the film script, but it already contains the two main characters of the story (Paul and Auggie), the two contrasting stories-within-the-story (the picture project and Auggie's Christmas story) and the two main themes (moral responsibility and the relationships between fact and fiction). Auster's main additions in the script are the subplots about Rashid-Cyrus and Ruby-Felicity, which reinforce the two main themes and add a very Austeresque one, the father-son relationships. The narrative already contains a very strong visual element, the description of Auggie's pictures, which may have been the reason why Wayne Wang was attracted to the story in the first place.

[8] The themes of visual representation and artistic and moral responsibility may also be related to Auster's *Moon Palace*, where different visual and verbal representations of the West are presented, together with their moral consequences. Blakelock's painting *Moonlight*, central to the book, presents an idyllic vision of the West, before the white man destroyed it in search of the American Dream (González 2006).

[9] I am using Mieke Bal's term as adapted by Shlomith Rimmon-Kenan (92) and Jacques Lacan's well-known distinction between perceivable "reality" and "the Real", impossible to attain or define in words.

[10] Even though *Smoke* was directed by Wang, Auster's implication in the film was such that Wang insisted in sharing the credits with him by writing the title "A film by Wayne Wang and Paul Auster". In *Blue in the Face*'s final credits there is no reference to a script or screenplay, just "Situations created by Paul Auster and

Wayne Wang in collaboration with the actors", and later "Directed by Wayne Wang and Paul Auster". One example of collective creation was the appearance of the ghost of Jackie Robinson, the first black baseball player to play in a major league team in 1947, which was a suggestion by Harvey Weinstein, president of Miramax. And the story of crime and redemption told by Giancarlo Esposito, which beautifully complements both Auggie's Christmas story and the tale acted out by Auggie and the Mira Sorvino character at the beginning of *Blue in the Face*, was created by Esposito himself.

[11] Mark Brown says that it "self-consciously carries its mode of production in its presentation" (Brown 2003, 138).

[12] Deleyto has pointed out the visual blurring of racial barriers in Auggie's final story. By virtue of black and white photography and high-hey lighting Auggie's and Ethel's faces look grey rather than black or white in their final embrace.

[13] The stone is blue (like Blue in "Ghosts" or the blue notebook in *Oracle Night*) with a red stripe (like Auster's *The Red Notebook*, for example). It looks natural, but it also has a man-made element, maybe suggesting the idea of opposites that will be seen in Celia/Lulu later. While it provides the 'Macguffin' which moves the thriller aspect of the story (like the phone call in "City of Glass", another combination of detective story and metaphysics), it has all kinds of metaphoric associations. For example, Celia says that it reminds her of a piece of the Berlin Wall, connecting it to *The Music of Chance* and to the double function of walls to separate and to connect people.

[14] The visual treatment of the Lulu/Black scene emphasizes contrasts: it is filmed in a white set, with the characters wearing just black and white clothes.

[15] He plays with his eyes closed, as if for himself, and does not notice the chaos in the club until he is shot. A visual metaphor of people's difficulty in receiving his musical messages is the scene of Celia trying to open his CD.

[16] This theme is also reinforced visually by the scene where Izzy finds the stone: he looks at the dead man as if it were a mirror ("the man isn't a stranger so much as another version of himself", 30), which may remind the viewer of a story told in *Smoke* about a mountaineer finding his dead father—his own image—in ice.

[17] This moral purpose is also shared by some of Auster's latest novels (*The Book of Illusions, Oracle Night, Brooklyn Follies*), which are all stories of redemption and recovery from tragedies and losses.

[18] The fall is another common Auster motif, which relates the film to *Leviathan, In the Country of Last Things* or *Mr. Vertigo*.

[19] The script gives all kinds of details of the preparation of the shot: *"The entire set is visible. Film crew, equipment, adjustable walls, etc. The scene begins with an overhead shot of CATHERINE sitting in a chair and studying the monitor. She is flanked by the SCRIPT SUPERVISOR and the DIRECTOR OF PHOTOGRAPHY. As the camera sweeps past her, she leans to her left and whispers something to the D.P. The camera continues to move, taking in the SOUNDMAN, the sound cart, and the FIRST ASSISTANT DIRECTOR; then, the CAMERA OPERATOR, the prop camera, the FOCUS PULLER, the SECOND ASSISTANT CAMERAMAN (clapper),*

and the two STAGEHANDS. Close-up of the clapper. It reads: "PANDORA'S BOX. Scene 3, Take 1" (Auster 1998, 75).

[20] Two more flaws that can be attributed to Auster as director, and which may explain the popular failure of the film, are the direction of actors and the special effects for the blue stone scenes. Harvey Keitel in love is never as convincing as he was in *The Piano*, and Mira Sorvino is too naïve and even childlike. As to the blue stone scenes, the Director of Photography, Ali Sakharov, has described the economical and technical problems he encountered in shooting and treating those scenes (Auster 1998, 172), but the result is certainly disappointing. According to the script, it is supposed to be a magical moment, but probably due to bad handling of special effects, editing and acting, the jump from script to film does not work properly.

[21] As a student at Columbia University, Auster was hired to write a "dirty book" by a pornography publisher, but he says he ran out of inspiration: "There were just so many ways to describe that one thing, I discovered, and my stock of synonyms soon dried up" (Auster 2003, 184).

[22] The story is very similar to "The Day I Disappeared", a comic story written by Auster and illustrated by Jacques de Loustal. It was published in *Little Lit: Strange Stories for Strange Kids*, a comic book edited by Art Spiegelman, author of *Maus*, the only comic book to have received the Pulitzer Prize, and his wife Françoise Mouly. "The Day I Disappeared" is about a man who wakes up to find that he has become invisible but later finds a visible image of himself. He is able to look at himself from the outside ("I thought I looked sad", Spiegelman and Mouly, 57), and appreciate the beauty of the world. He ends up saving his image from drowning, wakes up the following day as visible again and goes back to work in his office: the Bureau of Missing Persons.

[23] This situation is not very different from Auster's experience with *Lulu on the Bridge*, which was never released in cinemas in the US due to wrong business decisions taken by its producers (González 2009, 23).

[24] The burning of books has all kinds of associations, from *Don Quixote* to *Fahrenheit 451*, or the Spanish writer Vázquez Montalbán's detective stories. The burning of films is associated in the novel to a quotation by Luis Buñuel in his autobiography, *My Last Sigh*: "A while later, I suggested that we burn the negative on the place du Tertre … In fact, I'd still do it today; I can imagine a huge pyre in my own little garden where all my negatives and all the copies of my films go up in flames. It wouldn't make the slightest difference" (Buñuel 1984, 284).

[25] This technique is also used by Auster in *Moon Palace* and *In the Country of Last Things*, which turn out to have been written by Marco Stanley Fogg and Anna Blume, respectively. Incidentally, David Zimmer is the friend who rescues Marco in *Moon Palace*, and, after his Alma-Hector experience, marries Anna Blume, as we find out in *Travels in the Scriptorium* (Auster 2006, 22).

[26] In an interview in 1994, Auster had already stated: "I think my work has come out of a position of intense personal despair, a very deep nihilism and hopelessness about the world … And yet, at the same time, I've wanted to express the beauty and extraordinary happiness of feeling yourself alive" (Irwin 1994, 118).

[27] "I worked hard on those passages. It was difficult to find the right approach. The thing about a film is that it never stops, you can't go back the way you can in a book, you can't read the same passage five times in a row; it's just coming at you. I had to create that kind of speed, but at the same time I needed to put in enough detail, so the reader can see the images in his head. I had to walk a tight rope of not too much, not too little, just right" (González 2009, 24).

[28] Four years after the publication of *The Book of Illusions*, Auster decided to make a real film called *The Inner Life of Martin Frost*. It was shot in Portugal, rather than in New Mexico, and photographed in colour. The first half of the actual film follows very closely the fictional film of the novel. Then it continues the Martin-Claire story looking at the relationship between writers and muses from a rather disconcerting realistic point of view. All in all, *The Inner Life of Martin Frost* (2007) has been less successful with critics and audiences than its previous rendition in *The Book of Illusions*.

CHAPTER TEN

A "PORTRAIT OF A SOUL IN RUINS": PAUL AUSTER'S *THE BOOK OF ILLUSIONS*

MARK BROWN

Paul Auster begins his 2002 novel, *The Book of Illusions*, with this epigraph:

> Man has not one and the same life. He has many lives, placed end to end, and that is the cause of his misery.

The quotation comes from the works of Francois-René de Chateaubriand (1768-1848), whose autobiography, *Memoires d'outre-tombe* (*Memories From Beyond the Grave*), represents a significant key to understanding Auster's novel and how the device of the posthumous address, which we discover at the end of the narrative, can be seen emerging in earlier texts. By invoking Chateaubriand's sentiment, Auster suggests that the characters narrated in *Illusions* live a number of lives within the one life, and that in reading these literary lives we should be sensitive to the many phases contained in them.

Auster has meditated on the nature of identity and the relationship of both the individual and the writer to the wider social and material world since the very beginning of his literary career. In 1987 he said that by writing 'The Book of Memory' (in *The Invention of Solitude*, 1989 [1982]) in the third person he had fulfilled Rimbaud's dictum of "'Je est un autre'—I is another" (Auster 1997, 277). At the same time he suggested that the capacity to become somebody else writing about himself revealed an important truth about the solitude of the writer. For Auster, being alone in his room is, paradoxically, "the moment when you are not alone anymore, when you start to feel your connection with others" (Auster 1997, 277) because writing is both a solitary practice and the thing which connects the writer to the material world. This idea is explored again and again in Auster's work through the symbolic power of the writer's notebook.

It is possible to trace a distinct development in Auster's thinking about the relationship of the individual to the world through his writing. It is also possible to see how his work has developed to accommodate the complexity of lived lives and the phases that constitute his characters' lives. The early novels explore a period of intense isolation in the lives of his central characters. A few years after *Solitude*, in the striking opening page of *Moon Palace* (1992) for example, the extravagantly named Marco Stanley Fogg—whose name suggests both a manuscript (M. S.) and the insubstantiality and indistinctness of a dream—describes how the episode he will go on to relate marks the beginning of his life (Auster 1989, 1). After his Uncle Victor's death, Fogg undergoes a near catastrophic breakdown during which he attempts to erase himself through starvation in an act of "nihilism raised to the level of an aesthetic proposition" (Auster 1989, 20). He is rescued by friends and goes on to discover his paternal origins which, of course, contributes to his sense of identity. However, the view of the reader remains limited in this novel because it concludes at the end of that adventure. The later novels—*Mr. Vertigo* (1994), *Timbuktu* (1999), *The Book of Illusions* and more recently *Oracle Night* (2004)— have, in contrast, sought a broader view able to acknowledge Uncle Victor's observation in *Moon Palace* that "[e]very man is the author of his own life … The book you are writing is not finished yet. Therefore, it's a manuscript" (Auster 1989, 7). Only death will draw the manuscript to a close, and so M. S.'s manuscript lacks a conclusion. The later novels, though, show how phases in characters' lives accumulate to form a fuller sense of a single life—each shaped by a particular location. So, it also becomes clear that, as his literary career has progressed, Auster's temporal and geographical focus has gradually expanded to encompass a greater array of places in a single book. Each phase for the characters in these later texts is associated with a place, and, crucially, the time to move on marks the end of that identity and the emergence of a new one.

The notion of the many lives in the one life, then, adds a new and subtle dimension to looking down to the bottom of himself, which prompted Auster to tell an interviewer: "what I found there was more than just myself—I found the world" (Auster 1997, 315-316). While in *Solitude* Auster as a writer finds a world inside him to write from, the central characters in *Illusions* find a number of selves out in the world, each influenced by the material conditions of place. These characters journey in search of a harmony between their inner terrain and the external terrain, constantly in search of an inner peace.

The concern with place in Auster's work is persistent and can be traced back to the early poetry of the 1970s and to his best known novel, *The New York Trilogy* (1987). In this work of three thematically linked metaphysical detective stories, the central characters attempt to establish identities for themselves through the practices of writing and the records they make in their symbolic red notebooks, and through walking. For Quinn in the first story, "City of Glass",

> New York was an inexhaustible space, a labyrinth of endless steps, and no matter how far he walked, no matter how well he came to know its neighbourhoods and streets, it always left him with the feeling of being lost. Each time he took a walk, he felt as though he were leaving himself behind, and by giving himself up to the movement of the streets, by reducing himself to a seeing eye, he was able to escape the obligation to think, and this, more than anything else, brought him a measure of peace, a salutary emptiness within. (Auster 1987, 3-4)

Quinn, then, seeks to evacuate his sense of identity by giving himself up to the motion of the New York streets. Later, we see how Quinn's "excursions through the city had taught him to understand the connectedness of inner and outer" and how "drowning himself out of himself" was a strategy for controlling despair (Auster 1987, 61). Ultimately, Quinn and the other central writer-characters are unable to re-establish a relationship between the inner terrain of identity and the outer terrain of place. The consequence for each is the threat of textual erasure from his own narrative.

In this chapter I will be exploring how the concerns of place and identity, storytelling and illusion in Auster's literature and films have undergone a process of development, which finds its fullest expression in *The Book of Illusions*, his eighth novel. In the first section of my discussion, I will trace the ways in which Auster's geographical concerns developed in his earlier work. At times these texts explore locations that contrast with the New York representations he is renowned for and it is these episodes of movement that first demonstrate how Auster's characters can be challenged by new environments. At this early stage in his career, though, the concerns of place, mobility and identity remain constrained by the temporal scope of the works. I will then trace the lives of Auster's protagonists in *Illusions*, focusing on key narrative moments for each of the two central characters to illustrate how place and identity are linked in their stories. The final section will explore the power of storytelling and its relationship to illusion in *The Book of Illusions*, suggesting that storytelling and illusion, particularly in the fictional films that inhabit the text, are a way of making sense of a series of seemingly random experiences and places, and shaping them into an identity—a process that can only be completed or concluded at the end of the manuscript. I will conclude by considering the relationship in Auster's work of the narrative structures he adopts to the various identities his characters inhabit.

Place

I want to look first at how place has shaped both Auster's writing and the lives of some of his most memorable characters. Crucially for us here, different manifestations of self advance and recede for Auster's characters according to the various circumstances of place. Mobility and movement inevitably mean the abandonment of New York City—a constant presence in the earlier novels—and the introduction of a multitude of geographical locations across Europe and the American continent. The places beyond New York City which Auster's work visits, from his own experiences described in *The Invention of Solitude* through to the events described by the narrator of *Illusions*, embrace the capital cities of Western Europe (London, Paris, Amsterdam, Dublin), the cities and prairie-lands of America's mid-west (Chicago, Kansas), the cities and countryside of the north east (Boston, Baltimore, Vermont), and the western deserts of New Mexico. Each of the places has an effect on the lives and the sense of self experienced by the characters who visit them. This discussion will focus first on Amsterdam, before considering the events which take place in Vermont, the mid-west and New Mexico in *The Book of Illusions*. By moving from place to place, we shall see how these spaces operate in *Illusions*, and examine how constructions of self shift in the move from one place to another in Auster's work.

As I have argued elsewhere,[1] it is tempting to think that the extension of geographical scale from the metropolitan to the international—from New York to Amsterdam, for example—might represent a further opening of the fist to which Auster alludes in describing his move from poetry to prose. In an interview with Larry McCaffery and Sinda Gregory in 1989, he describes the movement from short, austere and uni-vocal poems "that resembled a clenched fist" (Auster 1997, 301), to an opening out of form and tone. This move has accompanied an expansion of focus from the intensely personal poetry and early prose to the metropolitanism of the early New York fiction, while the later fiction, from *Mr Vertigo* onwards, has taken Auster's characters out into America. So why not a further opening of form and focus to accompany this further geographical extension? The simple answer is that disconnection and emptiness are the defining experiences of these new places. Distant and foreign cities, unlike

Auster's home city of New York, lack the extended social circles that some earlier characters, like M. S. Fogg in *Moon Palace*, use to feed their gregarious natures. Equally, the reality of non-metropolitan spaces is that they can be literally empty, and the opportunities for locating references for self-formation and the social relationships for establishing a coherent identity are few.

It is important, then, first to examine the relationship between place and identity in Auster's thinking. New York in the early texts is clearly an important presence and Auster employs the city once again as the setting for the films of the mid-1990s.[2] Although the representation of New York in the *Trilogy* as a place for the construction of identity is negative, it is not entirely nihilistic. The New York of the *Trilogy* contains redemptive moments of social connection which allow even the most alienated and isolated characters a chance to re-connect with the familial or social realm. In "City of Glass", Quinn forms a friendship founded on a shared love of baseball with the counterman in a neighbourhood diner. Blue, in "Ghosts", similarly finds a connection at a Brooklyn Dodgers game. The anonymous narrator in "The Locked Room", though, is the character who has the clearest choice to make: between personal destruction in Boston or his new wife, Sophie, and their children in New York City.

The experience of place in the later texts, however, becomes much more complex. Here place, unlike the crowded anonymity of New York in the earlier novels, takes on an underdetermined quality that results from these spaces feeling relatively empty. As a consequence, and in contrast to the experience of place in the earlier texts, the characters experience these places in Europe, in the west and the northeast of the USA as "unengaging" not because they might be complex and overwhelming, but because they are empty, or sterile, or socially limiting. A prime example of this social sterility comes from Auster's own experience, recounted in *The Invention of Solitude*. He spent three days wandering around Amsterdam, visiting the Anne Frank House and the Van Gogh Museum, but also getting very lost. Auster's Kafka-esque third-person narrator, A., is disorientated by the experience of the city, and is forced further and further into himself:

> Cut off from everything that was familiar to him, unable to discover even a single point of reference, he saw that his steps, by taking him nowhere, were taking him nowhere but into himself. He was wondering inside himself, and he was lost. (Auster 1989 [1982], 86-7)

A.'s sense of self is undermined by the unfamiliarity of Amsterdam, symbolised by what he sees as the irrational organisation of the city into a circular pattern of roads, canals and bridges. As a result he often finds that he has been within a few feet of his destination before turning away in the wrong direction. Eventually A. feels "that the city had been designed as a model of the underworld, based on some classical representation of the place. … And if Amsterdam was hell, … then he realized there was some point to him being lost" (Auster 1989 [1982], 86). Place in this episode is unable to provide any support for the work of identity, forcing A. into himself and on to his own internal resources. A combination of A.'s youth and his perception of the chaotic organisation of Amsterdam means that he is unable to begin a coherent Dutch episode in his life and, as a consequence, he leaves and heads back to New York.

In Auster's work the open spaces of the American west have a similar effect on his characters as Amsterdam had on his younger self. Early novels such as *Leviathan* (1992) and *Moon Palace* adopt an almost conventional quest form as their central characters leave New York and head west searching for sites of potential revelation and discovery. However, the westward journeys that Sachs, Effing, and M. S. Fogg embark upon reveal only renewed experiences of disconnection, loneliness and confusion as they either return to New York, disintegrate further (literally in Sachs' case in *Leviathan* as he is blown up by his own bomb), or their story ends in irresolution.

The Book of Illusions, my primary focus here, also traces westward journeys. Professor David Zimmer pursues the silent film actor Hector Mann to a mysterious ranch in the New Mexico desert. Hector had himself embarked upon an epic journey of self-discovery across America in the 1920s. Auster presents the constant movement of these two men as attempts to achieve some kind of inner peace. Because Hector embarks on a second film career in the desert, this time as a director, *Illusions* also meditates on the relative values inherent in the practices of the film maker and the writer. The novel itself, I will argue, stands as a testament to the power of the word in comparison with that of the moving image.

The Book of Illusions: Place and Identity

The episodes from Zimmer's life recorded in *The Book of Illusions* encompass his life as an academic committed to the study of literature and the word, the despair he experiences at the loss of his family in an air crash, his spell as a translator, and his initial conversion to the power of the image as he writes a treatise on Hector's films as a way of dealing with his sorrow. Hector's life is similarly traumatic, oscillating between fame and anonymity, notoriety and obscurity. His many lives encompass his origins as a Jewish refugee named Chaim Mandelbaum, his slapstick film career in Hollywood as Hector Mann, his travels around America as an itinerant worker under the pseudonym Herman Loesser, and his final incarnation as Hector Spelling in New Mexico. But it is as Hector—significantly employing the artifices of acting—that he achieves his most secure and persistent self. As the novel progresses, the narratives of these men overlap until, at the very end of Hector's life, he and Zimmer meet—an event which ultimately prompts the telling of their stories and the establishment of some coherence in the construction of their lives and their narratives.

Loss and travel coincide in Zimmer's life when his comfortable family and professional life in Vermont is devastated by the death of his wife and two young sons in an air crash (Auster 2002, 5-6). Because of the loneliness that this tragedy causes, Zimmer disconnects from the world, by first withdrawing from his academic life and then plunging into "a blur of alcoholic grief and self pity" (Auster 2002, 7). Auster emphasises the depth of Zimmer's loneliness by presenting his desperate attempts to hold on to the memory of his family by playing with his children's toys, touching his wife's clothes and invoking her presence by smelling her perfume "to bring her back more vividly, to evoke her presence for longer periods of time" (Auster 2002, 7-8). Zimmer recognises that he is only "half human" without the family that had constituted so much of his identity and, until he has established who he is and what he wants, he cannot begin to construct a new self (Auster 2002, 56). So far this story echoes that of the disconnected characters in some of the early novels, particularly Quinn in *The New York Trilogy*. However, Zimmer's cultural connection to Hector opens up a whole new world to him.

The writing of a book, *The Silent World of Hector Mann*, provides Zimmer with a refuge from his grief (Auster 2002, 5). The research gives a purpose to his life, requiring him to travel to see the copies of Hector's films kept in six different film archives in Europe and America. Once his research is complete, Zimmer retreats to New York to write the book because it is, he insists, the city "least likely to wear on [his] nerves" (Auster 2002, 27). But, for once, New York does not play a significant role in this Auster story.

Hector's films reveal a new lexicon for Zimmer. His earlier academic work explored "books, language, the written word" (Auster 2002, 13). Now he has become an expert on silent film and cinema as a "visual language" (Auster 2002, 14). Auster is very precise in his descriptions of the physical language of Hector's slapstick art. He describes Hector as a "talented gag-man with exceptional body control" (Auster 2002, 12), adopting two tools of physical expression—his body and his moustache. Zimmer explains to the reader that the physical comedians of this time are more compelling for him because these actors "had invented a syntax of the eye, a grammar of pure kinesis … It was thought translated into action, human will expressing itself through the human body" (Auster 2002, 15).

In order to emphasise the emotional power of the physical language of slapstick, silent films adopt many facial close-ups. In an attempt to analyse the semiotic powers of Hector's face, Zimmer embarks upon a long discourse on the communicative powers of his moustache. Hector's facial adornment, we are told, is "the link to his inner self, a metonym of urges, cogitations and mental storms" (Auster 2002, 31). In other words, the moustache is a "seismograph" of Hector's "inner states" (Auster 2002, 29). In Hector's films, his moustache becomes a "twitching filament of anxieties, a metaphysical jump rope, a dancing thread of discombobulation, … it tells what Hector is thinking, … allows you into the machinery of his thoughts" (Auster 2002, 29). As a result of these new insights Zimmer is introduced to a form of non-verbal communication that opens the possibility for reading previously un-encountered cultural forms, and develops Auster's ever present theme of language.[3]

Once the book on Hector is finished, Zimmer begins a new phase of his life. He returns to Vermont and takes on the task of translating Chateaubriand's two-volume, two-thousand-page memoir, the title of which Zimmer interprets as *Memoirs of a Dead Man* (Auster 2002, 62). Chateaubriand was an imperious figure in nineteenth-century Europe. He was, in turn, a soldier, an ambassador, a politician and a writer. By placing Chateaubriand's autobiography at the beginning and centre of his own story, Auster is to some extent exposing the mechanics of *Illusions*, and illustrating the way in which the lives of both the narrator and his subject are a series of loosely connected episodes, posthumously presented. Chateaubriand's autobiography and his many lives haunt Auster's novel to provide clues to its literary method. The lives of Chateaubriand—contained in this book-within-the-book—are projected forward to become the many lives of Hector Mann, and then once again to those of David Zimmer, each spoken in the voice of a dead man.

"Everyone thought he was dead", Zimmer begins his narrative, because in January 1929

> without saying good-bye to any of his friends or associates, without leaving behind a letter or informing anyone of his plans, he walked out of his rented house on North Orange Drive and was never seen again … it was as if Hector Mann had vanished from the face of the earth. (Auster 2002, 1)

Two key concerns arise from this quotation. One is that of source material, or perhaps we might call it inspiration. There are distinct parallels here between Hector and the silent film actress Louise Brooks. She was tracked down by legendary film critic, Kenneth Tynan, living an ordinary life forty years after quitting Hollywood at the height of her fame. In his 1979 *New Yorker* article, 'Louise Brooks: the girl in the black helmet', Tynan describes how, after catching one of her films on an obscure channel, he tracked down both Brooks' films and the woman herself. Of their first meeting he writes: "She was seventy-one years old, and until a few months earlier I had thought she was dead" (Tynan 1979). Brooks' fame was due to her distinctive jet-black helmet haircut and her role as Lulu in Pabst's 1929 silent, *Pandora's Box*. Brooks herself inhabits Auster's work of this period, in a sense, as a muse and a figure of writerly inspiration. She provides him with the inspiration for the character of Hector in *Illusions*, but, as we shall see shortly, we can also identify writerly inspiration in an episode in which a writer-character conjures the figure of a beautiful woman to be his muse. Auster returns to Louise Brooks' almost mythical story in *Lulu on the Bridge* (1998) in which, in a dream, an ageing jazz musician embarks on a passionate affair with a beautiful young actress reprising the role of Lulu. We'll return to the role of dream and illusion in this film shortly.

The other issue is one that contributes to the structural device of posthumous address. This novel consists of three temporally distinct narratives—Hector's 1930s story, Zimmer's narrative of discovery and redemption in 1988, and finally the address from Zimmer's present through which he constructs his own and Hector's lives. The voice of a man presumed dead propels Zimmer out of his state of solipsistic mourning and into the next phase of his life. What happened to Hector Mann, and how he disappeared so effectively, is explained when a woman named Alma arrives with a gun to take Zimmer to Hector. After a violent confrontation, in which Zimmer blatantly courts his own death, Alma persuades him to accompany her to Hector's Blue Stone ranch in Tierra del Sueño where he is to bear witness to the genius of Hector's secret films before they are destroyed. It is vital to note here that Alma means *soul* in Spanish, and Tierra del Sueño means *land of dreams* as these insubstantial and illusory aspects of the narrative intervene at a critical moment in Zimmer's life (Max 2002, 6). In Alma, Zimmer finds a lover and an escape from his intense solitude. He records: "[a] series of accidents had stolen my life from me and then given it back, and in the interval, in the tiny gap between those two moments, my life had become a different life" (Auster 2002, 112). Zimmer describes how he experiences "microscopic holes in the universe" through which he has been able to pass and begin to build a new sense of his place in the world (Auster 2002, 115). In a sense, by passing through this irregularity in the fabric of his own life, Zimmer is able to move from one phase of his life to the next because he has achieved some degree of self-awareness.[4] However, Zimmer has to pass through a number of phases in his life before he is able to comprehend fully Alma's role in revealing new possibilities to him, and only then is he able to begin work on the manuscript which will give form to the various phases of his life.

Hector also moves from one life-changing event to another, gradually accumulating his experiences into the life related by Zimmer. Auster employs a complex narrative structure to set out Hector's life between 1929 and the novel's present in 1988. Auster narrates Zimmer, narrating Alma, recounting Hector's life from the recollections in his journal, from which Alma plans to write Hector's biography after his death. Despite the complexity of the narrative structure, this substantial passage (of seventy-two pages) provides one of the most compelling sections of the novel.

Hector's first narrated reincarnation results from the accidental killing of his pregnant lover, Brigid O'Fallon, by his fiancée.[5] Believing his movie career to be at an end, Hector flees to Seattle. Here he shaves off his trademark moustache, and adds a workman's hat found in a public bathroom. To complete his new identity he adopts the name inside the comfortably fitting cap, Herman Loesser. This name satisfies both Auster's sense of word play and Hector's need to retain some small part of his previous self, while at the same time acknowledging his remorse for his part in Brigid's death, an act of penance that haunts each of his subsequent incarnations. While he remains Herr Mann, he is also 'Lesser' or 'Loser', and "Hector figured that he had found the name he deserved" (Auster 2002, 144, original italics). Names and naming figure frequently in Auster's narratives, and contribute to his persistent focus on language. Mann is clearly a blank signifier onto which both Auster and Hector project multiple identities and "represents the plurality, and the consequent unknowability, of 'man' himself" (Peacock 2006, 63). Zimmer, on the other hand, is a name which offers a series of interpretations. He also appears as a character in *Moon Palace*, offering Fogg sanctuary in his apartment to recover after his aesthetic experiment in starvation. Zimmer is, of course, the German word for room. The writer's room is a frequent motif in Auster's early poetry and novels, able to represent the place from which the writer writes out into the world, his connection to that world and his sanctuary from it. Zimmer too is a writer—of the book on Hector and the notional "writer" of his own narrative—and we can conclude that his writing and his room provide a refuge from his loneliness.

Because Hector is not pursued for his part in Brigid's murder, he administers his own punishment, squirming "under the stringencies imposed on himself, to make himself as uncomfortable as possible" (Auster 2002, 146). Hector works in a series of manual jobs before embarking on the next phase of his life and his most tortuous and painful test yet: to live in the same city as Brigid's family. Hector works in the O'Fallon family sports store in Spokane, where he is required to deny his own identity at every turn and thus constantly destroy another part of his former self (Auster 2002, 163-164).

Hector is forced to deny himself once again when he flees to Chicago. Here he becomes the male half of a sex act with a prostitute called Sylvia Meers, giving live performances for the wealthy of Chicago, and he discovers a way to "go on killing himself without having to finish the job … to drink his own blood … devouring his own heart" (Auster 2002, 176-177). By wearing a mask during the act, he maintains his anonymity, but in doing so he constructs himself as a blank cipher onto which the audience can project their own desires.

When Sylvia becomes aware of Hector's identity and attempts to turn it to her own financial advantage, Hector is forced to flee once again and his sense of identity becomes so unstable that he barely has any coherent residue of selfhood left. The transition from one life to another, from one sense of self to the next, is gradually evacuating Hector's humanity until finally, in Sandusky, Ohio, Auster projects the emptiness of Hector's soul onto the bleak industrial landscape of America's mid-west. Here Hector finds himself

> looking at a dreary expanse of broken-down factories and empty warehouses. Cold gray weather, a threat of snow in the air, and a mangy three-legged dog the only living creature within a hundred yards. … [H]e was gripped by a feeling of nullity … . He couldn't remember his name. Bricks and cobblestones, his breath gusting into the air in front of it, and the three-legged dog limping around the corner and vanishing from sight. It was the picture of his own death, … the portrait of a soul in ruins, and long after he … had moved on, a part of him was still there, standing on that empty street in Sandusky, Ohio, gasping for breath as his existence dribbled out of him. (Auster 2002, 192)

Despite this despairing experience, Sandusky provides Hector with his salvation because it is here that he meets a young banking heiress, Frieda Spelling, who is to become his wife and much later the writer of the letter that brings Hector and Zimmer together. They move to New Mexico where they can live anonymously in a "blank and savage" landscape (Auster 2002, 204). The natural savagery of the environment leads to the death of their three-year-old son and, using Frieda's inheritance, Hector takes up filmmaking again, this time to displace his grief. This episode marks Hector's last environment, his last new self, and his last change of name. After Chaim Mandelbaum, Hector Mann and Herman Loesser, "Hector became Hector again" (Auster 2002, 202). This time, and in a play on the arbitrary nature of naming which has characterised much of his work, Auster christens his central character Hector Spelling.

Although he had vowed never to make films again as part of his life-long penance, Hector now seeks a way to justify breaking his own promise (Auster 2002, 145). In "an act of breathtaking nihilism" he "would make movies that would never be shown to audiences", Alma tells Zimmer (Auster 2002, 207). Hector's films are out of "the commercial loop" of Hollywood, and like Auster's own films which are independently produced, they are able "to work without constraints" of conventional style and subject matter (Auster 2002, 209). And like all of Auster's work, Hector's fourteen desert films have a "fantastical element running through them, a weird kind of poetry" (Auster 2002, 208-209), which at once breaks with narrative conventions while also suggesting an important imaginary and magical dimension to everyday life.

Hector dies soon after he first meets Zimmer, who returns to Vermont having seen only one of the films. Frieda is determined to destroy all traces of Hector's life after 1929 and sets about systematically burning his films, his journals and then Alma's biography. In a tussle with Alma, Frieda falls and is killed (Auster 2002, 302-305). Alma is unable to bear the tragic loss and takes her own life, leaving Zimmer alone once again. The remainder of the book sketches in brief details of the rest of Zimmer's life, before informing the reader that, like Chateaubriand, he speaks to us from beyond the grave (Auster 2002, 318).

Hector, then, journeys from LA to the mid-West and ultimately to New Mexico before achieving a degree of stability. Zimmer has journeyed around the film archives of the US and Europe, to New York to write his book, and then across the United States with Alma. The journey each of these men enacts is, ultimately, a search for some form of inner peace from which to build a stable sense of identity. The traditional quest form, with its westward journey of discovery, proves here and elsewhere in Auster's work to be insufficient for his characters to discover themselves or achieve a wholly adequate sense of self-awareness. Although Zimmer does journey west from Vermont to New Mexico, he is unable to achieve a sense of coherence or stability as a result of that journey. Similarly, in *Moon Palace*, Fogg feels that his arrival at "the end of the continent" will resolve "some important question for [him]" (Auster 1989, 297). Instead, his arrival in California represents not the end of his journey, but the place where his "life begins" (Auster 1989, 298). The family, for the characters of *Illusions* at least, provides another potential point of equilibrium and inner peace, which when removed causes catastrophic personal disintegration. Zimmer's loneliness, remember, caused him to try to recover his family through the physical things they had owned, while it is from Hector's despair and isolation in Sandusky that Auster fashions his portrait of a soul in ruins. The family as a site of self-formation then—as experienced by Zimmer and his wife, Hector and Frieda, and (potentially) Zimmer and Alma—is shown to be fragile and provisional and its work in identity creation remains prone to disruption. Importantly though, prior to her departure from the narrative, Alma begins to cure Zimmer's psychosis, allowing him to emerge into the world without being crushed. In time this new vision allows him the clarity to set down his own story, along with Hector's.

The Book of Illusions: Identity and Storytelling

The Book of Illusions, then, can be read as a meditation on the nature of love and the family, and the power they can exert, along with mobility and movement, on the process of identity construction. But can we also read the novel as an exploration of the power of illusion and storytelling in providing narrative coherence to the incoherent fragments of Hector's and Zimmer's lives? I shall come to this question shortly, but first I want to explore the extent to which we could also read the novel as a statement of the power of the word over the image. The one film of Hector's that Zimmer was able to see at the ranch, *The Inner Life of Martin Frost*,[6] suggests a significant power for storytelling and the imagination. In this text-within-a-text the eponymous author-character creates and falls in love with a beautiful female character who becomes his muse. As the pages of the story Martin is writing under Claire's inspiration begin to run out, he realises that to keep her alive in his imagination he needs to destroy the manuscript since, once it is finished, she will fully become a fiction—a character and nothing more. This reading prompts a metafictional interpretation of the *The Book of Illusions*, in which places, characters and texts are used by Auster to illustrate and explore both the nature of the fictional text and the process of its imaginative creation. Consequently, Tierra del Sueño becomes a literal dream place and a place of escape for the troubled Martin.[7] In this land of dreams, Claire is a character created by Martin Frost to act as his fantasy woman and his muse. Equally, Alma and Hector become the imaginative creations of the author-character David Zimmer in his attempt to free himself from his own solitude. This is reinforced by the birthmark on Alma's face, as Peacock notes in a comparison with Hawthorne's story 'The Birthmark', which reminds us that characters are authored. "The 'man's fist' on Alma's face", he argues, "speaks of the self-reflexive process of artistic representation in which Auster is engaged; the hand of the author is clearly visible" on his character (Peacock 2006, 57). And of course we must remember too that Zimmer is the creation of Paul Auster, whose name appears on the cover of the book.

By interpreting the novel through its *mise-en-abyme* film text, *The Inner Life of Martin Frost*, we can open up two further debates. Firstly, Auster goes on to develop the theme of linked story worlds in his next novel, *Oracle Night*, and again in *Travels in the Scriptorium* (2006).[8] Secondly, in *Illusions* the presence of different story forms prompts us to consider how Auster is setting up a comparison between the filmic and novelistic forms. This, in turn, invites us to consider the relationship between literary structure and the representation of identity in *The Book of Illusions*. Auster's return to the novel at this point in his career, after the disappointing reception of *Lulu on the Bridge* and in contrast to the smoky fate of Hector's canon, suggests that Auster believes the word to be more enduring than the image, while—most importantly—storytelling is held in common by the literary and the filmic. Consequently, the book itself—the object the reader holds in her or his hands—stands as a testament to both the power of storytelling and the primacy of the novelistic form over the cinematic medium.

We have already seen that the comparison between *Lulu* and *Illusions* is a compelling one. The dominant and central part of Auster's rarely commented upon film is constituted by a dream or reverie, just as we can see the majority of *Illusions* as a product of Zimmer's imagination. The central sequence in *Lulu* is framed by the shooting of jazz saxophonist, Izzy Maurer, and his trip to hospital in an ambulance. This short spell of "real" time encompasses a number of days of dream-time in both New York and Dublin (one of Auster's favourite cities). The story includes a glowing stone with magical properties, and an emotional relationship upon which the artist (here a musician, but elsewhere in Auster's work often a writer) is able to reconstruct some sense of self after a catastrophic loss—here Izzy's ability to play. Izzy endures kidnapping and danger to be with the woman in his dream, Celia. She helps him to come to terms with life without music and to investigate the mystery of the stone. This dream, like Zimmer's narrative, represents an escape from corporeal reality into the loving arms of a strange and beautiful woman. The film ends, however, on a nihilistic note when Izzy dies as his ambulance passes Celia on the street in New York: it is clear that the things he sought in his dream are intangible and ephemeral.

The projection of the image and the audience's desires onto the screen make film an ideal medium to explore the nature of illusion. In *The Book of Illusions*, both Zimmer and Hector use film to suspend the reality of loss. The slapstick of Hector's early silents draws laughter from Zimmer for the first time in months, and triggers a release from his misery (Auster 2002, 9-10). In the 1920s film-making was able to create a "delirium" and was "exhilarating" for Hector; besides, by forcing himself to abandon the happiness of making films, Hector cruelly punishes himself for his part in Brigid's death (Auster 2002, 147). By later returning to film-making at the Blue Stone Ranch—itself a reference to an illusion—after the death of his son, Hector rescues his marriage and saves himself from a mental disintegration similar to Zimmer's at the start of the novel. *The Inner Life of Martin Frost* demonstrates that film can present the inside of a man's head—the space of dream and illusion. In his imagination, Martin Frost conjures the image and person of Claire to appear in Tierra del Sueño (which is, of course, the land of dreams). Like Celia in *Lulu*, Claire is able to break Martin's solitude and provide focus for his work in the guise of what Auster describes as "a spirit, a figure born of the man's imagination, an ephemeral being sent to become his muse" (Auster 2002, 243). But to keep Claire alive, Martin Frost must destroy his work. The role that the insubstantial person of Claire plays in Frost's survival exemplifies how, in Auster's later work, the powerful forces of dream, imagination, illusion and, ultimately, storytelling are invoked.

Hector's lives, like the films he made in the desert, also have an underlying unresolved harmony which emerges, not from any fundamental origin or identity, but from an act of illusion and from his most vigorous incarnation: that of Hector Mann, actor. Chaim Mandelbaum is a character born in transition (on an immigrant boat from Holland), but he gains a conditional stability as Hector. When each disaster strikes, Hector moves on to a new self, each time retaining the persona of actor. In Spokane he is a salesman using the sporting goods as props, in Chicago he becomes an anonymous sexual spectacle for the audience to project their fantasies on to, and in the desert he becomes the consummate film-maker. But film and acting are themselves illusion and artifice. Ultimately, where harmonies do connect the phases of Hector's life and hold his identity together, they have no metaphysical basis, and are founded instead on the shifting sands of illusion and dream. Illusion—experienced or practiced in dream, film and storytelling—is the common thread which connects together the phases of these characters' lives and the places that are associated with each episode.

This brings us back to a possibility I opened up earlier: that there are interesting structural affinities between the way that Auster constructs both his narratives and the way he shapes the identity of his characters. Berge notes how "the narratives that are expressed as more coherent for the reader also approach solutions to these characters' identity crises" (Berge 2005, 118). But we can go further than this because, particularly in the later novels (*Illusions*, *Oracle Night*), Auster's texts are constructed as a series of narratives and texts-within-texts which fit inside each other like Chinese boxes. This can be seen in *Illusions* where both Chateaubriand's biography and *The Inner Life of Martin Frost* are texts-within-texts and so are secondary story worlds contained within a primary story. As we have also seen, the textual worlds presented in these contained texts offer significant clues about how we should read the novel. Brian McHale describes this narrative structure as *mise-en-abyme*, where "[s]trategies involving recursive structures—nesting or embedding, as in a set of Chinese boxes ....—have the effect of interrupting and complicating the ontological 'horizon' of the fiction, multiplying its worlds, and laying bare the process of world-construction" because the narrative worlds fall into and, crucially, resemble each other (McHale 1989, 112). Identity, similarly, takes on this quality of nested stories in Auster's work, with the phases of each character's life—each having structural similarities, each echoing the other—combining or accumulating into a coherent whole, and that coherence being achieved with the conclusion of the 'manuscript' of that life. The act of illusion is one of those structural affinities giving the lives of Auster's writer-characters form and clarity in the later novels, where disorganisation and disintegration characterised the lives of characters in the earlier texts. What we subsequently see emerging is a similarity between the structure of the stories-within-stories narratives of Auster's later novels and the lives-within-a-life of their characters. One brings about the construction of a coherent narrative, while the other posthumously shapes a series of incoherent events into a life. In *Illusions*, the text contains the nested narratives of Zimmer's life (the novel itself), Hector's life (his diary), *The Inner Life of Martin Frost* and Chateaubriand's memoir. If we then trace Hector's serial manifestations of self—his "many lives, placed end to end"—from his origins as Chaim Mandelbaum, through Hector Mann to Herman Loesser and eventually to Hector

Spelling, we can see a similar process of recursive narratives, but this time directed towards what McHale might call the process of identity-construction in fiction. As we have seen, his most stable manifestation of self is as Hector Mann, but this identity is located in the imaginary realm of acting and storytelling. These personal practices, vested in the imaginary, are key to Auster's aesthetic project, ultimately offering a bridge between the inner and outer terrains which Hector and Zimmer explore so thoroughly. Auster demonstrates through his central characters how the inclusion of the imaginary is the chance to escape the emblematic and miserable moment on the empty street in Sandusky when Hector was left "gasping for breath as his existence dribbled out of him" (Auster 2002, 192).

References

Auster, Paul. 1989 [1982]. *The invention of solitude*. London: Faber and Faber.
—. 1987. *The New York trilogy*. London: Faber and Faber.
—. 1989. *Moon palace*. London: Faber and Faber.
—. 1992. *Leviathan*. London: Faber and Faber.
—. 1994. *Mr. Vertigo*. London: Faber and Faber.
—. 1997. *The art of hunger*. London: Penguin.
—. 1999. *Timbuktu*. London: Faber and Faber.
—. 2002. *The book of illusions*. London: Faber and Faber.
—. 2004. *Oracle night*. London: Faber and Faber.
—. 2005. *The Brooklyn follies*. London: Faber and Faber.
Berge, Anne Marit K. 2005. 'The Narrated Self and Characterization: Paul Auster's Literary Personae'. *Nordic Journal of English Studies*. 41 (1): 101-120.
Blue in the face. 1995. Dir. Wayne Wang and Paul Auster.
Brown, Mark. 2007. *Paul Auster*. Manchester: Manchester University Press.
Lulu on the bridge. 1998. Dir. and Screenplay Paul Auster.
Max, D. T. 2002 'The Professor of Despair'. *New York Times*. 1st September.
McHale, Brian. 1987. *Postmodernist fiction*. London: Routledge.
Peacock, James. 2006. 'Carrying the Burden of Representation: Paul Auster's *The Book of Illusions*'. *Journal of American Studies*. 40 (1): 53-69.
Pandora's box. 1929. Dir. G W Pabst.
Smoke. 1995. Dir. Wayne Wang. Screenplay Paul Auster.

The inner life of Martin Frost. 2007. Dir. and Screenplay Paul Auster.
Tynan, Kenneth. 1979. 'Louise Brooks: the girl in the black helmet'. *New Yorker* http://www.geocities.com/debstj/tynan.html.

Notes

[1] An earlier version of parts of this discussion appeared in *Paul Auster* (Brown 2007). The author acknowledges the kind permission of Manchester University Press to reproduce these ideas here.

[2] New York City is the primary location of *The Invention of Solitude* (1982), *The New York Trilogy* (1987), *Moon Palace* (1989), *Leviathan* (1992), *Smoke* (1995), *Blue in the Face* (1995), *Oracle Night* (2004) and *The Brooklyn Follies* (2005).

[3] Language and its capacity to represent are central themes in Auster's early poetry and in *The Invention of Solitude*, as well as in the novels *The New York Trilogy*, *Moon Palace* and *Leviathan* (see Brown 2007, 12-19, 25-30, 37-49, 67-71).

[4] In a similar way, Fogg had also encountered these rents in the fabric of reality in the form of circles and holes in Blakelock's *Moonlight* painting in *Moon Palace* (Auster 1989, 141), while the Narrator in 'The Locked Room' finds a "tiny hole between self and not self" which reveals to him the power of his relationship with Sophie and leads to his reconnection with the world (Auster 1987, 232).

[5] Once again there is strong evidence that Auster is using the life of Louise Brooks as source material for his story. This time, though, the influence comes from the fictional part of her life. In *Pandora's Box*, Lulu accidentally shoots and kills her husband.

[6] This story from the book has now itself been turned into a film with screenplay and direction by Auster (2007).

[7] In *The Brooklyn Follies* (2005) Auster again proposes a place which emerges entirely from the imagination where escape and sanctuary are possible. The narrator's nephew, Tom, suggests that literature provides "non-existent worlds ... the inner refuge, ... the place a man goes to when life in the real world is no longer possible" (Auster 2005, 14-15). Later Tom proposes a utopian community called "Hotel Existence" where he, his uncle Nathan and their friend Harry can escape from the harsh realities of life (Auster 2005, 106).

[8] 'Oracle Night' is the title of a manuscript-within-a-story-within-a-novel. Writer-character Sidney Orr is trying to work out the destiny of his publisher-character in his writer's notebook which, though bought from the clearly insubstantial Paper Palace stationery store, appears to be so powerful that it can transport its user to the fictional world he is creating. "The first time I used the notebook", he tells his mentor Trause (an anagram of Auster), "Grace tells me I wasn't there anymore. ... That I disappeared" (Auster 2005, 165). In this novel, episodes from the different but concurrent narratives fall into each other, creating structural and thematic affinities which draw attention to the power of stories in Auster's aesthetic project. The nature of the exchange between textual worlds is subtly altered in *Travels in the Scriptorium* when characters, instead of falling into each other's worlds, leave

their storyworlds to visit that of their ageing creator in a mysterious room. The writer is then required to account for his actions in motivating their fates within their stories.

CHAPTER ELEVEN

IN THE KINGDOM OF SHADOWS:
PAUL AUSTER, *THE BOOK OF ILLUSIONS*
AND SILENT FILM

ALAN BILTON

Taking as my starting point Paul Auster's 2002 novel, *The Book of Illusions*, this chapter examines the relationship between Auster's fiction and the mysterious, phantasmal nature of silent film. One of the most striking characteristics of much early writing on film is its stress upon the ghostly; again and again, early commentators draw attention to the feeling that the flickering figures are mere shades, apparitions from the other side, and this chapter argues that the deathly nature of silent film is likewise central to Auster's novel, its spectral figures always glimpsed at the very moment of disappearing, paradoxically preserved at the point of vanishing forever. Just as elsewhere in Auster's fiction the act of writing always comes at a cost (a notion linked to the death of his own father), so too is silent film connected to the dialectical notions of Absence/Presence, There/Not there, and Reality/Illusion, that lie at the heart of his search for some kind of lost visionary art form—whether in terms of the buried paintings of *Moon Palace* (1989), Peter Stillman's perfect language in *The New York Trilogy* (1987), or the unseen films of Hector Mann. To this end, the chapter is structured in three parts. Part one examines the filmic sources underpinning Mann's phantom oeuvre, part two relates these to Auster's recurrent concern with material reality and shadowy disappearance, linking *The Book of Illusions* to Auster's engagement with the same themes in *Moon Palace,* whilst part three traces this concern back to the prehistory of Auster's own personal myth, and the sense of loss and absence that is, I would argue, central to his work.

I

So, who was the *real* Hector Mann? Or rather, which silent film star provided the model for the spectral clown at the centre of Auster's 2002 novel, *The Book of Illusions*? One might immediately think of Buster Keaton, whose stoical, woebegone countenance forms the dead centre of a suitably Auster-like absurdist universe, the world as a kind of metaphysical booby-trap, primed to go off at any minute.[1] After all, Auster writes of Hector's "spiritual calm in the face of adversity" (Auster 2002, 33), his unblinking attempt (akin to Keaton's stone-face gaze) to navigate his way through a world that stubbornly refuses to make sense, its substance closer to that of a "fever dream" or "hallucination" (Auster 2002, 163) than any kind of stable reality. The worlds of Keaton and Auster share a radical instability, a sense that the ground may give way at any moment. Here, walls are built to collapse, stairs to turn into trap doors, apparently sturdy buildings are in reality as flimsy as matchwood. In one of his most disconcerting and dreamlike shorts, *The Playhouse* (1921), Buster wakes up in the morning only for the walls of his bedroom to give way, the backdrop to be rudely retracted, and his bed left exposed on an eerily deserted stage; in Keaton's films, as in *The Book of Illusions,* the world is malleable and makeshift as a film set, forever in the process of being dismantled or deranged, broken apart by an army of invisible stagehands. Both Hector and Buster regard existence as a form of existential "obstacle course" (Auster 2002, 33), a spatial equation where the aim is to position oneself at the angle where one is least likely to get hurt. In *Mr Vertigo* (1994), Auster appropriates Keaton's extraordinary upbringing as part of a travelling medicine show for his central protagonist, Walt the Wonder Boy, who likewise dreams of moving to Hollywood to become a silent movie clown. Keaton's own career as much-abused child star 'The Human Mop' is echoed in Walt's physical trials at the hands of Master Yehudi, and it is these bodily travails that form the origin of his uncanny ability to levitate.[2] Indeed, in this sense, Walt's impossible agility is offered up as a kind of fictional equivalent to Keaton's own stunt work, both performers stressing the slapstick geometry of bodies propelled through space.

At the same time, however, Mann's "backpedals and dodges, his sudden torques and lunging pavenes" (Auster 2002, 33) are only one aspect of his comic persona. Auster also stresses his dapper threads and roué's moustache, a suave charm more akin to Valentino's foreign exoticism (one admirer speaks of his "smouldering magnetism, irresistible eyes, [a] heart-skipping handsome face" (Auster 2002, 87)) than Buster's melancholy totem pole.[3] The British publishers of the first edition of *The*

Book of Illusions opted for a still of Max Linder's gentleman-clown for the front cover, and it's easy to see why. Linder too played a dandyish man-about-town whose incessant skirt-chasing was constantly thwarted by the capricious nature of his world: sticky substances spilled onto his pristine suit, chairs abruptly pulled away just as he sought to make a grand entrance, his top-hat crushed by an ever-present array of oafish rivals. Like Linder, however, Hector "refuses to allow these petty frustrations to thwart his purpose or puncture his good opinion of himself" (Auster 2002, 11), his essential *shtick* that of insouciance in the face of calamity. Both men's comic personas are defined by a kind of studied nonchalance, a casual indifference wholly at odds with the tragic desperation of their actual, real lives. Like Linder, Hector's biographical trajectory unfolds as a series of tragic missteps, crises that necessitate the continuous exchange of one persona for another. Linder and his young wife attempted suicide twice, first by taking sleeping pills in Vienna in 1924, and then, successfully, in Paris the following year, this time simultaneously drinking Veronal, injecting a lethal dose of morphine and opening the veins on their arms: plainly, in such an untrustworthy world, it doesn't pay to take chances. Their daughter, Maude, went on to make a documentary of Linder's life and art, *The Man in the Silk Hat,* in 1985, a project that suggests an obvious link to Grund's biography in *The Book of Illusions.* Moreover, both Mann and Linder adopted a dazzling number of roles and invented personas throughout their lives, shedding their Jewishness (Hector's real name in the novel is Chaim Mandelbaum) along the way. Even Linder's tragic demise can be seen to echo the acts of violence in Auster's text, the murky details of Linder's suicide (and possible murder of his young wife) foreshadowing Hector's own mysterious death (where we never learn whether his wife kills him or not).

And yet, for all that, there seems to me to be a third silent film comedian who matches Hector's phantasmal silhouette even more closely. After all, whilst Linder and Keaton were enormous stars, their films preserved for posterity, Hector Mann is no more than a footnote in film history, a "late comer" (Auster 2002, 12) to the roster of silent clowns, appearing in no more than a dozen low-budget shorts just before the coming of sound. "[F]ew people seemed to know that he had ever existed" (Auster 2002, 1) notes David Zimmer, the novel's narrator and author of the sole book on Mann's career. His disappearance in 1926 (the year, of course, of *The Jazz Singer*) presages a second cinematic vanishing in the book: his films too have been lost, leaving behind only stills, plot synopsis, ghostly traces of the "extinct universe" (Auster 2002, 2) of silent film. Why then should anyone care about Hector Mann? Never granted the budget or independence to develop his persona, he flickers only briefly at the very twilight of silent slapstick, the practice itself "a dead art, a wholly defunct genre that would never be practiced again" (Auster 2002, 15). Nor did Mann seem to "add anything new to the genre" (Auster 2002, 11); rather, his persona seemed oddly miscast, "a second-rate leading man ... who had wandered onto the set of the wrong film" (Auster 2002, 32).

Enter, then, Raymond Griffith, perhaps the most mysterious, certainly least understood, of the great silent film comedians, and, I would argue, the real source material for Auster's fictional Hector Mann.[4] Film historian Kevin Brownlow characterises Griffith as a suave, silk-hatted fop, "a cross between Adolphe Menjou and Max Linder" (Brownlow 1968, 442), although, as Glenn Mitchell points out, Griffith always seemed a little too tubby and dispassionate to be a true lady-killer (Mitchell 1998, 107). Instead, just like Mann, Griffith seemed destined to play supporting roles in the bourgeois drawing-room comedies of his day, perennially cast as either a debonair bachelor or the hero's best friend, gazing on with ironical amusement at the romantic goings-on. Griffith was also, however, one of Mack Sennett's top gag men, and as such managed slowly to insinuate himself ever closer to the centre of Hollywood's slapstick universe: he began with bits of comic business in Sennett productions, then went onto small parts in romantic fripperies (usually playing a drunk or a fop or just a bemused bystander, always standing to one side of the action) before graduating to a short-lived career as leading man for Paramount. And yet even as the ostensible 'star' of his movies, there was always something strange about Griffith, something somehow misplaced, or in some ways out of joint. Walter Kerr in *The Silent Clowns* defines this displacement in terms of a "sweet, impudent detachment" (Kerr 1980, 307). Griffith never judges, never struggles, but rather observes the chaos with the same degree of interest he displays towards the lint at the bottom of his pocket. His defining characteristic, Kerr argues, is his "refusal to participate" (Kerr 1980, 300); in the Bebe Daniels vehicle, *Miss Bluebeard* (1925), for example, he steals each scene by the simple expedient of taking a nap amongst all the frantic action. Every time the heroine comes upon him, Griffith appears calmly curled up in an armchair or at the bottom of the stairwell, no more interested in the narrative drama swirling all around him than the family cat. Such benign narcolepsy also affects his surviving feature, *Hands Up!* (1926), where again his urbane hero seems constantly on the verge of abruptly dropping off. The film opens with his character receiving his military orders in a wooden shack in the process of exploding all around him, but Griffith still looks as if he is struggling to stay awake, the deafening shells no more real than the dreams inside his head (it is perhaps not entirely coincidental that one of his lost films was titled *Forty Winks*). Although *Hands Up!* is ostensibly a civil war movie with Western elements (its plot revolving around a secret Confederate gold mine), Griffith appears improbably dressed in silk hat, cloak and evening-attire: even given that his character is supposed to be under cover, his natty threads appear absurdly out of place as he crosses the desert, is taken prisoner by Indians or is pictured leaping onto the back of covered wagons. It is not so much that he appears to have dressed for the wrong film, but rather that his figure seems spliced into the wrong picture; indeed his very figure ("the habitué of drawing rooms and boudoirs", as Walter Kerr puts it (Kerr 1980, 299)) seems superimposed from another movie entirely, a continuity error or bad piece of editing, his character cut into the wrong scene at the wrong time. As Kerr notes, he "disturbs the landscape" (Kerr 1980, 304), like a smudge on the lens or a hair in the gate; ultimately, he appears like a guest in his own film, a tourist or disinterested bystander, a shadow just passing through.

Only half-present at the best of time, Griffith also gives the impression that he is able to appear or disappear at will. Sentenced to death by firing squad in *Hands Up!*, he leaves behind a wax replica to take his place (the card attached to it reads "Till We Meet Again"); later he inexplicably appears amongst his enemies on the back of a speeding wagon, unsure himself as to how he managed to get there. It seems as if he can be cut in or out of a scene, at will: now you see him, now you don't. In his only other surviving feature, *Paths to Paradise* (1925), a flickering torchlight catches Griffith's cheerfully unflappable jewel thief as he is first glimpsed enjoying a leisurely stroll, then pictured stumbling across a hidden safe, and finally caught tossing the comically enormously object carelessly up onto his back. When the torchlight comes back on again, he's gone.

In this sense, Griffith's comic persona seems predicated upon specifically cinematic notions of absence and vanishing, a disappearing act that Griffith turned into the basis of his short-lived movie career. Moreover, the notion of absence surrounds his character in other ways as well; even more so than his contemporaries, Griffith was a truly silent performer—a teenage illness meant that in real life he was unable to raise his voice above a whisper (he liked to tell journalists that this was a consequence of acting in a creaky old melodrama, *The Witching Hour,* where he was required to scream at the top of his voice every night; in reality his damaged vocal chords were the result of bronchial pneumonia). Was this the reason why his very persona at times seems no more than a murmur or trace? Certainly this hoarseness effectively sealed his fate with the coming of sound; after a couple of experiments with amplifying his vocal range, Griffith was forced to retire from the screen, his last melancholy appearance as a dying French soldier, rendered mute by a bullet wound, in *All Quiet on the Western Front* (1930).[5] As critics from Siegfried Kracaeur to Walter Kerr have pointed out, the absence of sound in early film (accompanied by its slightly faster than natural shooting speed) serves to "*dematerialise* silent film" (Kerr 1980, 35): bodies fall but make no thud, automobiles crash into the sea only to soundlessly sink, and ear-splitting explosions are reduced to no more than mute plumes of smoke. Silence robs matter of gravity and weight, creating what might be termed an unnatural lightness of being: blows land but no longer hurt, dynamite refuses to deafen, bodies themselves seem more insubstantial, less earthbound. The absence of sound is thus central to the phantasmal quality of silent film, and Griffith in his black and white tails, hovering at the very edge of the frame, is a particularly spectral example.

But Griffith's films are phantasmal in another important respect too: almost none of them survive. For a long time it was believed that only *Hands Up!* and a mutilated version of *Paths to Paradise* had been saved; in recent years, however, a second feature, *You'd be Surprised!* (1926), and a few partial scenes from his last feature, *Trent's Last Case* (1929) have emerged, albeit in rather dilapidated prints. Such a fate is not entirely unusual—it is estimated that only fifteen percent of silent films have been saved from the void—but it does render Griffith's disappearing act even more total. After all, unlike, say, Keaton or Chaplin, with Griffith we are left with merely a ghostly trace: misplaced stills, posters for features long gone, reviews and plot descriptions of movies that will never be seen again. In his persona, career and soundlessness, no other silent actor embodies the notion of absence as keenly as Raymond Griffith, a ghost of a star, a moustache floating in the half-light, a displaced dandy glimpsed only briefly in the shadows. And it is this key concept of absence (film as a "void", "a nothingness", a "haunted sphere" (Auster 2002, 45)), which is central to Auster's own silent movie text.

II

Notions of loss, absence and mourning haunt Auster's fiction, his perforated novels riddled with missing persons, mysterious voids and vanished works of art. Amongst the concrete sidewalks and vast desert spaces of Auster's work, gaps and fissures threaten to open up at any time: "I had slipped through a hole in the world", writes the unnamed narrator of *The Locked Room*, "I was falling into a place I had never seen before" (Auster 1986, 203). This vertiginous fear of the void is particularly strong in *The Book of Illusions*, which is full of holes, gulfs, cavities and lacunae of all kinds. The bullet hole in Brigid O'Fallon's left eye is terrifying not just in itself but as a kind of aperture in the very fabric of things; likewise, the hole in the desert where Hector and Dolores dispose of the body (Auster 2002, 140) suggests another, more troubling vacuity. Years later, when Hector is shot in a bank robbery, he stares down at "the hole that had appeared in his overcoat" (Auster 2002, 195) and again feels a profound dizziness. Breaches and ruptures open up in the novel like nitrate holes in an old reel of film. Even sex scenes employ the same honeycombed imagery, Auster's lovers "seeking out the holes and cavities in each other's bodies" (Auster 2002, 127). The narrator speaks of "microscopic holes in the universe" (Auster 2002, 115), the mysterious absence of things, matter either missing or somehow punctured or impaled. "The world was full of holes", Zimmer writes, "tiny apertures of meaninglessness, microscopic rifts that the mind could walk through, and once you were on the other side of one of those holes, you were free of yourself, free of your life, free of your death, free of everything that belonged to you" (Auster 2002, 109). At the close of the novel, this pinprick of otherness merges with the aperture of the projector as Hector's 'lost' film is screened; alongside the overwhelming presence of the objects and bodies on screen, Auster stresses a profound emptiness, the evacuation of materiality. Film is where one forgets one's sense of self, where one can loosen the bounds of ego-identity and instead merge with the flickering spectres on the screen. This constant swapping of personas, a radical mutability (and mobility) of identity, where one can become the hero, heroine, villain or faithful dog at will, suggests in turn Hector's constant shifting of name, role and appearance in the novel, but also suggests a more troubling sense of vacuity. One leaves one's selfhood behind for the free play of identities on the screen, but what if there is no going back (long-time Auster readers will immediately think of Quinn turning himself into the detective 'Auster', in *City of Glass*)? What if the space proves to be a black hole rather than any kind of opening? After all, the absence at the heart of the novel surrounds Hector's films themselves, lost and then found, only to sink back under the black waves of nothingness at the close of the narrative itself.

We have, of course, been here before in Auster's work, most explicitly in *Moon Palace*, a novel which possesses a number of close thematic links in terms of the visual and a paradoxical invisibility. There, as in *The Book of Illusions,* the hero's quixotic quest for lost artworks (in this case, Effing/Barber's missing desert paintings) ultimately ends in failure. *Moon Palace*'s mysterious canvases, linked to some kind of epiphanic revelation derived from the "emptiness" of desert space, are gone forever, flooded with the creation of Lake Powell, just as Hector's films go up in flames at the end of Auster's later text. In both novels, these missing artworks act as holes in the text, a fissure alternatively linked both to some kind of visionary transcendence and to a sense of utter loss, this empty space at once utopian and an awful, *terminal*, metonym for death. Moreover, in both works, the protagonist must undertake an extended initiation in how to approach these missing texts, a spiritual education predicated upon competing notions of presence and absence. In *Moon Palace,* Fogg is instructed by the now blind Effing to take long walks around New York where he must attempt to describe everything he sees as precisely and lucidly as possible. "My first attempts with Effing were dismally vague", he admits, "mere shadows flitting across a blurred background" (Auster 1989, 122). Accustomed to taking the city's sights and objects for granted, in his search for a perfectly neutral form of description Fogg is led to alter his understanding of the connection between words and things radically. "Until then, I had always had a penchant for generalizing", he admits, "for seeing the similarities between things rather than their differences. Now I was being plunged into a world of particulars, and the struggle to evoke them in words, to summon up the immediate sensual data, presented a challenge I was ill prepared for" (Auster 1989, 121). Unable to employ generic labels (a tree, a dog, a pile of trash), Fogg is forced to engage with specific, unique, wholly distinct *things*, colours, light and form. "No two things are alike", warns Effing (Auster 1989, 120), and these *things* are constantly changing (growing, crumbling, metamorphosising) too; in essence, what Fogg discovers is a sense of the overwhelming *presence* of the world, its detailed, multifarious, superabundant immediacy. As Mark Brown notes, Fogg's transformation of perception shares a great deal of similarity with Objectivist poetry, particularly with Charles Reznikoff's stress on "the primal art of seeing" (Brown 2007, 14), the need to see things as they truly are, free from generalizations or abstractions or habitual assumptions. At the same time, this sense of the concrete specificity of things also links Auster's project to the discoveries of early film, the notion that the camera captures and documents reality in a pure, similarly "over abundant" form (Trotter 2007, 4). As Fogg's mode of description becomes more and more accurate, reality suddenly reveals itself, its true, Platonic, contours perceptible to him for the very first time. Indeed, Plato's allegory of the cave—the image of humanity as prisoners staring at the flickering shadows on the walls rather than gazing at reality directly—has long been employed as an analogy for film, and in this sense

Effing's lost paintings (and the cave) can be seen to be drawing on the same source.

The second phase of Fogg's ocular education is, however, more mysterious. Effing now dispatches him to the Brooklyn Museum, where he is instructed to locate Ralph Albert Blakelock's Western landscape painting, *Moonlight*. There he is ordered to "look at the canvas for no less than an hour, ignoring everything else in the room" (Auster 1989, 135). In doing so he must both memorize the composition and "begin to enter the landscape" before him, giving himself up to the canvas as if "there were nothing else but this painting in the entire world" (Auster 1989, 135). Moreover, this spiritual exercise is to be accomplished in an aura of complete silence; whereas Fogg had earlier been required to seek out the correct words with which to describe the (almost monstrously present) physical world, here he must attempt to move beyond thought, language or any form of mimesis at all. When Fogg is finally face to face with the painting, he is immediately struck by the "perfectly round full moon in the middle of the canvas" (Auster 1989, 137), a disc that inexorably comes to resemble some form of portal or opening or hole. This absence (the polar opposite of the presence of the objects on the city street) is in turn linked with the shadowy figure of Native Americans glimpsed almost illegibly at the very left of the composition (Auster 1989, 138). The painting is no longer about what *is,* Fogg concludes, but rather what *is not*, the picture "meant to stand for everything we had lost ... a death song for a vanished world" (Auster 1989, 139). Blakelock's painting thus embodies an explicitly metaphysical sense of loss and vacuity, a vacancy positioned outside of language itself.[6] This shift from presence to absence, from materiality to what Jean-Paul Sartre would term "negation" or "nothingness" (Sartre 1992 [1946], 38)[7], is also mirrored in Effing's own lost paintings, which also evolve from an impressionistic attempt to portray the world ("the thick of things" (Auster 1989, 170), a dense, immediately tangible materiality) to a kind of unimaginable hollowness, a *tabula rasa* linked to the empty desert space itself. The paintings thus function as both a narrative gap in the text (unrecoverable, like the empty space of the cave in which they were painted) and as a trope of some kind of mysterious otherness. At the end of his quest, Fogg has to content himself with simply imagining them, the actual paintings positioned by Auster as *beyond language* (like Fanshawe's self-annulling red notebook at the close of *The Locked Room*) and therefore beyond the boundaries of the novel itself. These contradictory aesthetic impulses—to immerse oneself in the materiality of the world or to empty it out entirely—suggest a kind of structuring principle at work in Auster's universe, the syzygy of There/Not

There, which also underpins his use of film in *The Book of Illusions* in particularly striking ways.

After all, Hector Mann's career also shifts from a bodily presence (the gross materiality of slapstick comedy) to an enigmatic sense of absence and intangibility (one of Mann's lost films is suggestively titled *Report from the Anti-World*). As André Bazin (amongst others) has argued, slapstick films stress the inherently capricious nature of matter—its propensity to spill, stain, slip from one's grasp or break apart (Schickel 2006, 87). In *The Book of Illusions*, chairs suddenly splinter, wine glasses are dropped, objects or devices from locks to car boots stubbornly refuse to obey their owners. Auster terms this "the mutinous unpredictability of matter" (Auster 2002, 38), and the way in which *things* assume a malignant life of their own is one of the great subtexts of slapstick comedy, the physical world's clumsiness and crude inflexibility. However, alongside this stress on the awkward and the cumbersome—man's unerring ability to hit the banana skin or blunder over his unwieldy feet—slapstick movies also posit an impossible gracefulness, the balletic stunts and elegant pirouettes of the genre's jumping jacks. "Light-footed and nimble" (Auster 2002, 33), Mann "moves with uncommon grace and composure, never doubting that he'll soon be able to extricate himself from his predicament" (Auster 2002, 34). Whether clumsy or catlike, what defines silent film comedy is its stress on the physical, "a grammar of pure kinesis … thought translated into action, human will expressing itself through the human body" (Auster 2002, 15). In this sense, Zimmer's attempt to describe Mann's gyrations in his book, *The Silent World of Hector Mann*, is akin to Fogg's engagement with the concrete world in *Moon Palace*: both must search for the perfect word to describe bodies or things, the most apposite phrase or description, an impossible dream of perfect mimesis, the union of sign and subject. In this sense, Auster's description of a (wholly fictional but immediately believable) Mann short, *The Prop Man* (Auster 2002, 36-38) attempts to turn Mann's visual art into words, to balance physical gags with verbal puns.

Again, the links with Griffith seem inescapable. Auster writes of Hector's "sense of detachment, as if he were somehow mocking himself and congratulating himself at the same time" (Auster 2002, 35), of how Mann seems to "live in a state of ironical bemusement, at once engaged in the world and watching it from a great distance" (Auster 2002, 35). At the same time, however, Griffith's strange *lack of presence* also begins to infiltrate Zimmer's text. Unable to re-screen Mann's movies, and therefore reliant upon his inescapably sketchy memories, Zimmer describes the act of "writing about things I couldn't see anymore" as "like a hallucination"

(Auster 2002, 64), an eerie boxing with shadows. Moreover, Mann's final completed film, *Mr Nobody*, is described by Auster as an extended comic meditation on the theme of absence. After unsuspectingly drinking a potion that makes him invisible to all but the film's audience, Hector is transformed into a strange, corporeal ghost. "When he shouts in people's faces, his voice goes unheard", Zimmer notes. "He is a spectre made of flesh and blood, a man who is no longer a man … He has simply been erased" (Auster 2002, 40). Moving wraith-like through the visual world, the imperceptible Mann experiences a powerful sense of separation and banishment, his white-suited figure both there and not there on the screen. This sense of absence proves contagious: wandering the Los Angeles streets, Hector finds them curiously deserted, as if "he is the only person left in the city" (Auster 2002, 45). It is as if his symptom of nothingness has contaminated the very ground on which he walks; significantly, Auster repeats this scene later in the novel where the 'real' Hector wanders the streets of Sandburg, Ohio, sensing in the "empty landscape" a terrifying "nullity", "a picture of his own death" (Auster 2002, 192). Things become shadows, shapes flicker and vanish, chasms of darkness and light open up before him; in this context, one inescapably thinks of the mysterious intangibility of silent film, and also of Maxim Gorky's famous essay of 1896, "The Kingdom of Shadows", recording the Russian writer's first experience of the strange new invention, the Cinematograph:

> It is a world without sound, without colour. Everything there—the earth, the trees, the people, the water and the air—is dipped in monotonous grey. Grey rays of the sun across the grey sky, grey eyes in grey faces, and the leaves of the trees are ashen grey. It is not life but its shadow, it is not motion but its soundless spectre … Noiselessly, the ashen-grey foliage of the trees sways in the wind, and the grey silhouettes of the people, as though condemned to eternal silence and cruelly punished by being deprived of all the colours of life, glide noiselessly along the grey ground … Before you a life is surging, a life deprived of words and shorn of the living spectrum of colours—the grey, the soundless, the bleak and dismal life. It is terrifying to see, but it is the movement of shadows, only of shadows. Curses and ghosts, the evil spirits that have cast entire cities into eternal sleep, come to mind. (Gorky 1999 [1896], 10-11)

This terrifying afterlife is perceived by Gorky as first and foremost a kind of *lack*—the absence of sound, colour, speech—indeed, the absence of life itself, while cinema is a kind of underworld or purgatory, the "haunted sphere" (Auster 2002, 45) of Auster's book. Ultimately Zimmer, like Fogg in *Moon Palace*, moves from attempting to delineate the bodily or physical to an engagement with emptiness and negation, a shift foreshadowed by

Zimmer's previous book, "about writers who had given up writing, a meditation on silence" (Auster 2002, 14). The unwritten word (akin to *The New York Trilogy*'s description of the red notebook as a work in which "[e]ach sentence erased the sentence before it, each paragraph made the next sentence impossible" (Auster 1986, 313)), is thus replaced by the unseen film in the book, Hector's phantom movies becoming a kind of black hole at the centre of Zimmer's quest.

Presence and absence are therefore central to Zimmer's journey to the Blue Stone ranch—Mann's secretive, privately owned studio—at the end of the novel. The ranch is situated in a desert space that (as in *Moon Palace*), is both physically present (rocky, obdurate, composed of tangible, solid matter) and strangely absent: the text stresses the emptiness of the desert spaces, a "blankness" whose featureless space is akin to that of a movie screen before the projector is switched on, "like sitting in a room with the lights out and the shades drawn" (Auster 2002, 201). *Moon Palace* connects the Western landscape to the lunar surface, a lunar light traditionally seen in the Western tradition as enchanted or illusory, the moon's apparent presence (or absence) in the sky in reality a mere trick of the light; in this context, it is also almost impossible not to think of the iconic image of the man in the moon in Meliès' *Le Voyage dans la Lune* (1902). Similarly, when Zimmer finally gets to meet the aged Hector Mann, he is almost overwhelmed by the physical force of his existence, the fact that this mere shadow of a man has suddenly gained weight and presence, "that he was tangible, that he wasn't an imaginary being" (Auster 2002, 222). Hector can be touched, smelt, heard: however, within the course of the following twenty-four hours his body will be cremated, his bed stripped, and his films destroyed. With the burning of Alma's biography, no traces of Hector remain: like his cinematic persona, like Raymond Griffith's dapper ghost, he is returned to the ranks of the spectral.

Before his films disappear, their images crossed out from the world, Zimmer manages to watch one last short (*The Inner Life of Martin Frost*) and to hear Alma's oral descriptions of others. Although no longer slapstick comedies, Mann's 'lost' films are still concerned with the bodily: nudity, defecation, fornication, the primal physicality of childbirth (Auster 2002, 209) and that most basic kinetic unit of cinema, bodies in motion. By the end of the novel, however, all these things (like so much of silent film) are gone, never to be screened again. Like the brief appearance of Hector, his films' stress on what is physically present is displaced by a profound negativity, as if negation is (as Sartre would say) part of their constituent being, "non-being … a perpetual presence in us and outside of us" (Sartre, 1992 [1946], 43). Zimmer describes Mann's late films as "work whose central aim was nothingness" (Auster 2002, 279), an "ecstatic negation" (Auster 2002, 280), that is simultaneously both creation and destruction. Of Hector's art, Zimmer concludes, "it would come into being only at the moment of its annihilation—and then, as the smoke rose up into the New Mexico day, it would be gone" (Auster 2002, 280). With no proof left of their existence, no trace remaining, the films thus represent both a sense of aesthetic *possibility* (we are left to imagine them ourselves) and a synonym for death, the inevitable passing away of all things, the artist's fear that nothing will be left behind him.

But what of the film that (temporarily, at least) does remain, *The Inner Life of Martin Frost*, the only movie that Zimmer is able to see? Here, Auster runs an obvious risk of anti-climax or downright bathos: after all, the film, as described at great length in the text, cannot possibly live up to the intimations of the ineffable (that which *cannot* be put into words) associated with Mann's lost films.[8] In *Moon Palace,* Fogg never gets to see the lost paintings at the heart of the novel, but this loss is paradoxically uplifting.

> No matter how great an artist he might have been, Julian Barber's paintings could never match the ones that Thomas Effing had already given me. I had dreamed them for myself from his words, and as such they were perfect, infinite, more exact in their representation of the real than reality itself. As long as I did not open my eyes, I could go on imagining them forever. (Auster 1989, 232)

The *unseen* paintings thus continue to persist as a kind of perfect vision, the revelation of the real; *Martin Frost,* however, comes across as terribly stilted, a film about writing rather than a film about film, and as such a misjudged break with Auster's central theme. True, certain frames or images—"steam from a pot of boiling water, a puff of cigarette smoke, a pair of white curtains fluttering" (Auster 2002, 255)—suggest the motifs of absence and intangibility employed elsewhere, but the true meaning of the movie-within-the-text has less to do with Zimmer's description of its strangely flat cinematography, than with its recapitulation of one of Auster's most recurrent tropes: the notion that the act of writing can both create life and negate it. In Mann's film, the writer Frost literally brings the student, Claire, to life as the embodiment of all his masculine desires; she acts as his *anima,* his dream girl, a projection (like so many movie-stars) of his most intimate longings. However, as Frost approaches the end of his story, Claire falls ill and starts to fade: with the last full stop she will herself vanish, her life linked (like Scheherazade's) to the telling of the tale. Unwilling to lose her, Frost makes one last sacrifice: he burns his manuscript and the girl miraculously comes back to life, no longer a fictional character but a permanent, flesh and blood fixture. What are we to make of this seemingly inexplicable parable? After all, in many ways it acts as the exact opposite of the novel's main narrative: there, with the burning of Mann's films (and the cremation of his body), far from being resurrected, Hector is completely erased from the picture, his stripped bed a metaphor for his total elimination from the world. Once again, Auster's text seems balanced between reading this empty space as a metaphor for possibility (life) or negation (death), infinite potentiality (the *idea* of the films more real than the images themselves) or the eradication of all traces. As Frost types, the girl takes on weight and density, achieves a physical being; but whilst the destruction of Frost's manuscript allows Claire to live, the burning of Alma's biography serves to nullify Mann entirely.

III

These competing notions of presence and absence are also present in what one might term, depending on one's point of reference, as either Paul Auster's founding myth, or his very own Marvel Comics origin story. In 1978, Auster was, by his own admission, at an extremely low artistic and personal ebb. As he recounts in *Hand to Mouth* (1998), his marriage to Lydia Davies was disintegrating, his finances were dismal (and this with a baby to support) and even the sources of his artistic inspiration seemed to be drying up: his experimental play *Laurel and Hardy Go to Heaven* (1977) had been a disaster, his pulp novel *Squeeze Play* (1978) had earned less than a thousand dollars, and the less said about his attempt to launch his 'Action Baseball' card game at the New York Toy Fair, the better.

But then, in late December, Auster attended a rehearsal by a local, experimental dance group, where, as he wrote later, "the simple fact of watching men and women moving through space filled [him] with something close to euphoria" (Auster 1995, 132). Fired up by a sense of something indefinable, Auster spent the next month feverishly writing what would eventually become a long prose piece, *White Spaces*, an attempt, like Fogg describing the city streets or Zimmer describing Hector's silent films, to translate the physical or the bodily into words. As Mark Brown notes, *White Spaces* makes a link between "arms and legs … jumping up and down" (with obvious connections to slapstick comedy in *The Book of Illusions*) to "deserts" and "mountain ranges", the realm of the corporeal, the material real (Brown 2007, 19). The act of trans-coding the dancers' movements, the discovery of his own personal Rosetta Stone, deciphering the mysteries of the physical world, suggested to Auster a moment of profound revelation: "at any given moment I feel myself on the brink of discovering some terrible, unimagined truth" he wrote (Brown 2007, 20), a sublime opening teetering at the very edge of language. Delirious, Auster completed his piece on the 13th January 1979 and fell into a deep sleep: he was awoken by his uncle calling to tell him that his father had died some time during the night. Was this apparent coincidence the reason why his vision appeared so "terrible", awful in both senses of the word? Whilst Auster had been writing of the presence of living bodies moving physically through space, his own father had become an absence, lost forever to him, his existence vacated from the world.[9] At the same time, however, Auster also learnt that his father had left him a considerable sum of money, which would allow him to continue to write, and eventually complete both *The Invention of Solitude* (1982) and *The New York Trilogy*. "It's a terrible equation", he later admitted, "to think that my father's death saved my life" (Auster 1995, 132), but this linkage between physical bodies and immaterial ghosts, torsos in space and out-of-body delirium, presence and absence, would return to underpin much of Auster's subsequent writing, linked throughout by a recurrent sense of melancholia and loss.

Zimmer, of course, starts to write his book on Hector Mann as a means of coping with the death of his family, a grief-stricken absence that the physicality of Mann's antics is, in many ways, intended to counter. After their death, Zimmer returns to the family home where he feels an overwhelming sense of vacancy and emptiness; this was "a home that was supposed to have four people in it" (Auster 2002, 6), and as he walks from room to room, it feels as if it is occupied not by life but by a sense of unbearable loss. Zimmer responds to this sense of vacuity by trying to fill in the gaps himself, putting on his wife's clothes and make-up, playing with his kids' toys, "carrying on their little phantom lives for them by repeating the gestures they had made when they still had bodies" (Auster 2002, 8). Only clips of old films provide any measure of distraction from his grief—perhaps precisely because (as we have seen) silent film likewise embodies notions of presence and absence, a crude vitality of movement alongside a sense that these are pictures of a vanished world, messages, as it were, from the other side. Although the writing of his book slowly brings Zimmer back to life, the spectral figure of Mann is inescapably associated with death: Zimmer describes the dead genre as "like poems, like the renderings of dreams, like some intricate choreography of the spirit, and because they were dead, they probably spoke more deeply to us

now than they had to the audiences of the time" (Auster 2002, 15). The
flickering, phantasmal images, the play of shadow and mottled light, the
sense of another dimension—*the other side*—all link film to a strange kind
of cinematic afterlife, populated not by the living (no matter how much the
figures leap, fight or run) but by the long departed, a playground for
ghosts, a purgatorial pantomime.

Auster's book links silent film to Chateaubriand's *Memoirs of a Dead
Man* (1846), a memoir originally intended to be published only after the
author's death as a strange kind of intervention from beyond the grave. "I
prefer to speak from the depths of my tomb", writes Chateaubriand
(Auster 2002, 67), joining those "voices … which have something sacred
about them because they come from the sepulchre" (Auster 2002, 67). Just
as all the apparently lifelike actors and actresses of the silent screen have
now died, so too does Chateaubriand present himself as a shade straying
from the Stygian depths. Indeed, Auster makes the link between death,
film and the underworld quite clear: "I have suffered enough in this world
to be turned into a happy shadow in the next", Chateaubriand writes
(Auster 2002, 67), "a ray from Elysian Fields will throw a protective light
on these last pictures of mine", the flickering lights of the twentieth
century's Magic Lantern show merging with the spirit photography of a
nineteenth century séance. Again and again early commentators on film
drew attention to the suspicion that the flickering figures were phantoms,
revenants, apparitions from the great beyond; early Parisian newspaper
reports stressed film's uncanny ability to bring the dead back to life
("death would cease to be absolute" (Christie 1994, 111)), the camera's
capacity to save or preserve animated life. But what kind of life was this?
Mute, bodiless, the ghost of life rather than the real thing. Christian Metz
has argued that film, like a phantom limb, always signifies the absence of
something alongside its illusion of presence, which is to say, the visual
trace of that which is not (Metz 1982, 70). One might also think of this
'trace' in its Derridean sense as the 'specter' of something profoundly
anterior and unknowable, the ghost of "past norms" that cannot be
described except through their extinction, the "absence of a presence"
(Derrida 1992, 107). In this context, silent film appears particularly
insubstantial or phantasmal, the absence of sound suggesting other absences
and negations, the fact that their world of drooping moustaches, bustling
petticoats and ramshackle jalopies is itself long gone, lost to time like a
turn of the century Atlantis.[10] Paradoxically, the very presence of these
flickering shapes signifies the terrible absence of the original. In film,
notions of absence and presence become confused; figures are
mysteriously rescued from the grave and yet they are also simultaneously

erased, transformed into a different order of being, immortal yet ghostly. They still move, gambol, race from scene to scene, but (as in Gorky's essay) are condemned to a different order of existence, "as if these people have died and their shadows have been condemned to play ... for eternity" (Gorky 1999, 12).

Siegfried Kracauer writes that all slapstick comedy takes place "at the brink of an abyss" (Kracaeur 1960, xxii), that the animated vitality of the genre simultaneously banishes the idea of death (look how alive its clowns and pretty girls are!) and yet *almost against its will* inscribes this mortality within the very mechanisms of film (their white clown faces also a death mask). In his recent book *Cinema and Modernism* (2007), David Trotter stresses two competing notions of early film; its capacity to mechanically record reality in its entirety—a "super-abundance" (Trotter 2007, 4)—and its tendency to vacate the world, replacing it with flickering, transient rays of light. For Trotter, film always offers us both more and less of the world than we are immediately comfortable with, film simultaneously too much and too little. For early audience members, close-ups brought reality uncomfortably close to their faces (too much presence) but also confused audiences precisely through what had been left out of the frame, which is to say the loss of any background context (too much absence). In Trotter's fascinating study this paradigm becomes a way of understanding early film; on the one hand, the photographic image records reality in its entirety, producing a neutral optical document drawn toward the physical fabric of the world; at the same time, however, it also offers us a picture of what has now, inescapably, departed, the passage of time inscribing absence within the very frame of the image.[11] "The images [of early film] are so palpable", Trotter writes, "move in with such intensity upon the spectator not present at their creation, that they also speak of absence, of what is missing from them"—which is to say, the absence of the world they so meticulously bring back to life (Trotter 2007, 40).

From *White Spaces* to *The Book of Illusions* and beyond, Auster's work is fascinated by—even predicated upon—competing notions of presence and absence, what is there and what is not. His continued attempt to represent tangible, material, palpable reality is always linked to a sense of death: what the world would look like without us, the gaps or spaces left behind by those who have gone. Ideas of absence are inextricably conjoined with death and mourning, the space left behind forming what Trotter (by way of Sartre) defines as "a constitutive absence" (Trotter 2007, 169), the inescapable dark matter of existence. Empty rooms once occupied, seats once taken, beds once filled: moving pictures suggest both bodies in space and the spaces vacated by their parting.[12] Perhaps even more so than his other texts, *The Book of Illusions* is a death-haunted book; on virtually the final page, we learn that Zimmer has agreed for it to be published (like Chateaubriand) only after his death. The most important "hole" in the book is, of course, the grave itself, but against this void (Kracauer's "abyss") Auster continually stresses the gyrations and movements of a bodily presence. Little wonder then that silent film comedy serves his purposes so well.

References

Auster, Paul. 1982. *The invention of solitude*. London: Faber and Faber.
—. 1986. *The New York trilogy*. London: Faber and Faber.
—. 1989. *Moon palace*. London: Faber and Faber.
—. 1995. *Mr Vertigo*. London: Faber and Faber.
—. 1995.*The red notebook*. London: Faber and Faber.
—. 1998. *Hand to mouth*. London: Faber and Faber.
—. 2002. *The book of illusions*. London: Faber and Faber.
Brown, Mark. 2007. *Paul Auster*. Manchester: Manchester University Press.
Brownlow, Kevin. 1968. *The parade's gone by*. Berkeley, CA: University of California Press.
Christie, Ian. 1994. *The last machine*. London: BFI/BBC.
Derrida, Jacques. 1992. *Acts of literature*. London: Routledge.
González, Jesús Ángel. 2009. "Happy Accidents": An Interview with Paul Auster, *Literature/Film Quarterly*. 37 (1): 18-27.
Gorky, Maxim. 1999 [1896]. In The Kingdom of Shadows. In Gilbert Adair (ed.), *Movies*.10-13. London: Penguin.
Kerr, Walter. 1980. *The silent clowns*. New York: Da Capo Press.
Kracaeur, Siegfried. 1997 [1960]. *Theory of film: the redemption of physical reality*. Princeton, NJ: Princeton University Press.
Metz, Christian. 1982. *Psychoanalysis and cinema: the imaginary signifier*. London: Macmillan.
Mitchell, Glenn. 1988. *A-Z of silent film comedy*. London: Batsford.
Sartre, Jean-Paul. 1992 [1946]. *Being and nothingness*. trans. Hazel E. Barnes, New York: Washington Square Books.
Schickel, Richard (ed.). 2006. *The essential Chaplin*. Chicago: Ivan Dee.
Trotter, David, 2007. *Cinema and modernism*. Oxford: Blackwell.

Notes

[1] In an interview with Jesús Ángel González, Auster talks about writing a number of unproduced film scripts in his early twenties, "a bit in the spirit of Buster Keaton—not quite slapstick, but strange, strange stories" (González 2009, 18).

[2] Indeed, the Keaton Family act was known as the roughest in show business; Keaton Senior had handles sown onto his young son's pants so he could throw him across stage more easily. For a more detailed account of Keaton's extraordinary childhood, see Tom Dardis, *Keaton: The Man Who Wouldn't Lie Down*, New York: Proscenium Publishers, 1996.

[3] Hector's spotless white suit also suggests an unexpected kinship with Peter Stillmam Jr. in *The New York Trilogy*.

[4] Mann's surname may well have been suggested by Bertha Mann, Griffith's wife and a silent film star in her own right. Griffith is also name-checked on page ten of Auster's novel.

[5] After the end of his acting career, Griffith remained active in Hollywood, primarily as a producer first for Warner Brothers and then Twentieth Century Fox. He died in 1957, choking on his hors d'oeuvres in *The Masquer's Club* in Los Angeles: the inspiration, perhaps, for Hector's short-lived career as masked sex-worker in *The Book of Illusions*.

[6] Indeed, one might position Blakelock as another lost artist, at least in the sense that, whilst *Moonlight* was sold for a then record sum for an American painting during his lifetime, Blakelock himself received little remuneration (it was described as the most forged painting of its day) and eked out the remains of his life, abandoned and forgotten, in the Middletown State asylum.

[7] A nothingness, Sartre says, that "haunts" our "very understanding of being" (Sartre 1992 [1946], 38).

[8] Alas, and with the best will in the world, Auster's film-version of *The Inner Life of Martin Frost* (2007), only released on DVD in the UK, cannot be described as an unmitigated triumph either.

[9] Interestingly, in *The Invention of Solitude*, Auster connects his father with notions of absence, long before his actual demise. "Even before his death he had been absent", he writes, "and long ago the people closest to him had learned to accept this absence, to treat it as the fundamental quality of his being" (Auster 1982, 6).

[10] Watching old newsreels, Virginia Woolf remembers being overwhelmed by a sense of "beholding a world which has gone beneath the waves" (Trotter 2007, 165).

[11] Trotter describes this in terms of "the haptic" (from the German *hapstein,* to fasten), cinema's ability to invoke the sensory presence of the world (smells, texture, tangibility), in an illusory two-dimensional space (Trotter 2007, 28).

[12] Of film, Virginia Woolf writes: "We see life as it is when we have no part of it" (Trotter 2007, 12).

CHAPTER TWELVE

SPEAKING THE UNSPEAKABLE: AUSTER'S SEMIOTIC WORLD

FRANÇOIS HUGONNIER

> We *are* connected, we can't be isolated from one another because we all live inside of language.
>
> —Paul Auster

Starting at the brink of adulthood, Paul Auster's literary activity was inspired by "a set of questions" that have never stopped haunting him since then. When Larry McCaffery talks about the fact that Auster's books are really "the same book" and asks him about the nature of that book, he answers that it is "the saga of the things that haunt [him]. Like it or not", he continues, "all my books seem to revolve around the same set of questions, the same human dilemmas" (Auster 1995, 123). Auster endlessly questions the nature of reality and language, and his books always deal with language and the world's interconnectedness. As he explains to Jim Francis, "in poetry, a rhyme will yoke together two things that don't seem connected, yet the fact that they rhyme creates an association, and starts you thinking about new kinds of connections on the world. The same thing occurs with events in life" (Francis 1990, 15). Auster's world view started to take shape in his work as a poet and essayist, and even as early as his "Notes from a Composition Book" (Auster 2004b [1967], 203-5).

While most of Auster's essays deal with the output of various writers' traumatic and pathological relationship to language, his poems reveal his own failure to speak of the world. Jacques Dupin defines Auster's poetry as a "cold duel with language" and speaks of "the poem's complete uncertainty in its infinite approach, in its blind journey across language and the world" (Dupin 1994, 8; my translation). In the poem "Narrative", Auster writes that "if we speak / of the world / it is only to leave the world / unsaid" (Auster 2004b, 143).[1] This defeat is due to the inadequacy of language and the poet's inescapable interconnection with the semiotic world that surrounds him and dwells in him: "myself / the sound of a word / I cannot speak. ... / so much silence / ... so many words / lost in the wide world / within me" ("In Memory of Myself", Auster 2004b, 148).

In Auster's novels, the restrictions of language often confine the characters to the room and the act of writing (Quinn, Fanshawe, Anna Blume, Samuel Farr, David Zimmer, Sidney Orr, Mr. Blank, Adam Walker), depriving them of speech (especially in *The New York Trilogy*, *The Brooklyn Follies* and *Man in the Dark*) and memory (*In the Country of Last Things, Travels in the Scriptorium, Invisible*). Throughout his career Auster has tried to get through the walls of language and subjectivity. The limits of the self, of the book and of language generated a poetry that is reminiscent of the Objectivists and the Jewish tradition, and Auster's fiction still bears witness to these early influences.

This chapter focuses on the devices used by Paul Auster to overcome the limits of the say-able. After analyzing Auster's search for linguistic consistency in his essays and poems, we will show how he enhances the power of language by wandering in its margins, using new narrative forms and voices in order to speak the unspeakable in his post-9/11 fiction. Like Gilles Deleuze who considers literature as the creation of a people to come (1993, 15), *The Brooklyn Follies*' narrator Nathan Glass wants to "resurrect [people] in words" by writing their biography and concludes that "one should never underestimate the power of books" (Auster 2005a, 302). Auster's novels are seldom autobiographical as regards plots and stories. However, when it comes to metaphysics, the man is inseparable from the oeuvre. When I interviewed him on the act of writing and spirituality in his work, Paul Auster told me that he was

> not a believer. But there is always this idea that we haven't invented the world. We haven't created it. There are transcendental aspirations in each soul for something bigger than us. ... I see myself as belonging to the world. Most of the time people are cut off from the world, isolated, but sometimes we feel connected. Those are life's happiest moments, aren't they? (Hugonnier 2005, 2)[2]

As Jacques Derrida and the post-structuralists have pointed out, metaphysics is always built on a language and sign theory with which it forms a system (Agacinski 1994, 775). In Auster's latest novels, this system reaches maturity, but in order to access its full scope we first have to go back to its foundations.

***

Speaking of his early critical work, Auster claims that he "looked on those pieces as an opportunity to articulate some of [his] ideas about writing and literature, to map out some kind of aesthetic position" (Auster 1995, 130). As he explains to Joseph Mallia, "in some sense, these little pieces of literary journalism were the training ground for the novels" (Auster 1995, 106). Auster had the freedom to choose the authors he would write about, and he was particularly interested in the work of Jewish poets who have experimented new modes of representation after Auschwitz (Jabès, Reznikoff, Celan, Perec) and others "who have contributed something important to the language" (Auster 1995, 108). Most of them tackle the paradox of the over-communicative aspect of language and its malfunction when it comes to saying the things that have to be said. Auster's preface to his translation of Jacques Dupin's *Fits and Starts*, written in 1971, is his first public expression of an ever growing sense of the distance between the perceptive eye and the "creative word":

> The poetic word is essentially the creative word, and yet, nevertheless, a word among others, burdened by the weight of habit and layers of dead skin that must be stripped away before it can regain its true function. (Auster 1974, 3)

Auster deplores the fact that the word of man does not have the dreamed powers of the Word of God, even though "it is language that creates us and defines us as human beings" ("New York Babel" in Auster 2003, 329). This metaphysical statement was written in reaction to the work of schizophrenic Louis Wolfson who wanted to get rid of his mother tongue and form a new language based on phonetic and phonemic connections taken from various languages. Wolfson's mother played the opposite role of Stillman (who forbade his son Stillman Jr. to speak English in Auster's first novel "City of Glass"), since she would come into the room shrieking words in English, for both sound and obscure reasons, as Deleuze explains in his preface to *Le Schizo et les Langues* (1970). This strange out-of-print piece of work, which came from a highly disturbed relationship with language, is a cornerstone of Auster's groundwork. He enthusiastically refers to it as "one of those rare works that can change our perception of the world" (Auster 2003, 330). Wolfson's lonely and insane craft is reminiscent of young Stillman's poetry. After years of confinement in a locked room, Stillman pretends to be able to speak "God's language":

> I am the only one who knows what the words mean. They cannot be translated. ... They are God's language, and no one else can speak them.

… That is why Peter lives so close to God. That is why he is a famous
poet. (Auster 1987, 19-20)

Both Stillman and Wolfson's words "exclude all possibility of translation"
(Auster 2003, 325). After trying to reach a utopian linguistic purity in his
poems like his mentor William Bronk, Auster mocks it in his fiction.
While Stillman (father) conducts his experiments with the B-A-B-E-L
cartography and the Word of God, his abused son has become the ironical
archetype of a great poet.

Auster often uses poetry as a way to purify the eroded and polluted
word of man. This search for a language "prior to language" (Finkelstein
1995, 53) is a basic concern of the objectivists, and especially Auster's
friend George Oppen who, in his eyes, seems to get rid of the "layers of
dead skin" as "the language is almost naked, and the syntax seems to
derive its logic as much from the silences around words as from the words
themselves" (Auster 1981, 49-50). In "The Decisive Moment", Auster
makes a similar statement about another one of his great objectivist
influences:

> Reznikoff is essentially a poet of *naming*. One does not have the sense of a
> poetry immersed in language but rather of something that takes place
> before language and comes to fruition at the precise moment language has
> been discovered. (Auster 1990, 224)

Indeed, in Auster's poetry and as early as "Spokes" ("Lifted into speech, it
carries / Its own birth", 2004b, 33) and "Unearth", the act of naming
creates the poems as much as the poems struggle toward naming ("A
remnant / grief, merging / with the not yet nameable", Auster 2004b, 51).
Going farther than the basic proposition he wrote in his "Composition
Book",[3] Auster apprehends language as a means to organize experience
("from one stone touched / to the next stone / named", Auster 2004b, 50),
but the creation of language tends to be experienced too as we "become
the name / of what we name" (Auster 2004b, 41). The poem is a *mise en
scène* of the open eye as a passageway for the world ("He is alive, and
therefore he is nothing / but what drowns in the fathomless hole / of his
eye", in "Disappearances", Auster 2004b, 107), leaving nothing but a
vague remnant worded on the page: "You ask / words of me, and I / will
speak them—from the moment / I have learned / to give you nothing" (in
"Unearth", Auster 2004b, 48).

The poet breathes the sky in and out of his lungs, he internalizes the
external world, but his word can only translate the blind search for pure
objectivity. Consciousness and language disturb the poet's great "animal's

vision", as Rilke calls it in the *Duino Elegies* (1922). In *L'Espace littéraire* (1955), Blanchot explains that Rilke deemed the animal's small degree of consciousness to be a key to enter reality without being the center of it. It is a way for the disembodied subject to enter the world and to let the world enter him with a wide open eye. This eye does not feed the subject's inner world but always keeps on opening to the unique world at large (Blanchot 1955, 172-175). Auster's consciousness allows him to travel everywhere he likes when he is locked in a room, as he suggests in "White Spaces",[4] but this internal reverberation also compels him to relentless representation. Rilke and objectivists such as Reznikoff have tried to reach this "animal's vision" in order to overcome the limits of subjectivity:

> The *one* space extends through all beings:
> The world's inner space. The birds fly silently
> Through us. O, wanting to grow,
> I look out, and the tree grows in me. (Blanchot 1955, 174)

After Rilke in this 1914 poem entitled "All things almost summon us to feeling", Auster produces a similar interconnection and blurs the line between inside (the subject) and outside (the world) as he speaks of "A tree" that "will take root in us / and rise in the light / of our mouths" in the poem "Scribe" (Auster 2004b, 69). The inner image of a tree is named and can be communicated and re-presented thanks to the mouth. These lines allude to the linguistic reality that "extends through all beings". In Auster's seven-part poem "Disappearances" (1975), language is precisely what connects people and paradoxically builds a stone wall that prevents one from knowing someone else's interiority. The poet invents his own solitude by constituting himself as a subject ("and what he sees / is all that he is not: a city", Auster 2004b, 107). Like a child, when he says "I", he differentiates himself from the world that surrounds him even if he increasingly becomes conscious of his connectedness with it ("Therefore, he says I, / and counts himself / in all that he excludes, / which is nothing", Auster 2004b, 112).[5] The objectivists' goal is an intrinsic impossibility, and Auster's poetry acknowledges this paradox as the linguistic process of subjectivation ("and those who would speak / to give birth to themselves", Auster 2004b, 108) leads to erasure and nothingness ("I believe, then, / in nothing / these words might give you", in "Facing the Music", Auster 2004b, 151). Finkelstein thus speaks of the poem's "resolute unmaking" and he asserts that "all the reassuring materials of the objectivist lyric, quietly celebrated for their mere being—are gone" (Finkelstein 1995, 53).

Auster's deconstruction of language starts with Genesis. In Umberto Eco's words, "Creation itself arose through an act of speech; it is only by giving things their name that [God] created them and gave them an ontological status" (Eco 1995, 7). Auster's visceral approach to language is inscribed in the aftermath of the *confusio linguarum*, the confusion emanating from the fall of the Tower of Babel. The subsequent diversity of languages is a process of irreversible linguistic fragmentation. The loss of the original perfect language (the Word of God used by Adam in the Garden before the Fall) and the chaos involved by the inadequacy of human languages are a fundamental leitmotiv in Auster's work. It first appears in the "Composition book" and then in the poetic work, for instance in "Scribe": "The name / never left his lips: he talked himself / into another body: he found his room again / in Babel" (Auster 2004b, 69). In the poem "Gnomon", Auster reaches a certain purity of the word, a perfect harmony at the brink of silence, when all the words have been used up. The ancient Greek word *gnomon* refers to the part of a sundial that projects the shadow. By extension the gnomon refers to man, and the poetic "I" stands as this one man in the "enormous / vineyards of the living" (Auster 2004b, 128). But is the poetic "I" able to cast the shadow of his perception of the world? The gnomon suggests a rare *conformal* system of representation, which is the aim of the universal search for the perfect language, as explained by Umberto Eco:

> In Hjelmslev's terms the two planes of a natural language (form and content) are *not comformal*. This means that the expression-form and the expression-content are structured according to different criteria: the relationship between the two planes is arbitrary, and variations of form do not automatically imply a point-to-point variation of the corresponding content. ... However, this feature of natural languages is not necessarily a feature of other semiotic systems, which can be *conformal*. Think of an analogue clock: here the movement of the hands corresponds to the movement of the earth around the sun, but the slightest movement (and every new position) of the hands corresponds to a movement of the earth: the two planes are point-to-point conformal. (Eco 1995, 22-3)

Contrary to the gnomon, poetry and language are not conformal systems of representation. In "Facing the Music", Auster's "valediction to poetry" (Finkelstein 2004, 14), the poet deplores:

> our own lack
> of knowing what it is
> we see, and merely to speak of it
> is to see

> how words fail us, how nothing comes right
> in the saying of it, not even these words
> I am moved to speak. (Auster 2004b, 151)

The last poems written between 1976 and 1979 often point at the impossibility of rendering experience faithfully in a nutshell. The poet is unable to abolish time, to capture the outside world and turn it into speech. The poet's impossible "purity and consistency of language" (Auster 1995, 133) is stated in the concluding lines of "Facing the Music" ("as if / there could never be another word / that would hold me / without breaking", Auster 2004b, 152). Auster's early works of prose confirm that his vision cannot be communicated by a single word. In "White Spaces"—Auster looks back on this piece as "the bridge between writing poetry and writing prose" (Auster 1995, 132)—he expresses his frustration with unprecedented clarity: "It comes from my voice. But that does not mean these words will ever be what happens" (Auster 2004b, 155). Facing the unspeakable, Auster starts using language's irrevocable flaws in a new and extended form.

In *The Invention of Solitude* (1982), Auster draws a parallel between "suffocating" and his inability to say. "Never before have I been so aware of the rift between thinking and writing", he concludes, adding that "the story [he is] trying to tell is somehow incompatible with language" (Auster 1988, 32). Auster's farewell to poetry is enclosed in the predicament of Freuchen, the arctic explorer stuck in his igloo surrounded by starving wolves (in "White Spaces"). If he breathes, he will wall himself to death with his own freezing breath, but if he does not breathe, he will certainly die too. As this metaphor illustrates, Auster needs to use language in order to be in the world, and yet it increasingly smothers him. In "Interior", after using a similar image ("a scarab devoured in the sphere of its own dung", Auster 2004b, 67), Auster divulges the duality of his condition in one of his most accomplished concluding stanzas: "In the impossibility of words, / in the unspoken word that asphyxiates, / I find myself" (Auster 2004b, 69). Even though its eggs could not hatch, Auster's "reptilian writing" (Dupin, 1994, 9) managed to slough off its skin and wind its way from poetry to prose. As Auster tells Joseph Mallia, "if it really has to be said, it will create its own form" (Auster 1995, 104).

***

In order to shed new light on Auster's early dilemmas, we need to move on to the study of the unspeakable in his fiction. After becoming a narrative motivator in his very first novels—rising from the linguistic remnants of the Tower of Babel and the Holocaust—the unnameable suddenly reappeared in the aftermath of the attacks on the Twin Towers. Genesis and the episode of the Tower of Babel inspired Stillman's insane linguistic experiments and wanderings in the first volume of *The New York Trilogy* (1987). In Auster's next novel *In the Country of Last Things* (1987),[6] Anna Blume intimates that man must act as a daily Adam in the city where language gradually disappears and melts into oblivion: "you must encounter each thing as if you have never known it before. No matter how many times, it must always be the first time" (Auster 1989, 7). The text is suffused with silent connections with Babel. Isabel loses the power of speech before dying, making

> an awful noise that sounded like chaos itself. Spittle was dribbling down from the corners of her mouth, and the noise kept pouring out of her, a dirge of unimaginable confusion and pain. (Auster 1989, 78)

Isabel's spittle recalls the crumbling of stones in poems such as "Meteor" ("the dust / of the smallest stone / that falls from the eaves / of Babel", Auster 2004b, 133). Anna portrays a *confusio linguarum* in which "chaos itself" precedes the "confusion". Besides, we may observe the paronomasia between Babel and Isabel. In the post-Holocaust landscape of *In the Country of Last Things*, Anna Blume explains how words fail her when she is exposed to unbearable visions such as a dead child with her head crushed: "Your mind seems to balk at forming the words, you somehow cannot bring yourself to do it" (Auster 1989, 19). In "Ghosts", Blue's "stability into his relationship with a small and very narrowly defined world" (Brown 2007, 46) is based on language. Blue reenacts the linguistic creation of the world:

> It will not do to call a lamp a bed, he thinks, or the bed a lamp. No, these words fit snugly around the things they stand for, and the moment Blue speaks them, he feels a deep satisfaction, as though he has just proved the existence of the world. (Auster 1987, 148)

Twenty years later, Auster goes back to these considerations in *Travels in the Scriptorium* (2006), which reads like a matrix of his overall work. The name of the main character Mr Blank refers to the character's erased memory, to the writer's blank page, a clean slate ready to be filled with names and stories. After Anna, who is a central character again, Mr Blank is a new daily Adam literally naming the things that are in front of his eyes and who feels guilty for having done "something terrible… unspeakable…" to Anna (Auster 2006, 21). Every day he is the first man and he creates the world as he tries to make sense of the clues that surround him in the room. His irrational behavior is evocative of the Pilgrim Fathers who lived in the confinement of the first colonies (their new Garden of Eden) and stayed away from the wilderness of the outside world (the Devil's realm). The initial situation includes words attached to each object in the room. The strips of paper are the substantive proof of the irreducible distance between words and objects. Towards the end of the novella, Mr Blank experiences a new kind of *confusio linguarum*:

> After a thorough investigation, he is horrified to discover that not a single label occupies its former spot. The wall now reads CHAIR. The lamp now reads BATHROOM. The chair now reads DESK. ... He always took great pains to write up his reports on their activities in a language that would not betray the truth of what they saw and thought and felt at each step along the way. To indulge in such infantile whimsy is to throw the world into chaos, to make life intolerable for all but the mad. Mr Blank has not reached the point where he cannot identify objects that do not have their names affixed to them, but there is no question that he is in decline, and he understands that a day might come ... when his brain will erode still further and it will become necessary for him to have the name of the thing on the thing in order for him to recognize it. (Auster 2006, 103-5)

The word *chaos*[7] is used again, and Mr Blank's situation is similar to Anna's when she makes an inventory of the lexical disappearances (Auster 1989, 89). The allusion to "Ghosts" is also obvious here, but this time, Auster breaks the linguistic order of things. This will to destroy language and test its workings when words and characters are pushed to their limit is a constant in Auster's fiction. The characters always have to restore peace to a broken universe.

Two decades after *The New York Trilogy*, the theme of the Word of God is revisited in *The Brooklyn Follies* (2005) with Reverend Bob's experiment:

> Every time we talked, we drowned out the voice of God. Every time we listened to the words of men, we neglected the words of God. From now on, he said, every member of the church above the age of fourteen would spend one day a week in total silence. In that way, we would be able to restore our connection with God, to hear him speaking within our souls. (Auster 2005a, 265)

The confrontation and the fusion of silence and speech are at the center of *The Brooklyn Follies*' plot. They form a pattern that encompasses the slightest details such as character names, semantic fields and literary references. Starting as soon as the opening sentence in which Nathan Glass explains that he "was looking for a quiet place to die" (Auster 2005a, 1), nothing seems to escape this silence/speech grid. The whole novel is infused with the irreducible difference between sign and object. The underlying ontological questioning is also raised through the constant duality between presence and absence ("The absent Aurora" is representative of Auster's philosophy of presence, as "if she's anywhere now, it is only in her daughter's face, in the little girl's loyalty to her, in Lucy's unbroken promise not to tell us where she is", Auster 2005a, 198), and through several dichotomies including male/female (as illustrated by the transsexual character Tina Hott), inside/outside (Aurora is locked in a room and reduced to silence by David Minor while Nathan goes on a trip to save her), body/soul (Nathan speaks of his mystical near-death experience, Auster 2005a, 297), and original/fake. As Auster reminds us in "White Spaces", faking is a characteristic of language as "words falsify the things they attempt to say" (Auster 2004b, 158) and therefore it is impossible to make out the originals from the facsimiles. Reverend Bob is referred to as a "fraud", a "scam-artist" (Auster 2005a, 263). Many characters are fakes ("the ersatz James Joyce", Auster 2005a, 221[8]) and the plot is built around a nonexistent original manuscript of Hawthorne ("an elaborate hoax within a hoax", Auster 2005a, 210). The proliferation of fake works of art and the presence of transsexual characters make *The Brooklyn Follies* read as a rewriting, or as a copy of William Gaddis's *The Recognitions* (1955). In *The Brooklyn Follies*, Gaddis's name appears on the shelves of original first editions in Brightman's Attic, and *The Recognitions* is precisely a novel about art forgery. William Gaddis borrowed the title from the Clementine *Recognitions* whose original version is lost and simply seems to have never existed. Just as in *The Recognitions*, the fake paintings in *The Brooklyn Follies* turn out to be better than the originals:

> not only had Dryer duplicated the look and feel of one of Smith's canvases, … but he had taken Smith even so slightly farther than Smith had ever gone himself. It was Smith's *next painting*. (Auster 2005a, 44)

As Brigitte Félix explains, in *The Recognitions* the origin is out of reach in a world filled with all kinds of forgers, fake objects and copies whose originals were lost (Félix 1997, 37). In *The Brooklyn Follies*, this phenomenon extends to language. Like the fake Hawthorne manuscript, the Word of God is an unattainable origin. We soon realize that every element of the plot can be seen as an exploration of the impossibilities inherent to language. Sign and object are analogue to fake and original, and with a closer look, the reader will get a glimpse of the linguistic construction of the text. The plumbing often shows, and especially when it comes to naming: Harry Brightman/Dunkel (*Dark* in German) is yet another representative dichotomy of Paul Auster's two-sides-of-the-coin alchemist game. Harry is first presented by what he is not:

> Harry Brightman did not exist. ... Nearly everything Tom thought he knew about Harry was false. Forget the childhood in San Francisco ... . Forget Exeter and Brown. (Auster 2005a, 32)

Harry is reduced to a play on words, which emphasizes his illusory presence.[9] We may also note the generic reference to simulacra and hyper-reality contained in the title of the book (a "folly" is, among other things, an *imitation* castle). In a semiotic world based on thriving forgery since day one, reality and fiction are no longer separate entities. Words falsify, and any book and any "Hotel Existence" is "built on a foundation of 'just talk'" (Auster 2005a, 181). As Harry explains, the Hotel Existence was fantasized as a shelter for WWII orphans in the first place, and Tom, Nathan and Harry refer to their utopia as a linguistic construction. However, the word "just" keeps appearing throughout the novel and it has crucial consequences on the plot. Lucy's linguistic confusion with the word "just" in "just let him know that I'm okay, that I'm doing fine" (Auster 2005a, 270) turns out to be the reason for her unflinching silence, the central riddle of *The Brooklyn Follies*.

All those developments on the deceptive nature of language also point at the things that cannot be spoken, that defy our modes of representation. In *The Invention of Solitude*, Auster had reformulated Wittgenstein's concluding proposition of the *Tractatus Logico-Philosophicus* (1921) that excluded the unspeakable from the field of philosophy. What resists linguistic representation should be expressed differently. After refraining from quoting Wittgenstein as the foreword of "City of Glass" (Auster 1995, 110), Auster abides to Wittgenstein's principle by invoking in silence things that cannot be said. In *The Brooklyn Follies*, Nathan simply alludes to an anecdote about the philosopher's life without speaking about his work, hence avoiding the paradox of putting the unspeakable into words. What seems to be a trivial remark hides a key to the reading of the novel. Auster adheres to Wittgenstein's famous proposition by not mentioning it. Presence, absence, speech and silence guide the reader into the margins of language. Silence is a powerful tool to summon up what words cannot put across. During the ceremony held after Brightman's death, Tina Hott performs as a "faux-singer":

> He was one of the most beautiful women I had ever seen. … He had turned
> himself into an incarnation of absolute femininity, an idea of the feminine
> that surpassed anything that existed in the realm of natural womanhood. …
> Tina's legs were so long and lovely to look at, it was impossible to believe
> that they were attached to a man.
>
>   But there was more to the effect she created … The inner light of the
> feminine was there as well. … All through the ceremony, she didn't say a
> word, standing among us in total silence. … This was how Tina Hott
> performed in her Saturday night cabaret appearances: not as a singer, but
> as a faux-singer, mouthing the words. … It was magnificent and absurd. It
> was funny and heartbreaking. It was moving and comical. It was
> everything it was and everything it wasn't. … It was one of the strangest,
> most transcendent moments of my life. (Auster 2005a, 222-3)

This passage has all the features of the grotesque we find in the overall
novel and its "follies", but at the same time it is given an almost mystical
depth. Tina is mouthing the words; she is pretending to pronounce them.
No words are needed. When the narrator starts the next paragraph, the
metamorphosis is completed, and the *he* is turned into a *she*. The fake
woman has become the symbol of womanhood *par excellence*, the
archetypal occurrence of the notion (it "surpassed anything that existed in
the realm of natural womanhood"). Auster blurs the line between fake and
original, reality and fiction, silence and speech. He evokes a certain
creative purity without naming it, an un-say-able language as shapeless as
the Word of God. Many characters who are estranged from language
people the novel, such as Nathan's ex-wife "the now unmentionable one"
who is later referred to as "(name deleted)" (Auster 2005a, 229, 230).
Lucy—who etymologically brings the (mystical) light—is the best
representative of this phenomenon. She embodies silence and exposes
Nathan and Tom to the inefficiency of language when she refuses to
speak:

> I had been hoping to trick a few words out of her, but all I got were the
> same nods and shakes … . Strange unsettling little person. … We talked
> for a good thirty or forty minutes, but nothing came of it except ever-
> mounting confusion and worry. … Round and round we went, the two of
> us traveling in circles, talking, talking, talking, but unable to answer a
> single question. (Auster 2005a, 135-6)

The speech/silence duel between Nathan, Tom and Lucy recalls Derrida's
deconstruction of Plato's *pharmakon* (Derrida 1972).[10] Language carries a
useless leftover, it is a series of signs that do not mean so much as they are
poisonous. Tina Hott is the personification of the *pharmakon*'s ambivalence

as he/she is the center of all oppositions. The story of Freuchen's freezing breath (in "White Spaces") and the image of the "scarab devoured in the sphere of his own dung" (in "Interior") were already heading toward this conception of language as both a cure and a poison. Language is not a conformal system of representation and the linguistic signs carry a dangerous supplement. This ambiguous leftover engenders negativity, fashions multiple readings and gives birth to poetic and literary games: words inside the word, books inside the book, and worlds inside the world.

***

Auster explores the "limits of the known world" (Auster 1988, 98) through characters who undergo various forms of deprivation and who are almost reduced to nothingness, a concept which was already taking shape in his work of poetry. His poetry reformulates the tale of Creation by recounting the origins of nothingness ("And if nothing / then let nothing be" in "Gnomon", Auster 2004b, 128). The poems are flooded with "un-words" ("unpronounceable", "unsigned", "unquenchable", "unapproachable", "unknowable", "unland" echoing the collection *Unearth*—the word being used again in "Riding Eastward": "A word, unearthed"—"unappeasable", "unspoken", "untellable", "unseen", "unborn", "unblessed", "undead") along with negations and the systematic repetition of words conveying nothingness: "never", "nowhere", "nothing", "to say nothing", "nothing but", "no more", "no home", "no meaning", "nothingness", "you will leave unsaid—and nothing / will be lost", and by extension "inaudible", "invisible", "irreducible". The climax is reached with "Impossible" surrounded by extra white spaces making the word pop out precisely in the middle of "Facing the Music".[11] "The list is inexhaustible" as Auster puts it in his novel *Invisible* (2009, 139), which is haunted by such "un-words" throughout. All these words carry their own erasure even though they paradoxically give birth to the poems, coming back to life from the edge of absence by a double negation ("as nothing / that will not haunt you" in "Aubade", Auster 2004b, 130), and in the introduction of "Wall Writing": "Nothing less than nothing. / In the night that comes / from nothing / for no one in the night / that does not come" (Auster 2004b, 81).[12]

The upshot is the striking unification of these poems in the process (and I can't help assuming that this most French of American writers would have thought of "un", the French word for "one"). The poetic work thus finds its unity in *nothingness*,[13] a word about which Auster questions Edmond Jabès as follows:

PA: There are a dozen or so words and themes that are repeated constantly, on nearly every page of your work: desert, absence, silence, God, nothingness, the void, the book, the word, exile, life, death… and it strikes me that each of these words is in some sense a word on the other side of speech, a kind of limit, something almost impossible to express.

EJ: Exactly. But at the same time, if these are things that cannot be expressed, they are also things that cannot be emptied of meaning. ... God is perhaps a word without words. A word without meaning. And the extraordinary thing is that in the Jewish tradition God is invisible, and as a way of underscoring this invisibility, he has an unpronounceable name. What I find truly fantastic is that when you call something 'invisible', you are naming something, which means that you are almost giving a representation of the invisible. In other words, when you say 'invisible,' you are pointing to the boundary between the visible and the invisible; there are words for that. But when you can't say the word, you are standing before nothing. And for me this is even more powerful because, finally, there is a visible in the invisible, just as there is an invisible in the visible. And this, this abolishes everything. (Auster 1990, 202-3)

Most of these words are repeated by Auster himself in his own work, especially *desert, absence, silence, invisible, God, nothingness, the book, the word, life* and *death*. Like Jabès, Auster is a secular Jewish author inspired by the Jewish tradition as if by intuition. In Norman Finkelstein's words,

Auster is haunted by Jewish themes, and perhaps more importantly, by the Jewish attitude toward writing: to witness, to remember, to play divine and utterly serious textual games. (Finkelstein 1995, 49)

Auster's mystical games with *logos* and chance, with the reading of clouds and weirdly connected events have kabalistic overtones. The invisible God of the Jews who "has an unpronounceable name" is presented in detail in "White Spaces":

Each of the ninety-nine names tradition ascribes to this God was in fact nothing more than a way of acknowledging that-which-cannot-be-spoken, that-which-cannot-be-seen, and that-which-cannot-be-understood. (Auster 2004b, 157)

The poet's concerns with the unspeakable and his games with the outside of language start to find their own voice, so to speak. YHWH is alluded to in "City of Glass":

> The last two letters remained: the 'E' and the 'L'. Quinn's mind dispersed. He arrived in a neverland of fragments, a place of wordless things and thingless words. Then, struggling through his torpor one last time, he told himself that El was the ancient Hebrew for God. (Auster 1987, 71)

As Jabès scholars have noted, chiasm is a literary trope that enables him to evoke that-which-cannot-be-spoken, seen or understood. In his interview with Paul Auster, Jabès uses one of those in order to go beyond the limits of the say-able ("visible" / "invisible"). The young Auster was so influenced by Jabès that he articulated a chiasm that mirrors the irreducible difference between the linguistic sign and the tangible object ("wordless things and thingless words") even if he had better leave it unsaid, as the mention of El implies.[14]

Following the example of Jabès, Auster works with the invisible and the incommunicable in order to exceed the limits of our modes of communication. For instance, Mark Brown explains that Quinn "anticipates the end of the notebook by exploring modes of representation that go beyond the visible inscriptions of writing" (Brown 2007, 45). Convincingly enough, the American hard-cover edition of Auster's *Invisible* (Henry Holt) manages to represent the visible in the invisible as the invisible God's omniscient eye and/or the poet's "I"/eye are graphically embedded in the title. But there are unspeakable elements lurking under the smooth surface of the novels as well, not the infinite possibilities of the text nor what mystically stands outside the borders of speech and do not have any corresponding substantive, but what cannot be said because it is unnamable and inhuman, because it suggests that inhumanity is part of humanity.

> The dead children. The children who will vanish, the children who are dead. Himmler: "I have made the decision to annihilate every Jew child from the face of the earth". Nothing but pictures. Because, at a certain point, the words lead one to conclude that it is no longer possible to speak. Because these pictures are the unspeakable. (Auster 1988, 98)

Before *Oracle Night* (2004) and *Man in the Dark* (2008), Auster had written little about the Holocaust except for these early remarks in *The Invention of Solitude* and his commentaries on the works of post-holocaust writers. In his essay on Reznikoff's *Holocaust* (1975), Paul Auster expresses dissatisfaction with this text, which was made out of the objective court reports of the Eichmann and Nuremberg trials. His criticism enables him to formulate his personal vision:

> The Holocaust, which is precisely the unknowable, the unthinkable, requires
> a treatment beyond the facts in order for us to be able to understand it—
> assuming that such a thing is even possible. (Auster 1990, 224)

"A treatment beyond the facts" means using fiction and imagination.
Death cannot be experienced nor put into words. But what happens when
the living are no longer able to speak? According to Primo Levi and
Giorgio Agamben, the "integral witness" of the Holocaust is the half
human and half inhuman *muselmann*, a "living corpse" who was no longer
able to testify. The Holocaust is a concrete proof of the inhuman which is
now officially part of humanity. As Agamben explains, the *muselmann* is
not only the limit between life and death but also the threshold between
man and un-man. The frontier has been blurred, and witnessing and
literature have gradually opened up to new terrifying modes of
representation. Contrary to Reznikoff's factual depiction of the Holocaust,
Auster tentatively infuses his fiction with unspeakable horrors inspired
from historical facts. *In the Country of Last Things* evokes the Holocaust
and many horrible events that actually happened throughout the twentieth
century. The unbearable inhuman visions such as the "ghost people"
(Auster 1989, 11)—who are described in the exact same way as the
muselmann, the "crematoria" (Auster 1989, 31, 17) and the human
slaughterhouse Anna Blume is lured into—have been absent from Auster's
work for almost two decades. Uncertain hope seemed to come out of
Anna's discussions with the rabbi in the library. But now it is as if the
terrorist attacks and repeated massacres in Yugoslavia had restarted
nurturing Auster's "writing of the disaster".[15]

The Holocaust paradigm increasingly surfaces in Auster's latest
novels, starting with *Oracle Night*, which is haunted by Ed Victory's
testimony of the concentration camps. The story-within-the-story character
Ed Victory is Nick Bowen's new boss at the Bureau of Historical
Preservation. As the narrator explains, his job is a "mad enterprise of
collecting telephone books", a way for Ed to "translate the experience of
the death camp into an enduring lifelong action" (Auster 2004a, 93). Ed
seems to be Nick's spiritual guide, a contemporary "interpreter", as he is
"the man who was delivered to him by God" (Auster 2004a, 90). Like
Christian in John Bunyan's *The Pilgrim Progress* (1678),[16] "Nick peers
into the darkness before him, unable to see a thing" (Auster 2004a, 89)
when they enter the bomb shelter. In the main narrative thread, John
Trause (an anagram for Auster and a father-figure) is Sidney Orr's
interpreter. Sid's "What do you think that means?" (Auster 2004a, 46)
echoes Christian's "What means this?" (Bunyan 1967 [1678], 28), but
Trause makes fun of his apprentice: "It doesn't mean a thing, Sid" (Auster

2004a, 46). Ed Victory uses allegorical pseudonyms (*"Lightning Man, New York,* and *Mr Goodshoes"*, Auster 2004a, 96) and the main character's wife is called *Grace*. Auster hints at Bunyan's characters *Grace, Mr Worldly Wiseman* and *Goodwill* (the last being the name of the place where Nick bought his second-hand clothes). Contrary to Christian who is shown a portrait of the Christ holding "the best of books" in the House of the Interpreter (Bunyan 1967 [1678], 28), Bowen reads a Warsaw phone book[17] in the bomb shelter where Victory initiates him to a post-holocaust Godless world: "that was the end of mankind, Mr Good Shoes, God turned his eyes away from us and left the world forever" (Auster 2004a, 92). The story within the story ends when Nick is trapped in the bomb shelter. The allusion to Bunyan is made more obvious: "Although he doesn't believe in God, he tells himself that God is testing him—and that he mustn't fail to accept his misfortune with grace and equanimity of spirit" (Auster 2004a, 105). The bomb shelter symbolises a refuge to war disasters including Auschwitz, Hiroshima and the World Trade Center.

Auster has not written much about the 9/11 attacks, and the end of *The Brooklyn Follies* is all the more striking as it gives an unexpected glimpse of the horror which is representative of the way the real attacks happened. It is conveyed through the singular point of view of a Brooklynite and his silence that go beyond the worldwide known images of the attacks, what Art Spiegelman[18] intended to do with his comic entitled *In the Shadow of No Towers* (2004). Only two lines erase the three hundred pages of light humor and the dreams of the Hotel Existence. Nathan simply explains that "the smoke of three thousand incinerated bodies would drift over toward Brooklyn and come pouring down on us in a white cloud of ashes and death" (Auster 2005a, 304), but he instantly goes back to his cheerful tone ("my friends") and talks about his greatest feeling of happiness. He is no longer able to speak of it. In *Man in the Dark* (2008), Auster steps further in the representation of the unspeakable. August Brill imagines stories taking place in a divided America where the 9/11 attacks have never happened.[19] Katya, his granddaughter, who is a cinema student, develops a little theory about silence and "inanimate objects as a means of expressing human emotions. That's the language of film", she concludes, insisting on the inappropriateness of verbalization: "without using a single word of dialogue. … No words. No words needed" (Auster 2008, 16, 21). Watching (silent) movies is the only way for Katya to cope with loss, which recalls Zimmer watching Hector Mann's silent films in *The Book of Illusions* (2002).[20] The shocking death of Katya's boyfriend Titus, who was beheaded by terrorists, is pushed back until the end of the novel. Like

Nathan Glass in *The Brooklyn Follies*, August Brill "doesn't want to go there" (Auster 2008, 2) and postpones the insufferable thought. The suspense occasioned by the repeated allusions to this unspeakable vision gives an unforgettable strength to the inhuman images that finally "drown in the fathomless hole of [our] eye" (Auster 2004b, 107). Titus is the embodiment of the line between human and inhuman as his head is chopped off from his body. He is "no longer quite human … , a person and not a person" (Auster 2008, 176). The effect on the reader is indelible. The scene is highly visual. One of the terrorists precisely "stabs out the boy's eyes" (Auster 2008, 176). Titus is now an un-man in the dark. He is defined in the same way as the *muselmann* was described by camp survivors.[21] Auster emphasizes the visual aspect of the unspeakable scene by referring to Titus as a *"nature morte"*, which harks back to the beginning of the novel when Brill makes an analogy between Titus and Rembrandt's famous painting of his own son Titus "ravaged by illness" (Auster 2008, 176, 2).[22] By using the French term for still life (*nature morte*), Auster alludes to his friend Don DeLillo's novel *Falling Man* (2007), published the year before. In this fiction about the 9/11 attacks, the narrator makes a digression about art and the unspeakable. He describes a character contemplating a painting by Giorgio Morandi which holds "a mystery she could not name", and adds that it is a *"Natura Morta*. The Italian term for still life" (DeLillo 2007, 12).[23] The *nature morte* enables both Auster and DeLillo to express the inexpressible thanks to the sublime. Auster goes beyond the power of words by throwing these unbearable pictures at us. They are part of a silent web movie ("mercifully, there is no sound", 2008, 175) which confirms that such events need not and cannot be put into words.

In Jabès's view, the simple mention of the Holocaust, or by extension here, of terrorism, "tells the whole story" (Auster 1990, 202). No further comment is needed. A whole range of human emotions are instantly stirred by these notions. They are universal capitals on the map of human consciousness. The images of Titus's death haunt the family members in silence, and they don't want to discuss it. Even thinking about it is impossible: "You're a brave girl, I said, suddenly thinking about Titus. / Stop it, Grandpa. I don't want to talk about him" (Auster 2008, 18). Step by step, the narrator slowly comes to the point until his digressions bring us to a series of WWII stories. The first one deals with the rescue of a Jewish family who was about to be sent to a concentration camp. Another one recounts the torture of a Belgian prisoner in the death camps. Again, the atrocities are committed in silence: "the woman didn't cry out, didn't make a sound as one limb after another was pulled off her body" (Auster

2008, 121). Like Art Spiegelman and Elie Wiesel's families who were told about the death camps while they stayed in the ghettos and wouldn't take the stories for granted, Brill questions the veracity of the facts: "Is such a thing even possible?" (Auster 2008, 121) Unspeakable events are inhuman and as a matter of fact, unimaginable. The story-teller loses the power of speech: "Jean-Luc couldn't look at us when he spoke the words. ... He wasn't capable of talking" (Auster 2008, 121-2). During an interview with the French website *Rue89*,[24] Auster explained that all those digressions reflect August Brill's state of shock after seeing the pictures of Titus's murder. *Man in the Dark* is dedicated to Auster's friend David Grossman, whose son was actually killed by terrorists in Lebanon. The death of Titus illustrates the fact that Auster's imagination is overwhelmed by the darkness of the real. At the dawn of his literary career, Auster had visited Anne Frank's room in Amsterdam, and he wrote about this shattering experience in *The Invention of Solitude*:

> As he stood in Anne Frank's room, the room in which the diary was written, ... he suddenly found himself crying. Not sobbing, as might happen in response to a deep inner pain, but crying without sound, the tears streaming down his cheeks, as if purely in response to the world. It was at that moment, he later realized, that the Book of Memory began. As in the phrase: "she wrote her diary in this room". (Auster 1988, 83)

Auster presents literature as a way to testify and to cry for the world in silence. He notes that what he felt was not an inner pain but a rare moment of openness, a communion with the world. The visit of Anne Frank's room has epiphanic overtones. It is a new starting point in Auster's career. "The Book of Memory" is Auster's first successful attempt at desubjectivation, that is, writing about himself with a distance in the third person. This technique was inspired by Rimbaud's famous phrase "Je est un autre"—"I is another". The trip to Amsterdam marks the end of Auster's poetic aphasia and the beginning of his prolific dialogism, voicing such characters as Anna Blume, whose first name and writing-in-wartime activity recall the most famous child victim of the Holocaust. Speaking about Auster's characters, Mark Brown reminds us that

> aphasia causes a disjunction in the mind of the sufferer between their experience of the world and their ability to deploy language to describe it. In short, words and things no longer correspond. (Brown 2007, 8)

It seems that Auster's inability to deploy language to describe his experience of the world, which was at the core of his early poems, paradoxically voiced

countless fictional writer-characters. In other words, it is precisely because
things and words no longer correspond that Auster finds his place as a
writer and speaks the unspeakable. The attacks on the WTC and the war
on terror have unearthed Auster's ghosts. New unspeakable pictures of
annihilation burn the writer's eyes. The fall of the towers have put the
world into chaos. A linguistic profusion and confusion revives the ancient
myth of Babel, as the numerous architectural metaphors suggest in *The
Brooklyn Follies.*[25] According to Genesis, God punished men for their
arrogance as they wanted to build a tower that would reach the sky. The
connection with two of the world biggest *skyscrapers* is striking. One may
wonder whether Jihadists wanted to inflict a holy punishment, assaulting
the WTC as the symbol of capitalism and globalization. In the seventies,
French philosopher Jean Baudrillard studied simulacra and claimed that
the Twin Towers contemplated each other in their Siamese superiority and
in this way abolished world concurrence, putting an end to the symbolic
colonization of the sky. According to Baudrillard, the Twin Towers used
to symbolize "the death of the original and the end of representation", like
Andy Warhol's serigraphy, like the thousands Al Wilsons and Gordon
Dryer's fake Alec Smiths, like Paul Auster's name on the cover and in the
fiction, like the two Stillmans, the real James Joyce and his homonymous
ersatz, and the two Tituses. But what about the Twin Towers' destruction?
The end of the end of representation, or in Art Spiegelman's view, a black-
on-black picture?

In "The Art of Worry", Auster addresses the impossibility of picturing
or writing about the Holocaust and the terrorist attacks on the WTC. The
following excerpt reveals the importance of these historical events in
Auster's eyes. In his work, they are synonymous with absence and silence,
and yet they are artistically inspiring and ground-breaking:

> Then came September 11, 2001. In the fire and smoke of three thousand
> incinerated bodies, *a holocaust was visited upon us*, and nine months later
> the city is still grieving over its dead. In the immediate aftermath of the
> attack, in the hours and days that followed that murderous morning, few of
> us were capable of thinking any coherent thoughts. The shock was too
> great, and as the smoke continued to hover over the city and we breathed
> the vile smells of death and destruction, most of us shuffled around like
> sleepwalkers, numb and dazed, not good for anything. But *The New Yorker*
> had an issue to put out, and when they realized that someone would have to
> design a cover—the most important cover in their history, which would
> have to be produced in record time—they turned to Spiegelman.
>   That black-on-black issue of September 24 is, in my opinion,
> Spiegelman's masterpiece. In the face of absolute horror, one's inclination
> is to dispense with images altogether. Words often fail us at moments of

extreme duress. The same is true of pictures. If I have not garbled the story Spiegelman told me during those days, I believe he originally resisted that iconoclastic impulse: to hand in a solid black cover to represent mourning, an absent image to stand as a mirror of the ineffable. ... But still it wasn't enough. ... Then, just as he was about to give up, he began thinking about some of the artists who had come before him, ... in particular Ad Reinhardt and his black-on-black canvases from the sixties, those supremely abstract and minimal anti-images that had taken painting to the farthest edge of possibility. Spiegelman had found his direction. Not in silence—but in the sublime. You have to look very closely at the picture before you notice the towers. They are there and not there, effaced and yet still present, shadows pulsing in oblivion, in memory, in the ghostly emanation of some tormented afterlife. When I saw the picture for the first time, I felt as if Spiegelman had placed a stethoscope on my chest and methodically registered every heartbeat that had shaken my body since September 11. Then my eyes filled up with tears. Tears for the dead. Tears for the living. Tears for the abominations we inflict on one another, for the cruelty and savagery of the whole stinking human race. (Auster 2003, 462-3, emphasis added)

This passage is Auster's most explicit mention of the delocalization of the Holocaust trauma. He finds himself crying again in a way that silently echoes the visit of Anne Frank's room in *The Invention of Solitude*. Auster describes the 9/11 attacks as the "holocaust" re-"visited", in other words an occurrence, a re-presentation of the Holocaust.[26] Spiegelman draws a similar parallel between Auschwitz and 9/11 in *The Shadow of No Towers*. After Auster in "The Book of Memory", Spiegelman concedes that he can only write about himself in the third person when it comes to the immediate aftermath of the trauma (Spiegelman 2004, 8). Like Titus whose eyes are stabbed out, Spiegelman's self-portrait is red-eyed as the incandescent towers prevent him from seeing and drawing anything else. Representation, be it visual or linguistic, is taken to the "farthest edge of possibility" (Auster 2003, 463) by contemporary artists such as Auster and Spiegelman. But what happens when one stands in front of the unimaginable, the unspeakable, the un-presentable? Auster seems to go some way towards answering these questions here. As it is no longer possible to speak, the contemporary artist will have to find new modes of representation to cope with a reality that goes out of control and hinders rational thinking. Speaking of the inhuman scenes of *In the Country of Last Things*, Auster had told Joseph Mallia that "reality is far more terrible than anything we can imagine" (Auster 1995, 115). In his overall oeuvre, reality and fiction are unstable categories and metalepsis is often used to render the unreal aspects of life. Reality interferes with the fiction just as unimaginable things happen in the world. Evoking Borges as Auster would, Baudrillard considers the attacks on the WTC as "a fiction beyond fiction" (in "The Spirit of Terrorism", 2001). Since "White Spaces" and *The Invention of Solitude*, Paul Auster has never stopped trying to exceed "the limits of the known world" (Auster 1988, 98) in order to discover "some terrible, unimagined truth" (Auster 2004b, 159). Hell is a human invention. It is less frightening than reality. No wonder that God left the world. As Auster implored in "Hieroglyph", "Do not / emerge, Eden. Stay / in the mouths of the lost / who dream you" (Auster 2004b, 86).

At the center of his latest novel *Invisible*, Auster invites us to think the unthinkable by speaking of an unspeakable taboo. After "City of Glass" and *The Brooklyn Follies*, *Invisible*'s New York is once again a new Garden of Eden, a Promised Land where Adam Walker and his sister Gwynn commit "a monumental transgression" (Auster 2009, 144). For a while they are "the last two people left in the universe" (Auster 2009, 146), and their father addresses Adam as "Son, as in my son, my creation, my heir" (Auster 2009, 151), all of which depict a pre-lapsarian Adamic setting. Contrary to Cormac McCarthy's incestuous couple in *Outer Dark* (1968), they make love every day for several weeks using contraceptives and consequently "the unmentionable will never come to pass" (Auster 2009, 146). The narrator can only speak the unspeakable with a distance between him and himself, here thanks to the second person narrative, forty years after the facts:

> You and your sister never talk about what you are doing. You don't even have a conversation to discuss why you don't talk about it. You're living in the confines of a shared secret, and the walls of that space are built by silence, an insane silence that can be broken only at the risk of bringing those walls down upon your heads. (Auster 2009, 150)

This coming-of-age novel is composed of four parts alternating between present and past tenses, first, second and third person narratives. Again, Auster focuses on the questions that haunt him. A thorough scientific discussion on aphasia is even reported (Hélène Juin is a "speech pathologist", Auster 2009, 196-7). The three parts of Adam's memoir— "Spring", "Summer" and "Autumn", respectively written in the first, second and third person—are edited and published by the narrator, Walker's old college friend. After hinting at his own experimentation in desubjectivation,[27] Auster takes the poet Adam Walker one step further. Following a narrative logic that embraces nothingness, "Winter" remains untold. As his name implies, Adam is the first man, but at the end of his life, after having drifted from first to second and third person, the poet's desubjectivation is complete through death. The missing chapter stands for the unspeakable point of view of the non-person. Just like Rilke and Blanchot before him, Auster is fascinated by the limits of human experience, and blurs the line between life and death, inner and outer,[28] person and non-person, reality and fiction. In *The Brooklyn Follies, Man in the Dark* and *Invisible*, Auster conveys the speakable and the unspeakable in the same piece. Just as "there is a visible in the invisible" (Auster 1990, 202), there is a speakable in the unspeakable.

Towards the end of *Invisible*, the narrator meets the aging Gwynn who tells him that she did not commit that "monumental transgression" with her brother. It is then impossible for the reader to decide whether Walker's book is a memoir or a work of fiction. The narrator finally explains that everything we have been reading was transformed and altered for privacy purposes. The fact of the matter is that no integral witness will be heard, as human beings are bound to subjectivity. Although the writer leaves the world unsaid, he does not leave it unchanged. In Auster's semiotic world, each and every interconnected event involves the participation of language, imagination, memory and chance in the creation of the real.

References

Agacinski, Sylviane and Jean-Luc Nancy. 1994. Jacques Derrida. In *Dictionnaire des philosophes*, A-J, ed. Denis Huisman. Presses Universitaires de France.

Agamben, Giorgio. 1999. *Remnants of Auschwitz: The witness and the archive*. Brooklyn, NY: Zone Books.

Auster, Paul. 1974. Preface to *Fits and starts, selected poems of Jacques Dupin translated by Paul Auster*. Weston, Connecticut: Living Hand.

—. 1981. Private I, public eye, a few words in praise of George Oppen. *Paideuma* 10 (1, Spring): 49-52.

—. 1987. *The New York trilogy*. London: Faber and Faber.

—. 1988 [1982]. *The invention of solitude*. London: Faber and Faber.

—. 1989 [1987]. *In the country of last things*. London: Faber and Faber.

—. 1990. *Groundwork (selected poems and essays 1970-1979)*. London: Faber and Faber.

—. 1995. *The red notebook*. London: Faber and Faber.

—. 2002. *The book of illusions*. London: Faber and Faber.

—. 2003. *Collected prose*. New York: Picador.

—. 2004a. *Oracle night*. London: Faber and Faber.

—. 2004b. *Collected poems*. Woodstock, NY: One Overlook Press.

—. 2004c. Introduction to *Running through fire: How I survived the Holocaust*, by Zosia Goldberg, as told to Hilton Obenzinger, xv-xvii. San Francisco: Mercury House. NEA Heritage and Preservation Series.

—. 2005a. *The Brooklyn follies*. London: Faber and Faber.

—. 2005b. *Manhattan, Ground Zero: A sonic memorial soundwalk*. New York: Soundwalk.

—. 2006. *Travels in the scriptorium*. London: Faber and Faber.

—. 2008. *Man in the dark*. London: Faber and Faber.

—. 2009. *Invisible*. New York: Henry Holt.

Auster, Paul, Paul Karazik and David Mazzucchelli. 2004d. *City of glass, the graphic novel*. New York: Picador.

Baudrillard, Jean. 1976. *L'échange symbolique et la mort*. Paris: Gallimard.

Baudrillard, Jean. 2001. The spirit of terrorism. In *Le Monde*, 2 Novembre.

Blanchot, Maurice. 1955. *L'espace littéraire*. Paris: Gallimard.

—. 1980. *L'écriture du désastre*. Paris: Gallimard.

Brown, Mark. 2007. *Paul Auster*. Manchester: Manchester University Press.

Bunyan, John. 1967 [1678]. *The pilgrim's progress*. London: Penguin Books.

Deleuze, Gilles. 1970. Preface to *Le schizo et les langues*, by Louis Wolfson. Paris: Gallimard.

—. 1993. *Critique et clinique*. Paris: Minuit.

DeLillo, Don. 2007. *Falling man*. New York: Picador.

Derrida, Jacques. 1972. *La dissémination*. Paris: Seuil.

Dupin, Jacques. 1994. Preface to *Disparitions*, by Paul Auster, translated by Danièle Robert. Arles: Editions Unes/Actes Sud.

Eco, Umberto. 1995. *The search for the perfect language*. Oxford: Blackwell Publishers Ltd.

Félix, Brigitte. 1997. *William Gaddis, l'alchimie de l'écriture*. Paris: Belin.

Finkelstein, Norman. 1995. In the realm of the naked eye, the poetry of Paul Auster. In *Beyond the red notebook*, ed. Dennis Barone. University of Pennsylvania Press.

—. 2004. Introduction to *Collected poems*, by Paul Auster. Woodstock, NY: One Overlook Press.

Francis, Jim. 1990. "Living inside of language". Interview with Paul Auster. In *Rampike* (Tenth anniversary issue: Part 1), Toronto, Ontario.

Gaddis, William. 1993 [1955]. *The recognitions*. New York: Penguin.

Hugonnier, François. 2005. Interview with Paul Auster. Saint Malo. Festival des Etonnants Voyageurs.

Jabès, Edmond. 1988 [1963, 1964, 1965]. *Le livre des questions, I (Le livre des questions, Le livre de Yukel, Le retour au livre)*. Paris: Gallimard.

McCarthy, Cormac. 1968. *Outer dark*. New York: Random House.

Spiegelman, Art. 2004. *In the shadow of no towers*. New York: Pantheon Books, Random House.

Wolfson, Louis. 1970. *Le schizo et les langues*. Paris: Gallimard.

Notes

[1] Reference to all poems by Paul Auster: *Collected Poems*, 2004b.

[2] I translated the interview, which was conducted in French.

[3] "Language is not experience, it is a means of organizing experience" (Auster 2004b, 204).

[4] "I remain in the room in which I am writing this. I put one foot in front of the other. I put one word in front of the other, and for each step I take I add another word, as if for each word to be spoken there were another space to be crossed, a distance to be filled by my body as it moves through this space" (Auster 2004b, 158-9). In *Travels in the Scriptorium*, Mr Blank paces back and forth in a room and he only travels thanks to his imagination and his poor memory. *Man in the Dark* begins in a similar way as August Brill, an old man in a wheelchair, imagines stories when he cannot sleep.

[5] This early conception of metropolitan loneliness is acknowledged by Paul Karasik who pictures Quinn—the main character of "City of Glass"—disappearing with the stones of a wall in his graphic novel adaptation (Auster 2004d, 111).

[6] In fact Auster started working on *In the Country of Last Things* "back in the days when [he] was a college student" (Auster 1995, 114).

[7] The phrase "the word *something*" is systematically used (with italics) to debate the accuracy of certain words in *Travels in the Scriptorium* ("the word *all* is an absolute term", Auster 2006, 22). The same pattern is used in *The Book of Illusions* (2002) and in the following novel *Man in the Dark*, and again it calls the reader's attention towards word choice. It unveils the writing process and it points at the inadequacy of language which becomes an unstable referential system.

[8] Contrary to the well known Irish author, Auster's James Joyce is an insignificant character in *The Brooklyn Follies*.

[9] Since Auster invites us to find hidden meanings in the characters' names, we could read Alex Smith as *Al-Ex-Myth*, in other words an *Al* (one of the "thousand[s] Al Wilsons" [Auster 2005a, 163] from the crowds of fakes buried in "unmarked grave[s]", a "Mr Nobody" from "City of Glass" or *The Book of Illusions*), a nameless dead character (an *ex/X*—"Mr. X" is actually the name Born chooses for his fake biography at the end of *Invisible*, Auster 2009, 302-304), and an extremely talented artist who has actually never existed (a *myth*). The "unmarked grave"—which is mentioned by Aurora and then by Tom when he speaks of Poe's death (2005a, 150, 273)—alludes to the anonymous metropolitan

death as it was described by Musil in *The Man without Qualities* (1930-1942). Moreover it is connected to the title of the last chapter "X marks the spot" which focuses on the attacks on the targeted World Trade Center (through the eyes of the unnoticed Nathan Glass, whose new project is to write the biographies of the anonymous dead). Ground Zero is implicitly referred to as a *mass grave*.

[10] The Greek term *pharmakon* can either mean "cure" or "poison". According to Derrida (1972), the *pharmakon* is an outside element which forces a living creature to be connected to a fellow creature, risking an allergic pain in the process. This is precisely how language is presented in *The Brooklyn Follies*. This ambivalence appears in Auster's overall work, in which language can alternately be a curse or a blessing.

[11] Here is a complete reference list of "un-words" and additional words of nothingness taken from Auster's *Collected Poems*, 2004b: "unleashed" ("Spokes", 25, "Late Summer", 98), "unlike" ("Spokes", 30), "unsprung" ("Spokes", 32), "unseen" ("Unearth", 37, "Search for a Definition", 145, "White Spaces", 159), "unwritten" ("Unearth", 38), "unquelled" ("Unearth", 42), "unraveled" ("Unearth", 47, "Hieroglyph", 86), "unaborted" ("Unearth", 49), "unpronounceable" ("Unearth", 56), "unborn" ("Unearth", 57, "Search for a Definition", 146), "unsigned" ("Matrix and Dream", 66), "unspoken" ("Interior", 67), "unapproachable" ("Lies. Decrees. 1972", 73, "Northern Lights", 125), "unwitnessed" ("Lies. Decrees. 1972", 73), "undyingly" ("Lies. Decrees. 1972", 73), "unquenchable" ("Prism", 80), "unknowable" ("Ascendant", 89, "White Spaces", 157), "unbrokenly" ("Heraclitian", 99), "undeciphered" ("Disappearances", 107), "unland" ("Reminiscence of Home", 126), "unearthed" ("Riding Eastward", 127), "unsaid" ("Aubade", 130, "Narrative", 143), "unappeasable" ("Meteor", 133), "untellable" ("Siberian", 135), "unfallen" ("Narrative", 143), "unblessed" ("Between the Lines", 147), "undead" ("Bedrock", 149), "unpronounceable" ("White Spaces", 157), "unimagined" ("White Spaces", 159), "nothing" ("Spokes", 24, "Unearth", 37, 38, 48, 55, "White Nights", 65, "Fore Shadows", 78, "Wall Writing", 81, "Covenant", 83, "Song of Degrees", 94, "Autobiography of the Eye", 102, "Disappearances", 107, 111, 112, "Gnomon", 128, "Aubade", 130, "Quarry", 138, "Credo", 141, "Narrative", 143, "Search for a Definition", 145, 146, "Facing the Music", 151, 152, "White Spaces", 155, 157, 158, 159, 160, 161), "nothing left" ("Incendiary", 93), "nothing but" ("Fragment from Cold", 129, "Facing the Music", 150), "nothing more" ("Lackawanna", 72, "Viaticum", 76, "White Spaces", 157), "never" ("Unearth", 39, 53, 56, "White Nights", 65, "Scribe", 69, "Heraclitian", 99, "Effigies", 118, "Quarry", 138, "Obituary in the Present Tense", 142, 143, "Search for a Definition", 145, "Facing the Music", 150, "White Spaces", 157, 158, 159), "not even" ("Unearth", 58, "Interior", 67, "Aubade", 130), "nowhere" ("Unearth", 61, "Wall Writing", 81, "Disappearances", 108, 110, 113, "Facing the Music", 151, "White Spaces", 158), "no one" ("White Nights", 65, "Fore-Shadows", 78, "White Spaces", 156), "no one's voice" ("Unearth, 60), "no one's flesh" ("Transfusion", 134), "no longer" ("White Nights", 65, "Matrix and Dream", 66, "Lackawanna", 72, "Fire Speech", 96, "Braille", 100, "Testimony", 131, "White Spaces", 155), "no more" ("Obituary in the Present Tense", 142, "S.A. 1911-1979", 144, "Search

for a Definition", 145), "no less" (Obituary in the Present Tense", 142), "none" (Obituary in the Present Tense", 142), "no home" ("Facing the Music", 151), "no farther" ("White Spaces", 157), "no room" ("White Spaces", 161), "no name" ("White Spaces", 158), "no names" ("Interior", 67), "no meaning" ("S.A. 1911-1979", 144), "no memory" ("White Spaces", 155), "no importance" ("White Spaces", 160), "no room" ("White Spaces", 161), "nothingness" ("Visible", 132, "Notes from a Composition Book", 205), "to say nothing" ("Unearth, 37), "to be nothing" ("Disappearances", 109), "invisible" ("Unearth", 49, "Wall Writing", 81, "Autobiography of the Eye", 102, "Effigies", 121, "Narrative", 143, "Search for a Definition", 146, "White Spaces", 157), "invisibly" ("White Spaces", 159), "inaccessible" ("Unearth", 50), "inaudible" ("Matrix and Dream", 66), "illegible" ("Disappearances", 108), "impossible" ("Effigies", 118, "Facing the Music", 151), "impossibility" ("White Spaces", 157), "irreducible" ("Bedrock", 149), "ineffable" ("Notes from a Composition Book", 205).

[12] In *Invisible*, "true" and "untrue" tend to overlap. Most landmarks are finally erased and they end up in a double negation ("the remarks about Dante's Inferno on the first page of this book were not in not-Walker's original manuscript", Auster 2009, 260).

[13] Auster's heroes are zeros. Let us consider Owen Brick and Nick Bowen, the anagrammatic heroes of *Man in the Dark* and *Oracle Night*'s stories within the story. In the light of the poetic work, the first is a stone in the wall, but he is also emptied out by his own name which reads "new O" backwards (he has fallen into a "cylindrical hole" which forms a "perfect circle", not to mention the "double knot" which laces his boots, Auster 2008, 3). As for Nick Bowen, it reads "new o B", which makes sense if we follow the reversed order of publication. *The Brooklyn Follies*' *Uncle Nat* ("Un"/"Not") could also be seen as a personification of Auster's "unity in nothingness".

[14] One can also read the silent connection between "City of Glass" and Auster's essay on Jabès entitled "Book of the Dead", in which he notes that the last book of the *Book of Questions* is called *El* (Auster 2003, 367). In *The Brooklyn Follies*, Nathan *Glass*—New York is the city of *Glass*—speaks of "the book of the living" (Auster 2005a, 9). Like *Oracle Night* and *Travels in the Scriptorium*, Jabès's *The Book of Questions* is the title of the book inside the book. The narrator appropriates the name of one of the characters (Yukel), which is similar to Auster's use of his own name in "City of Glass".

[15] In *The Brooklyn Follies*, Nathan's dark considerations on Yugoslavia are a common *delocalization* of the trauma of the Holocaust and an illustration of what Blanchot called the "writing of the disaster". Another instance is the anti-atomic shelter, the concentration camp stories and Sidney Orr's need to write in reaction to a sordid newspaper article that represents "the end of mankind" in *Oracle Night* (2004a, 105). As for the non-fictional world, Paul Auster—who is a third generation Jewish American from an unscathed family—finally enabled Hilton Obenzinger to publish Zosia Goldberg's Holocaust memoirs after several years of repeated efforts. In the introduction, Auster mentions the "unspeakable horrors" Zosia went through (Auster 2004c, xvii).

[16] In *The Pilgrim Progress*, Christian flees from the City of Destruction and goes on an allegorical journey to the Celestial City. His spiritual guide is called the Interpreter. The main paradox of Bunyan's story is the fact that Christian leaves his family behind in order to achieve his spiritual goal. In *Oracle Night*, it is also the starting point of the story of Nick Bowen who simply walks out of his marriage one night, never to return.

[17] During the Saint Malo Festival (2005), Auster explained that the phone book—whose cover appears in *Oracle Night* (Auster 2004a, 113)—was actually given to him by his Hungarian editor.

[18] In "The Art of Worry", his preface for a 2003 Spiegelman exhibition, Auster praises the author of *Maus*, "the brilliant two-volume narrative of his father's nightmare journey through the camps in the Second World War" (Auster 2003, 458). Spiegelman also wrote the introduction—entitled "Picturing a glassy-eyed private I"—to the graphic novel adaptation of "City of Glass" (Auster 2004d).

[19] In a 2002 article entitled "NYC=USA", Auster states that he thought about the "possibility of New York seceding from the Union and establishing itself as an independent city-state" (Auster 2003, 510). This fantasy is the initial situation of August Brill's story in *Man in the Dark*. This piece, along with "Random Notes—September 11, 2001—4:00 PM" (Auster 2003, 505-6) and *Manhattan, Ground Zero: A Sonic Memorial Soundwalk* (Auster 2005b) all bear witness to the 9/11 attacks.

[20] *The Book of Illusions* is a meditation on loss which was published one year after September 11, 2001. In "NYC=USA"—written on July 31, 2002, and first published in *The New York Times* on September 9, 2002, that is to say at the time *The Book of Illusions* was published—Auster makes the following remark on 9/11: "we experienced that day as *a family tragedy*. Most of us went into a state of *intense mourning*, and we *dragged ourselves around* in the days and months that followed engulfed by a sense of *communal grief*" (Auster 2003, 509, emphasis added). For chronological reasons (in both real and fictional time), reading *The Book of Illusions* as Auster's first fictional reaction to the national tragedy is arguable. Even if it is set in the 1980's, the initial situation of the novel strongly resonates with "NYC=USA". After losing his entire *family* in a *plane crash*, the narrator David Zimmer is "*wandering around* the house" and even speaks of "*communal mourning*" (Auster 2002, 7, emphasis added). Throughout the novel, the words "plane", "jump" and "crash" are often repeated, and most of all, "the word *fall*" (Auster 2002, 200). A list of plant names ("a random collection of syllables from a dead language") features "Fall panicum" (Auster 2002, 295, 296). It alludes to Zimmer's panic in the aftermath of the plane crash (he suffers from post-traumatic stress disorder and cannot take a plane without his Xanax pills). In the first phase of his mourning, he plays with his dead kids' toys: "as I [...] played with their Lego pieces, *building ever more complex and baroque structures*, I felt that I was temporarily inhabiting them again—carrying on their little phantom lives for them by repeating the gestures they had made when they still had bodies" (Auster 2002, 7-8, emphasis added). This passage could be read as a *mise en*

abyme of absence and memorial at Ground Zero and of the (re)building of the WTC. But this hidden subtext remains uncertain and unsaid. Indeed, silence is central to *The Book of Illusions.* Zimmer overcomes his unspeakable sorrow thanks to Hector Mann's silent films and his mustache, "a metaphysical jump rope" which "speaks a language without words" (Auster 2002, 29).

[21] The chopped head is a recurrent motif in *The Book of Illusions* and *Invisible.*

[22] Auster speaks about Rembrandt's son Titus before drawing his conclusion on the "dead children" as the "pictures" of "the unspeakable" in "The Book of Memory" (Auster 1988, 97-8).

[23] Contrary to *Falling Man,* which puts the reader in the ashes of 9/11 right from the opening sentence, the unspeakable events are first circumvented in *The Brooklyn Follies* and *Man in the Dark.* Both Auster and DeLillo represent the unspeakable trauma thanks to a still life. Like August Brill and Katya who cannot get rid of the image of Titus's chopped head, Martin and Lianne "keep seeing the towers in [Morandi's] still life" (DeLillo 2007, 49): "Two of the taller items were dark and somber, with smoky marks and smudges, and one of them was partly concealed by a long-necked bottle. The bottle was a bottle, white. The two dark objects, too obscure to name, were the things that Martin was referring to. "What do you see?" he said. She saw what he saw. She saw the towers" (DeLillo 2007, 49). Such projective visions are symptomatic of post-traumatic stress disorder.

[24] http://www.dailymotion.com/video/x82mgl_paul-auster-sur-rue89-1interview-in creation (January 6, 2009).

[25] Tom gave up his thesis entitled "Imaginary Edens: The Life of the Mind in Pre-Civil War America" (Auster 2005a, 14). *The Brooklyn Follies* is about the life of the mind in Pre-War on Terror America, and the title of Tom's thesis echoes Stillman's: "The Garden and the Tower: Early Visions of the New World", composed of two parts: "The Myth of Paradise" and "The Myth of Babel". Thoreau's *Walden* and the utopia of the "Hotel Existence"—both described as a "sanctuary" (Auster 2005a, 16, 189)—are central references, along with Brightman's Attic, which is a "paradise of tranquility and order" (57), but ends up in failure. All of which questions the modernist conception of art as a redemptory refuge and leads us to the final scene of the 9/11 attacks.

[26] We may also note that when the phrase "smoke of three thousand incinerated bodies" (Auster 2003, 462) is repeated at the end of *The Brooklyn Follies* (Auster 2005a, 304), the word "incinerated" hints at the Holocaust without naming it.

[27] "By writing about myself in the first person, I had smothered myself and made myself invisible. ... *I* became *He*..." (Auster 2009, 89).

[28] When Nathan Glass testifies of his mystical near-death experience in *The Brooklyn Follies,* he finds himself "nowhere", i.e., "inside myself and outside myself at the same time" (Auster 2005a, 297). This chapter ("Inspiration") silently pays homage to Blanchot's "L'inspiration" (1955, 211-48), a study of death as the unknowable and unsayable "other side" of human experience. For further reading on the unspeakable, see also Blanchot's *Death Sentence* (1948), which is quoted by Auster in *The Invention of Solitude*: "'What is extraordinary begins at the moment I stop. But I am no longer able to speak of it'" (Auster 1988, 63).

CONTRIBUTORS

Michelle Banks teaches American Literature at the University of Windsor in Windsor, Ontario, Canada, and is working on a book about connection and narrative.

Alan Bilton is Lecturer in literature and film at Swansea University, Wales. He is the author of *An Introduction to Contemporary American Fiction* (Edinburgh/New York University Press, 2002) and co-editor of the three-volume *America in the 1920's* (Helm 2004). He has also published articles and book chapters on subjects as diverse as Buster Keaton, Saul Bellow, F. Scott Fitzgerald, Don DeLillo and F. W. Murnau. His first novel, *The Sleepwalkers' Ball,* described by one critic as "Mary Poppins meets Kafka", was published by Alcemi in 2009. He is currently at work on a monograph on American silent film comedy, *Constantly Moving: Happiness Machines,* as well as a second novel.

Mark Brown is Senior Lecturer in English and American Literature at the University of Northampton in England. He is the author of *Paul Auster* (Manchester University Press, 2007) and essays on Auster's films, novels and poetry.

Stefania Ciocia is Senior Lecturer in Contemporary Literatures in English at Canterbury Christ Church University (UK). Her main research interests lie broadly in the areas of postmodernism and postcolonialism. She has published, amongst others, on Sarah Waters, Derek Walcott, Tim O'Brien and, more recently, on crossover fiction.

Anita Durkin is currently finishing a dissertation in nineteenth-century American literature at the University of Rochester in Rochester, NY (USA). Her research interests include the organization of literary canons and the aesthetic connections between seemingly disparate writings. She has published previously on Toni Morrison's *Beloved*, and has presented papers at numerous conferences.

Ginevra Geraci has earned her Ph.D. from Università di Roma 3 (Italy) with a dissertation on black-Jewish relationships entitled "Imagining the Other: the Representation of the Jew in Zora Neale Hurston, Chester Himes and Alice Walker". She has worked on James Baldwin, Richard Wright, Ann Petry and Bernard Malamud. Her research interests also include Ralph Ellison and Philip Roth.

Jesús Ángel González is Professor of English at the University of Cantabria, Spain. He holds an M.A. in Spanish from the Pennsylvania State University and a Ph.D. in English from the University of Salamanca, Spain. He has published *La narrativa popular de Dashiell Hammett: Pulps, Cine y Cómics* (Valencia University Press, 2002) and *An Introduction to North American Culture and Literature* (Ediciones TGD, 2006) as well as a number of articles on Applied Linguistics, the detective novel and the West in American Literature.

François Hugonnier is a French scholar and poet. He is a Ph.D. student at the University of Paris X-Nanterre, and a former student of the École Normale Supérieure (Ulm, Paris, France). His research focuses on the works of post-Holocaust and post-9/11 Jewish American writers Paul Auster and Jerome Rothenberg. He is the author of a Master's thesis on the unspeakable in *The Brooklyn Follies* (University of Le Mans), and a recent article on the writing of the disaster in *Man in the Dark* (University of Provence/UQAM).

Ulrich Meurer studied Comparative Literature in Munich (Germany) and received his Ph.D. in American and Media Studies at Constance University. He is the author of *Topographien. Raumkonzepte in Literatur und Film der Postmoderne*, has edited several books on cinema and widely published on the relationship between written word and (moving) image. Currently he holds the position of Visiting Professor for Film and Media Sciences at Vienna University.

James Peacock is Lecturer in English and American Literatures at Keele University in the UK. He is the author of *Understanding Paul Auster* (University of South Carolina Press, 2009) and has published articles on Auster, Jonathan Lethem, Brooklyn in contemporary fiction, and Quakerism in American literature.

Paolo Simonetti holds a Ph.D. in Anglophone Literatures from "Sapienza" University of Rome, Italy, and he is currently teaching Anglo-American Language and Culture at the Communication Sciences Department of the same university. His research areas include literary theory, historical fiction, postmodernist and contemporary American literature. His publications include essays on Sylvia Plath, Thomas Pynchon, Don DeLillo, Robert Coover, and Paul Auster. He is the author of *Paranoia Blues*, a monograph on postmodernist American fiction.

Aliki Varvogli lectures in English at the University of Dundee in Scotland. She is the author of *The World That is the Book: Paul Auster's Fiction*, and she has published essays on several American authors, including Philip Roth, Jay McInerney, Jonathan Safran Foer and Annie Proulx. She is currently working on a book called *Travel and Dislocation in Contemporary American Literature*.

INDEX

A

Art of Hunger, The, 134, 145, 150, 197
"Auggie Wren's Christmas Story", 194
authenticity, 5, 76–77, 84, 90–91
authorship, 6, 41, 44, 46–49, 51–52, 56–57, 83, 85, 87, 100, 112, 125–127, 129, 132–136, 138, 144–145, 158, 174–176, 179–180, 185, 232

B

Bakhtin, Mikhail, 164–166
Barone, Dennis, 1, 9, 15, 175
Barthes, Roland, 58, 173–174, 176, 196, 211–212
Baudrillard, Jean, 87, 194, 278, 280
Beckett, Samuel, 2, 3, 6, 8, 126–127, 130, 133–136, 145
Berlatsky, Eric, 62, 67
Blakelock, Ralph, 209, 247
Blanchot, Maurice, 129, 185, 263, 281
Bloom, Harold, 3
Blue in the Face, 76–77, 92, 194, 198–201, 204, 211
Book of Illusions, The, 4, 7–8, 40, 42, 56–57, 75–76, 91, 100, 116, 127, 130, 150, 155, 156, 164, 176–179, 206, 208–209, 219–222, 224, 231–233, 239–241, 245, 248, 252, 255–256, 275
Briggs, Robert, 163–164
Brooklyn, 4, 16–17, 45, 63, 76, 80, 91, 195, 198–199

Brooklyn Follies, The, 4–5, 9, 13–14, 16, 18–19, 21, 24, 28, 31, 40–44, 46–47, 49–50, 55–58, 60, 62, 68, 72–73, 76–78, 80–81, 84, 88, 90–93, 117, 130, 177, 260, 267–269, 275–276, 278, 280–281
Brown, Mark, 2, 7, 42, 97, 198–199, 246, 252, 273, 277
Buñuel, Luis, 216
Bush, George W., 5, 16–17, 22–23, 26, 29, 40–41, 43, 48–49, 60
Butler, Martin, 23–24, 47–49

C

Calle, Sophie, 7, 103, 183–188
Cervantes, Miguel de, 190
chance, 6, 15–16, 18, 85, 103, 157–158, 162, 167, 188, 193, 272, 281
Chateaubriand, Francois-René de, 208, 219, 226, 230, 234, 254, 256
Chénetier, Marc, 2, 15–16, 21–22
city, 67, 199, 221–223, 266
City of Glass, 16, 32, 43, 49, 57–58, 78, 81, 98, 126, 134–135, 137, 152–153, 156–157, 159, 163, 181, 194, 221, 223, 245, 261, 269, 272, 280
coincidence. *See* chance
Collected Poems, 284

D

Dante, 98, 121, 285